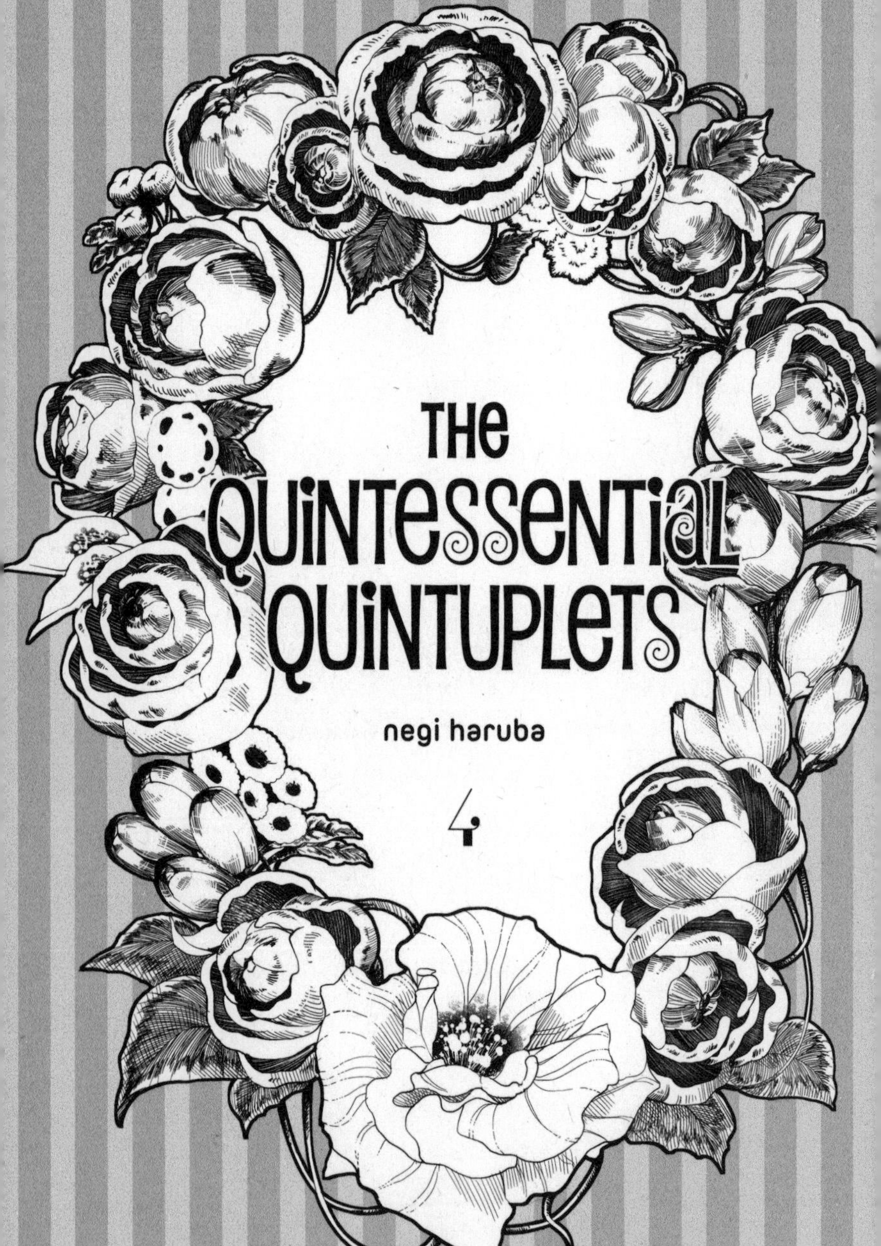

THE QUINTESSENTIAL QUINTUPLETS

negi haruba

4

Character intros

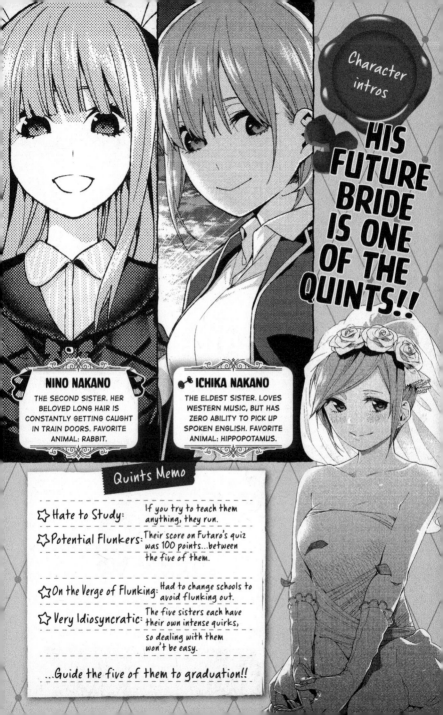

HIS FUTURE BRIDE IS ONE OF THE QUINTS!!

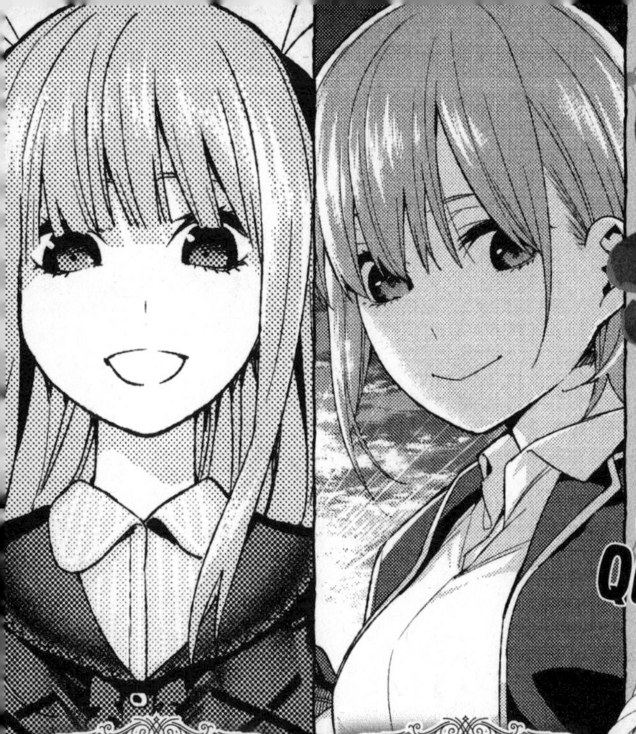

NINO NAKANO

THE SECOND SISTER. HER BELOVED LONG HAIR IS CONSTANTLY GETTING CAUGHT IN TRAIN DOORS. FAVORITE ANIMAL: RABBIT.

ICHIKA NAKANO

THE ELDEST SISTER. LOVES WESTERN MUSIC, BUT HAS ZERO ABILITY TO PICK UP SPOKEN ENGLISH. FAVORITE ANIMAL: HIPPOPOTAMUS.

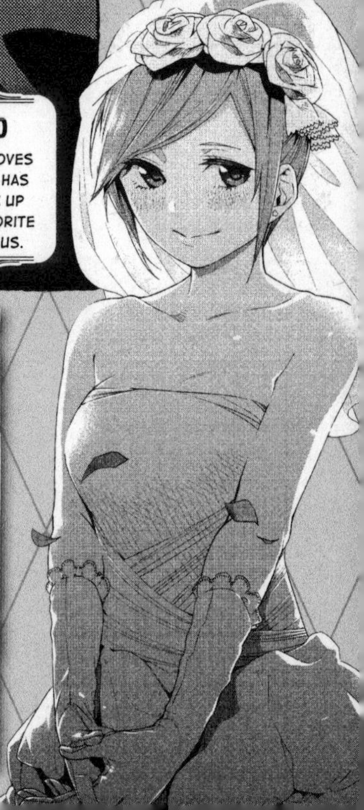

Quints Memo

- ☆ Hate to Study: If you try to teach them anything, they run.
- ☆ Potential Flunkers: Their score on Futaro's quiz was 100 points...between the five of them.
- ☆ On the Verge of Flunking: Had to change schools to avoid flunking out.
- ☆ Very Idiosyncratic: The five sisters each have their own intense quirks, so dealing with them won't be easy.

...Guide the five of them to graduation!!

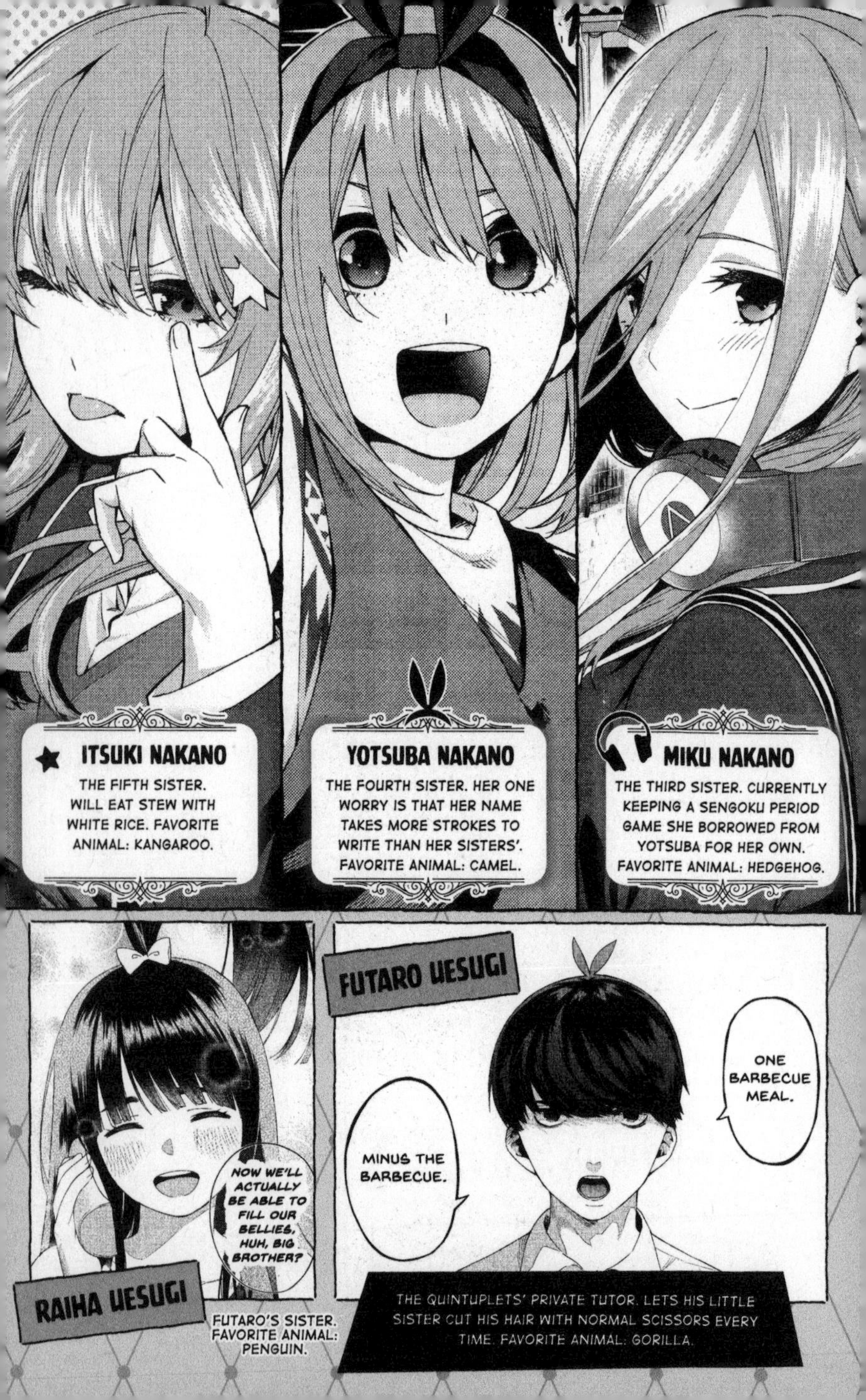
MIKU NAKANO
THE THIRD SISTER. CURRENTLY KEEPING A SENGOKU PERIOD GAME SHE BORROWED FROM YOTSUBA FOR HER OWN. FAVORITE ANIMAL: HEDGEHOG.
YOTSUBA NAKANO
THE FOURTH SISTER. HER ONE WORRY IS THAT HER NAME TAKES MORE STROKES TO WRITE THAN HER SISTERS'. FAVORITE ANIMAL: CAMEL.
ITSUKI NAKANO
THE FIFTH SISTER. WILL EAT STEW WITH WHITE RICE. FAVORITE ANIMAL: KANGAROO.
FUTARO UESUGI
ONE BARBECUE MEAL.
MINUS THE BARBECUE.
THE QUINTUPLETS' PRIVATE TUTOR. LETS HIS LITTLE SISTER CUT HIS HAIR WITH NORMAL SCISSORS EVERY TIME. FAVORITE ANIMAL: GORILLA.
NOW WE'LL ACTUALLY BE ABLE TO FILL OUR BELLIES, HUH, BIG BROTHER?
RAIHA UESUGI
FUTARO'S SISTER. FAVORITE ANIMAL: PENGUIN.

CONTENTS

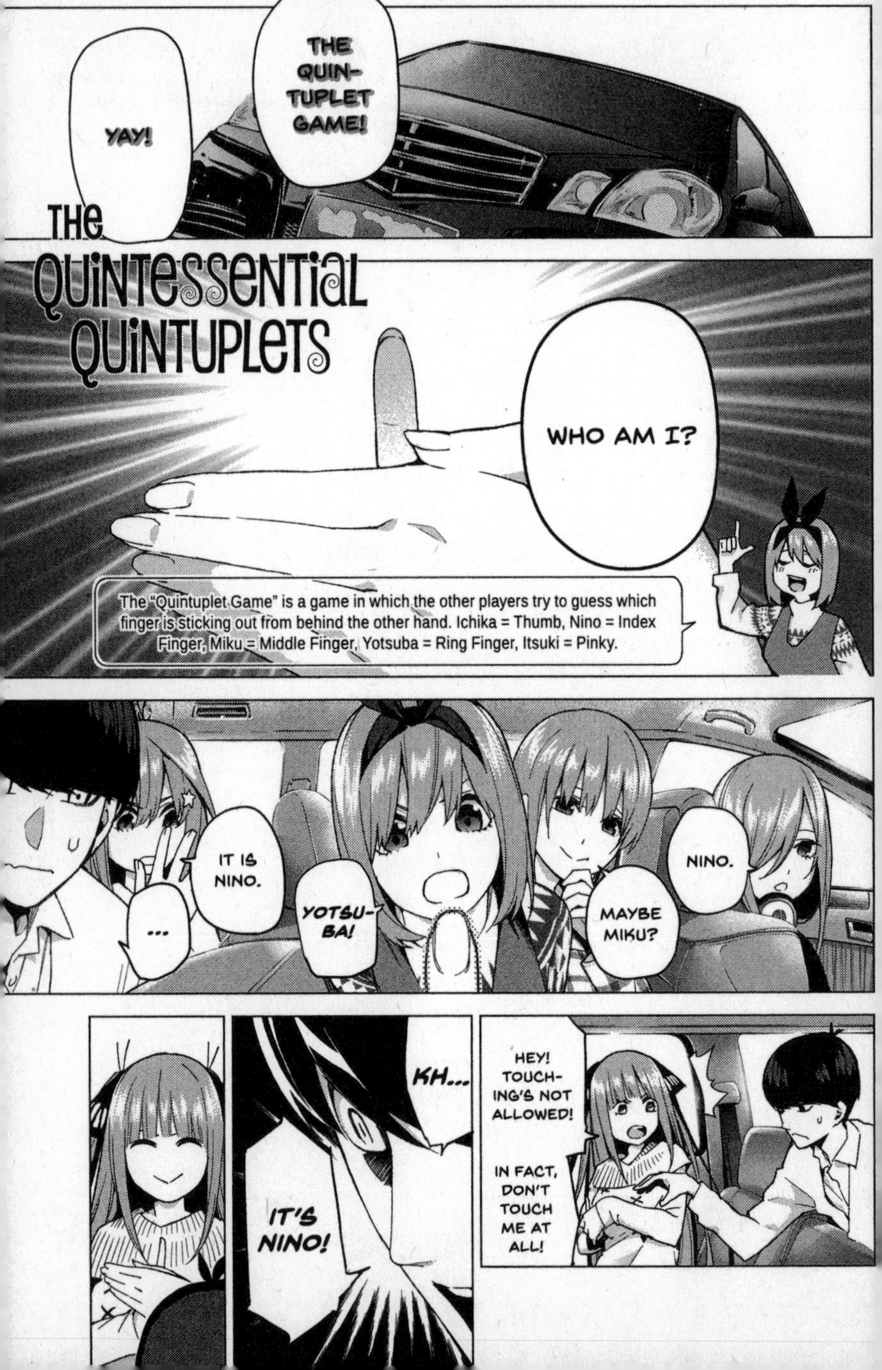
THE QUINTUPLET GAME!
YAY!
The Quintessential Quintuplets
WHO AM I?
The "Quintuplet Game" is a game in which the other players try to guess which finger is sticking out from behind the other hand. Ichika = Thumb, Nino = Index Finger, Miku = Middle Finger, Yotsuba = Ring Finger, Itsuki = Pinky.
NINO.
MAYBE MIKU?
YOTSUBA!
IT IS NINO.
...
HEY! TOUCHING'S NOT ALLOWED!
IN FACT, DON'T TOUCH ME AT ALL!
KH...
IT'S NINO!

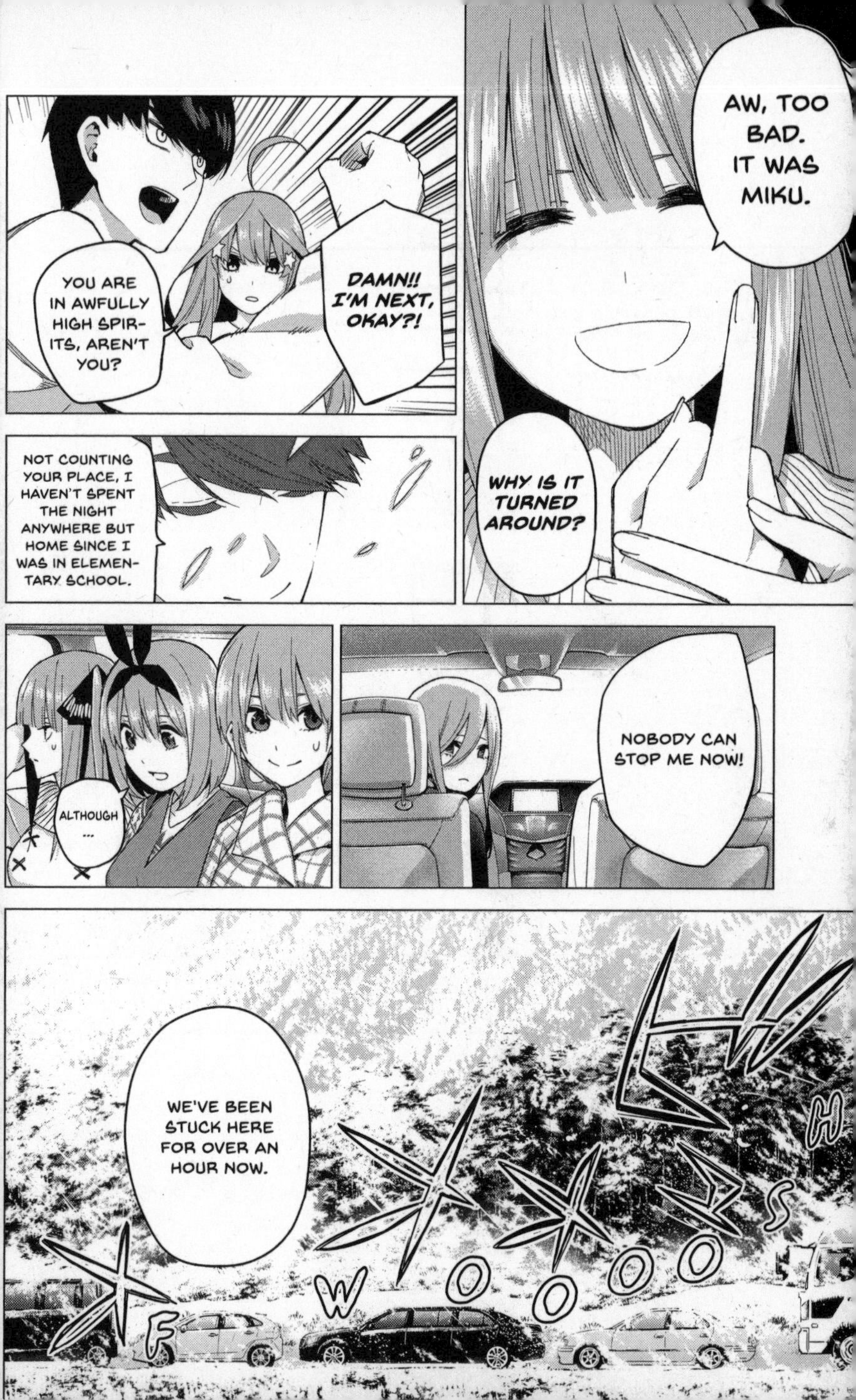
AW, TOO BAD. IT WAS MIKU.
WHY IS IT TURNED AROUND?
DAMN!! I'M NEXT, OKAY?!
YOU ARE IN AWFULLY HIGH SPIR-ITS, AREN'T YOU?
NOT COUNTING YOUR PLACE, I HAVEN'T SPENT THE NIGHT ANYWHERE BUT HOME SINCE I WAS IN ELEMEN-TARY SCHOOL.
NOBODY CAN STOP ME NOW!
ALTHOUGH...
WE'VE BEEN STUCK HERE FOR OVER AN HOUR NOW.
FWOOOOSH

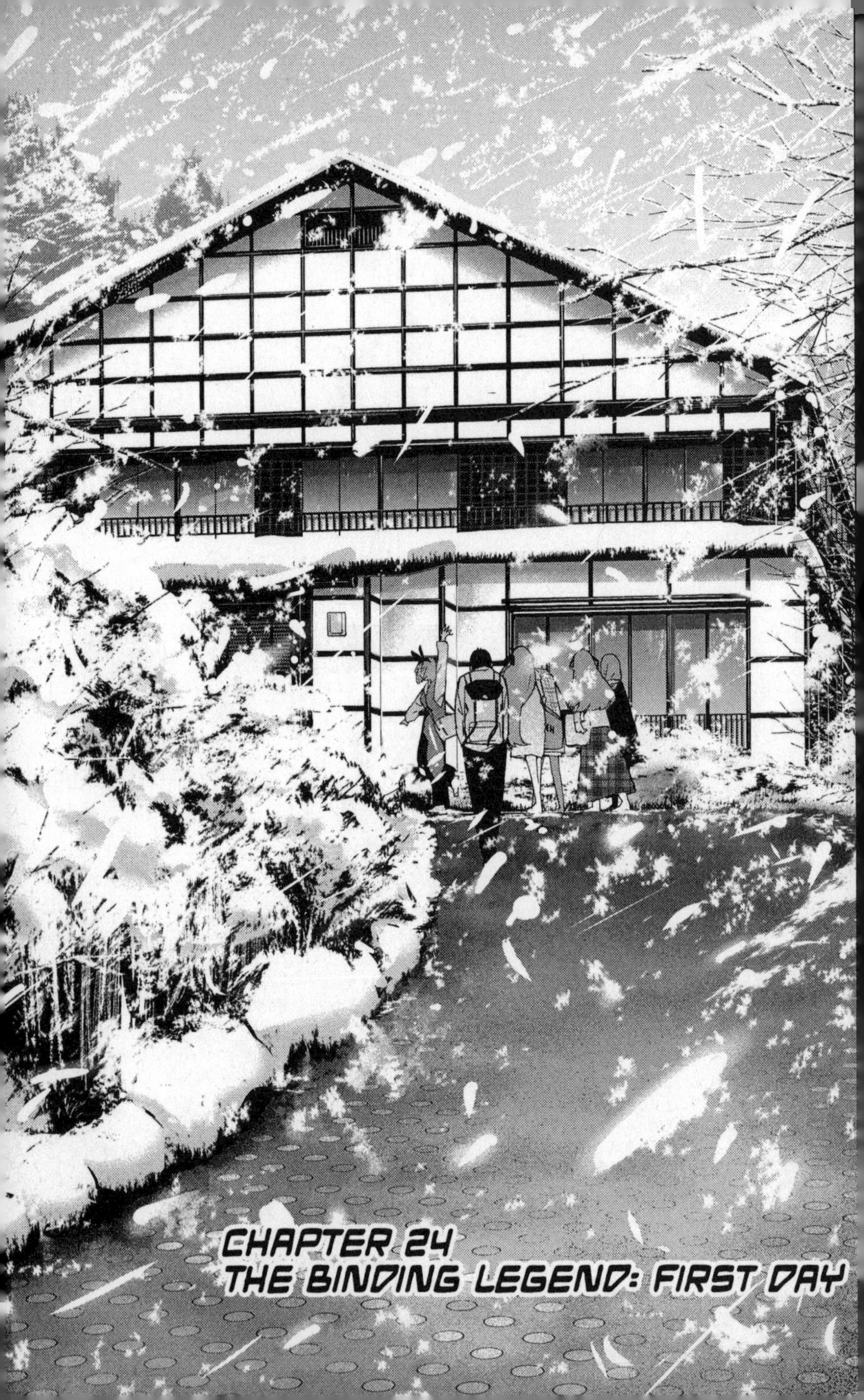
CHAPTER 24
THE BINDING LEGEND: FIRST DAY

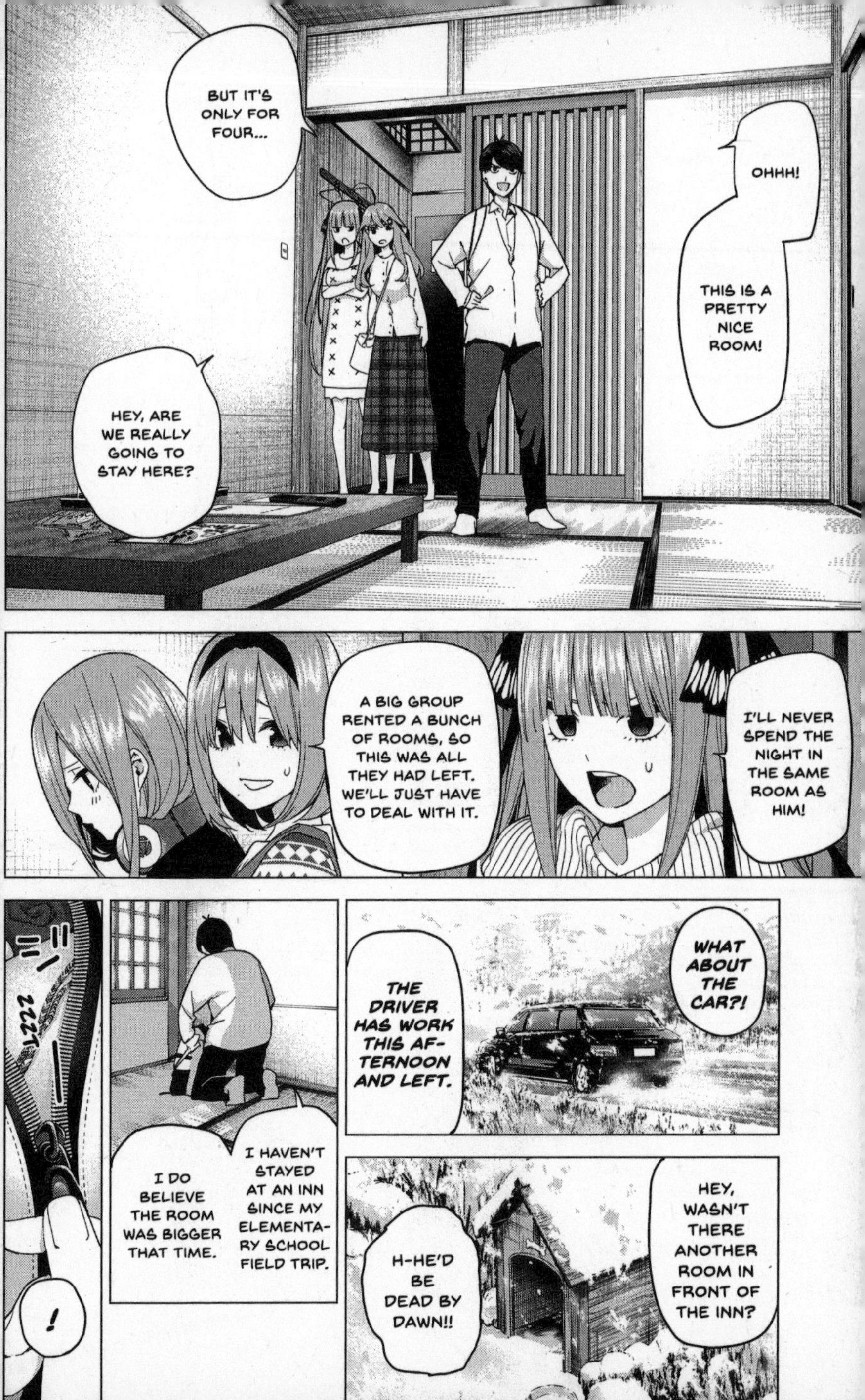
OHHH!
THIS IS A PRETTY NICE ROOM!
BUT IT'S ONLY FOR FOUR...
HEY, ARE WE REALLY GOING TO STAY HERE?
I'LL NEVER SPEND THE NIGHT IN THE SAME ROOM AS HIM!
A BIG GROUP RENTED A BUNCH OF ROOMS, SO THIS WAS ALL THEY HAD LEFT. WE'LL JUST HAVE TO DEAL WITH IT.
WHAT ABOUT THE CAR?!
THE DRIVER HAS WORK THIS AFTERNOON AND LEFT.
HEY, WASN'T THERE ANOTHER ROOM IN FRONT OF THE INN?
H-HE'D BE DEAD BY DAWN!!
I HAVEN'T STAYED AT AN INN SINCE MY ELEMENTARY SCHOOL FIELD TRIP.
I DO BELIEVE THE ROOM WAS BIGGER THAT TIME.
ZZZ
!

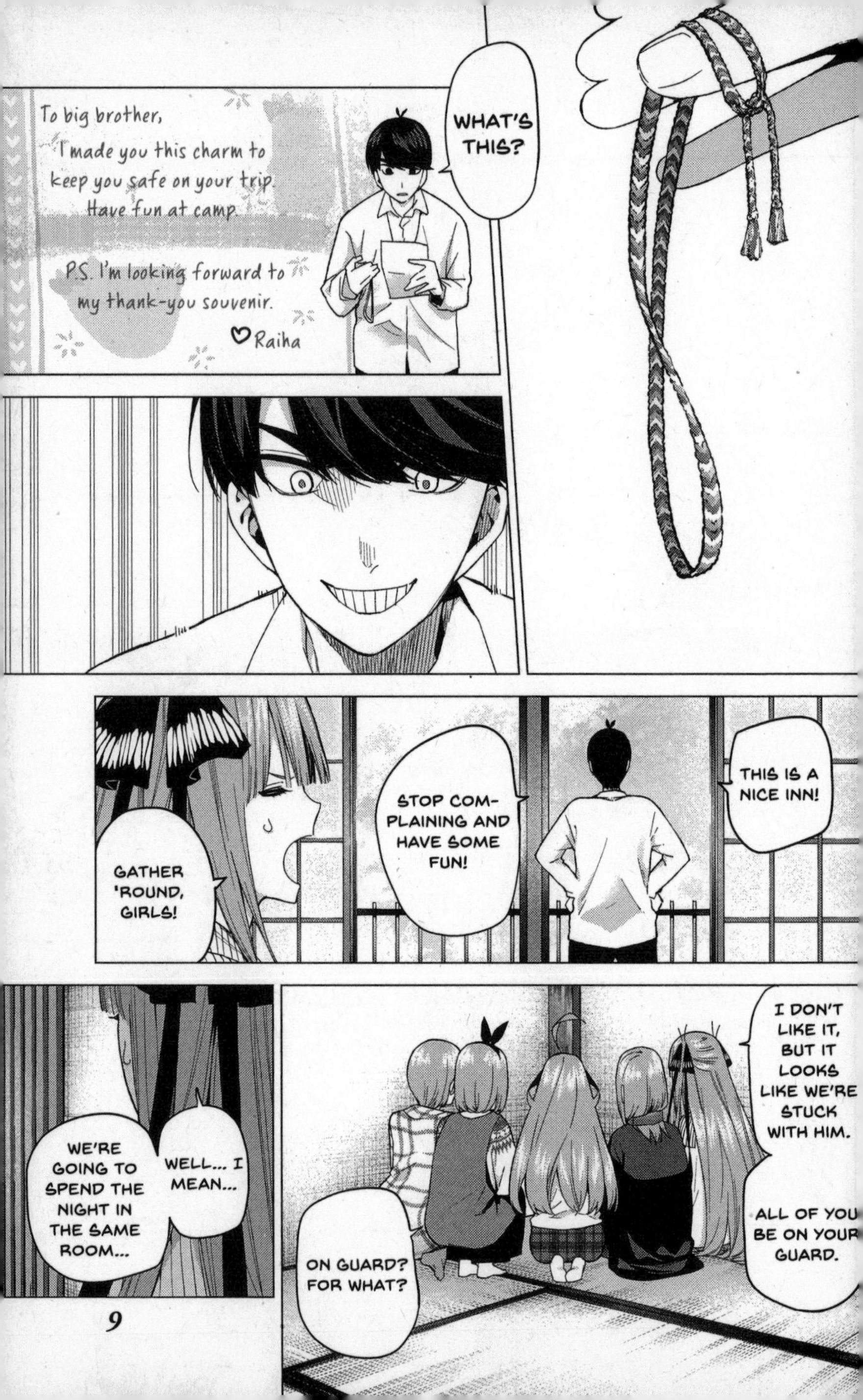
WHAT'S THIS?
To big brother,
I made you this charm to keep you safe on your trip. Have fun at camp.
P.S. I'm looking forward to my thank-you souvenir.
Raiha
THIS IS A NICE INN!
STOP COMPLAINING AND HAVE SOME FUN!
GATHER 'ROUND, GIRLS!
I DON'T LIKE IT, BUT IT LOOKS LIKE WE'RE STUCK WITH HIM.
ALL OF YOU BE ON YOUR GUARD.
ON GUARD? FOR WHAT?
WELL... I MEAN...
WE'RE GOING TO SPEND THE NIGHT IN THE SAME ROOM...

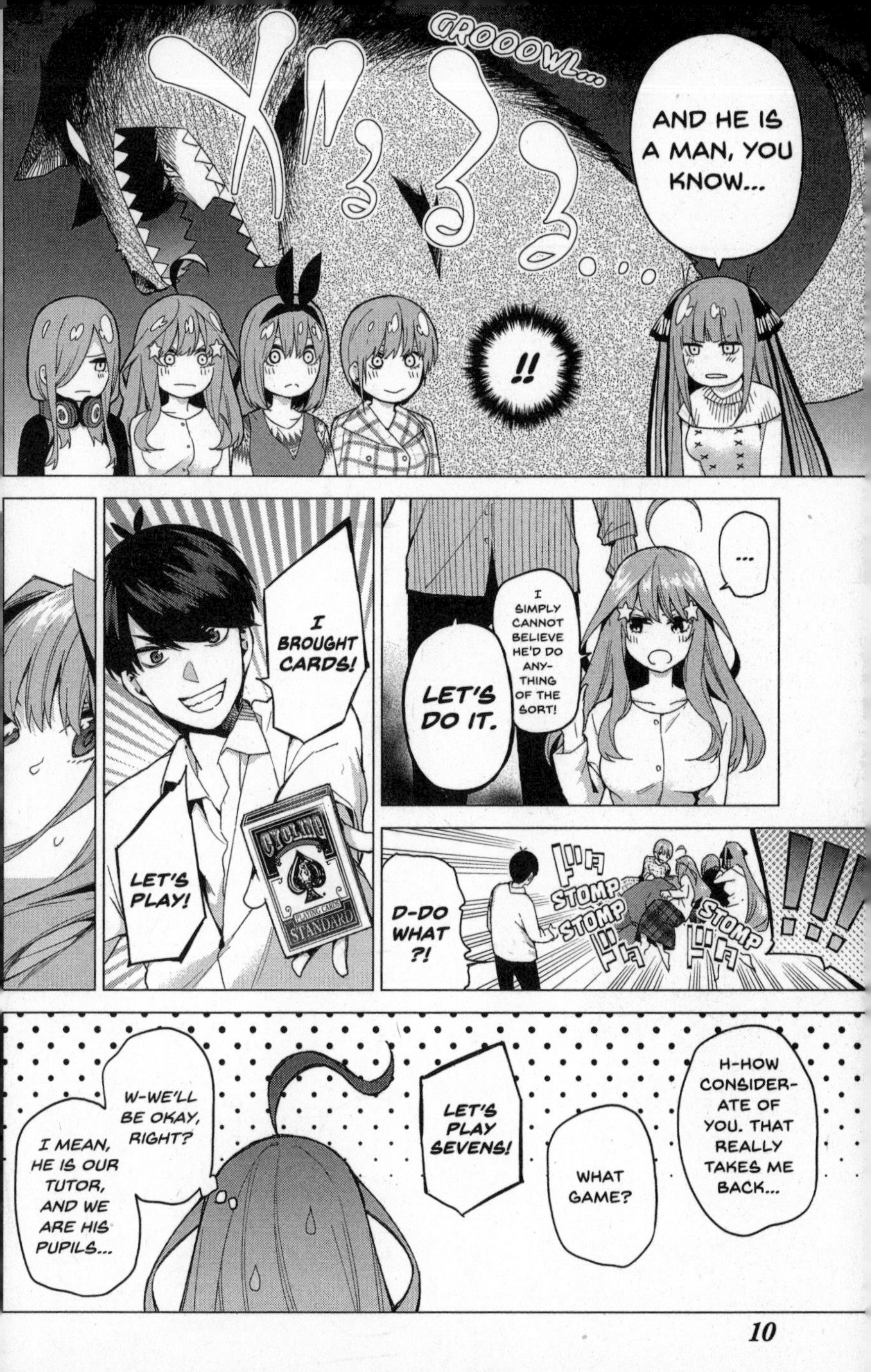
GROOOWL...
AND HE IS A MAN, YOU KNOW...
!!
...
I SIMPLY CANNOT BELIEVE HE'D DO ANYTHING OF THE SORT!
LET'S DO IT.
!!!
STOMP
STOMP
STOMP
D-DO WHAT?!
I BROUGHT CARDS!
LET'S PLAY!
CYCLING
PLAYING CARDS
STANDARD
H-HOW CONSIDERATE OF YOU. THAT REALLY TAKES ME BACK...
WHAT GAME?
LET'S PLAY SEVENS!
W-WE'LL BE OKAY, RIGHT?
I MEAN, HE IS OUR TUTOR, AND WE ARE HIS PUPILS...

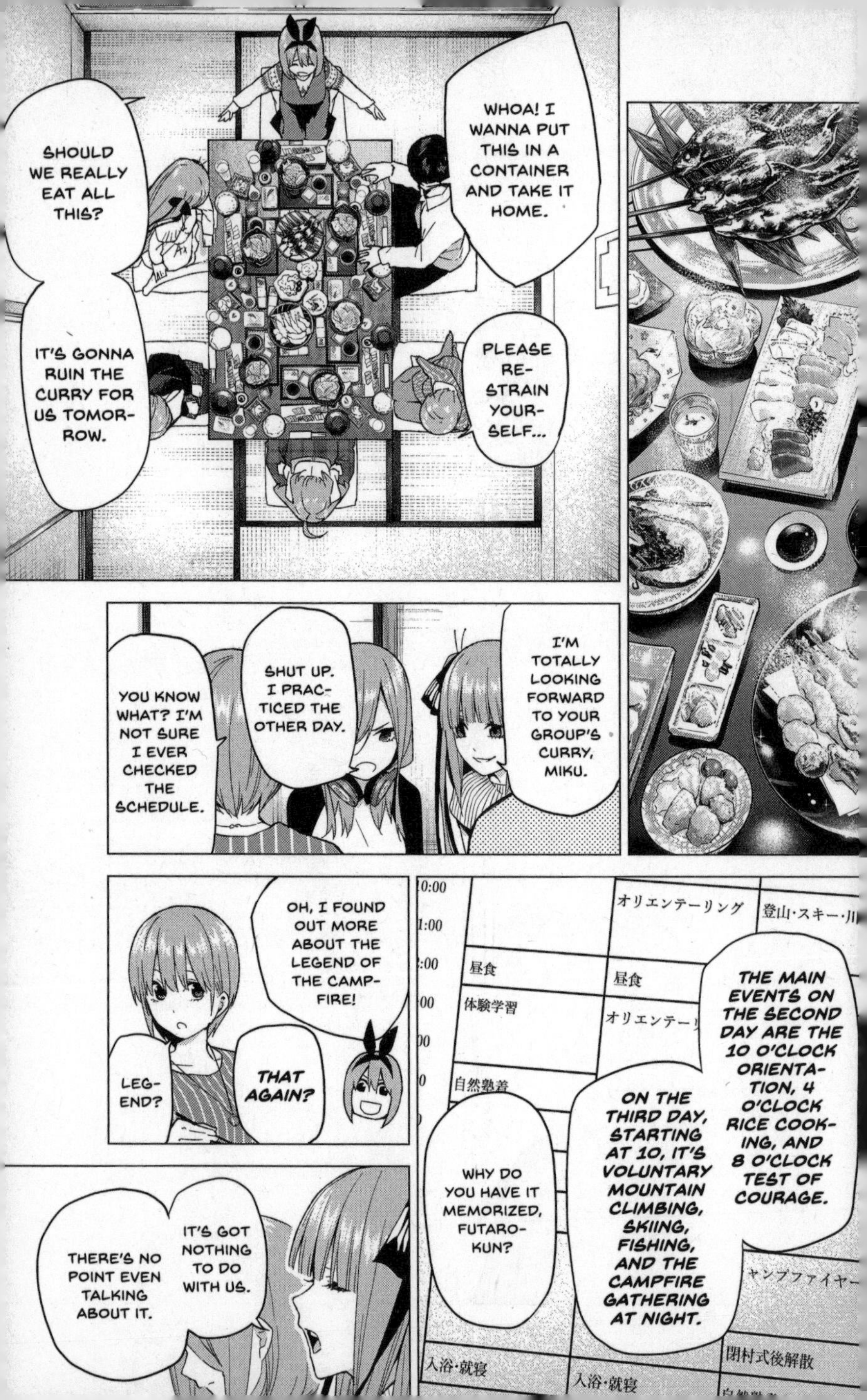
WHOA! I WANNA PUT THIS IN A CONTAINER AND TAKE IT HOME.
PLEASE RE-STRAIN YOUR-SELF...
SHOULD WE REALLY EAT ALL THIS?
IT'S GONNA RUIN THE CURRY FOR US TOMOR-ROW.
I'M TOTALLY LOOKING FORWARD TO YOUR GROUP'S CURRY, MIKU.
SHUT UP. I PRAC-TICED THE OTHER DAY.
YOU KNOW WHAT? I'M NOT SURE I EVER CHECKED THE SCHEDULE.
オリエンテーリング
登山・スキー・川
昼食
昼食
体験学習
自然塾着
閉村式後解散
入浴・就寝
入浴・就寝
THE MAIN EVENTS ON THE SECOND DAY ARE THE 10 O'CLOCK ORIENTA-TION, 4 O'CLOCK RICE COOK-ING, AND 8 O'CLOCK TEST OF COURAGE.
ON THE THIRD DAY, STARTING AT 10, IT'S VOLUNTARY MOUNTAIN CLIMBING, SKIING, FISHING, AND THE CAMPFIRE GATHERING AT NIGHT.
WHY DO YOU HAVE IT MEMORIZED, FUTARO-KUN?
OH, I FOUND OUT MORE ABOUT THE LEGEND OF THE CAMP-FIRE!
THAT AGAIN?
LEG-END?
IT'S GOT NOTHING TO DO WITH US.
THERE'S NO POINT EVEN TALKING ABOUT IT.

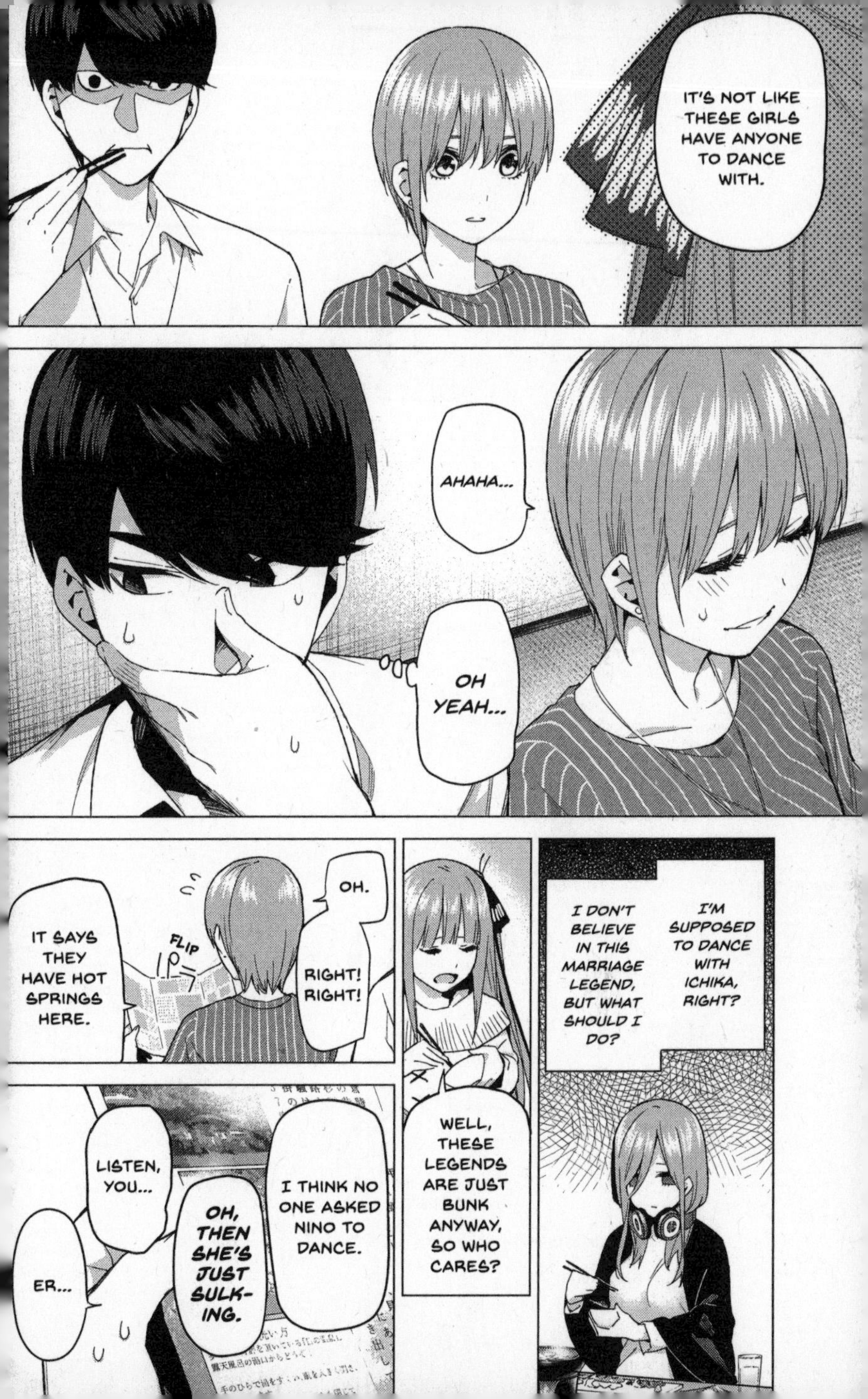

IT'S NOT LIKE THESE GIRLS HAVE ANYONE TO DANCE WITH.
AHAHA...
OH YEAH...
I'M SUPPOSED TO DANCE WITH ICHIKA, RIGHT?
I DON'T BELIEVE IN THIS MARRIAGE LEGEND, BUT WHAT SHOULD I DO?
WELL, THESE LEGENDS ARE JUST BUNK ANYWAY, SO WHO CARES?
OH.
RIGHT! RIGHT!
FLIP
IT SAYS THEY HAVE HOT SPRINGS HERE.
I THINK NO ONE ASKED NINO TO DANCE.
OH, THEN SHE'S JUST SULKING.
LISTEN, YOU...
ER...

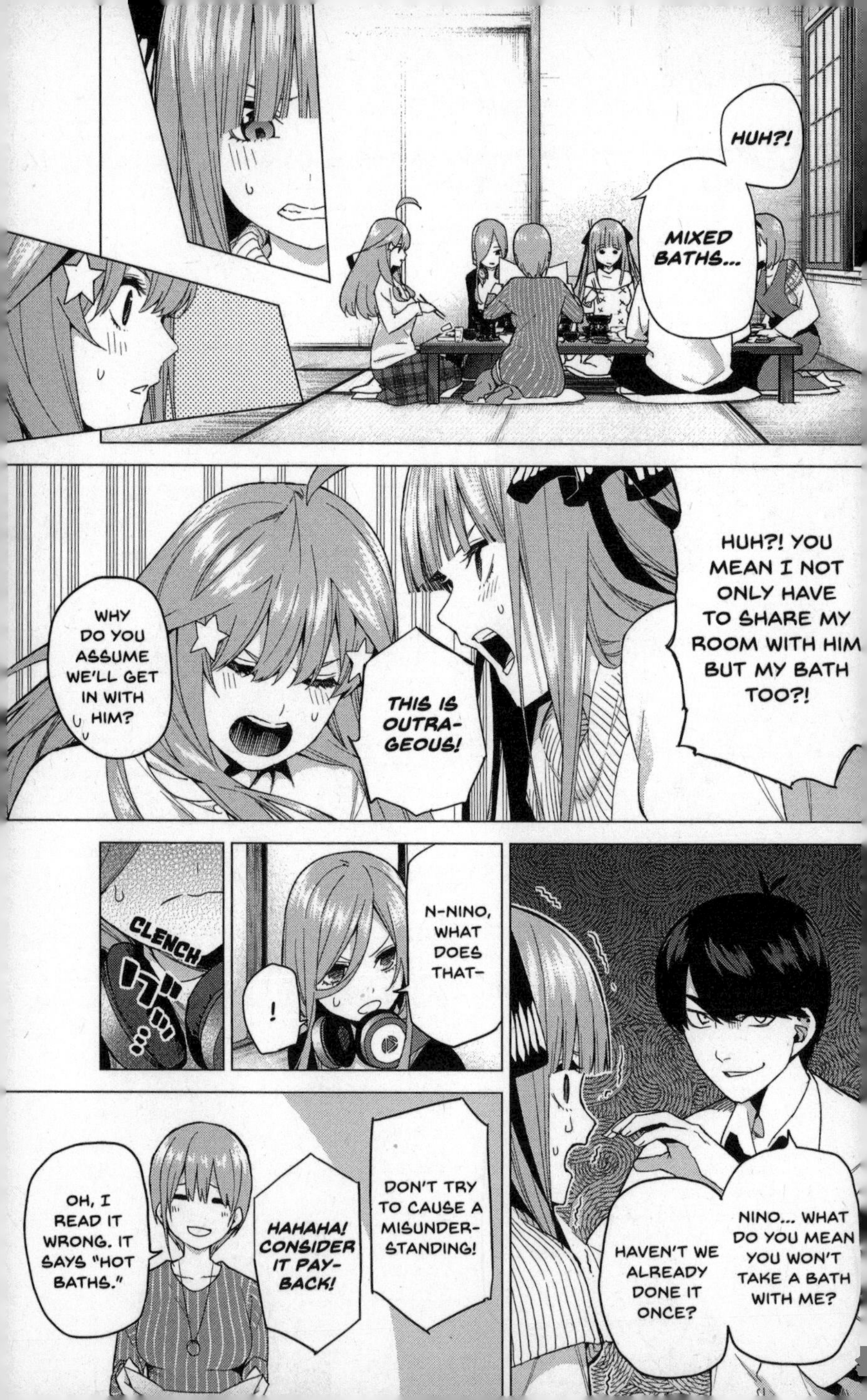
HUH?!
MIXED BATHS...
HUH?! YOU MEAN I NOT ONLY HAVE TO SHARE MY ROOM WITH HIM BUT MY BATH TOO?!
THIS IS OUTRAGEOUS!
WHY DO YOU ASSUME WE'LL GET IN WITH HIM?
NINO... WHAT DO YOU MEAN YOU WON'T TAKE A BATH WITH ME?
HAVEN'T WE ALREADY DONE IT ONCE?
N-NINO, WHAT DOES THAT-
!
CLENCH
DON'T TRY TO CAUSE A MISUNDER-STANDING!
HAHAHA! CONSIDER IT PAY-BACK!
OH, I READ IT WRONG. IT SAYS "HOT BATHS."

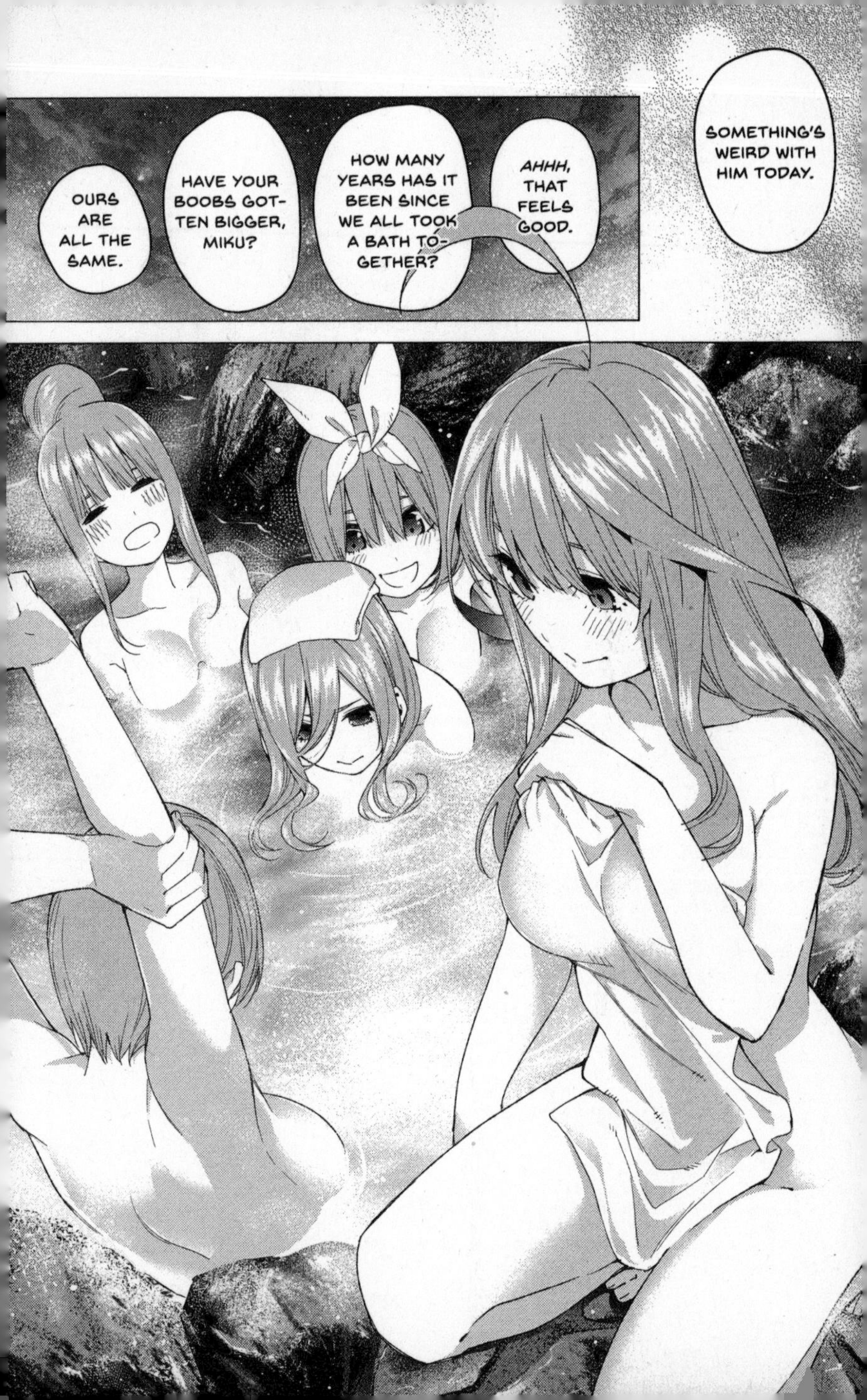
SOMETHING'S WEIRD WITH HIM TODAY.
AHHH, THAT FEELS GOOD.
HOW MANY YEARS HAS IT BEEN SINCE WE ALL TOOK A BATH TO-GETHER?
HAVE YOUR BOOBS GOT-TEN BIGGER, MIKU?
OURS ARE ALL THE SAME.

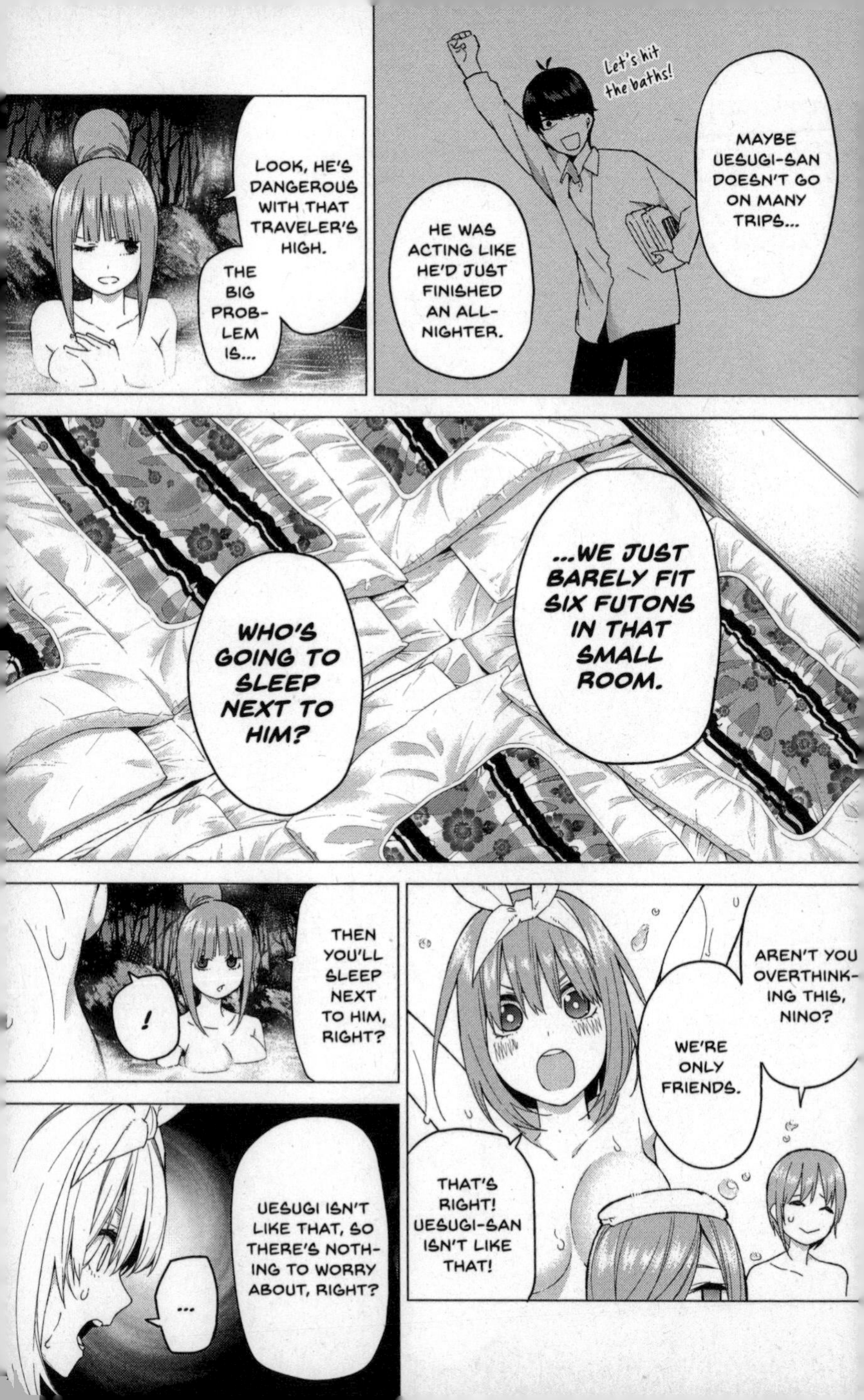
MAYBE UESUGI-SAN DOESN'T GO ON MANY TRIPS...
Let's hit the baths!
HE WAS ACTING LIKE HE'D JUST FINISHED AN ALL-NIGHTER.
LOOK, HE'S DANGEROUS WITH THAT TRAVELER'S HIGH.
THE BIG PROBLEM IS...
...WE JUST BARELY FIT SIX FUTONS IN THAT SMALL ROOM.
WHO'S GOING TO SLEEP NEXT TO HIM?
AREN'T YOU OVERTHINKING THIS, NINO?
WE'RE ONLY FRIENDS.
THAT'S RIGHT! UESUGI-SAN ISN'T LIKE THAT!
THEN YOU'LL SLEEP NEXT TO HIM, RIGHT?
!
UESUGI ISN'T LIKE THAT, SO THERE'S NOTHING TO WORRY ABOUT, RIGHT?
...

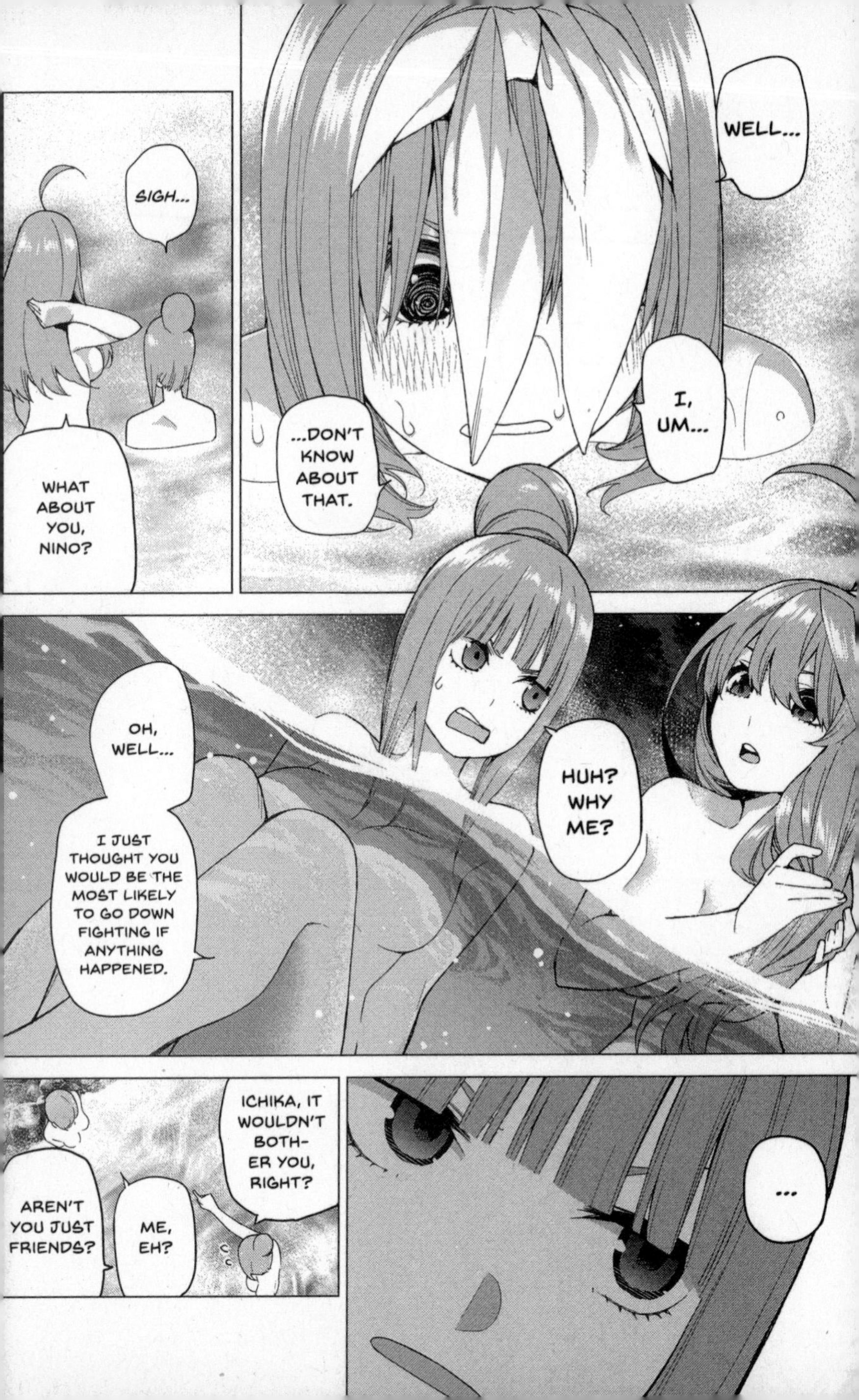
WELL...
I, UM...
...DON'T KNOW ABOUT THAT.
SIGH...
WHAT ABOUT YOU, NINO?
HUH? WHY ME?
OH, WELL...
I JUST THOUGHT YOU WOULD BE THE MOST LIKELY TO GO DOWN FIGHTING IF ANYTHING HAPPENED.
...
ICHIKA, IT WOULDN'T BOTH-ER YOU, RIGHT?
ME, EH?
AREN'T YOU JUST FRIENDS?

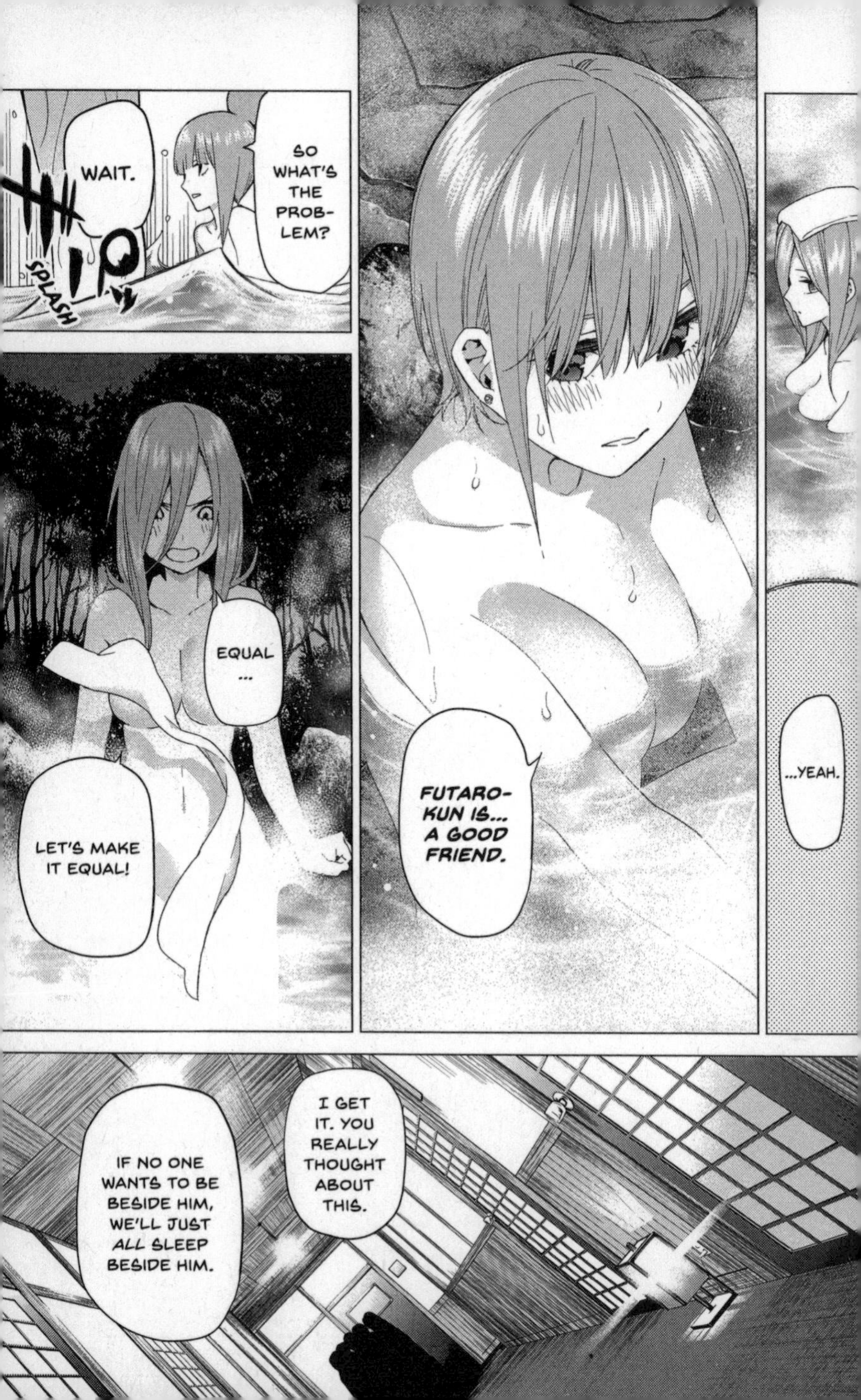

...YEAH.
FUTARO-KUN IS... A GOOD FRIEND.
SO WHAT'S THE PROB-LEM?
WAIT.
SPLASH
EQUAL...
LET'S MAKE IT EQUAL!
I GET IT. YOU REALLY THOUGHT ABOUT THIS.
IF NO ONE WANTS TO BE BESIDE HIM, WE'LL JUST *ALL* SLEEP BESIDE HIM.

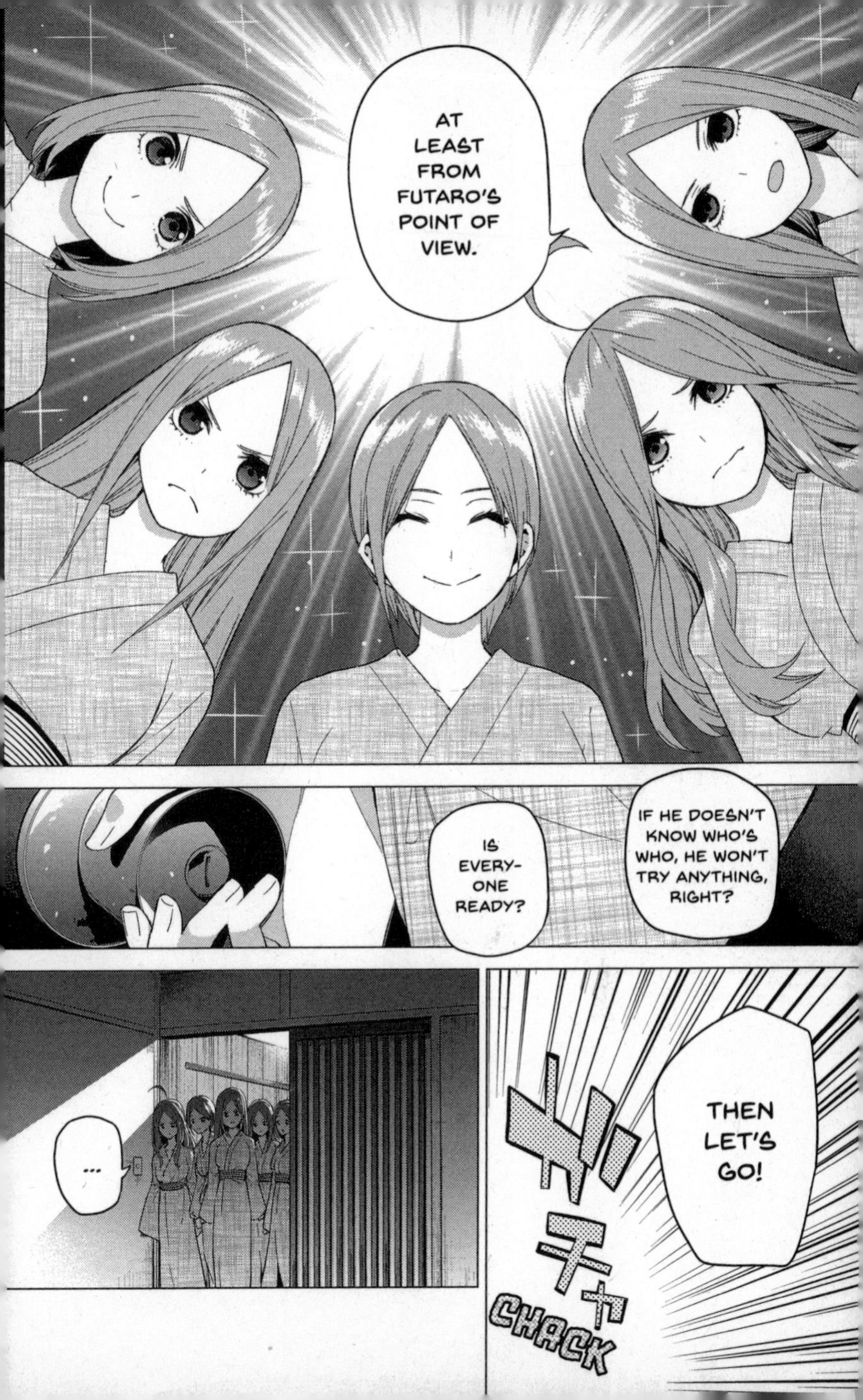
AT LEAST FROM FUTARO'S POINT OF VIEW.
IF HE DOESN'T KNOW WHO'S WHO, HE WON'T TRY ANYTHING, RIGHT?
IS EVERY-ONE READY?
THEN LET'S GO!
CHACK
...

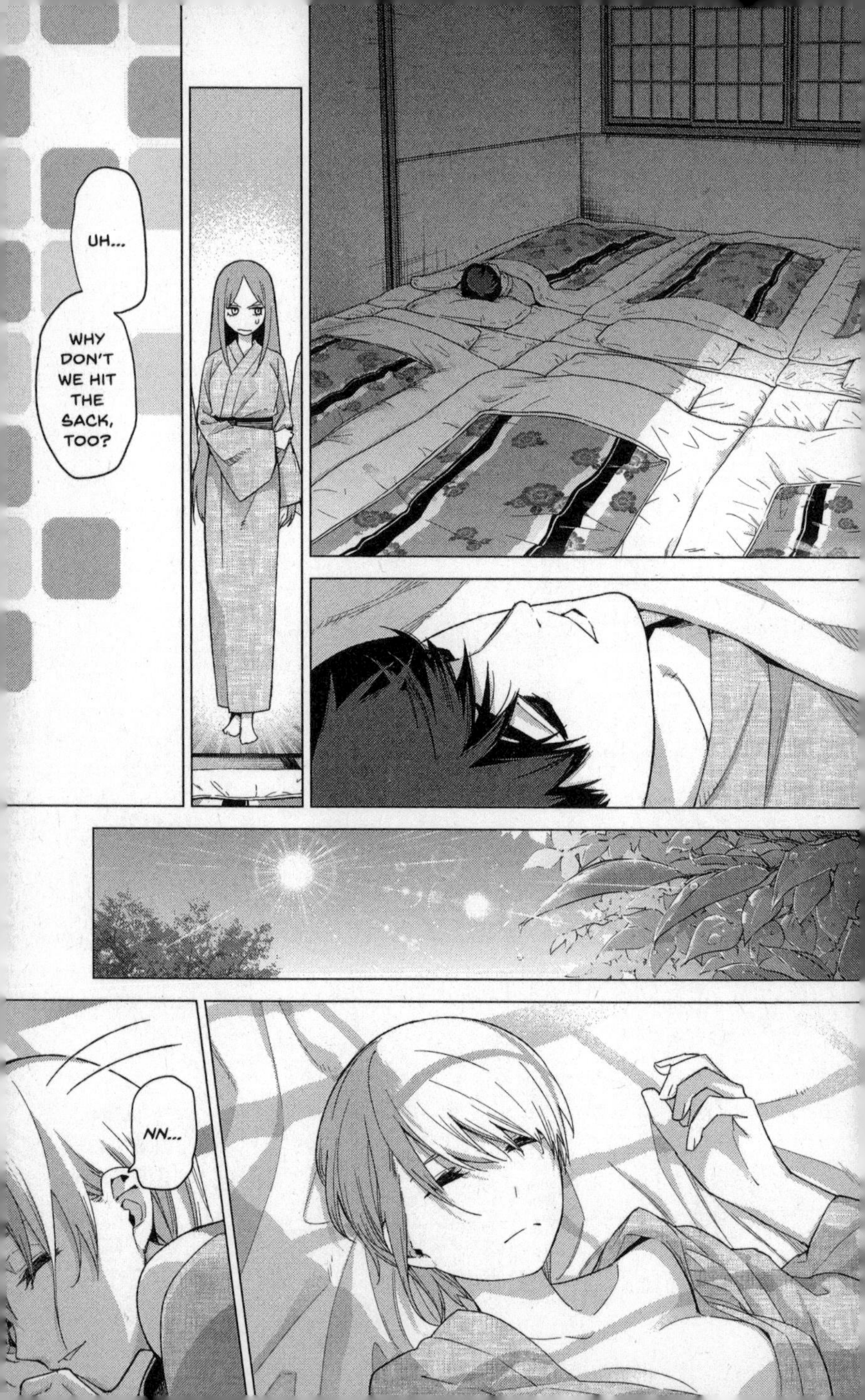
UH...
WHY DON'T WE HIT THE SACK, TOO?
NN...

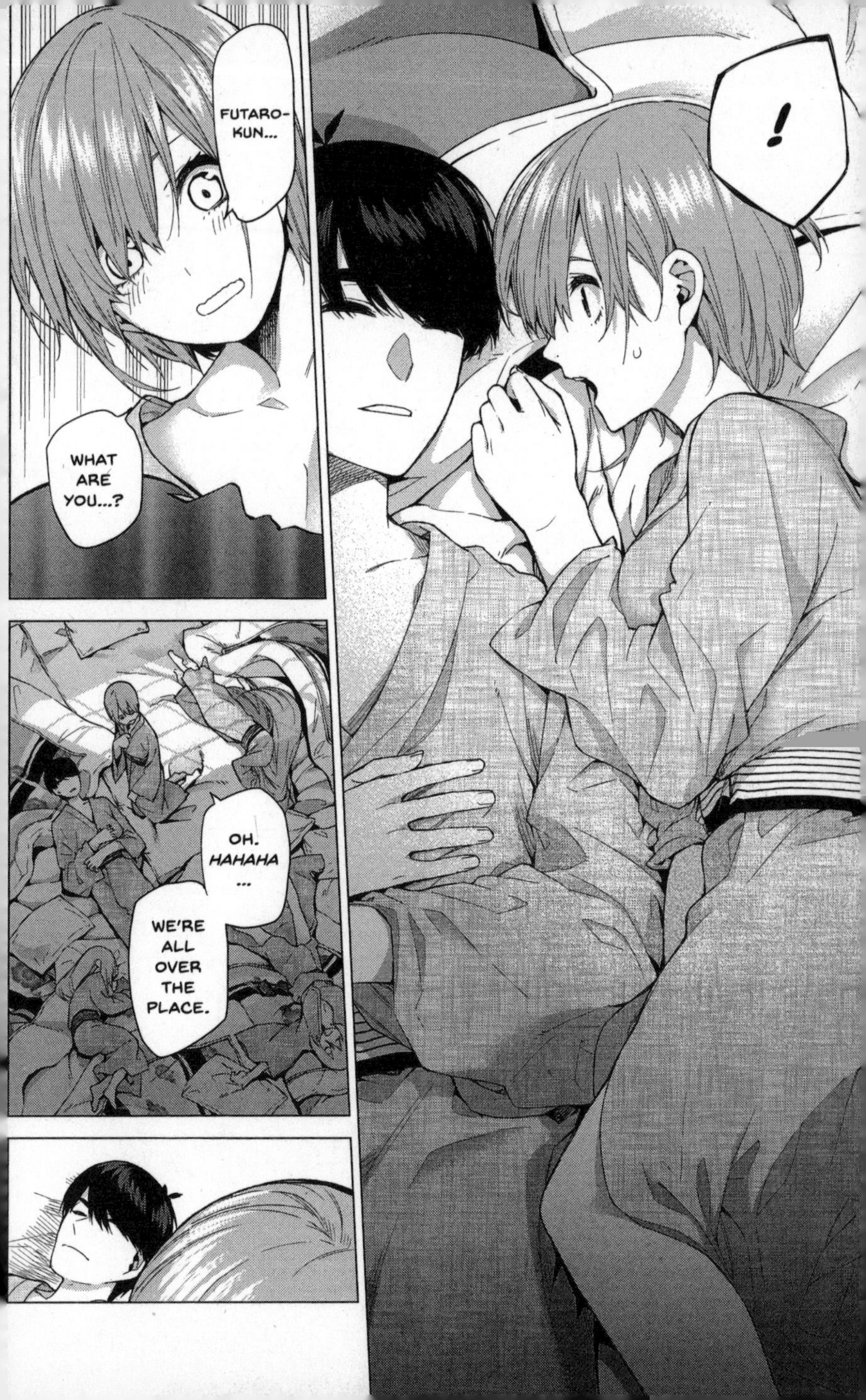
!
FUTARO-KUN...
WHAT ARE YOU...?
OH. *HAHAHA* ...
WE'RE ALL OVER THE PLACE.

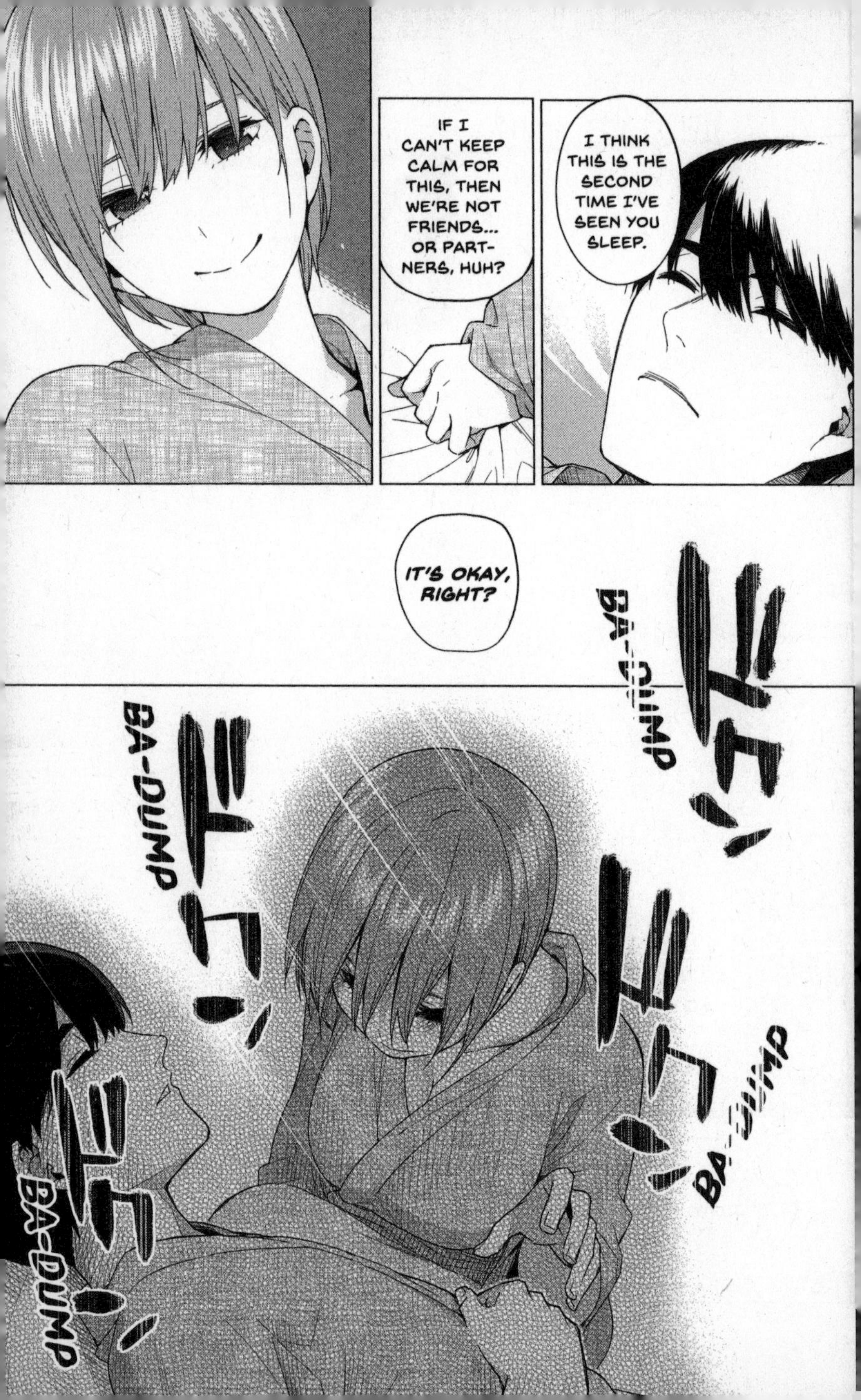
I THINK THIS IS THE SECOND TIME I'VE SEEN YOU SLEEP.
IF I CAN'T KEEP CALM FOR THIS, THEN WE'RE NOT FRIENDS... OR PART-NERS, HUH?
BA-DUMP
IT'S OKAY, RIGHT?
BA-DUMP
BA-DUMP
BA-DUMP

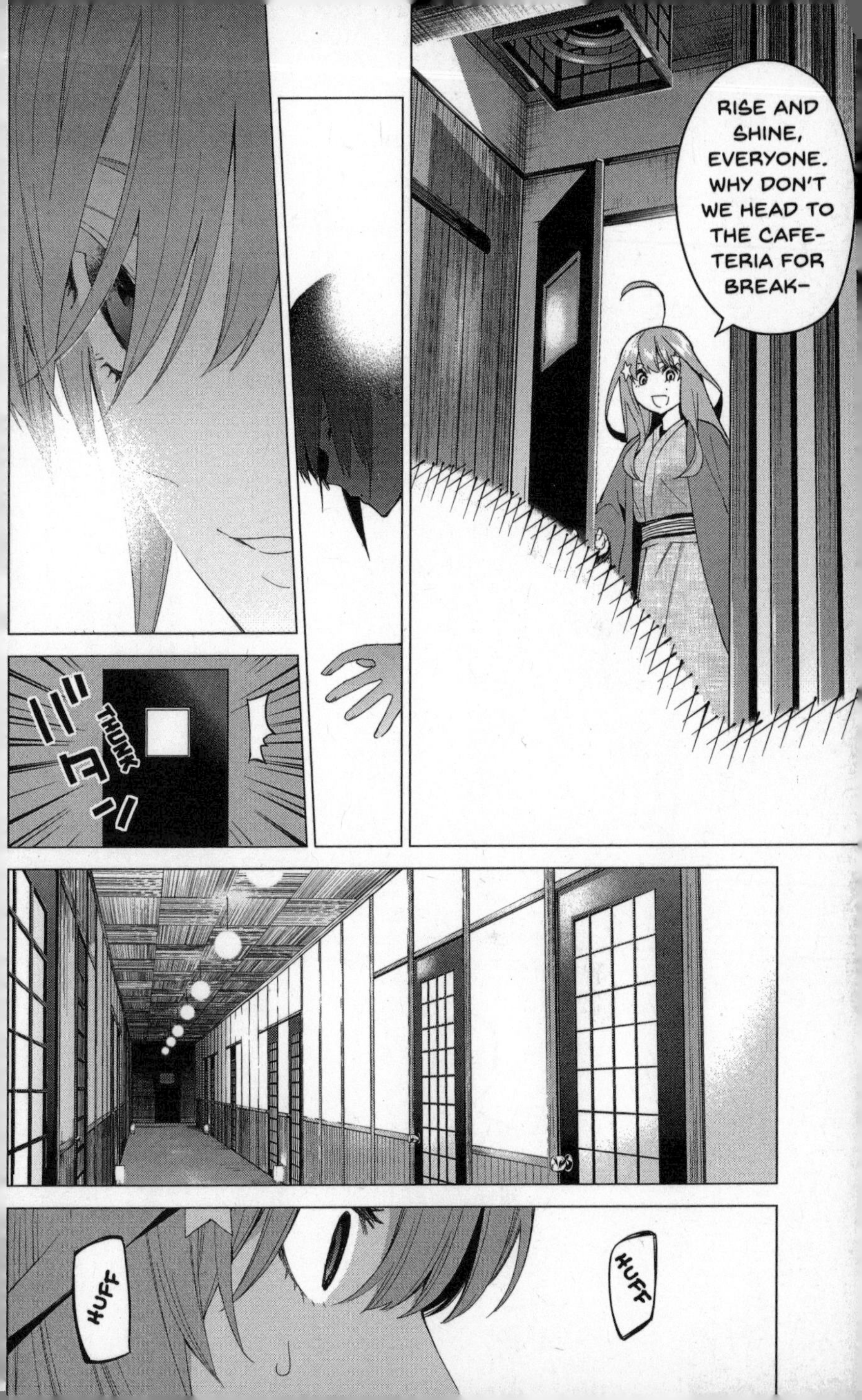
RISE AND SHINE, EVERYONE. WHY DON'T WE HEAD TO THE CAFETERIA FOR BREAK–
THUNK
HUFF
HUFF

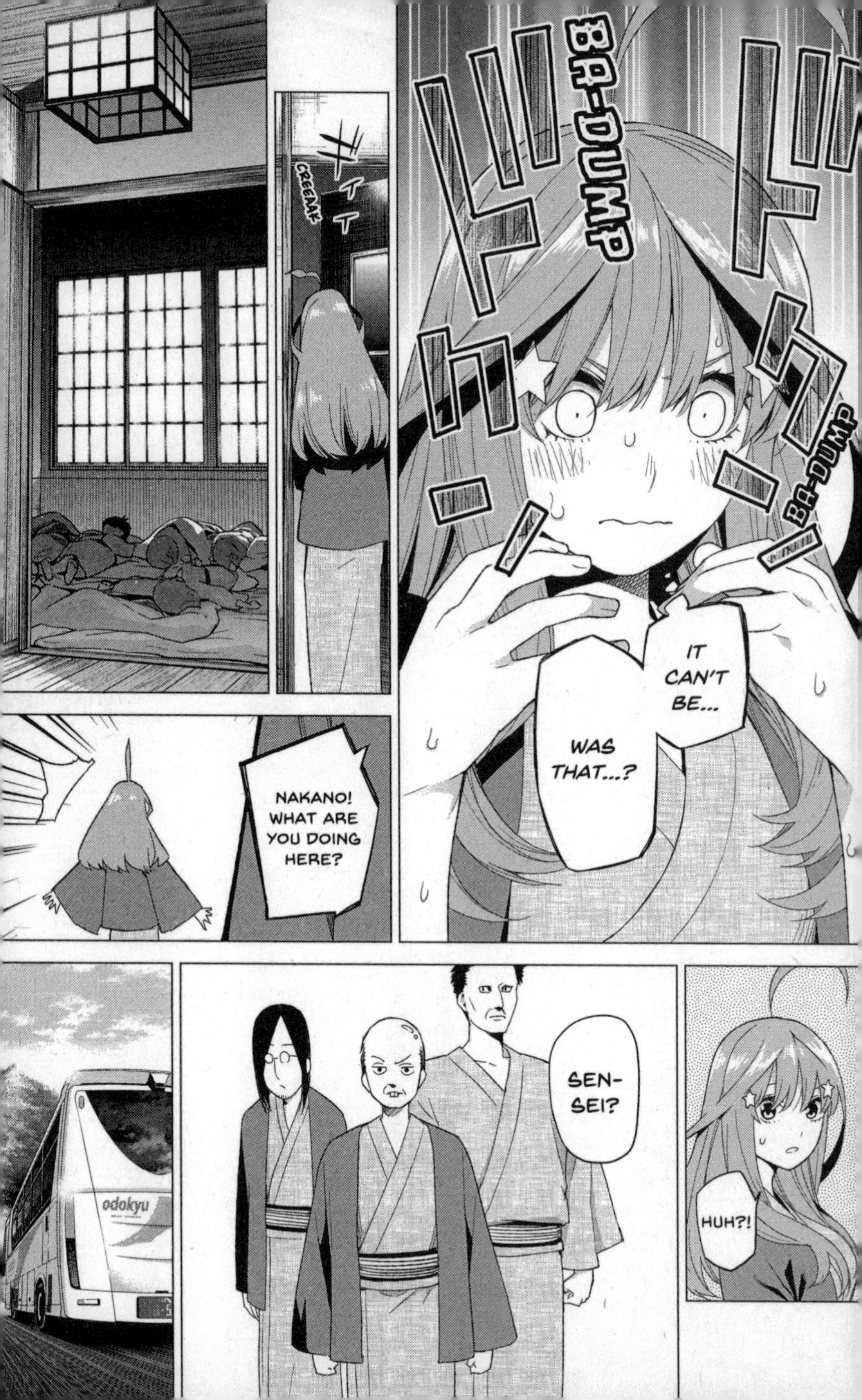
BA-DUMP
BA-DUMP
IT CAN'T BE...
WAS THAT...?
CREEAAK
NAKANO! WHAT ARE YOU DOING HERE?
HUH?!
SEN-SEI?
odakyu

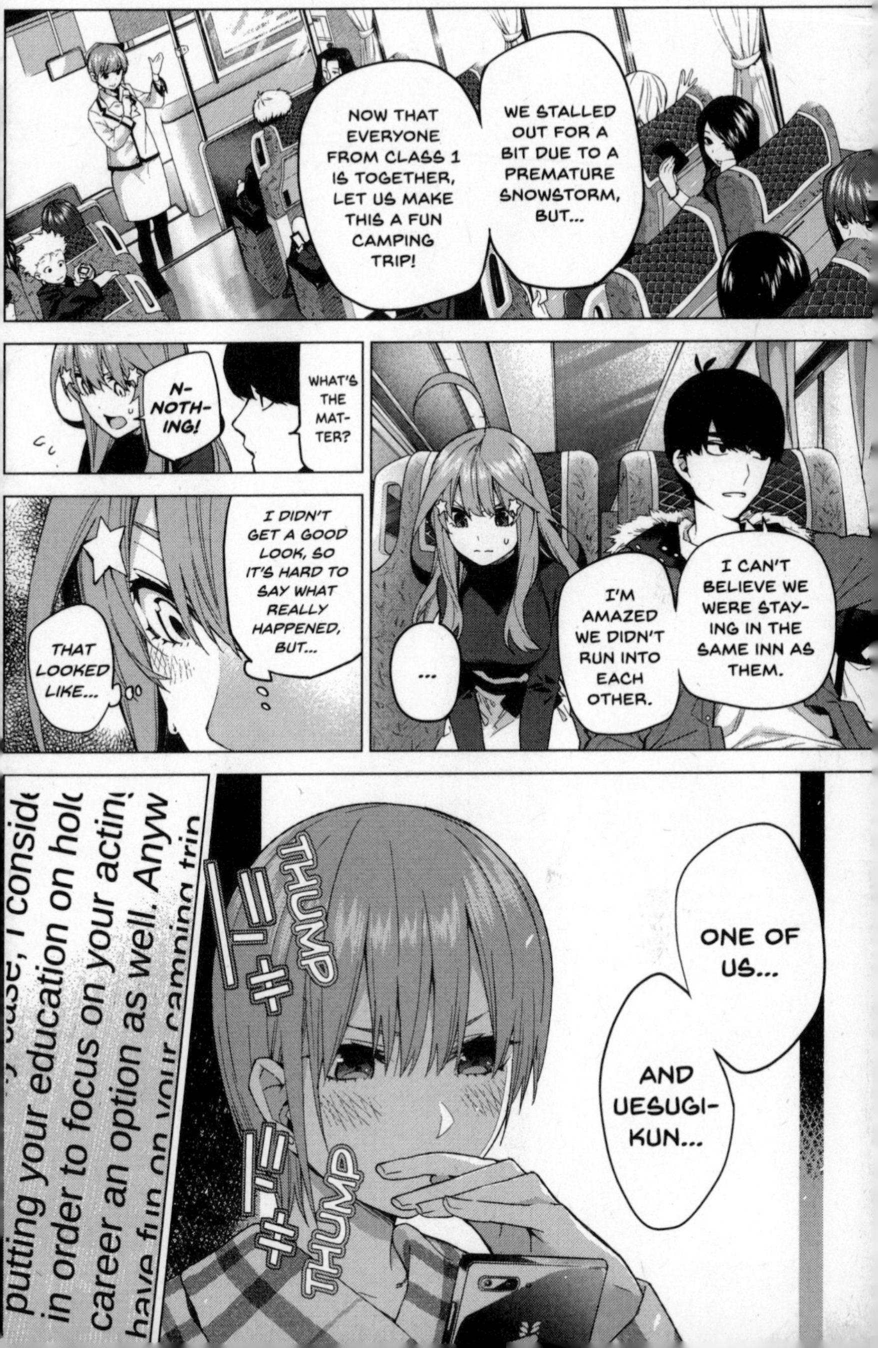
WE STALLED OUT FOR A BIT DUE TO A PREMATURE SNOWSTORM, BUT...
NOW THAT EVERYONE FROM CLASS 1 IS TOGETHER, LET US MAKE THIS A FUN CAMPING TRIP!
I CAN'T BELIEVE WE WERE STAYING IN THE SAME INN AS THEM.
I'M AMAZED WE DIDN'T RUN INTO EACH OTHER.
...
WHAT'S THE MATTER?
N-NOTHING!
I DIDN'T GET A GOOD LOOK, SO IT'S HARD TO SAY WHAT REALLY HAPPENED, BUT...
THAT LOOKED LIKE...
ONE OF US...
AND UESUGI-KUN...
THUMP
THUMP

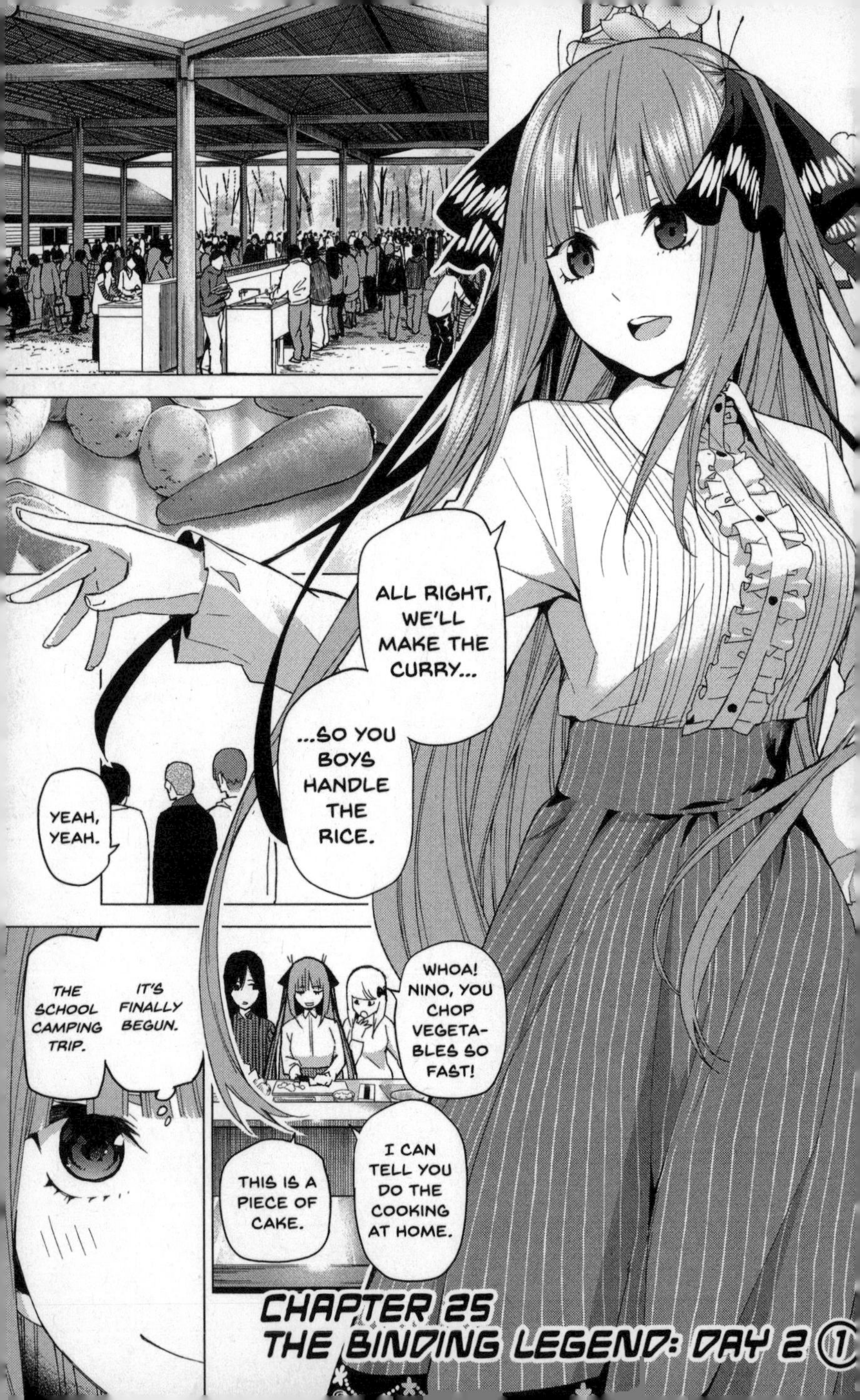
ALL RIGHT, WE'LL MAKE THE CURRY...
...SO YOU BOYS HANDLE THE RICE.
YEAH, YEAH.
WHOA! NINO, YOU CHOP VEGETA-BLES SO FAST!
I CAN TELL YOU DO THE COOKING AT HOME.
THIS IS A PIECE OF CAKE.
IT'S FINALLY BEGUN.
THE SCHOOL CAMPING TRIP.
CHAPTER 25
THE BINDING LEGEND: DAY 2 ①

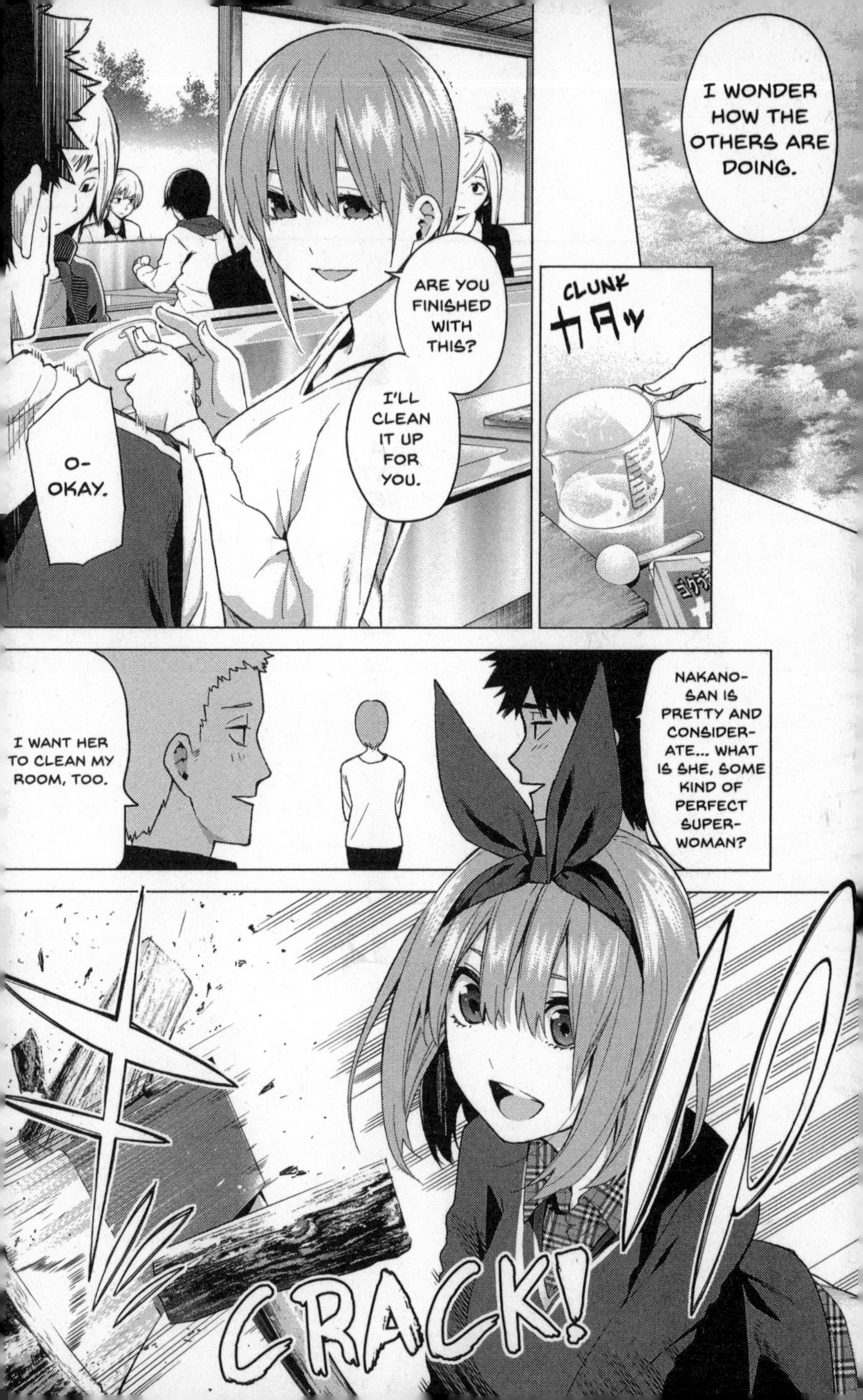
I WONDER HOW THE OTHERS ARE DOING.
CLUNK
カタッ
ARE YOU FINISHED WITH THIS?
I'LL CLEAN IT UP FOR YOU.
O-OKAY.
NAKANO-SAN IS PRETTY AND CONSIDER-ATE... WHAT IS SHE, SOME KIND OF PERFECT SUPER-WOMAN?
I WANT HER TO CLEAN MY ROOM, TOO.
CRACK!

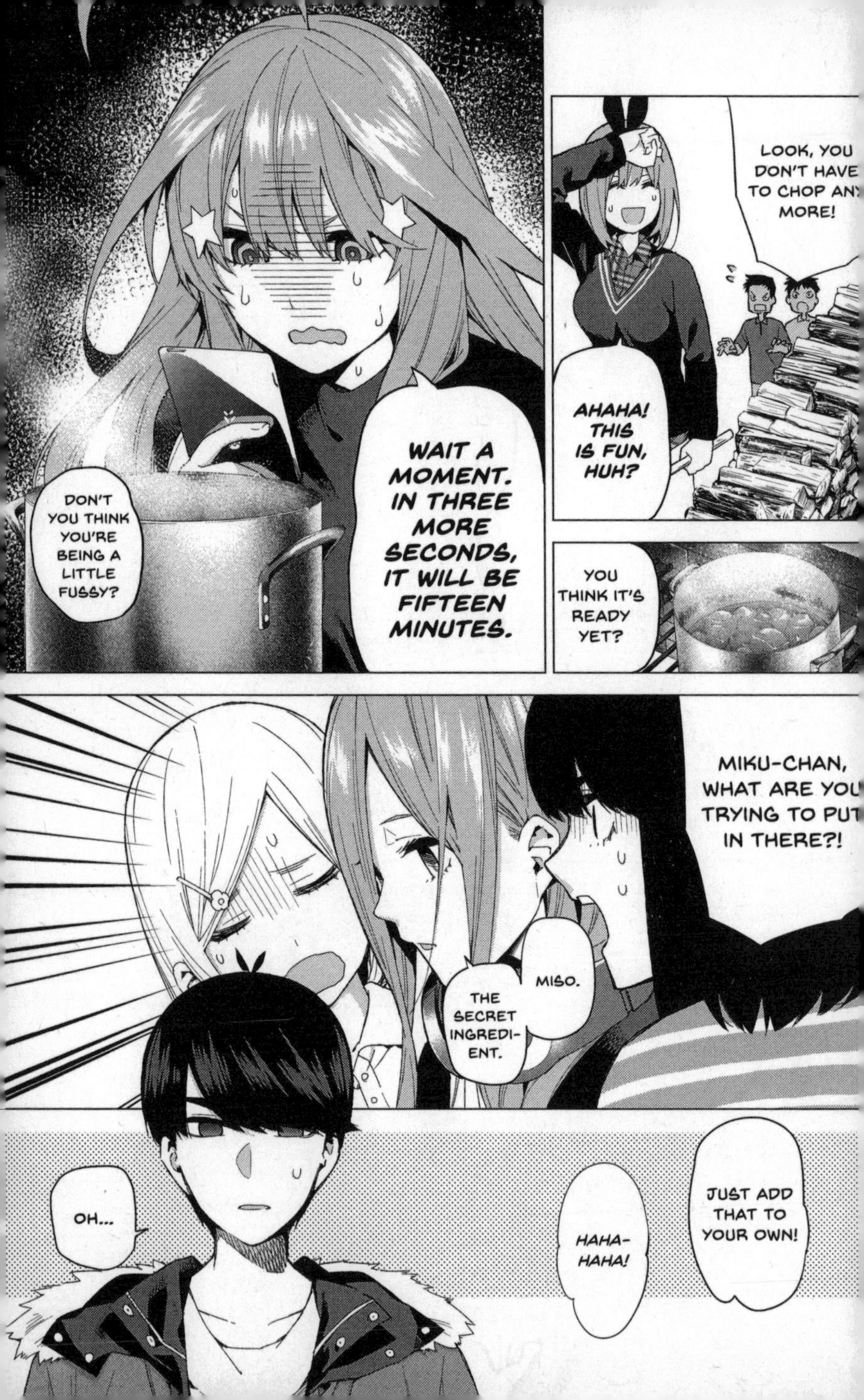
LOOK, YOU DON'T HAVE TO CHOP ANY MORE!
AHAHA! THIS IS FUN, HUH?
YOU THINK IT'S READY YET?
WAIT A MOMENT. IN THREE MORE SECONDS, IT WILL BE FIFTEEN MINUTES.
DON'T YOU THINK YOU'RE BEING A LITTLE FUSSY?
MIKU-CHAN, WHAT ARE YOU TRYING TO PUT IN THERE?!
MISO.
THE SECRET INGREDI-ENT.
JUST ADD THAT TO YOUR OWN!
HAHA-HAHA!
OH...

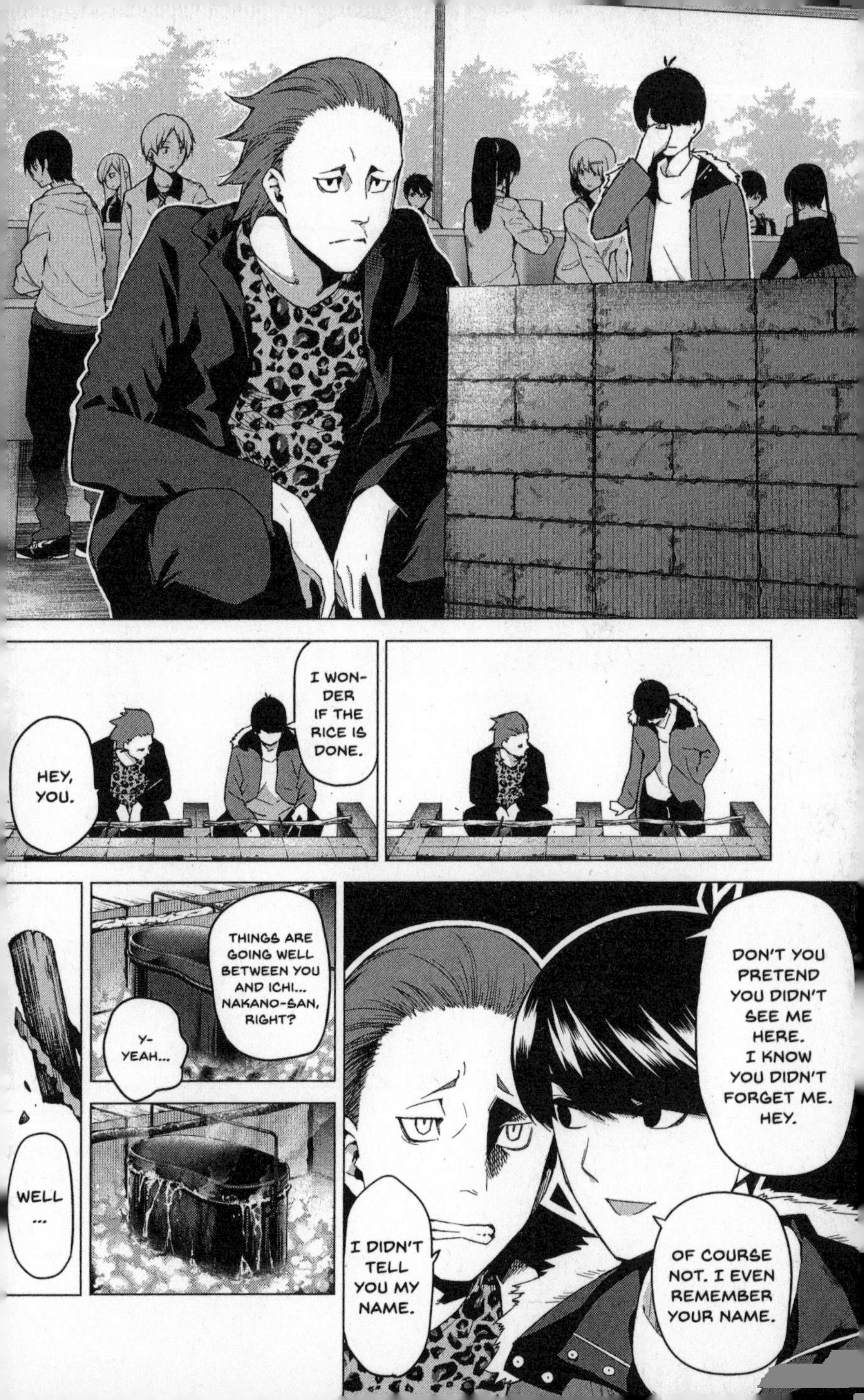
I WON-DER IF THE RICE IS DONE.
HEY, YOU.
DON'T YOU PRETEND YOU DIDN'T SEE ME HERE. I KNOW YOU DIDN'T FORGET ME. HEY.
OF COURSE NOT. I EVEN REMEMBER YOUR NAME.
I DIDN'T TELL YOU MY NAME.
THINGS ARE GOING WELL BETWEEN YOU AND ICHI... NAKANO-SAN, RIGHT?
Y-YEAH...
WELL ...

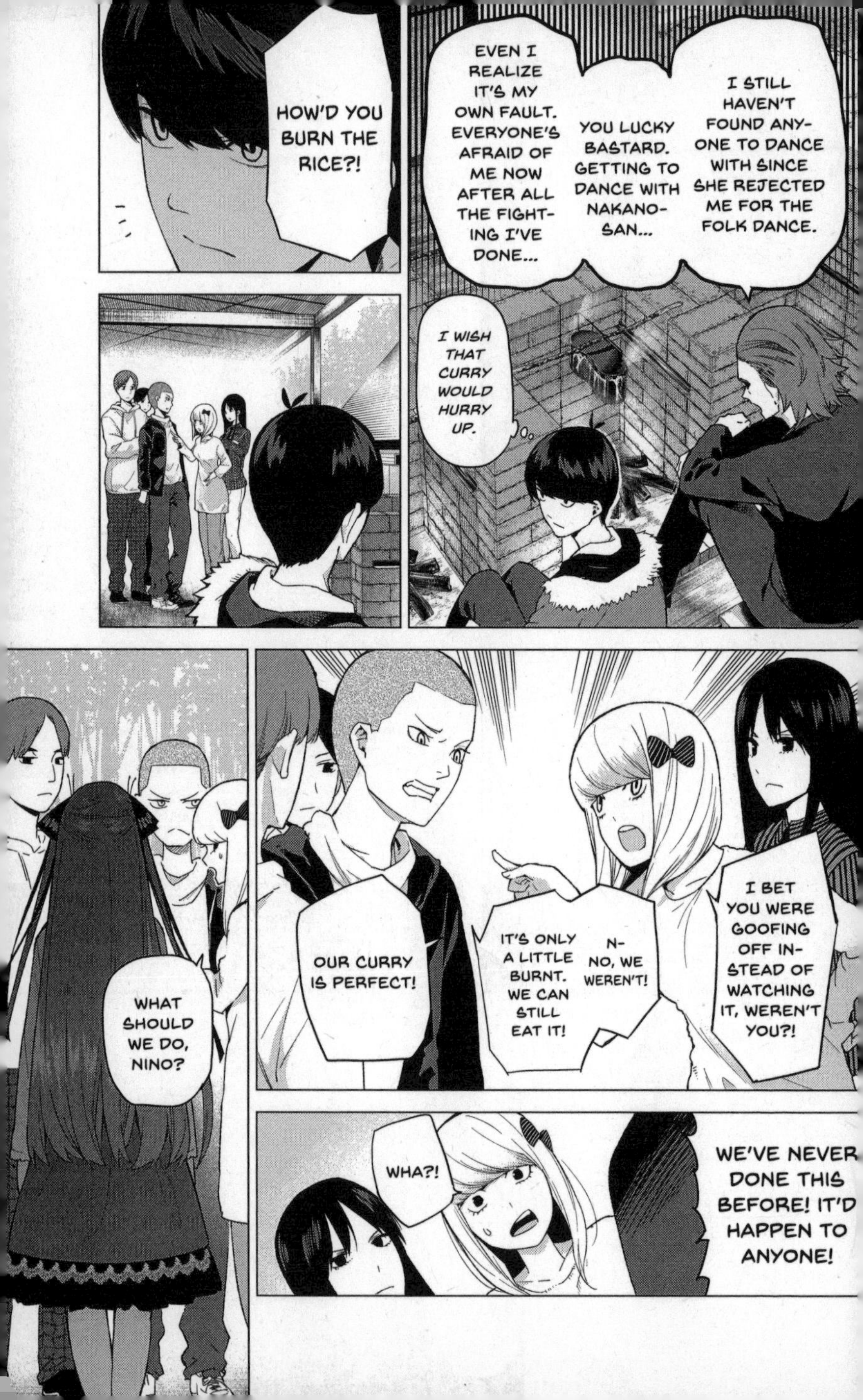
I STILL HAVEN'T FOUND ANYONE TO DANCE WITH SINCE SHE REJECTED ME FOR THE FOLK DANCE.
YOU LUCKY BASTARD. GETTING TO DANCE WITH NAKANO-SAN...
EVEN I REALIZE IT'S MY OWN FAULT. EVERYONE'S AFRAID OF ME NOW AFTER ALL THE FIGHTING I'VE DONE...
I WISH THAT CURRY WOULD HURRY UP.
HOW'D YOU BURN THE RICE?!
I BET YOU WERE GOOFING OFF INSTEAD OF WATCHING IT, WEREN'T YOU?!
N-NO, WE WEREN'T!
IT'S ONLY A LITTLE BURNT. WE CAN STILL EAT IT!
OUR CURRY IS PERFECT!
WE'VE NEVER DONE THIS BEFORE! IT'D HAPPEN TO ANYONE!
WHA?!
WHAT SHOULD WE DO, NINO?

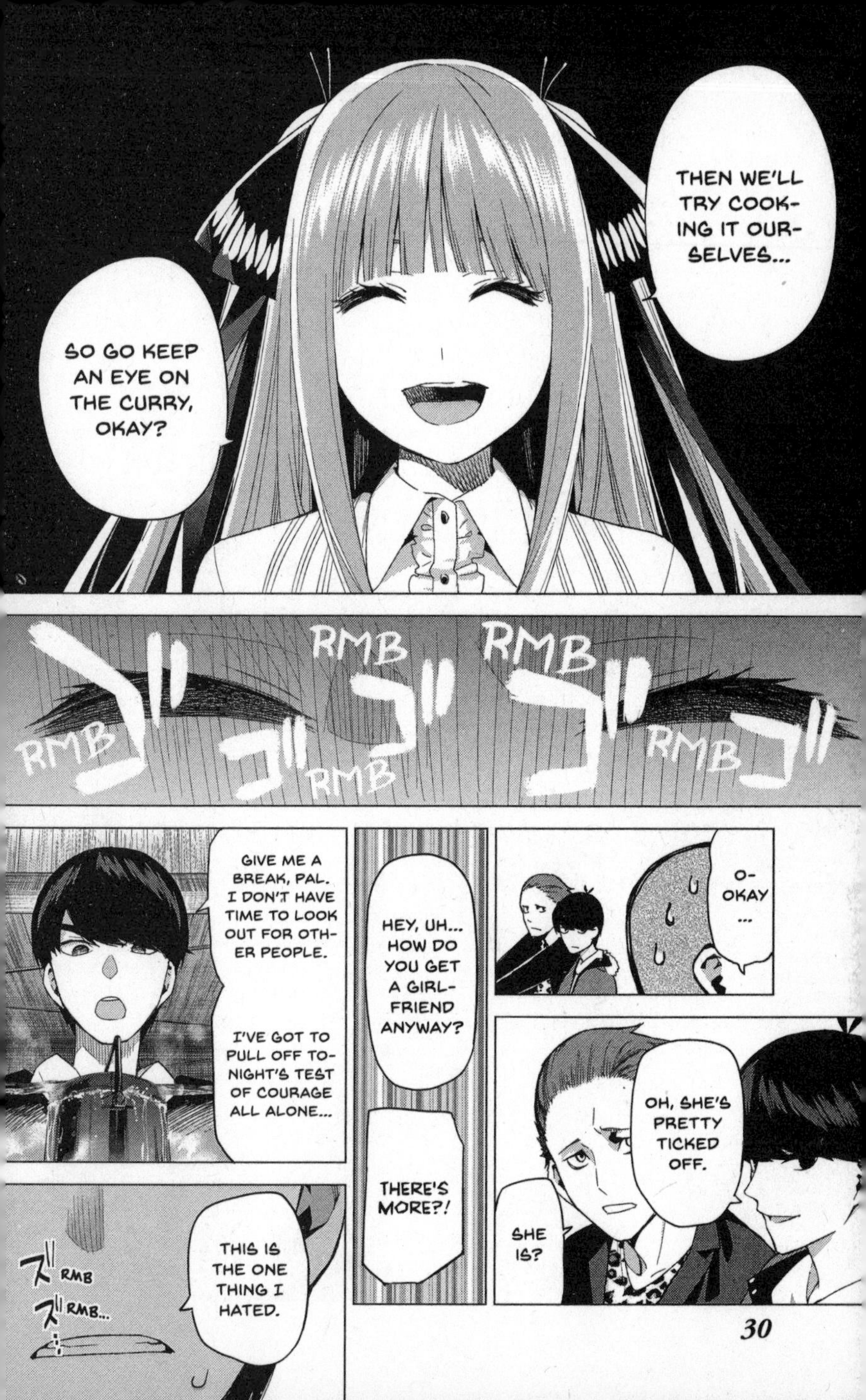
THEN WE'LL TRY COOKING IT OURSELVES...
SO GO KEEP AN EYE ON THE CURRY, OKAY?
RMB RMB RMB RMB RMB RMB
O-OKAY...
OH, SHE'S PRETTY TICKED OFF.
SHE IS?
HEY, UH... HOW DO YOU GET A GIRLFRIEND ANYWAY?
THERE'S MORE?!
GIVE ME A BREAK, PAL. I DON'T HAVE TIME TO LOOK OUT FOR OTHER PEOPLE.
I'VE GOT TO PULL OFF TONIGHT'S TEST OF COURAGE ALL ALONE...
THIS IS THE ONE THING I HATED.
RMB
RMB...

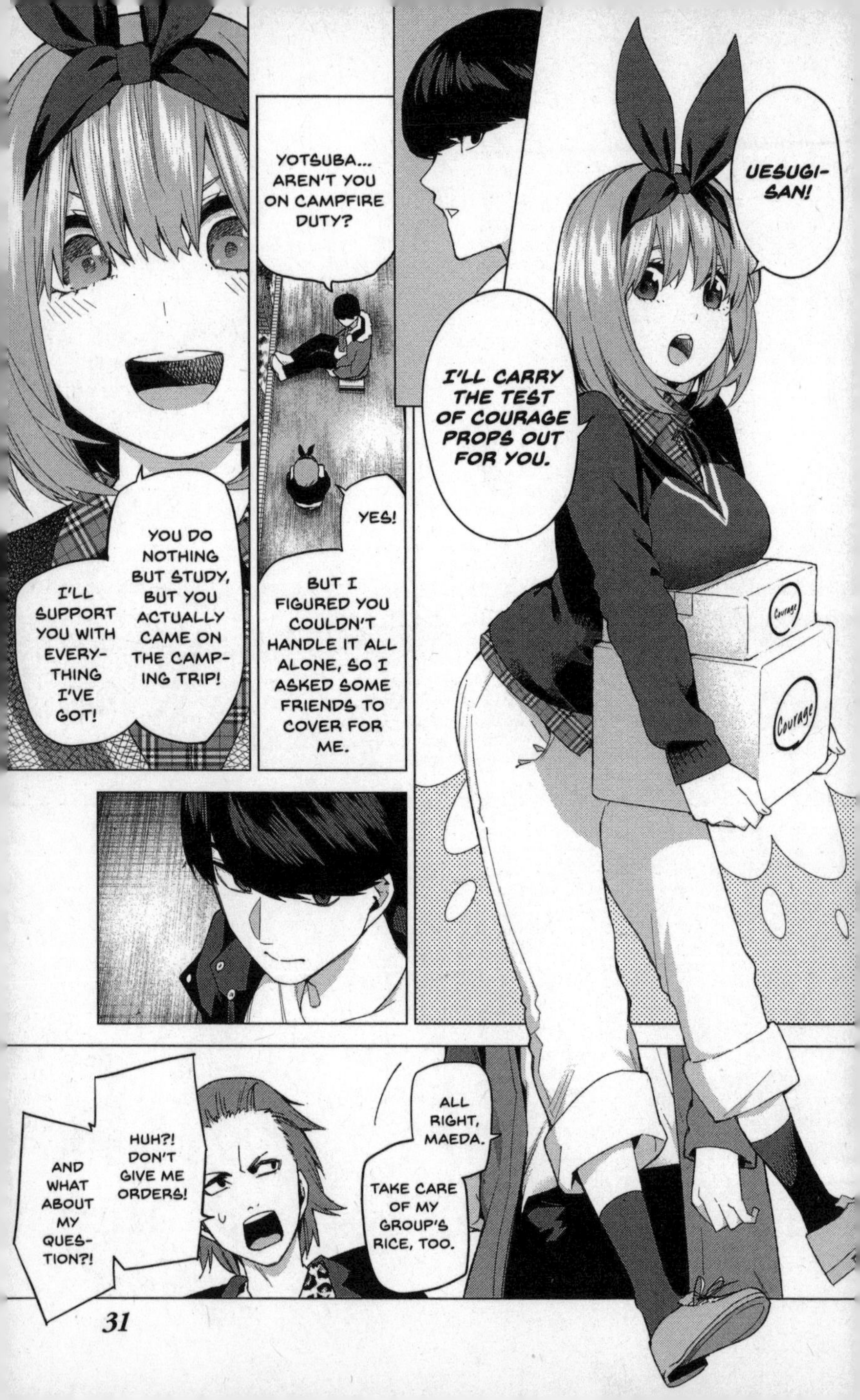
UESUGI-SAN!
I'LL CARRY THE TEST OF COURAGE PROPS OUT FOR YOU.
YOTSUBA... AREN'T YOU ON CAMPFIRE DUTY?
YES!
BUT I FIGURED YOU COULDN'T HANDLE IT ALL ALONE, SO I ASKED SOME FRIENDS TO COVER FOR ME.
YOU DO NOTHING BUT STUDY, BUT YOU ACTUALLY CAME ON THE CAMPING TRIP!
I'LL SUPPORT YOU WITH EVERYTHING I'VE GOT!
Courage
Courage
ALL RIGHT, MAEDA.
TAKE CARE OF MY GROUP'S RICE, TOO.
HUH?! DON'T GIVE ME ORDERS!
AND WHAT ABOUT MY QUESTION?!

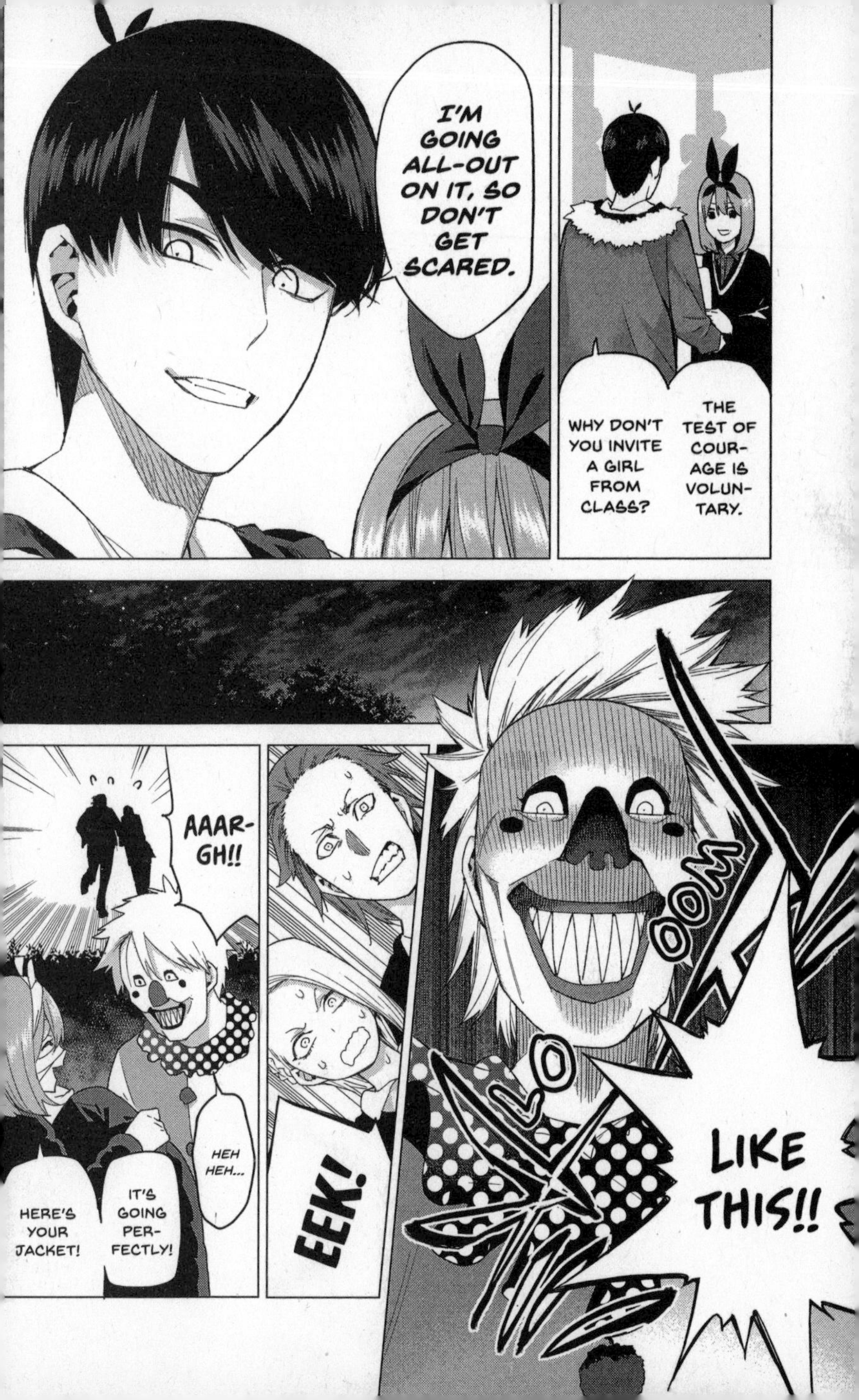
THE TEST OF COUR-AGE IS VOLUN-TARY.
WHY DON'T YOU INVITE A GIRL FROM CLASS?
I'M GOING ALL-OUT ON IT, SO DON'T GET SCARED.
LOOOM
LIKE THIS!!
EEK!
AAAR-GH!!
HEH HEH...
IT'S GOING PER-FECTLY!
HERE'S YOUR JACKET!

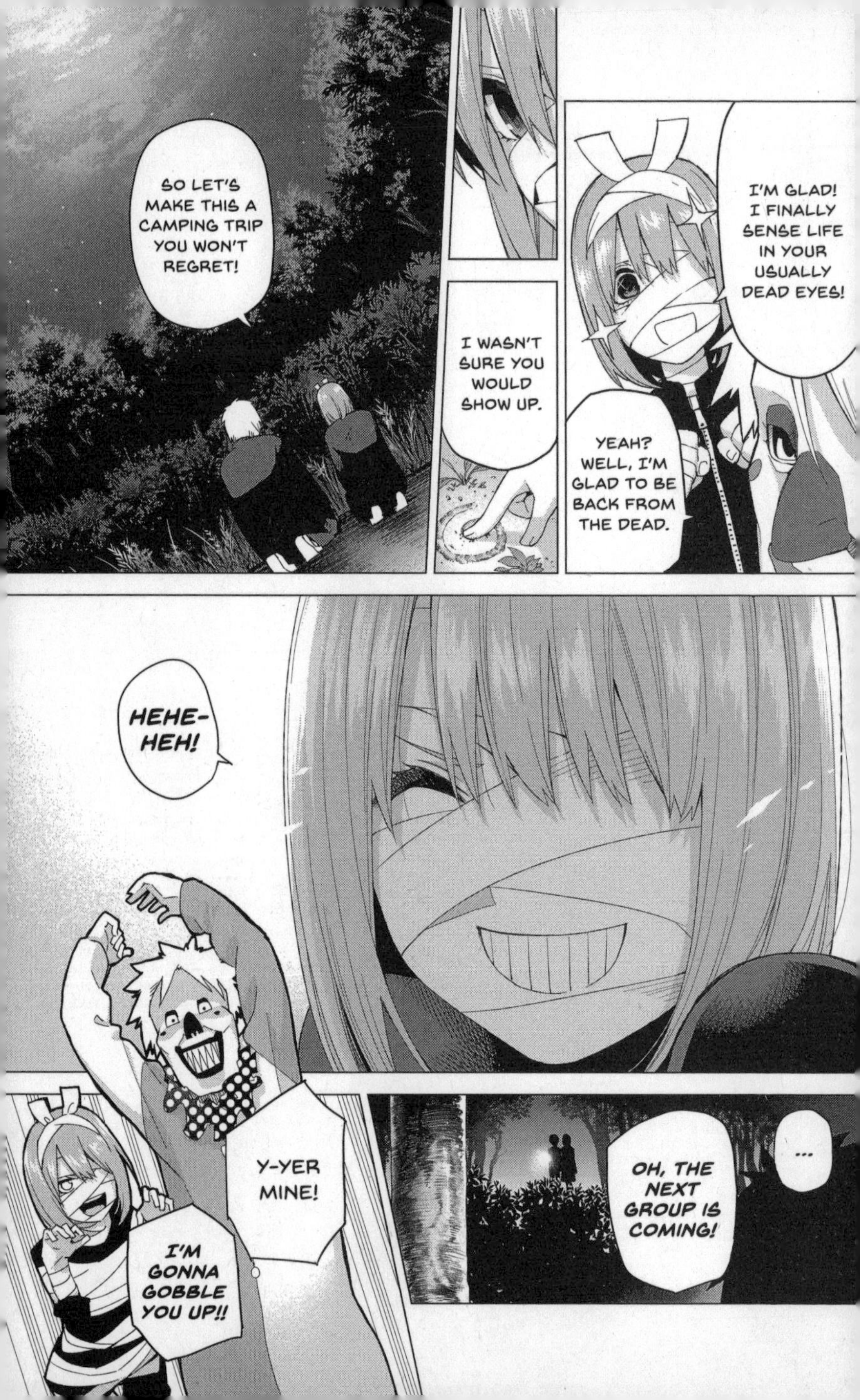
I'M GLAD! I FINALLY SENSE LIFE IN YOUR USUALLY DEAD EYES!
YEAH? WELL, I'M GLAD TO BE BACK FROM THE DEAD.
I WASN'T SURE YOU WOULD SHOW UP.
SO LET'S MAKE THIS A CAMPING TRIP YOU WON'T REGRET!
HEHE-HEH!
...
OH, THE NEXT GROUP IS COMING!
Y-YER MINE!
I'M GONNA GOBBLE YOU UP!!

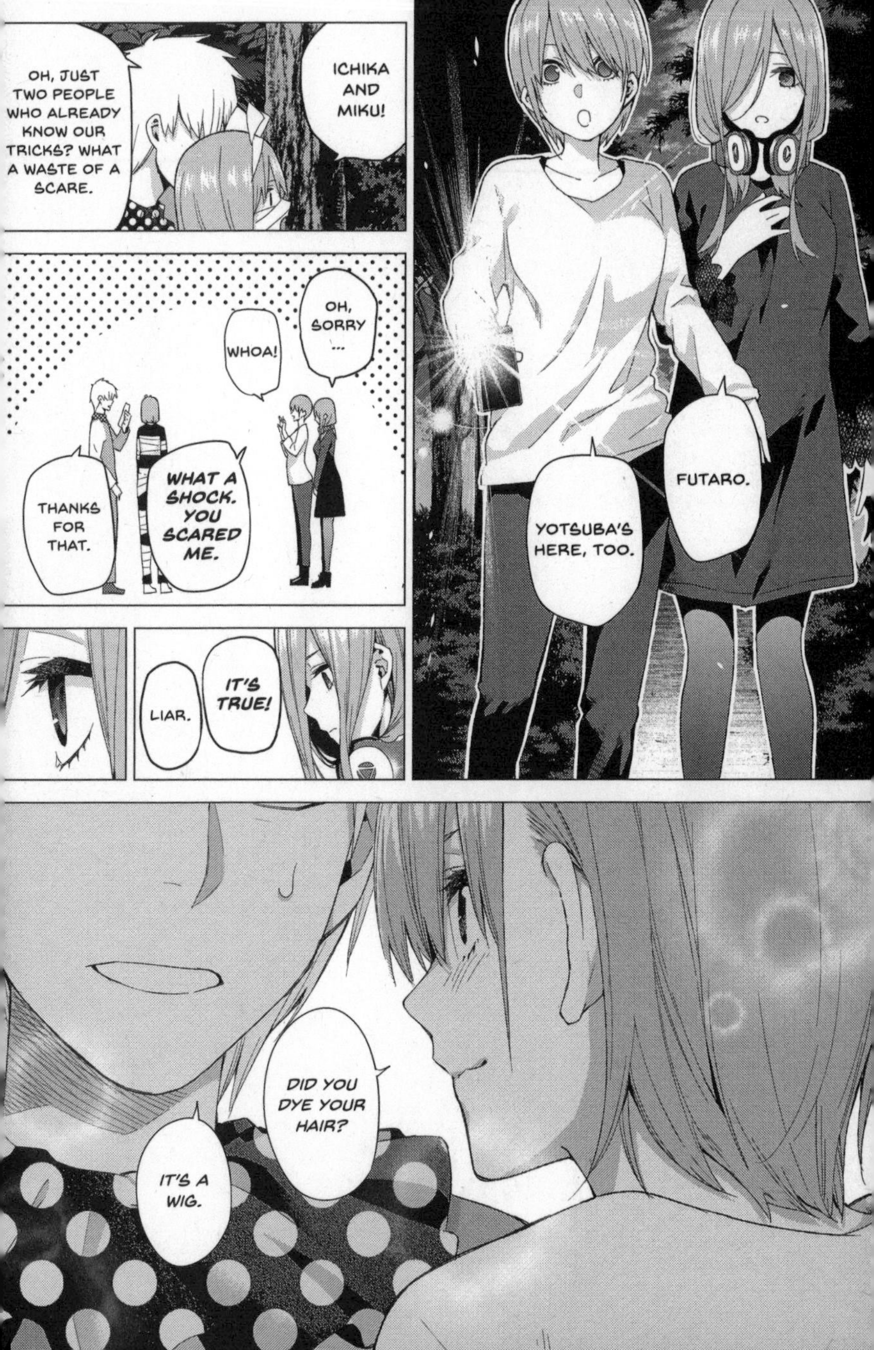
FUTARO.
YOTSUBA'S HERE, TOO.
ICHIKA AND MIKU!
OH, JUST TWO PEOPLE WHO ALREADY KNOW OUR TRICKS? WHAT A WASTE OF A SCARE.
OH, SORRY ...
WHOA!
WHAT A SHOCK. YOU SCARED ME.
THANKS FOR THAT.
IT'S TRUE!
LIAR.
DID YOU DYE YOUR HAIR?
IT'S A WIG.

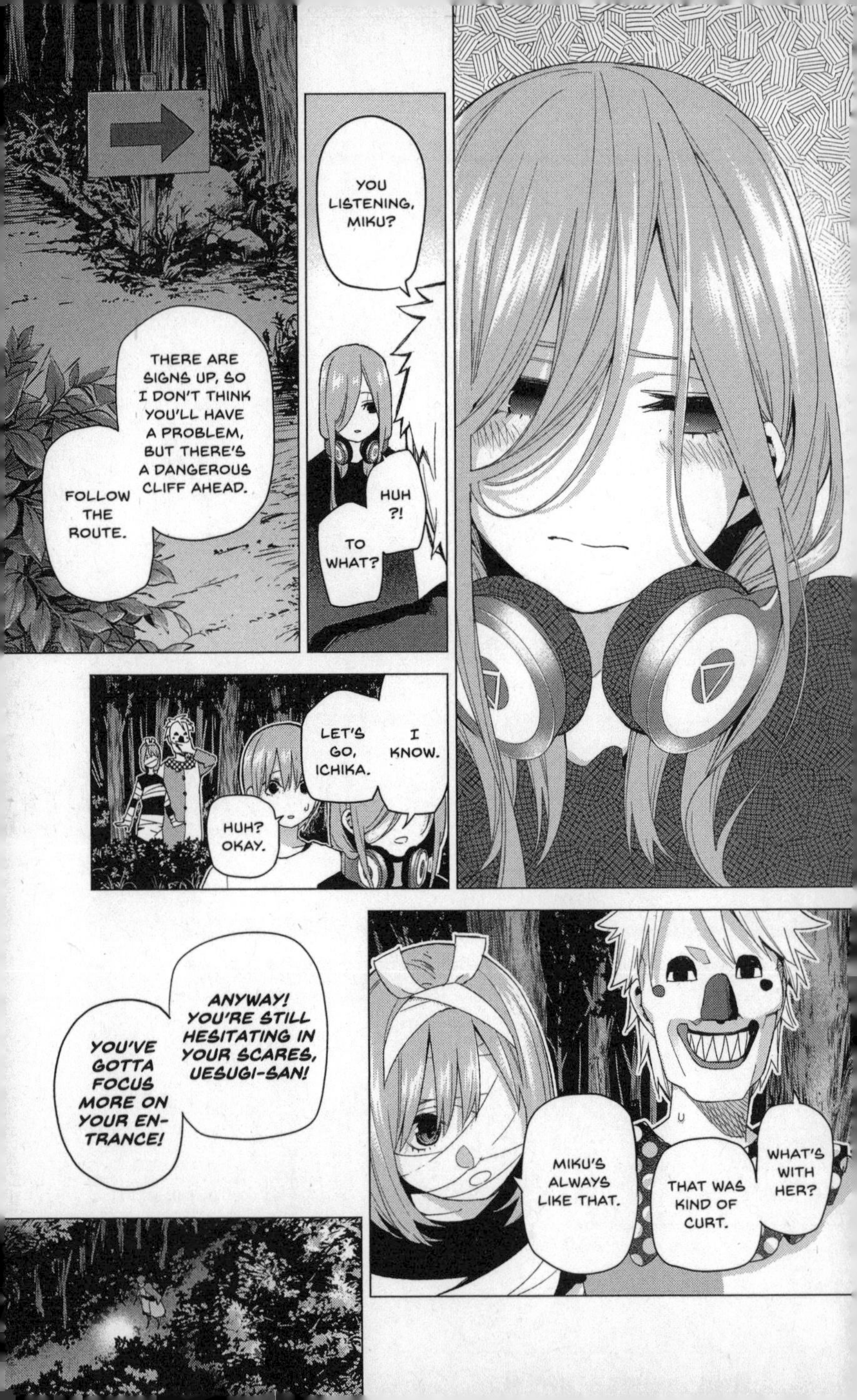
YOU LISTENING, MIKU?
HUH ?!
TO WHAT?
THERE ARE SIGNS UP, SO I DON'T THINK YOU'LL HAVE A PROBLEM, BUT THERE'S A DANGEROUS CLIFF AHEAD.
FOLLOW THE ROUTE.
I KNOW.
LET'S GO, ICHIKA.
HUH? OKAY.
WHAT'S WITH HER?
THAT WAS KIND OF CURT.
MIKU'S ALWAYS LIKE THAT.
ANYWAY! YOU'RE STILL HESITATING IN YOUR SCARES, UESUGI-SAN!
YOU'VE GOTTA FOCUS MORE ON YOUR EN-TRANCE!

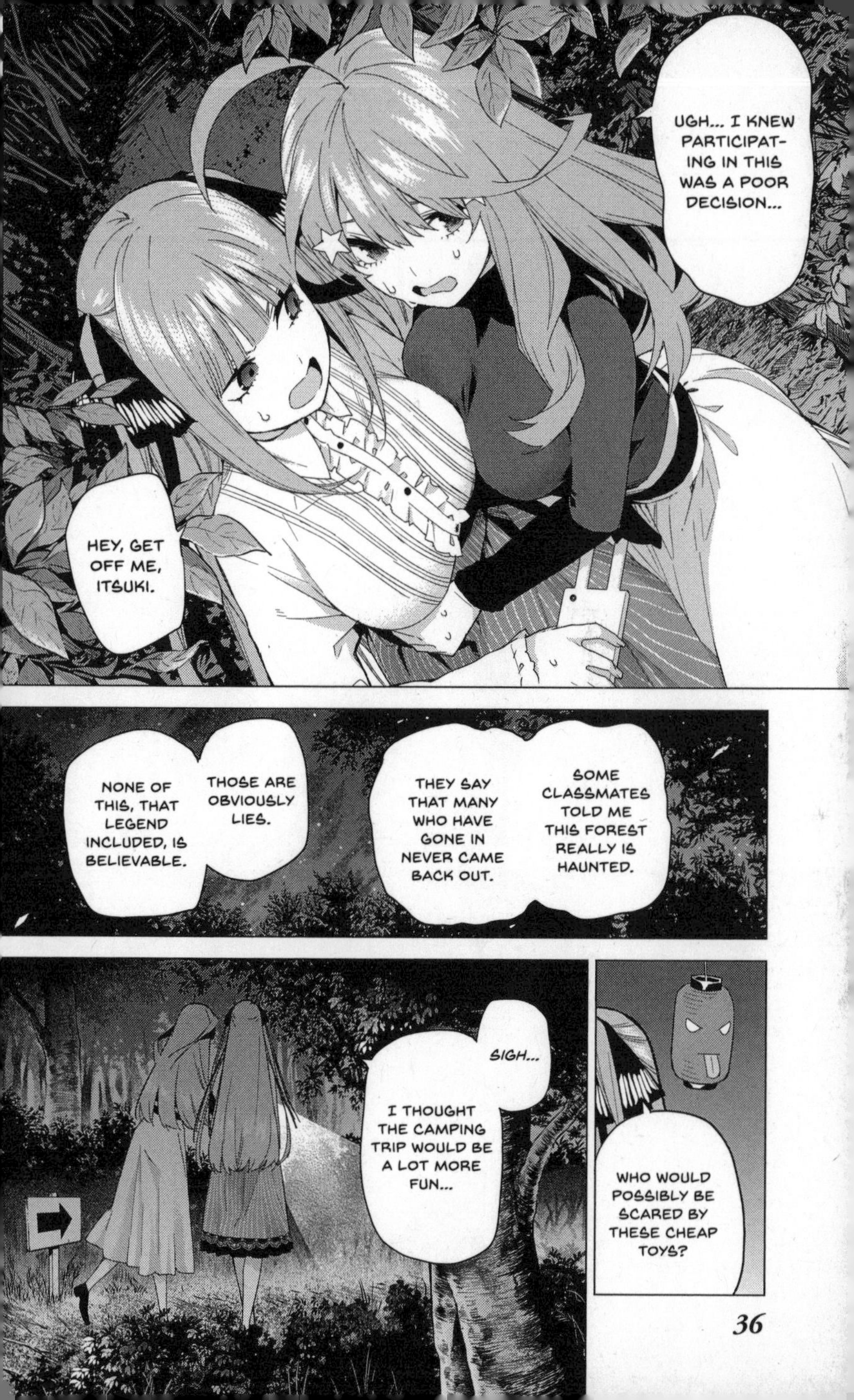
UGH... I KNEW PARTICIPAT-ING IN THIS WAS A POOR DECISION...
HEY, GET OFF ME, ITSUKI.
SOME CLASSMATES TOLD ME THIS FOREST REALLY IS HAUNTED.
THEY SAY THAT MANY WHO HAVE GONE IN NEVER CAME BACK OUT.
THOSE ARE OBVIOUSLY LIES.
NONE OF THIS, THAT LEGEND INCLUDED, IS BELIEVABLE.
WHO WOULD POSSIBLY BE SCARED BY THESE CHEAP TOYS?
SIGH...
I THOUGHT THE CAMPING TRIP WOULD BE A LOT MORE FUN...

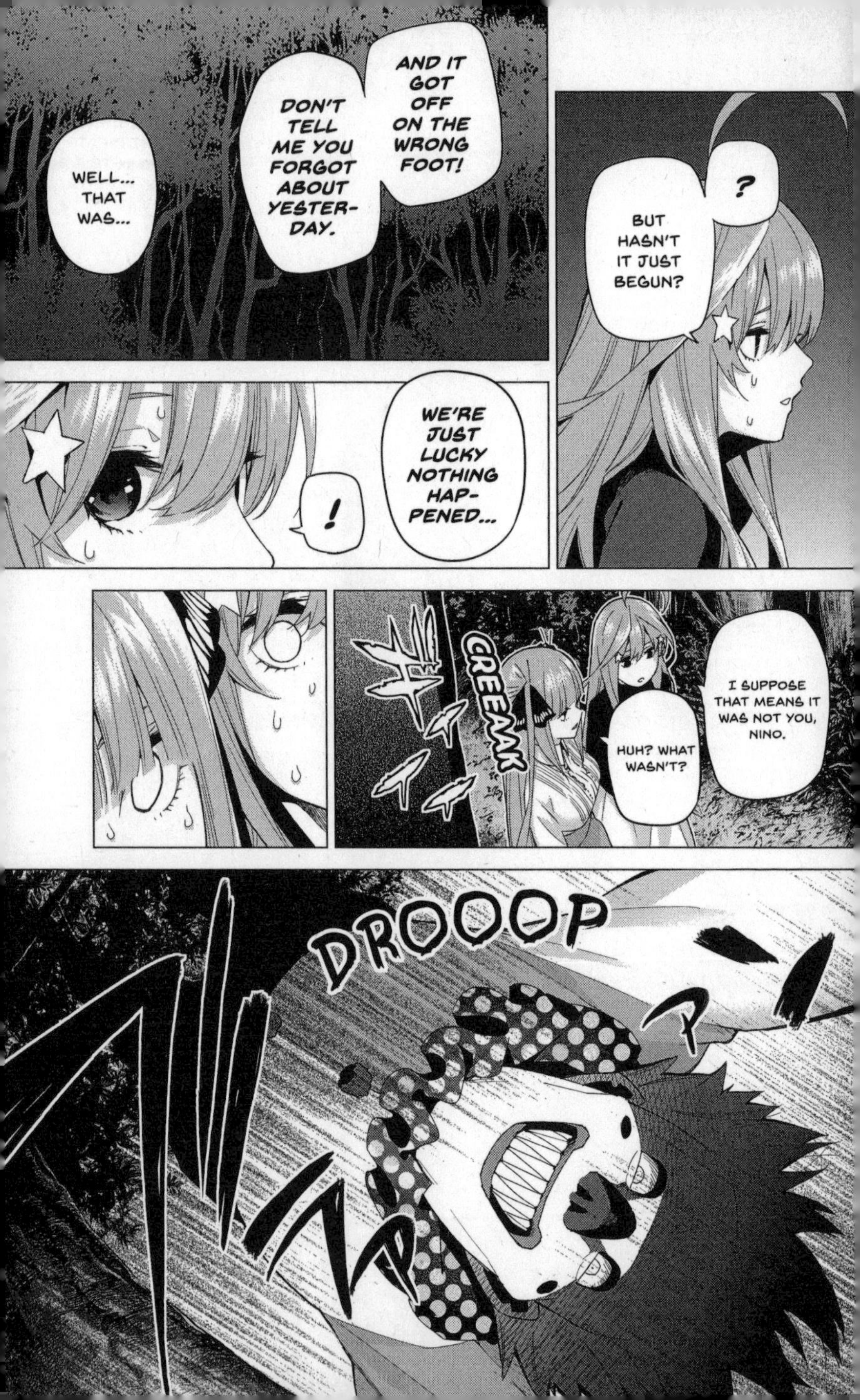
?
BUT HASN'T IT JUST BEGUN?
AND IT GOT OFF ON THE WRONG FOOT!
DON'T TELL ME YOU FORGOT ABOUT YESTER-DAY.
WELL... THAT WAS...
WE'RE JUST LUCKY NOTHING HAP-PENED...
!
I SUPPOSE THAT MEANS IT WAS NOT YOU, NINO.
HUH? WHAT WASN'T?
CREEAAK
DROOOP

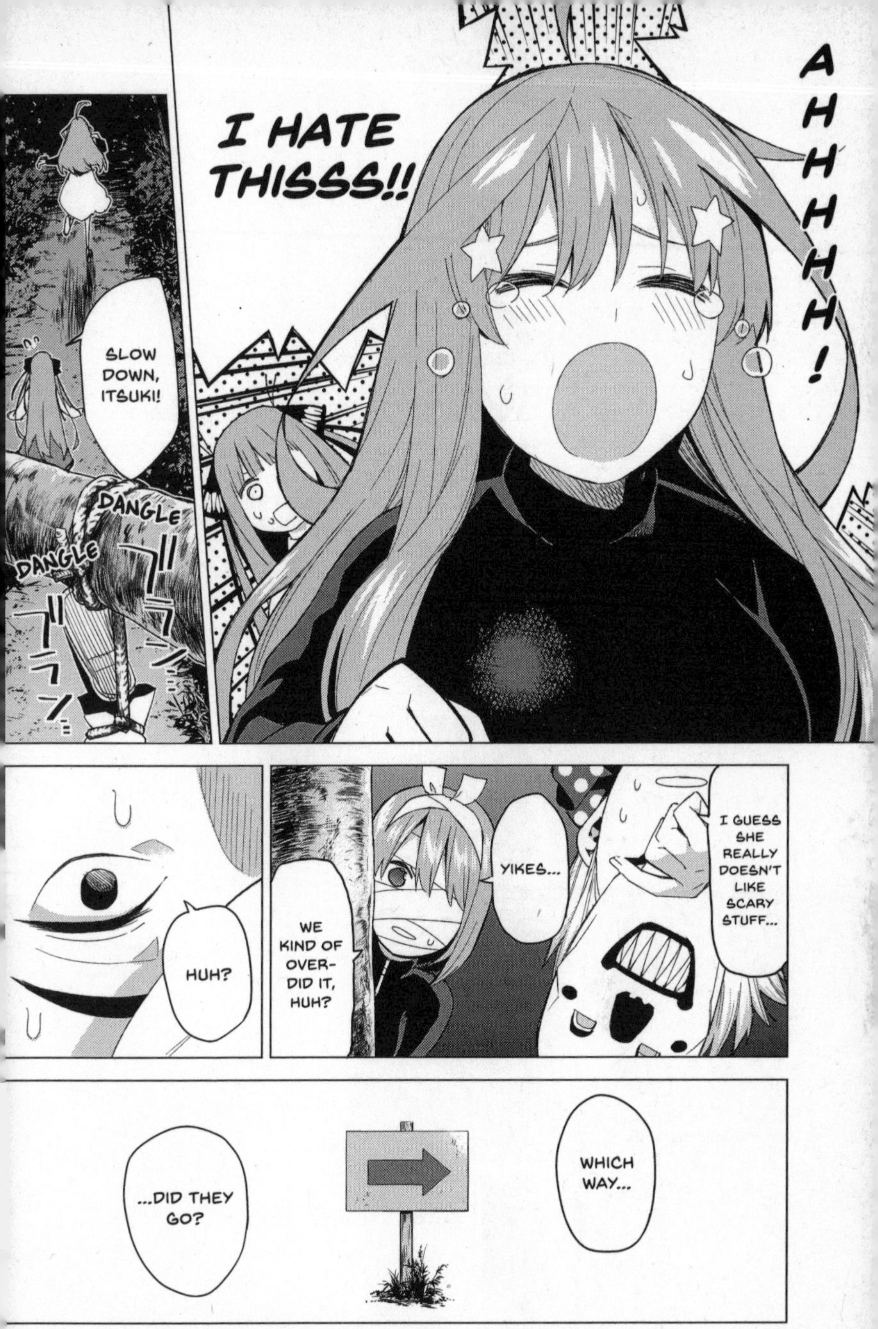
AHHHHHH!
I HATE THISSS!!
SLOW DOWN, ITSUKI!
DANGLE
DANGLE
I GUESS SHE REALLY DOESN'T LIKE SCARY STUFF...
YIKES...
WE KIND OF OVER-DID IT, HUH?
HUH?
WHICH WAY...
...DID THEY GO?

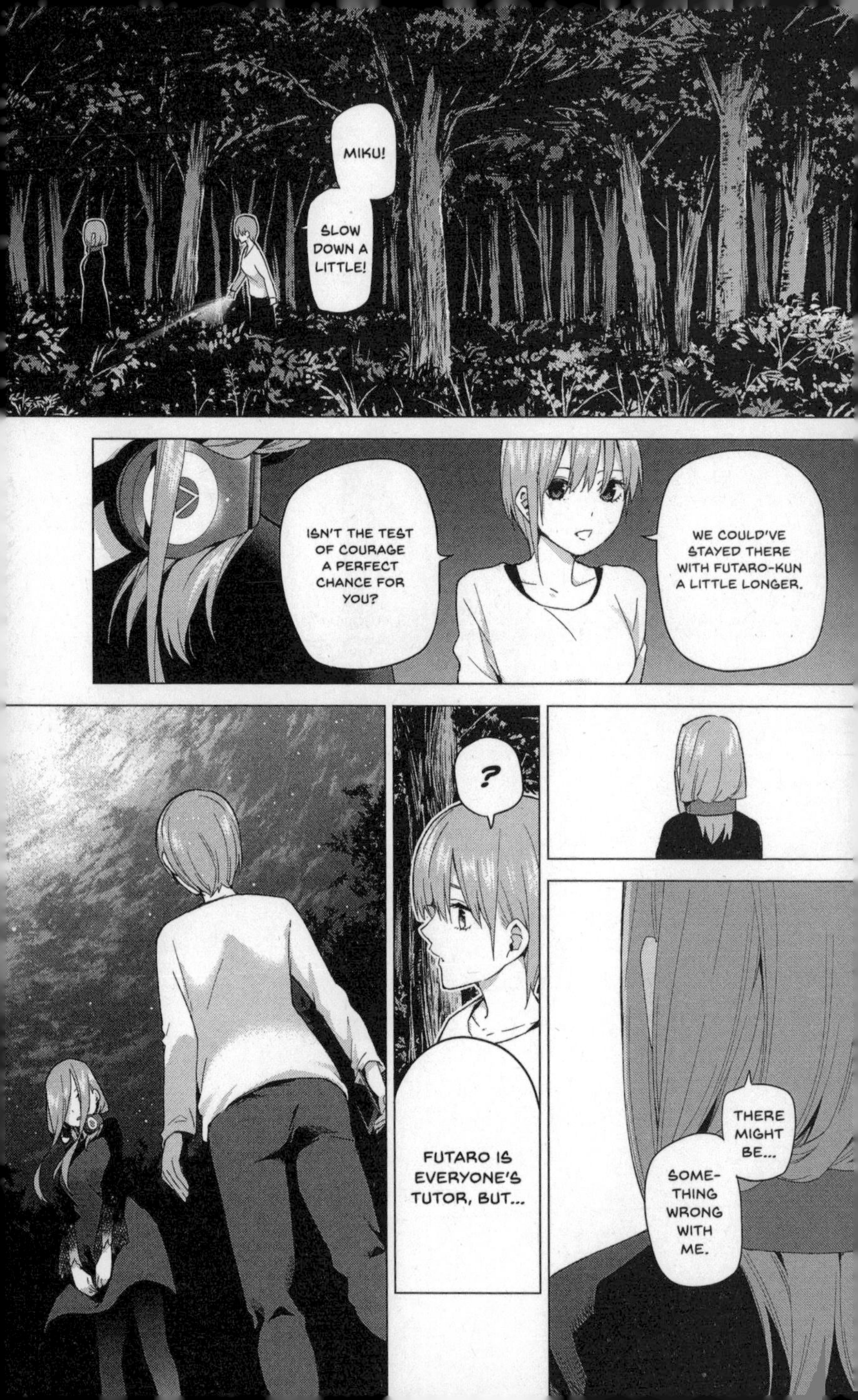
MIKU!
SLOW DOWN A LITTLE!
WE COULD'VE STAYED THERE WITH FUTARO-KUN A LITTLE LONGER.
ISN'T THE TEST OF COURAGE A PERFECT CHANCE FOR YOU?
THERE MIGHT BE...
SOME-THING WRONG WITH ME.
?
FUTARO IS EVERYONE'S TUTOR, BUT...

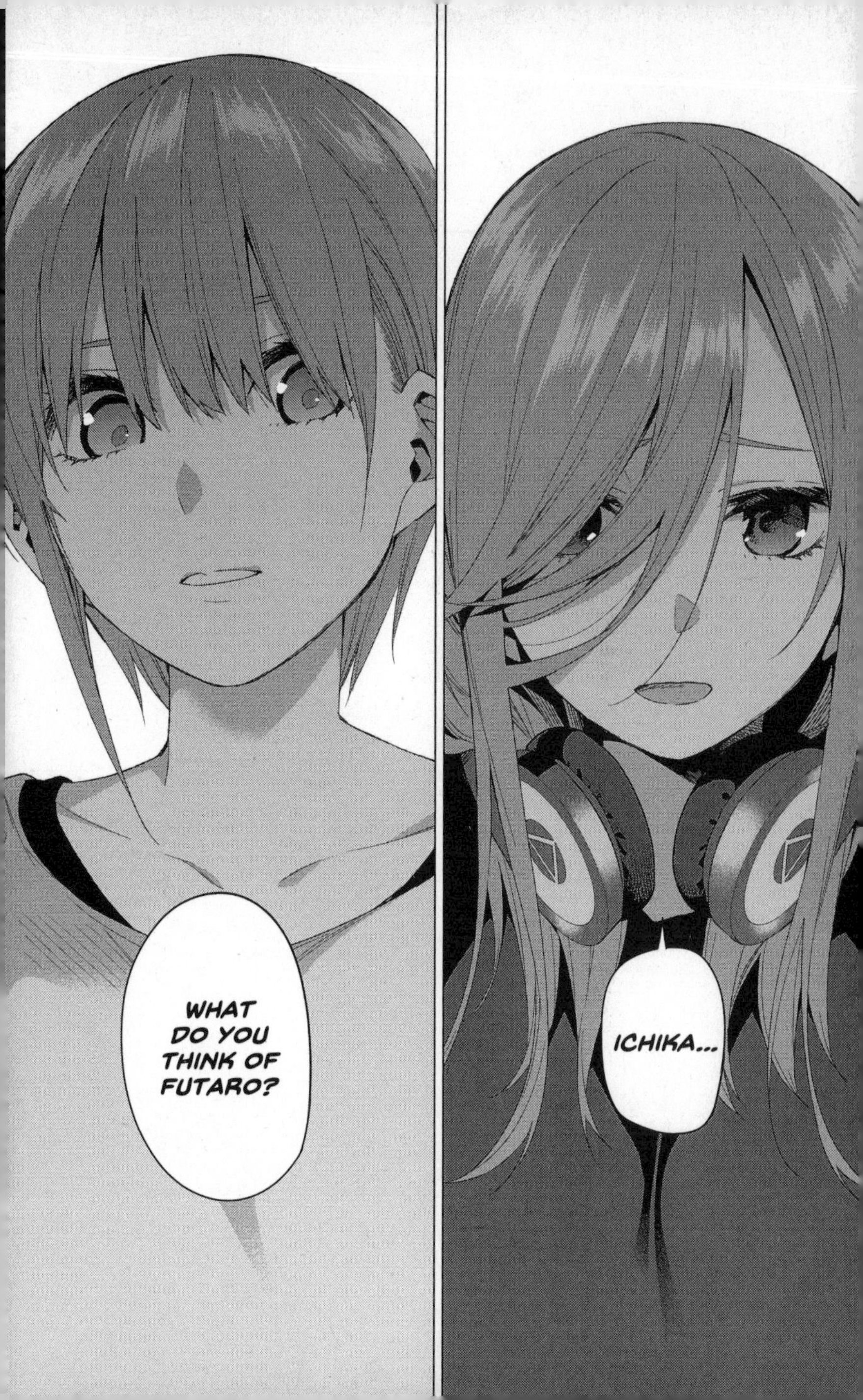
ICHIKA...
WHAT DO YOU THINK OF FUTARO?

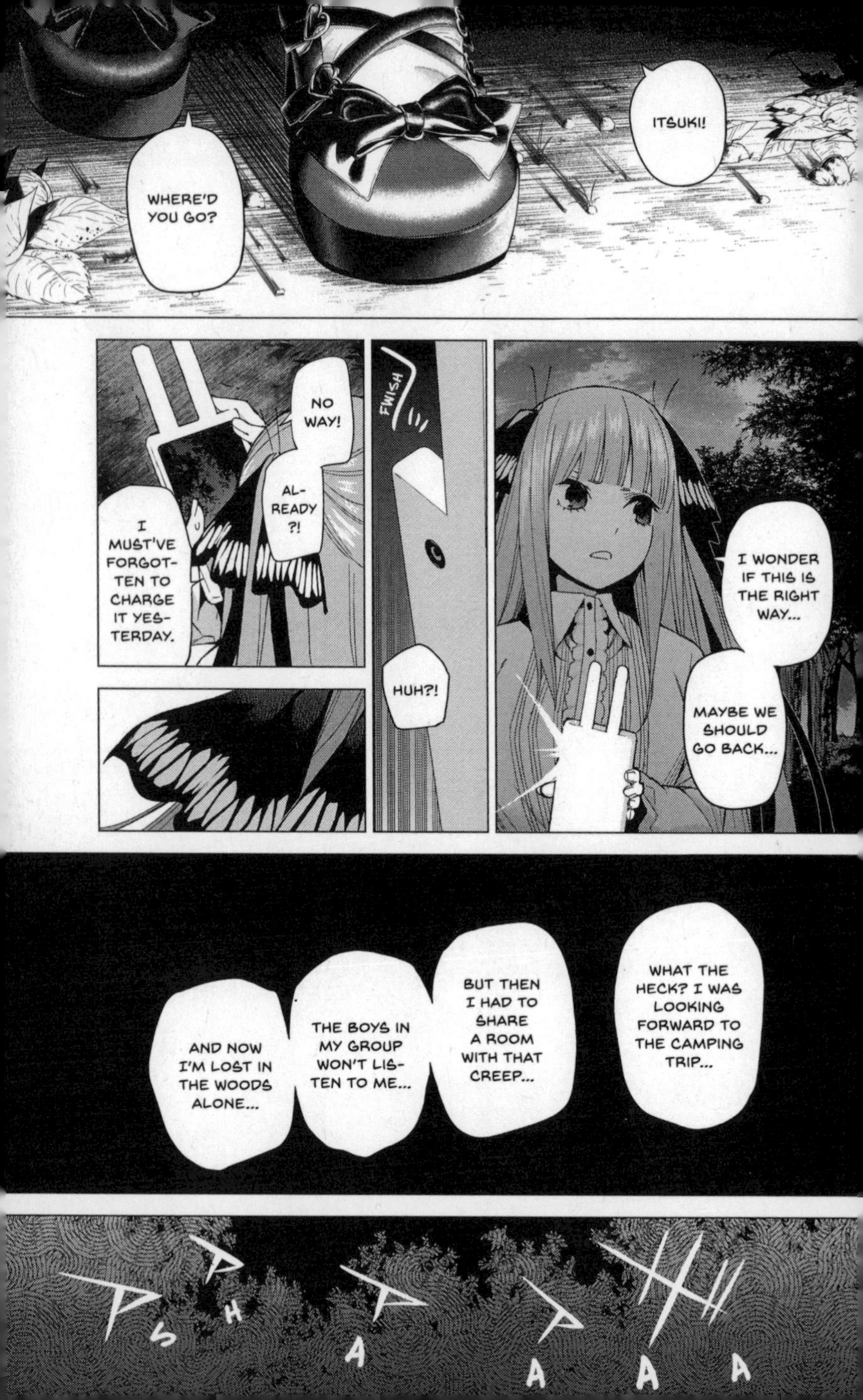
ITSUKI!
WHERE'D YOU GO?
I WONDER IF THIS IS THE RIGHT WAY...
MAYBE WE SHOULD GO BACK...
FWISH
HUH?!
NO WAY!
AL-READY?!
I MUST'VE FORGOT-TEN TO CHARGE IT YES-TERDAY.
WHAT THE HECK? I WAS LOOKING FORWARD TO THE CAMPING TRIP...
BUT THEN I HAD TO SHARE A ROOM WITH THAT CREEP...
THE BOYS IN MY GROUP WON'T LIS-TEN TO ME...
AND NOW I'M LOST IN THE WOODS ALONE...

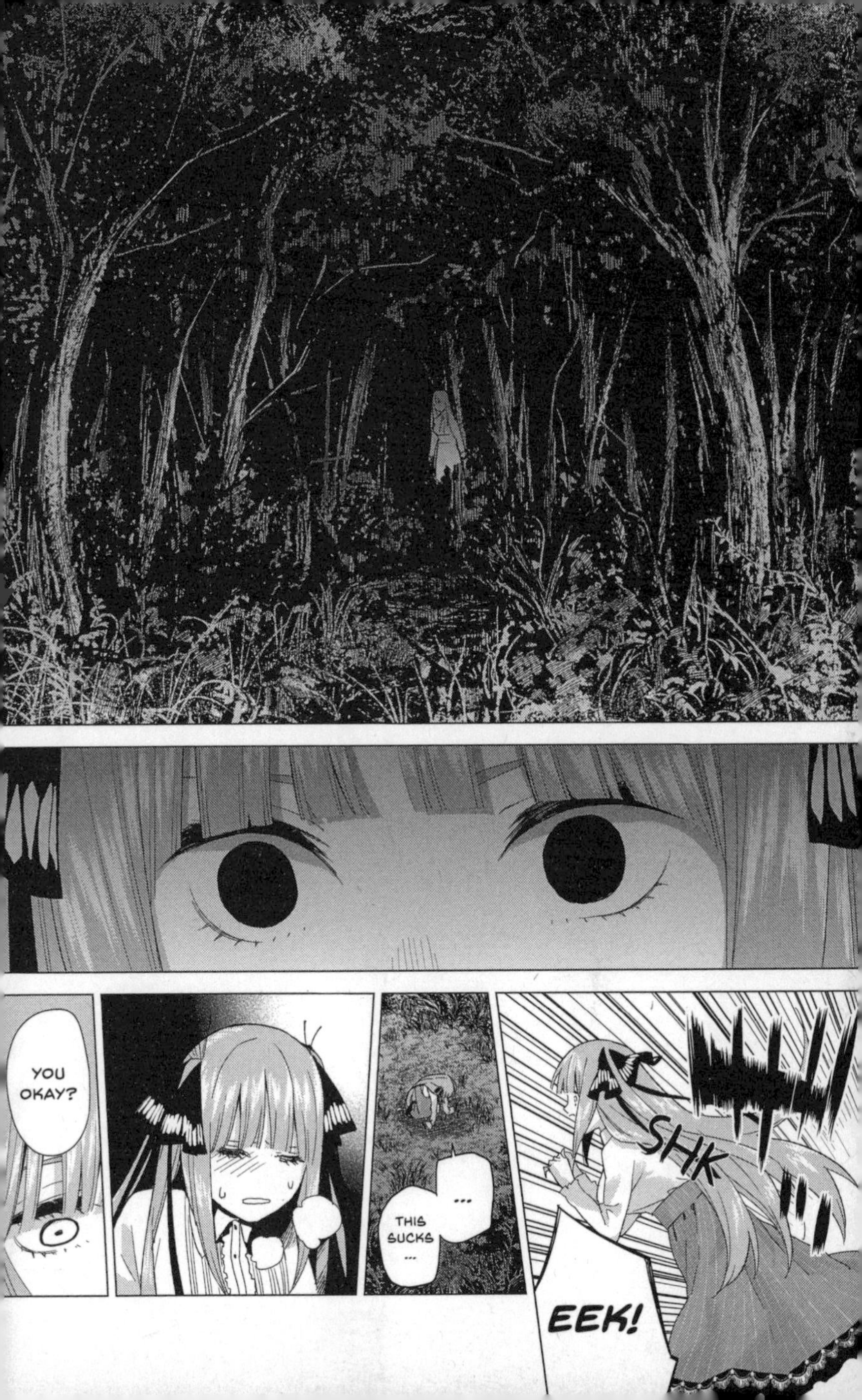
SHK
EEK!
... THIS SUCKS ...
YOU OKAY?

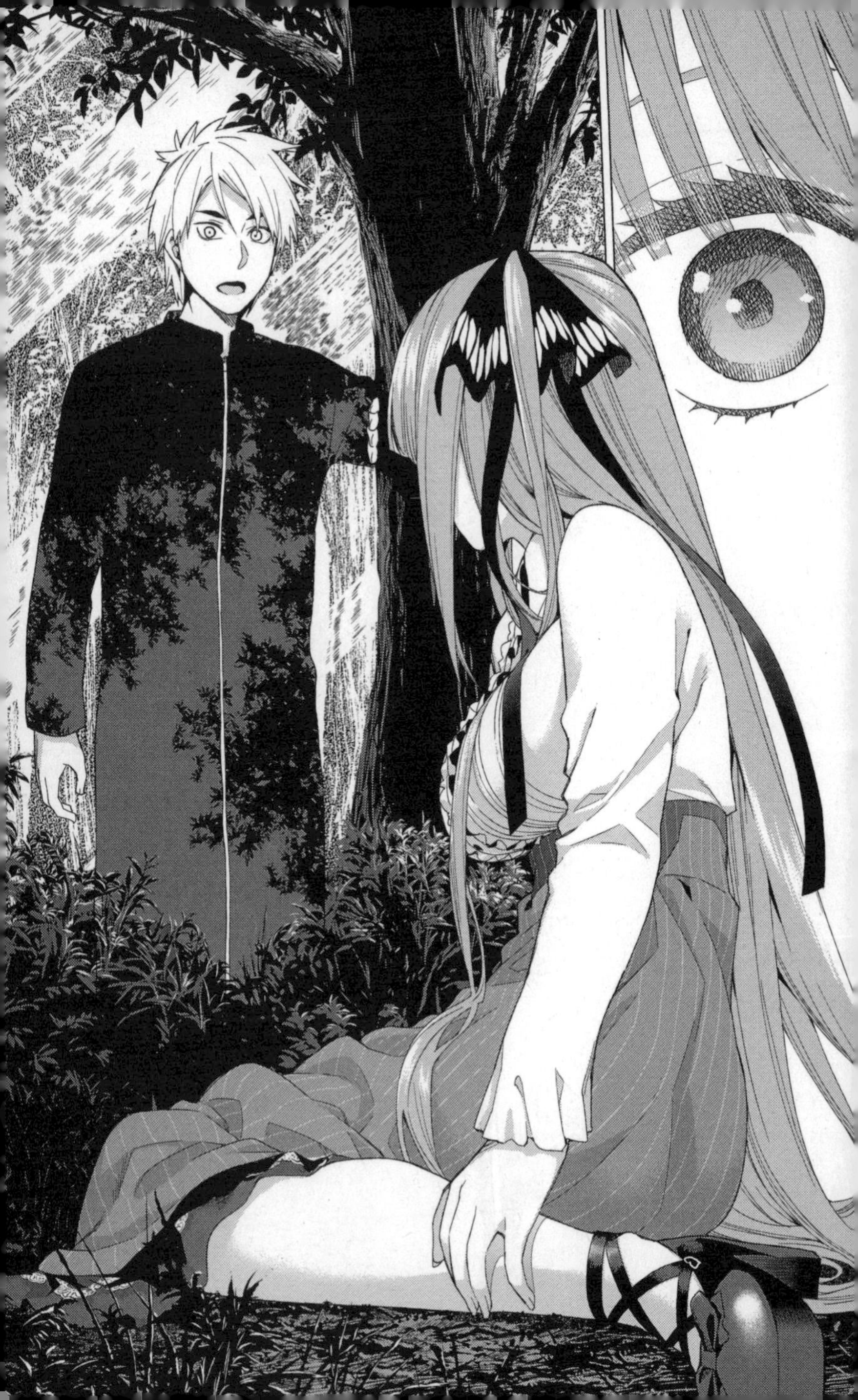

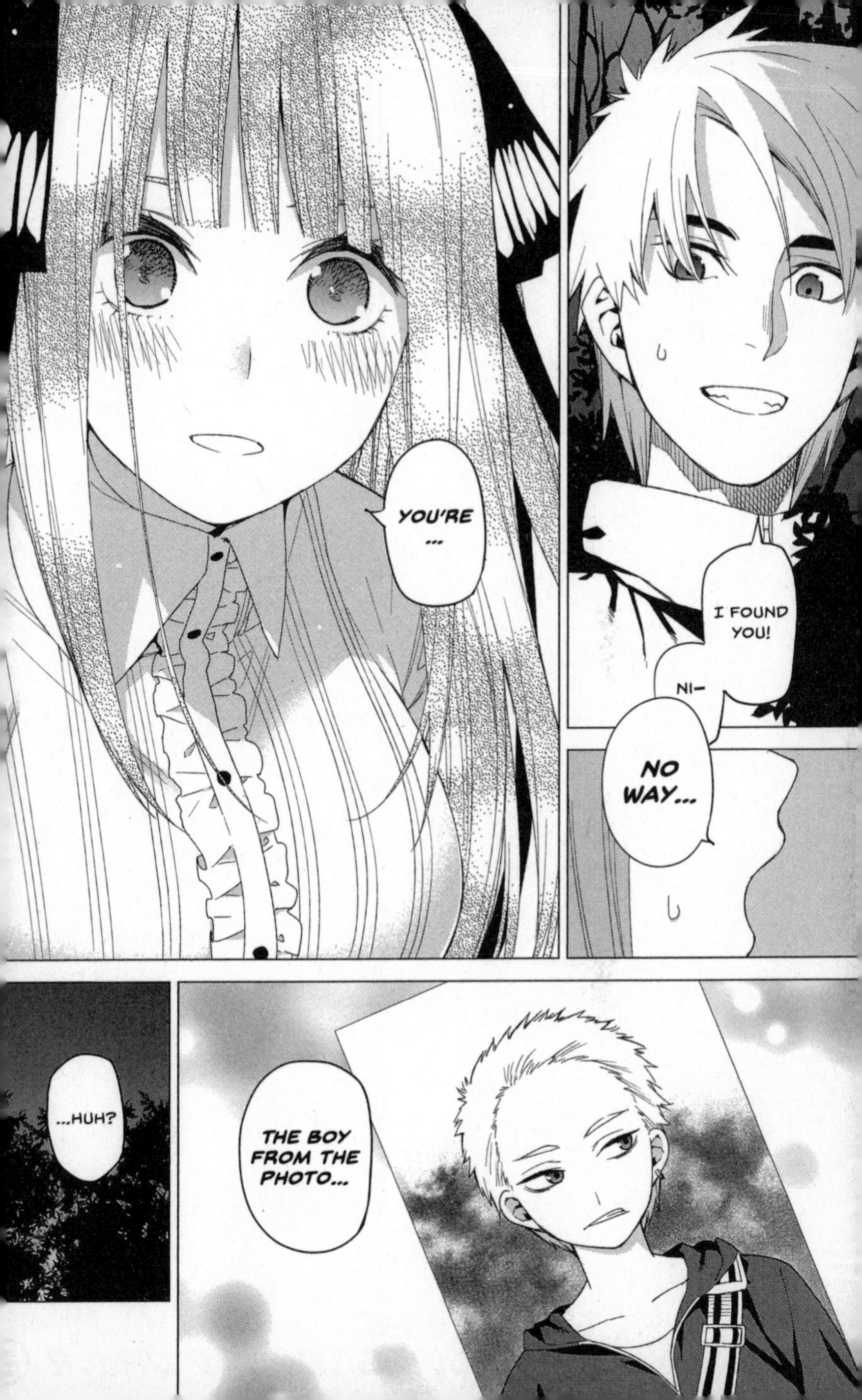
I FOUND YOU!
NI—
NO WAY...
YOU'RE ...
THE BOY FROM THE PHOTO...
...HUH?

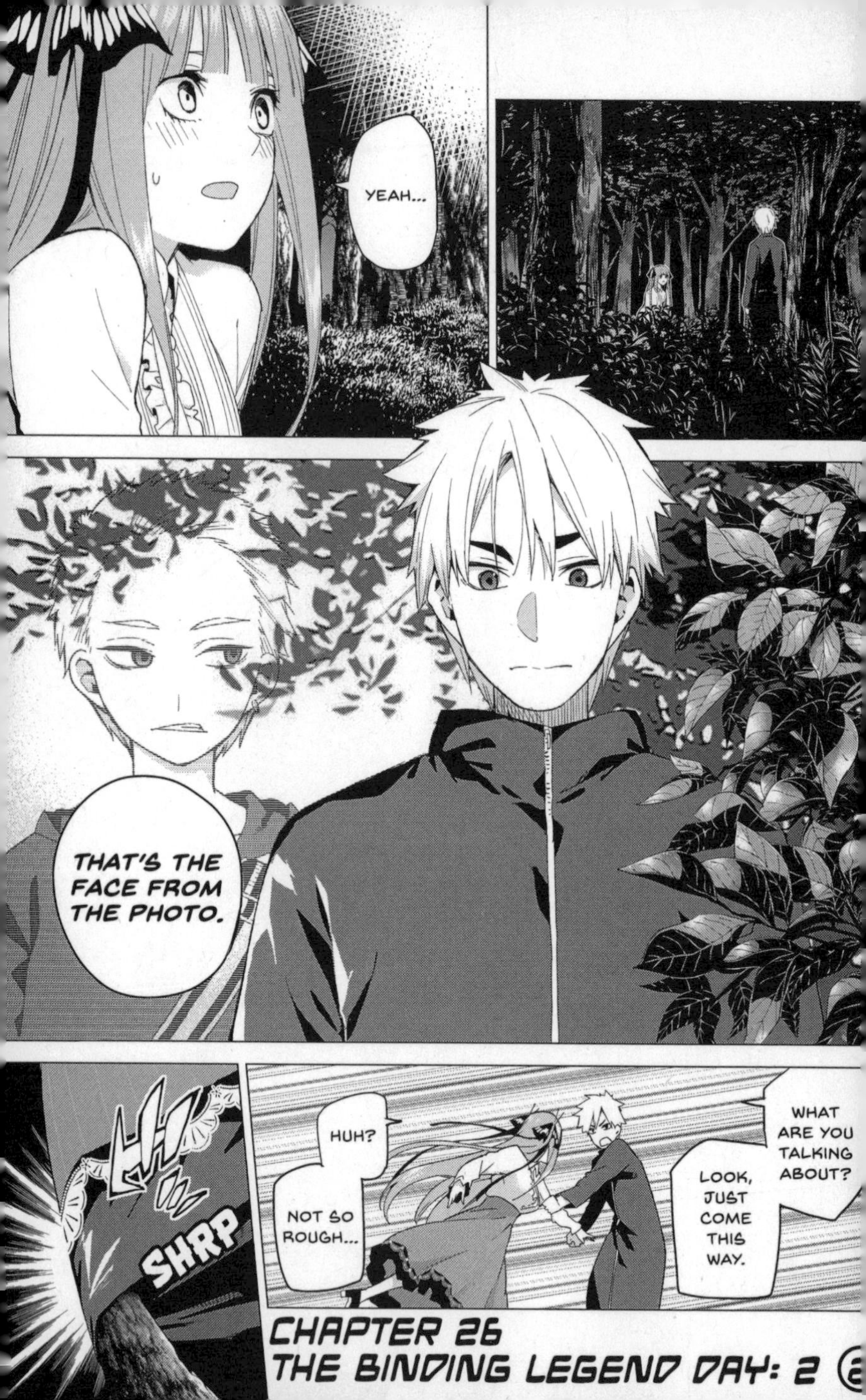
YEAH...
THAT'S THE FACE FROM THE PHOTO.
WHAT ARE YOU TALKING ABOUT?
LOOK, JUST COME THIS WAY.
HUH?
NOT SO ROUGH...
SHRP

CHAPTER 26
THE BINDING LEGEND DAY: 2

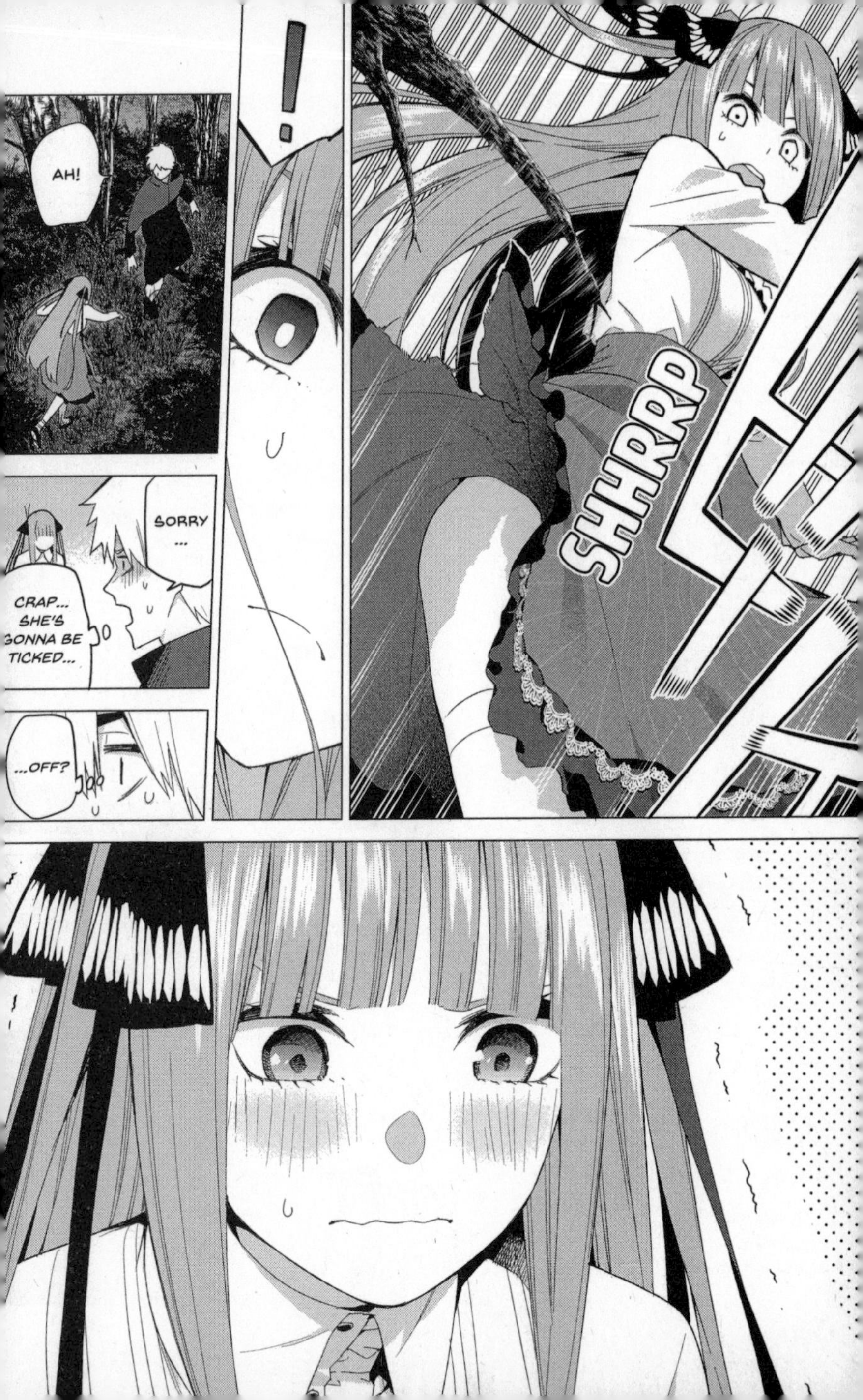
SHHRP
!
AH!
SORRY ...
CRAP... SHE'S GONNA BE TICKED...
...OFF?

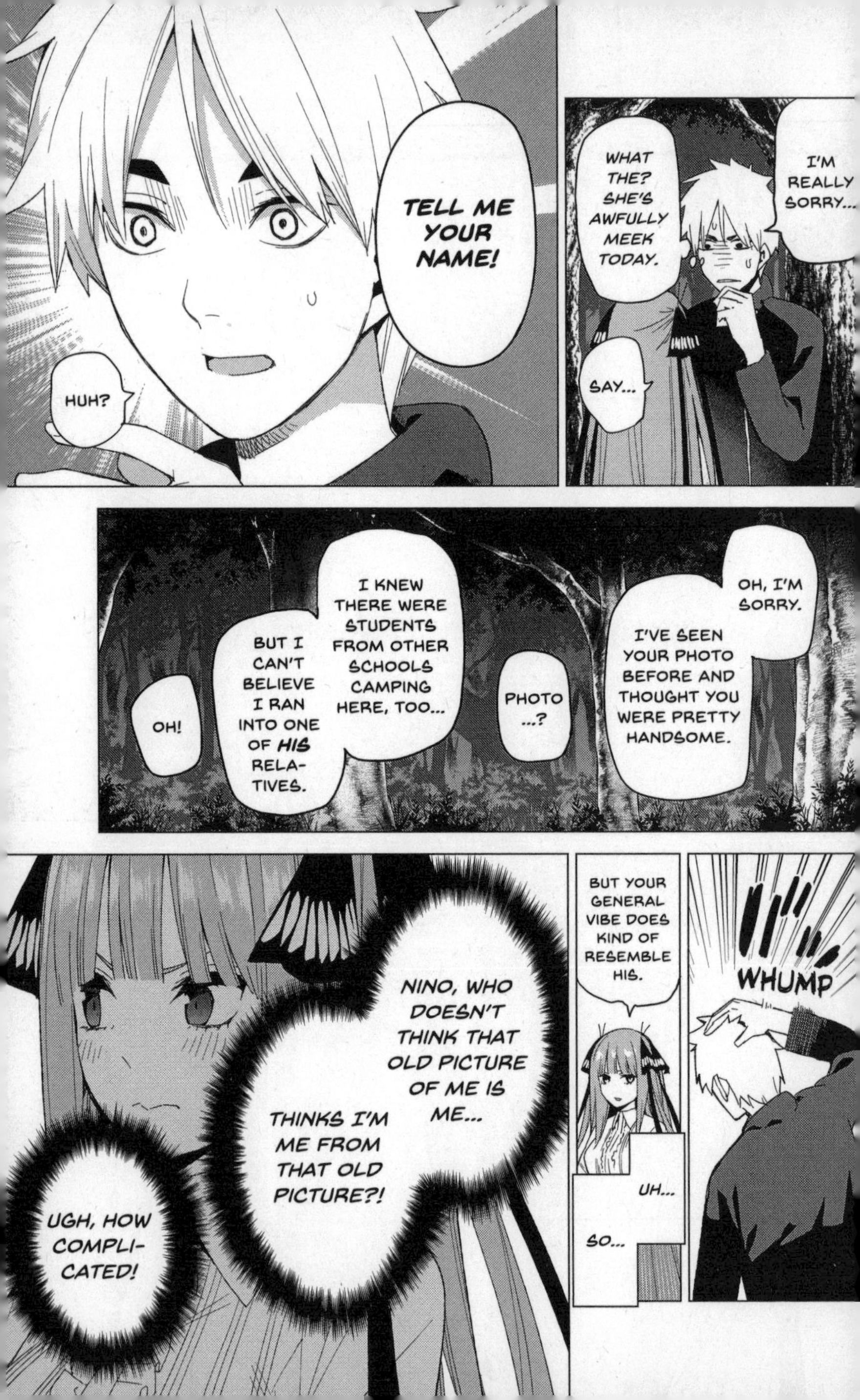

I'M REALLY SORRY...
WHAT THE? SHE'S AWFULLY MEEK TODAY.
SAY...
TELL ME YOUR NAME!
HUH?
OH, I'M SORRY.
I'VE SEEN YOUR PHOTO BEFORE AND THOUGHT YOU WERE PRETTY HANDSOME.
PHOTO ...?
I KNEW THERE WERE STUDENTS FROM OTHER SCHOOLS CAMPING HERE, TOO...
BUT I CAN'T BELIEVE I RAN INTO ONE OF HIS RELATIVES.
OH!
WHUMP
BUT YOUR GENERAL VIBE DOES KIND OF RESEMBLE HIS.
UH...
SO...
NINO, WHO DOESN'T THINK THAT OLD PICTURE OF ME IS ME...
THINKS I'M ME FROM THAT OLD PICTURE?!
UGH, HOW COMPLICATED!

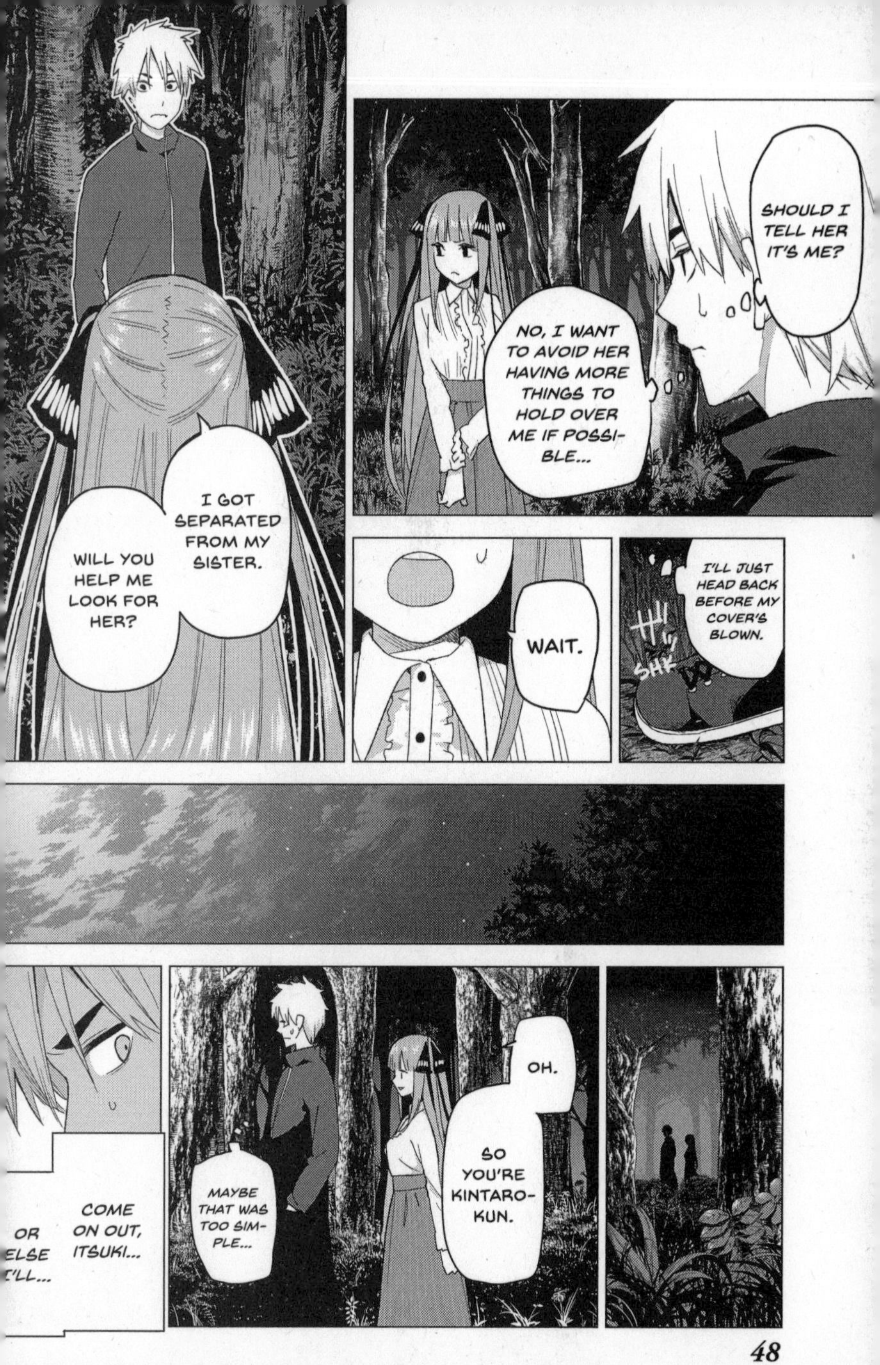
SHOULD I TELL HER IT'S ME?
NO, I WANT TO AVOID HER HAVING MORE THINGS TO HOLD OVER ME IF POSSI-BLE...
I'LL JUST HEAD BACK BEFORE MY COVER'S BLOWN.
SHK
WAIT.
I GOT SEPARATED FROM MY SISTER.
WILL YOU HELP ME LOOK FOR HER?
OH.
SO YOU'RE KINTARO-KUN.
MAYBE THAT WAS TOO SIM-PLE...
COME ON OUT, ITSUKI...
OR ELSE I'LL...

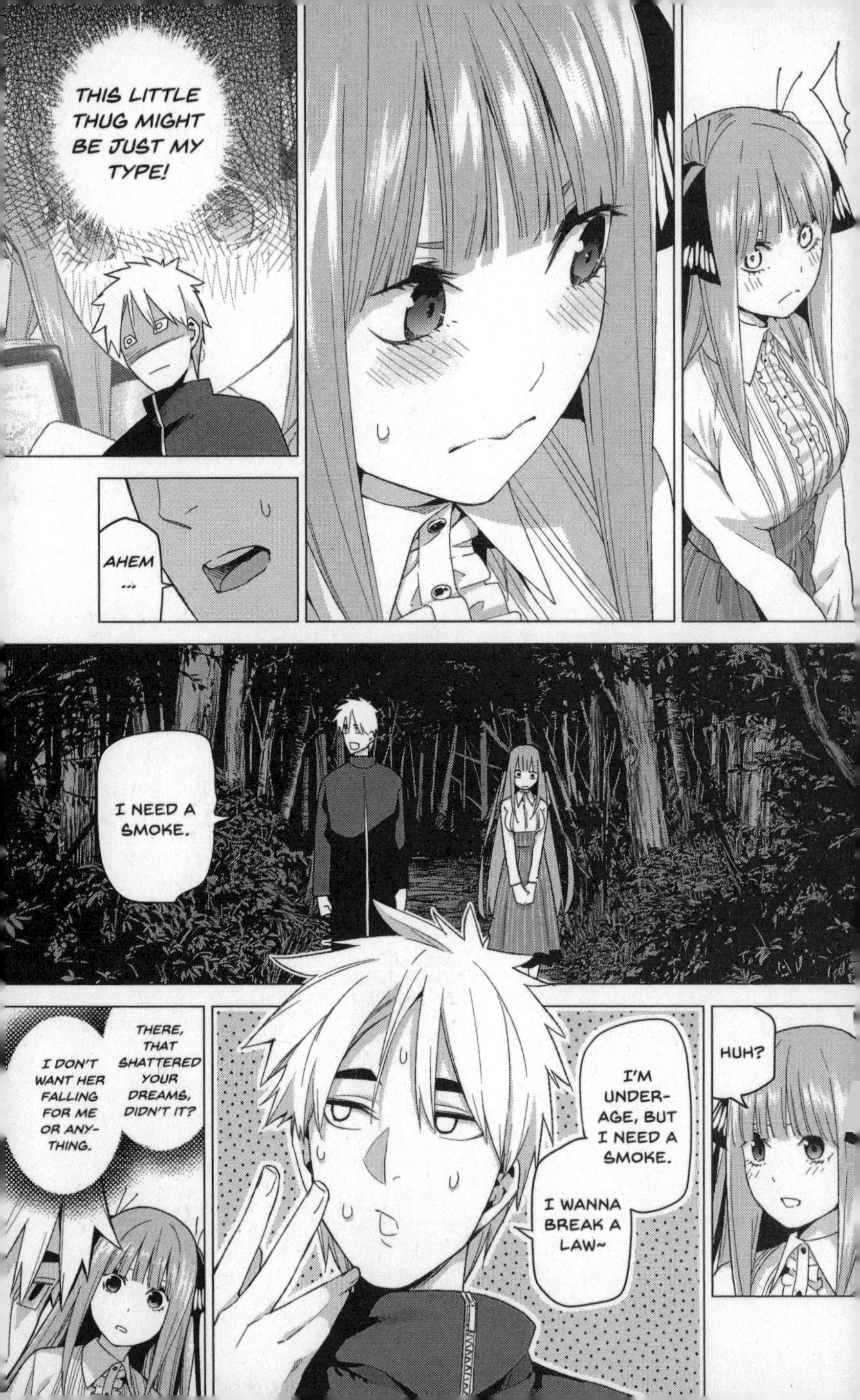
THIS LITTLE THUG MIGHT BE JUST MY TYPE!
AHEM ...
I NEED A SMOKE.
HUH?
I'M UNDER-AGE, BUT I NEED A SMOKE.
I WANNA BREAK A LAW~
THERE, THAT SHATTERED YOUR DREAMS, DIDN'T IT?
I DON'T WANT HER FALLING FOR ME OR ANYTHING.

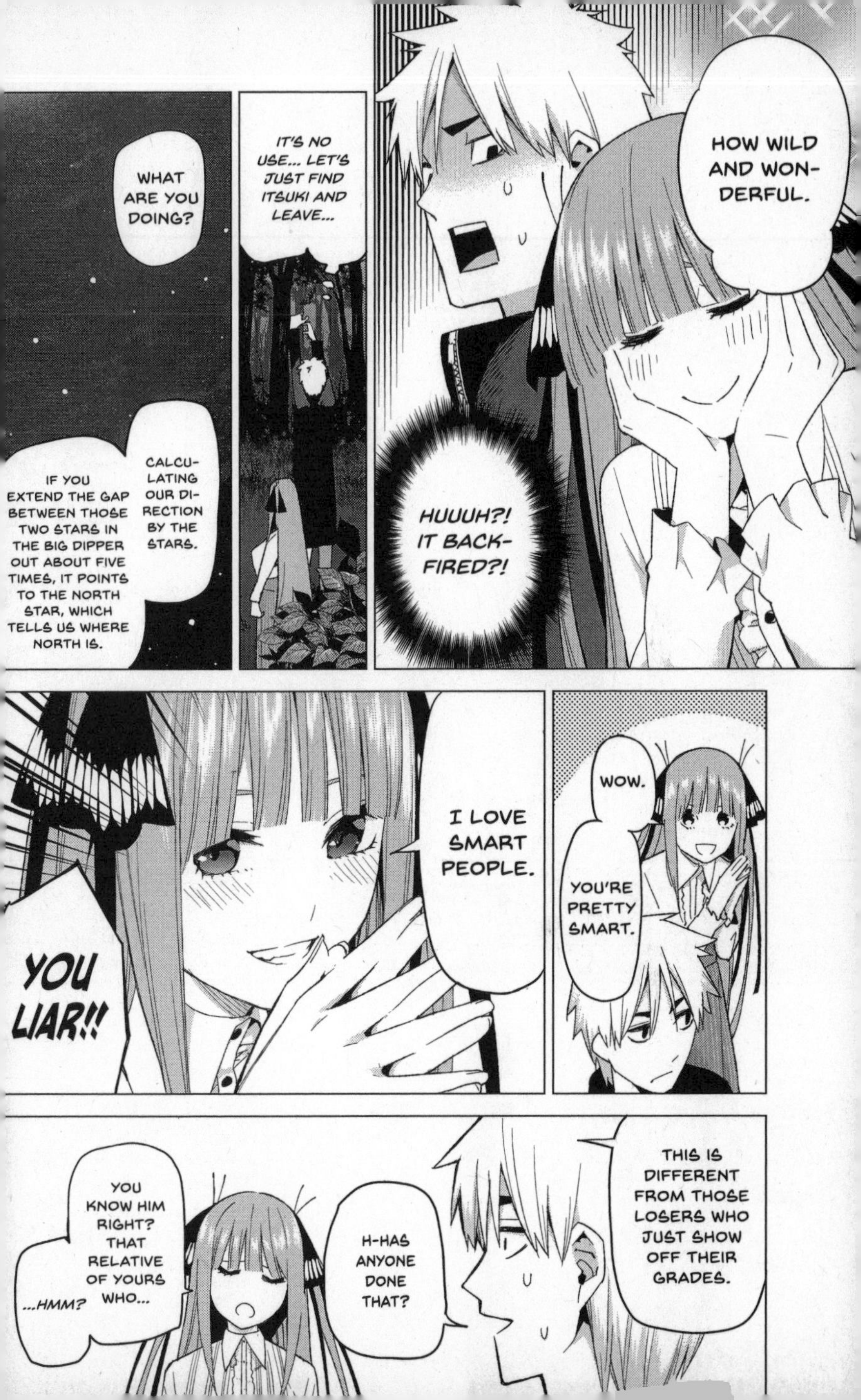
HOW WILD AND WON-DERFUL.
HUUUH?! IT BACK-FIRED?!
IT'S NO USE... LET'S JUST FIND ITSUKI AND LEAVE...
WHAT ARE YOU DOING?
CALCU-LATING OUR DI-RECTION BY THE STARS.
IF YOU EXTEND THE GAP BETWEEN THOSE TWO STARS IN THE BIG DIPPER OUT ABOUT FIVE TIMES, IT POINTS TO THE NORTH STAR, WHICH TELLS US WHERE NORTH IS.
WOW.
YOU'RE PRETTY SMART.
I LOVE SMART PEOPLE.
YOU LIAR!!
THIS IS DIFFERENT FROM THOSE LOSERS WHO JUST SHOW OFF THEIR GRADES.
H-HAS ANYONE DONE THAT?
YOU KNOW HIM RIGHT? THAT RELATIVE OF YOURS WHO...
...HMM?

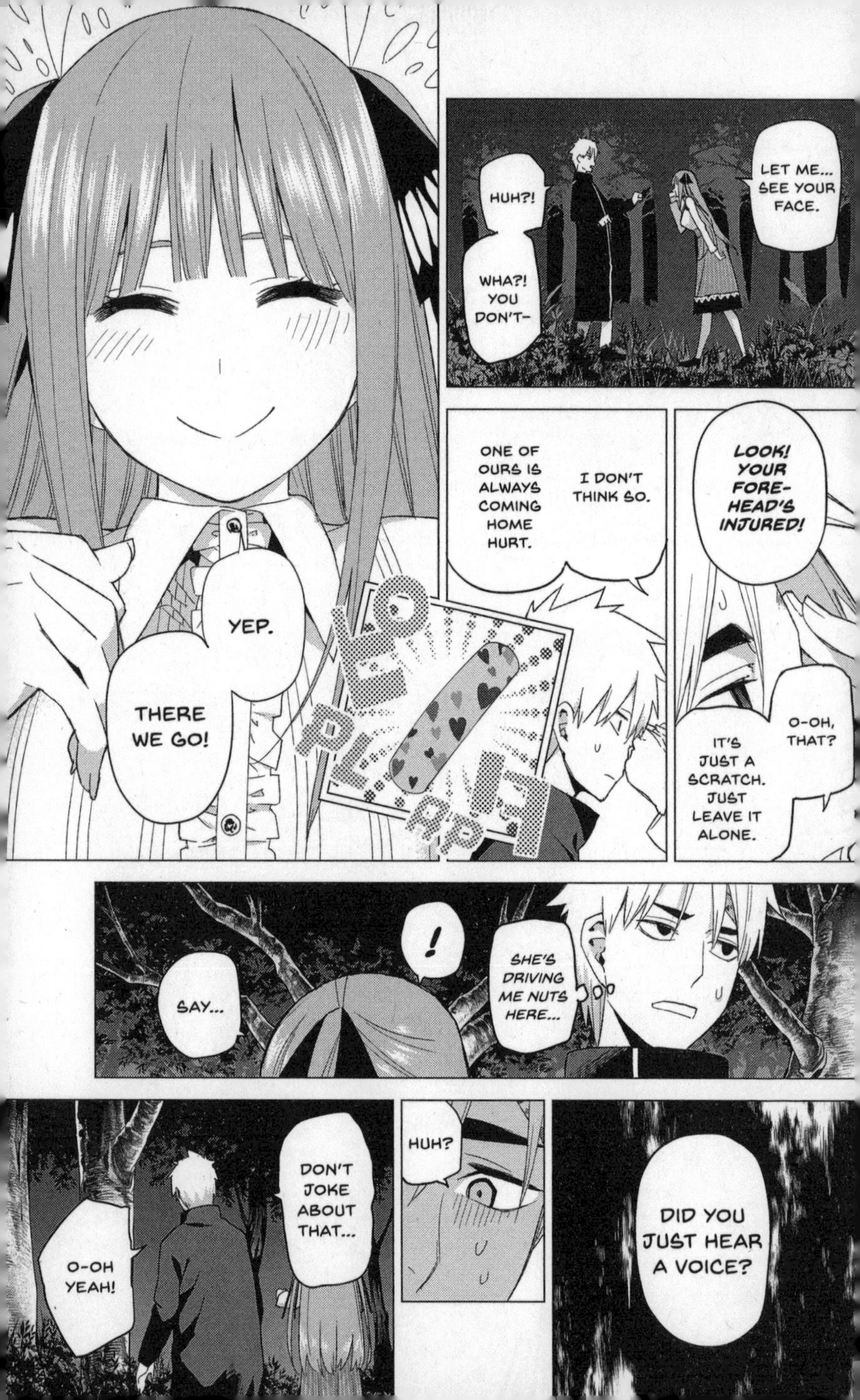
LET ME... SEE YOUR FACE.
HUH?!
WHA?! YOU DON'T-
LOOK! YOUR FORE-HEAD'S INJURED!
O-OH, THAT?
IT'S JUST A SCRATCH. JUST LEAVE IT ALONE.
I DON'T THINK SO.
ONE OF OURS IS ALWAYS COMING HOME HURT.
PLAP
YEP.
THERE WE GO!
SHE'S DRIVING ME NUTS HERE...
!
SAY...
DID YOU JUST HEAR A VOICE?
HUH?
DON'T JOKE ABOUT THAT...
O-OH YEAH!

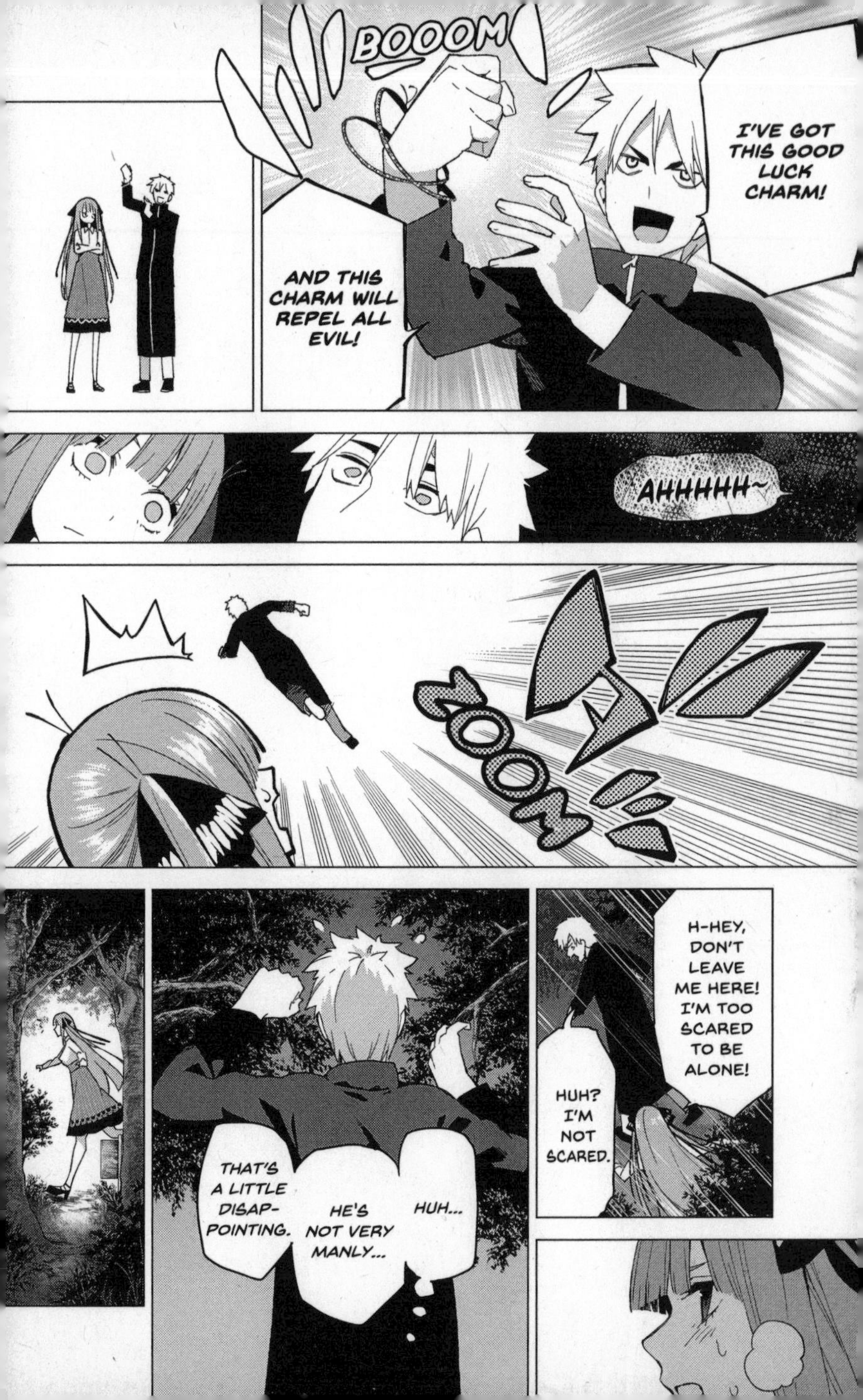
BOOOM
I'VE GOT THIS GOOD LUCK CHARM!
AND THIS CHARM WILL REPEL ALL EVIL!
AHHHHH~
ZOOM
H-HEY, DON'T LEAVE ME HERE! I'M TOO SCARED TO BE ALONE!
HUH? I'M NOT SCARED.
HUH...
HE'S NOT VERY MANLY...
THAT'S A LITTLE DISAP-POINTING.

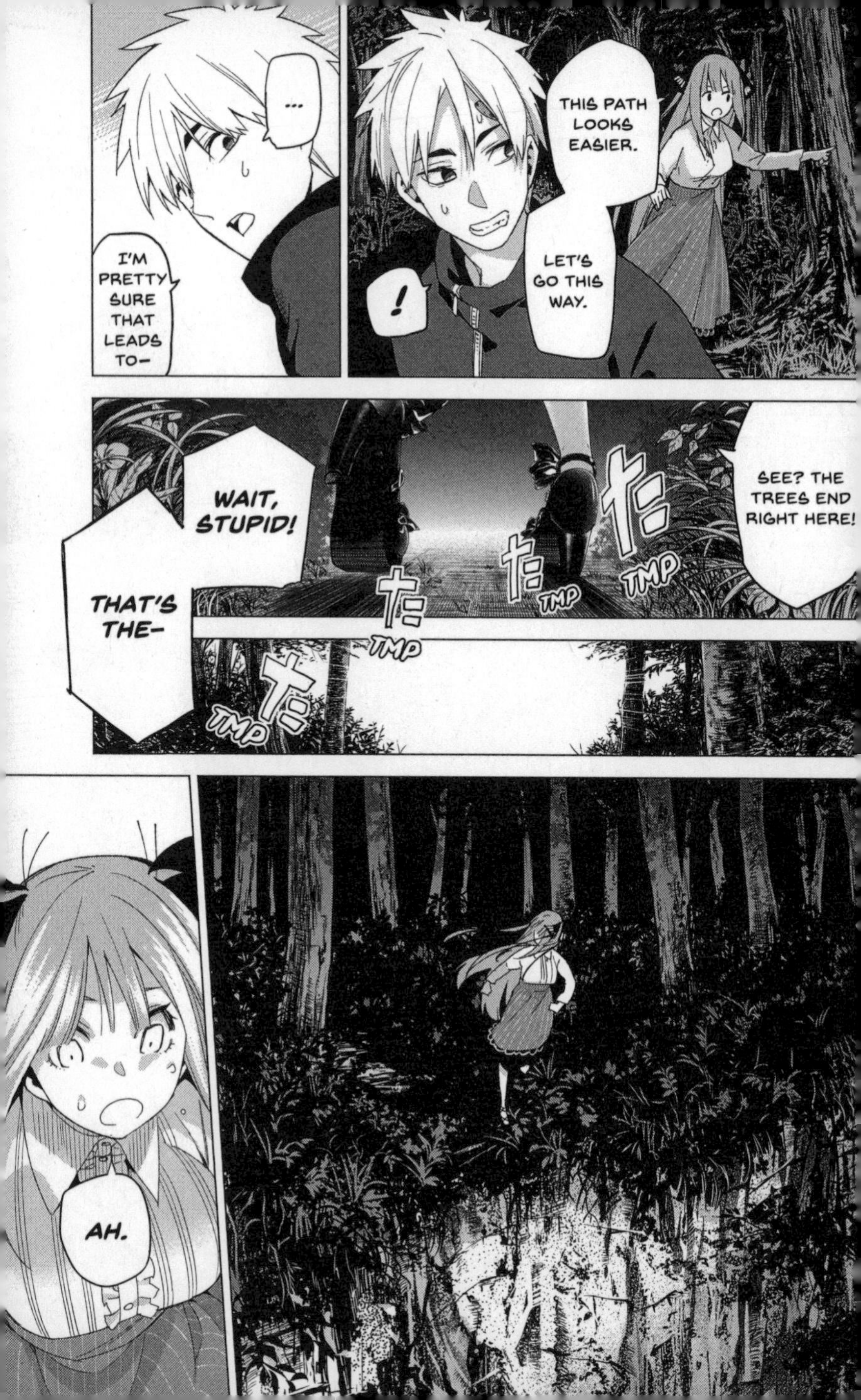
THIS PATH LOOKS EASIER.
LET'S GO THIS WAY.
!
...
I'M PRETTY SURE THAT LEADS TO-
SEE? THE TREES END RIGHT HERE!
TMP
TMP
TMP
WAIT, STUPID!
THAT'S THE-
TMP
AH.

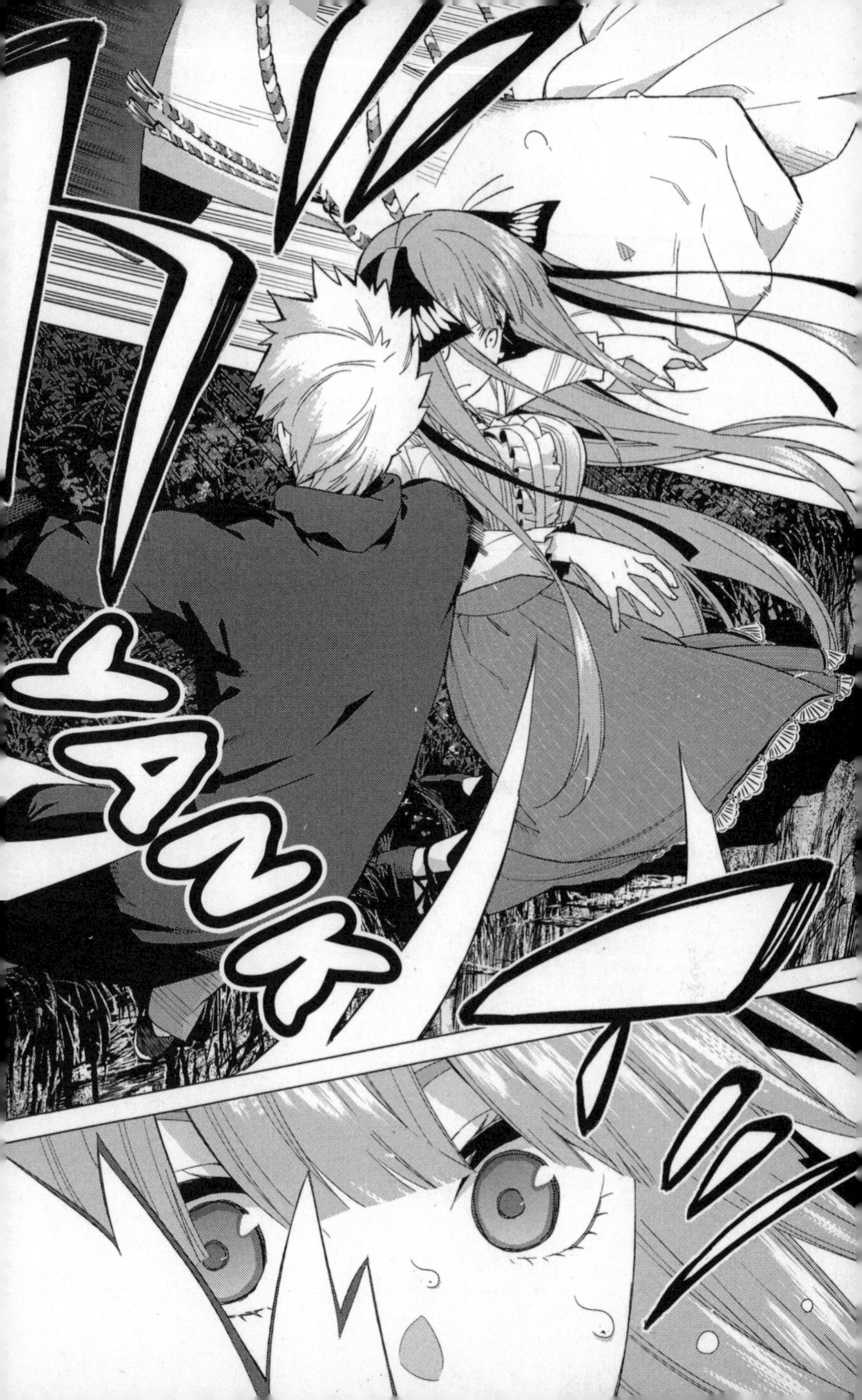
YANK

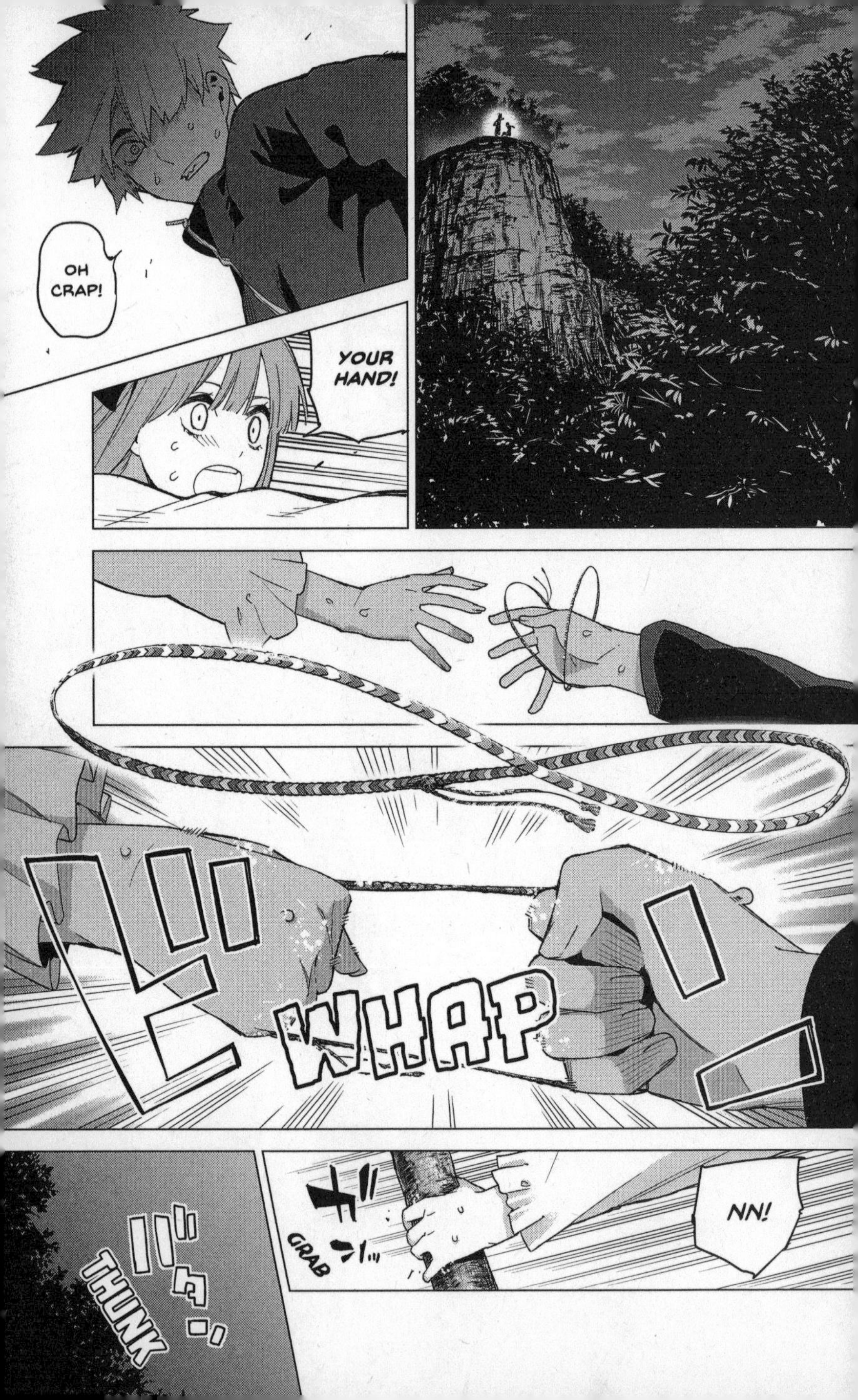
OH CRAP!
YOUR HAND!
WHAP
NN!
GRAB
THUNK

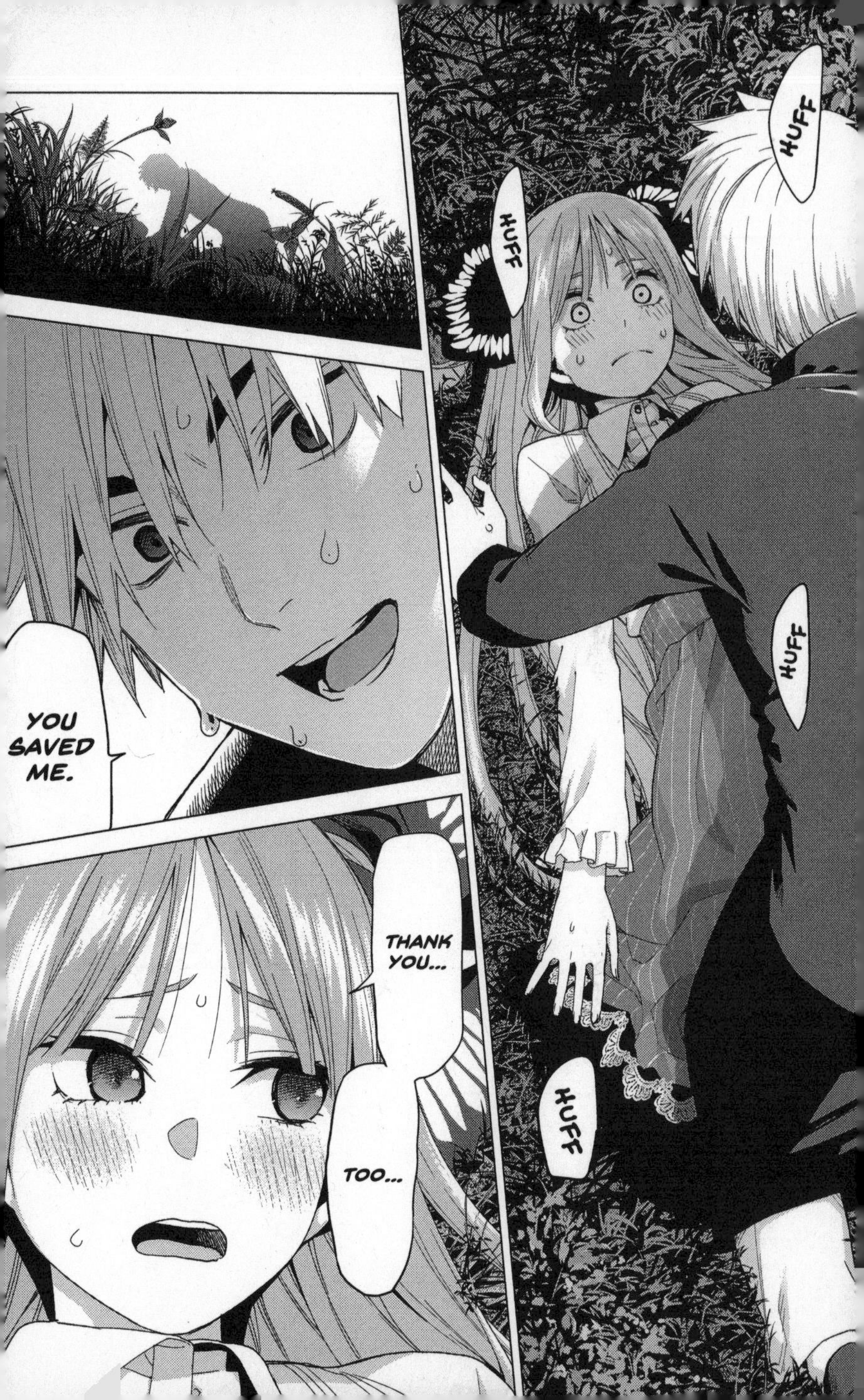
HUFF
HUFF
HUFF
HUFF
YOU SAVED ME.
THANK YOU...
TOO...

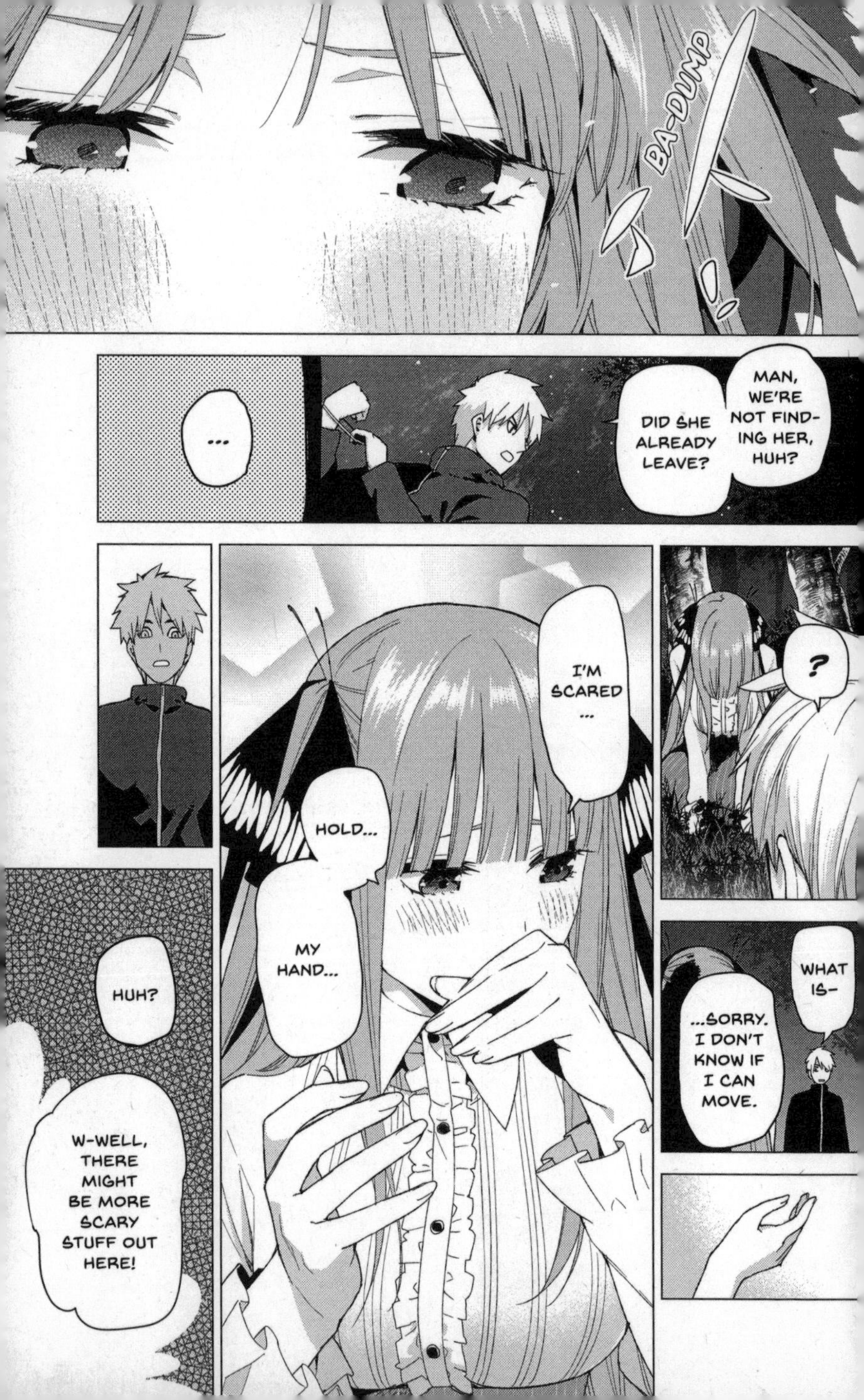
BA-DUMP
MAN, WE'RE NOT FINDING HER, HUH?
DID SHE ALREADY LEAVE?
...
?
WHAT IS-
...SORRY. I DON'T KNOW IF I CAN MOVE.
I'M SCARED ...
HOLD...
MY HAND...
HUH?
W-WELL, THERE MIGHT BE MORE SCARY STUFF OUT HERE!

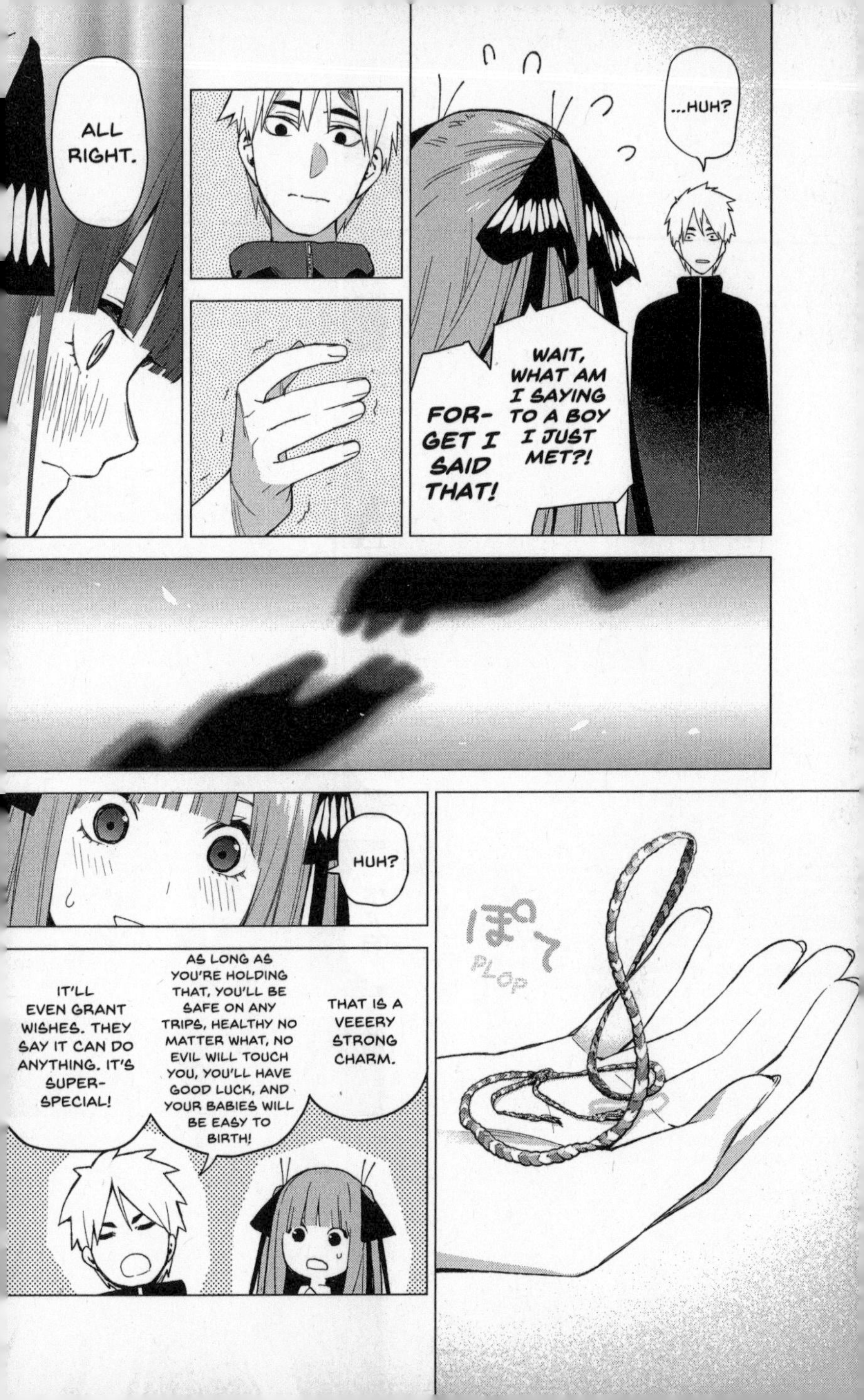
...HUH?
WAIT, WHAT AM I SAYING TO A BOY I JUST MET?!
FOR-GET I SAID THAT!
ALL RIGHT.
ぽて
PLOP
HUH?
THAT IS A VEEERY STRONG CHARM.
AS LONG AS YOU'RE HOLDING THAT, YOU'LL BE SAFE ON ANY TRIPS, HEALTHY NO MATTER WHAT, NO EVIL WILL TOUCH YOU, YOU'LL HAVE GOOD LUCK, AND YOUR BABIES WILL BE EASY TO BIRTH!
IT'LL EVEN GRANT WISHES. THEY SAY IT CAN DO ANYTHING. IT'S SUPER-SPECIAL!

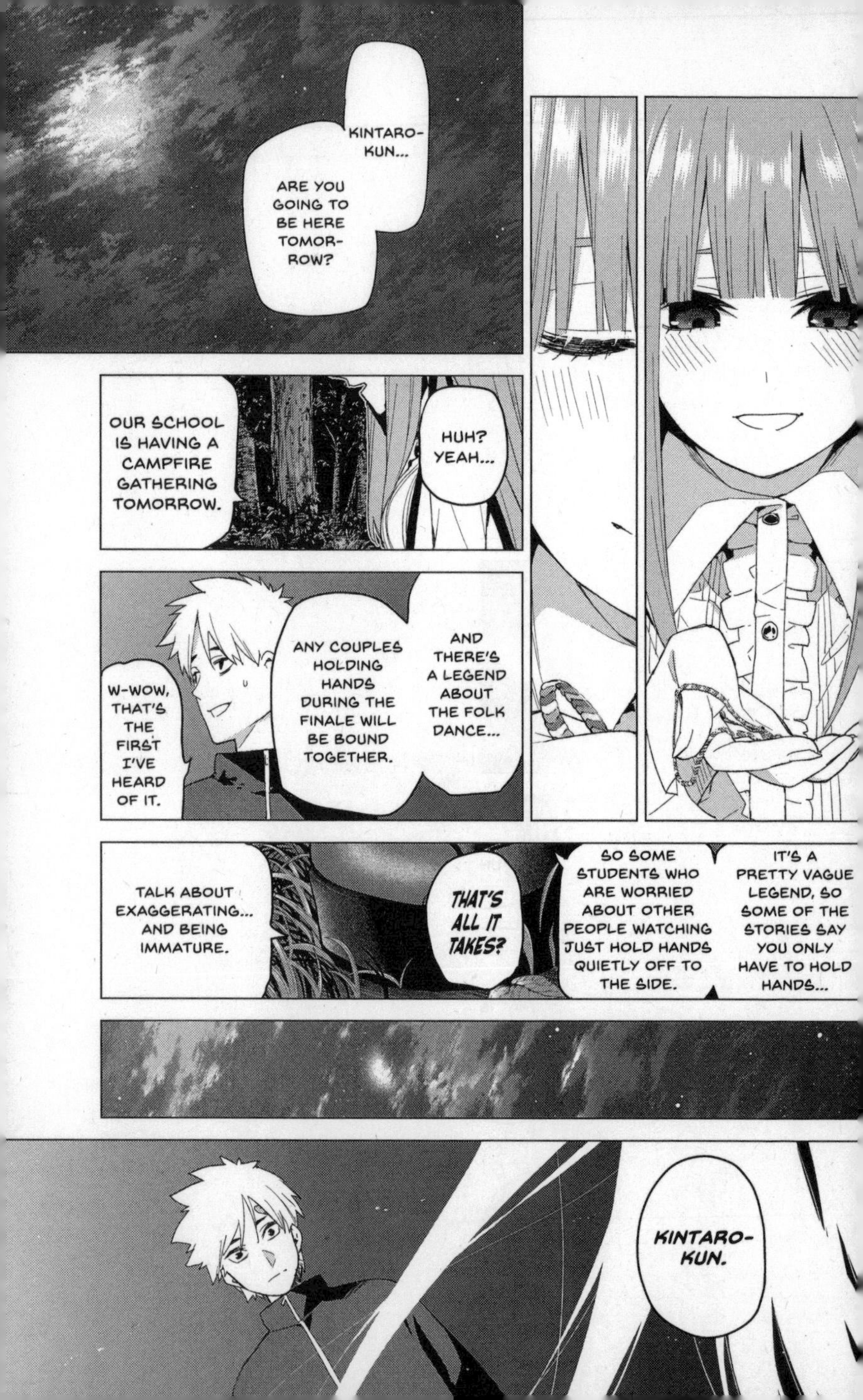
KINTARO-KUN...
ARE YOU GOING TO BE HERE TOMORROW?
HUH? YEAH...
OUR SCHOOL IS HAVING A CAMPFIRE GATHERING TOMORROW.
AND THERE'S A LEGEND ABOUT THE FOLK DANCE...
ANY COUPLES HOLDING HANDS DURING THE FINALE WILL BE BOUND TOGETHER.
W-WOW, THAT'S THE FIRST I'VE HEARD OF IT.
IT'S A PRETTY VAGUE LEGEND, SO SOME OF THE STORIES SAY YOU ONLY HAVE TO HOLD HANDS...
SO SOME STUDENTS WHO ARE WORRIED ABOUT OTHER PEOPLE WATCHING JUST HOLD HANDS QUIETLY OFF TO THE SIDE.
THAT'S ALL IT TAKES?
TALK ABOUT EXAGGERATING... AND BEING IMMATURE.
KINTARO-KUN.

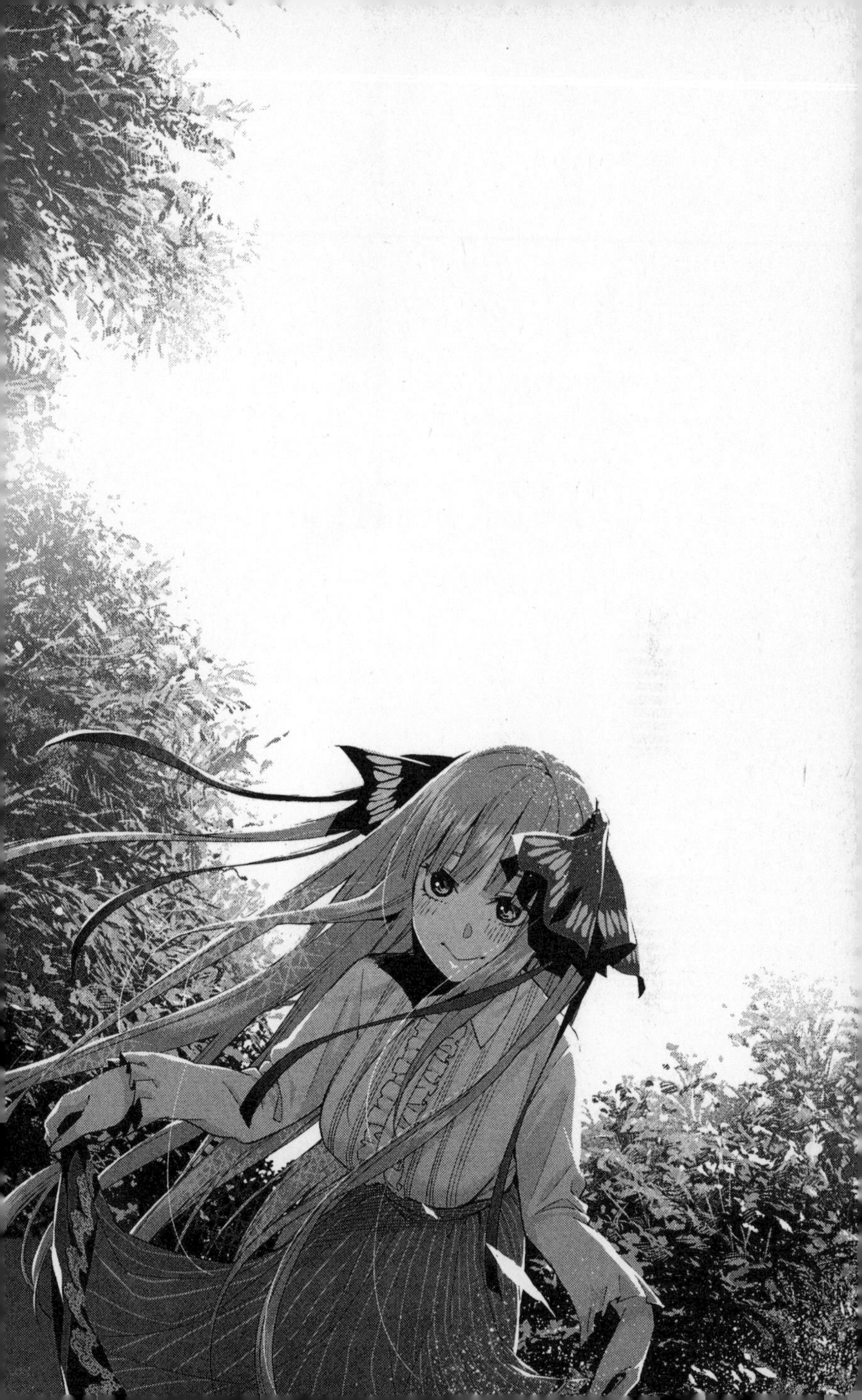

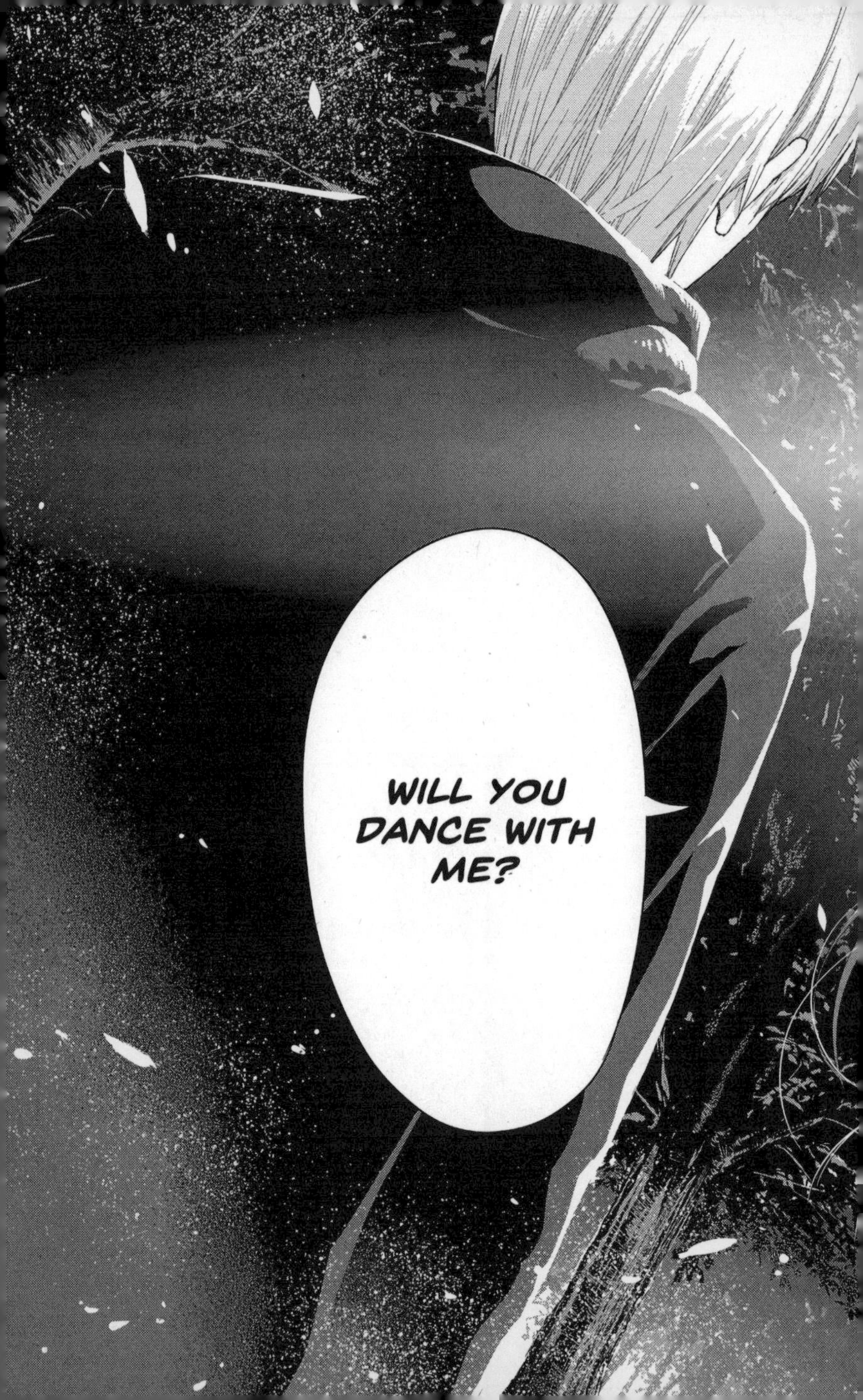
WILL YOU DANCE WITH ME?

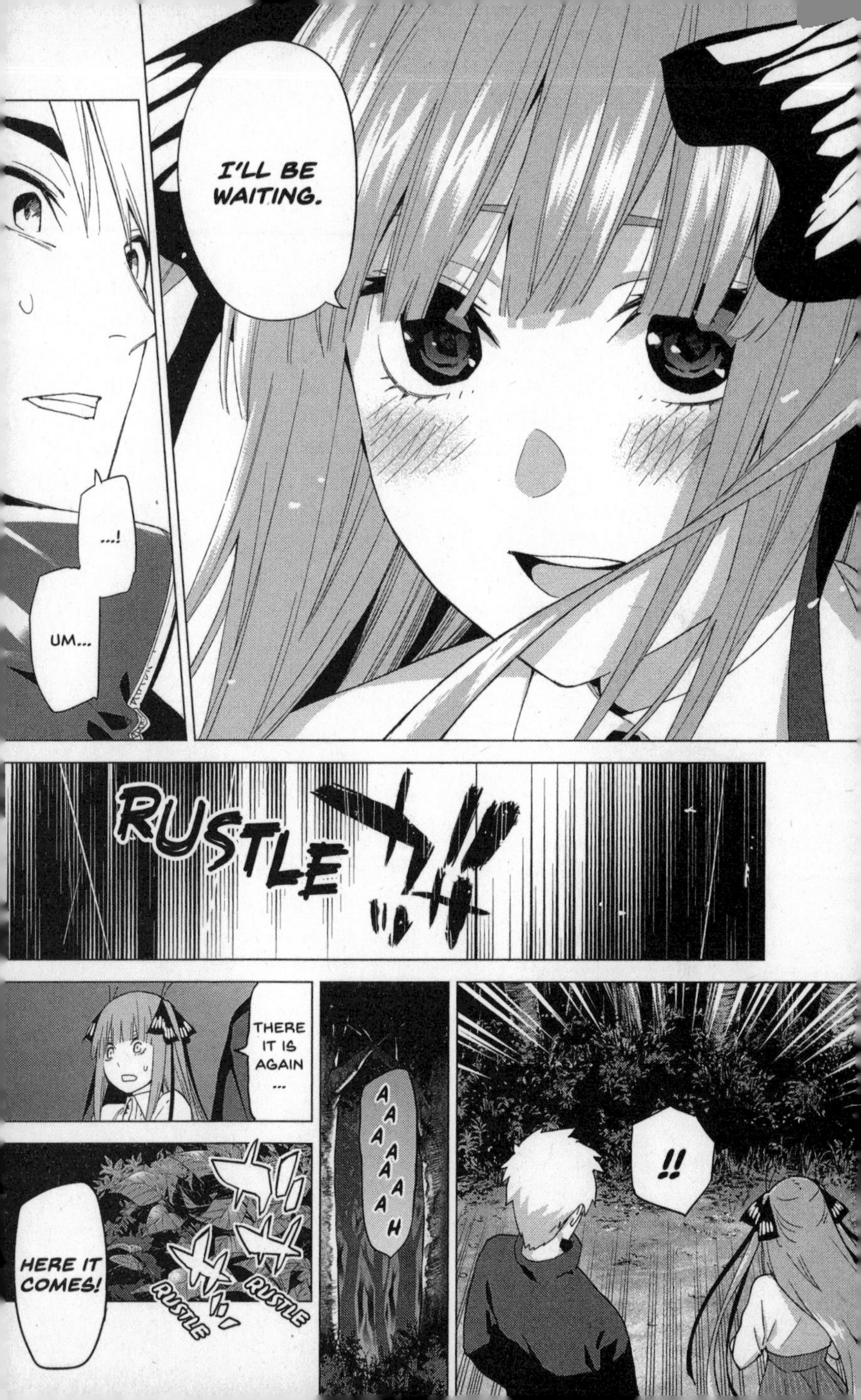

I'LL BE WAITING.
...!
UM...
RUSTLE
!!
AAAAAAAH
THERE IT IS AGAIN ...
HERE IT COMES!
RUSTLE
RUSTLE

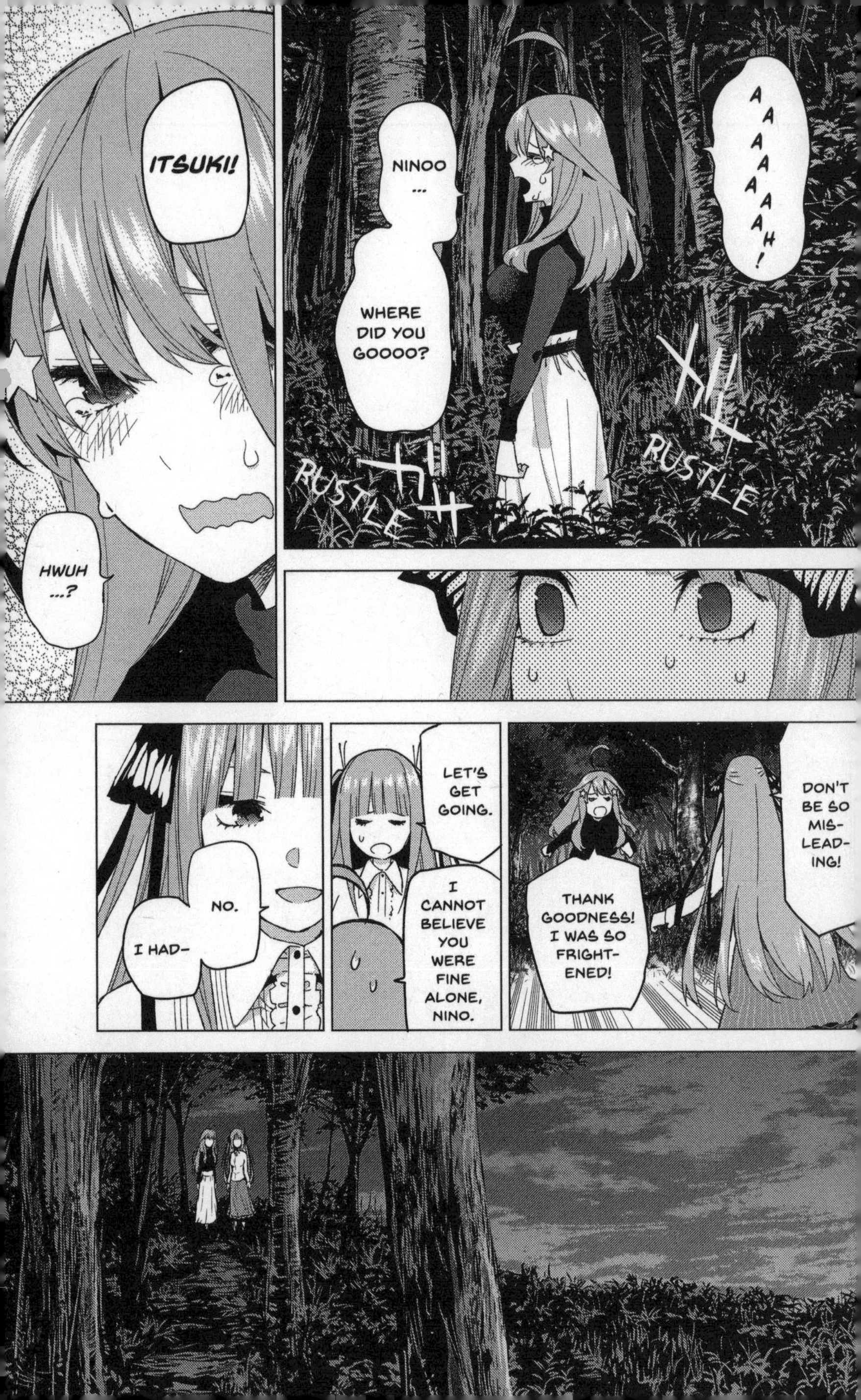
AAAAAAAH!
NINOO ...
WHERE DID YOU GOOOO?
RUSTLE
RUSTLE
ITSUKI!
HWUH ...?
DON'T BE SO MIS-LEADING!
THANK GOODNESS! I WAS SO FRIGHT-ENED!
LET'S GET GOING.
I CANNOT BELIEVE YOU WERE FINE ALONE, NINO.
NO.
I HAD-

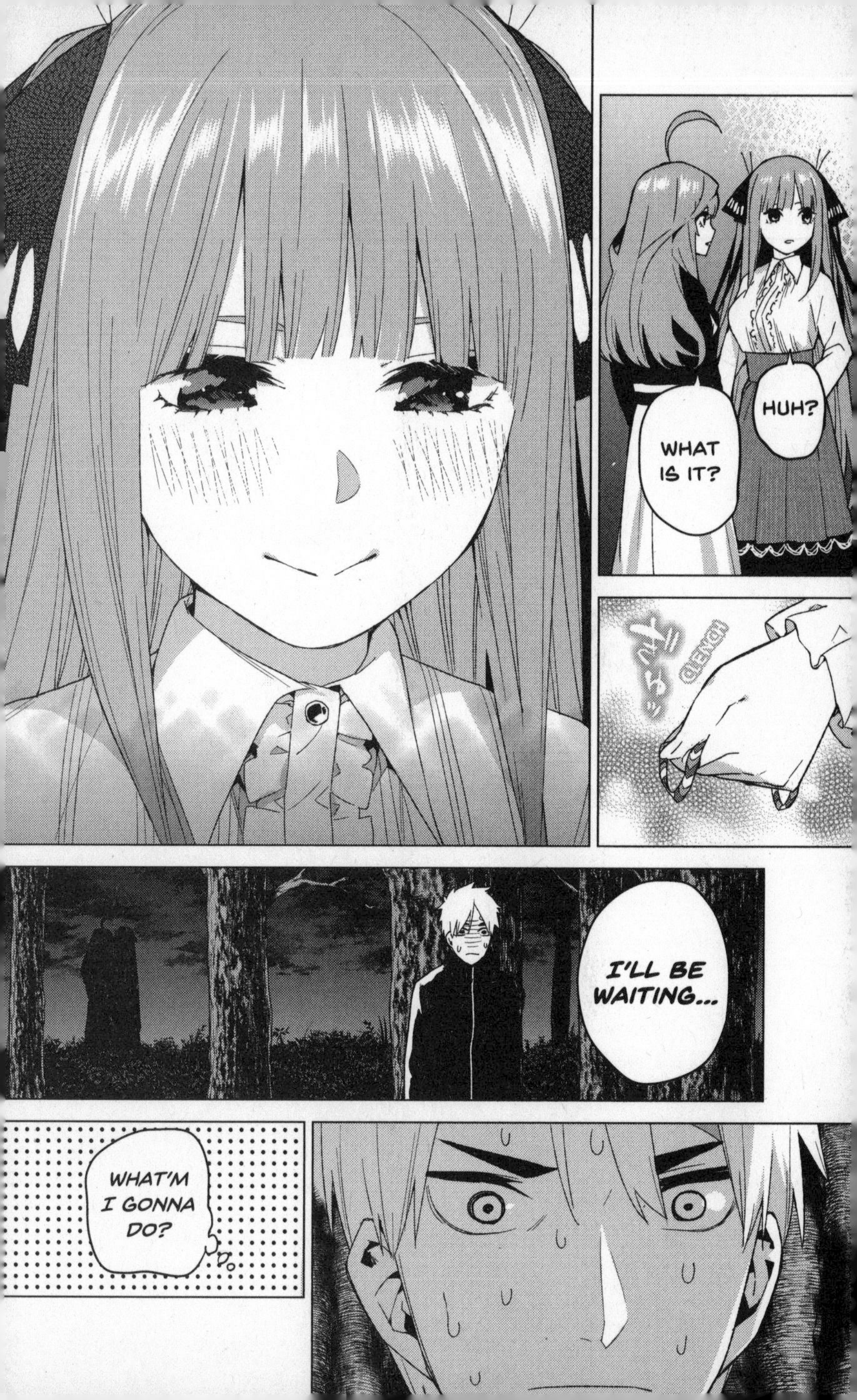
HUH?
WHAT IS IT?
I'LL BE WAITING...
WHAT'M I GONNA DO?

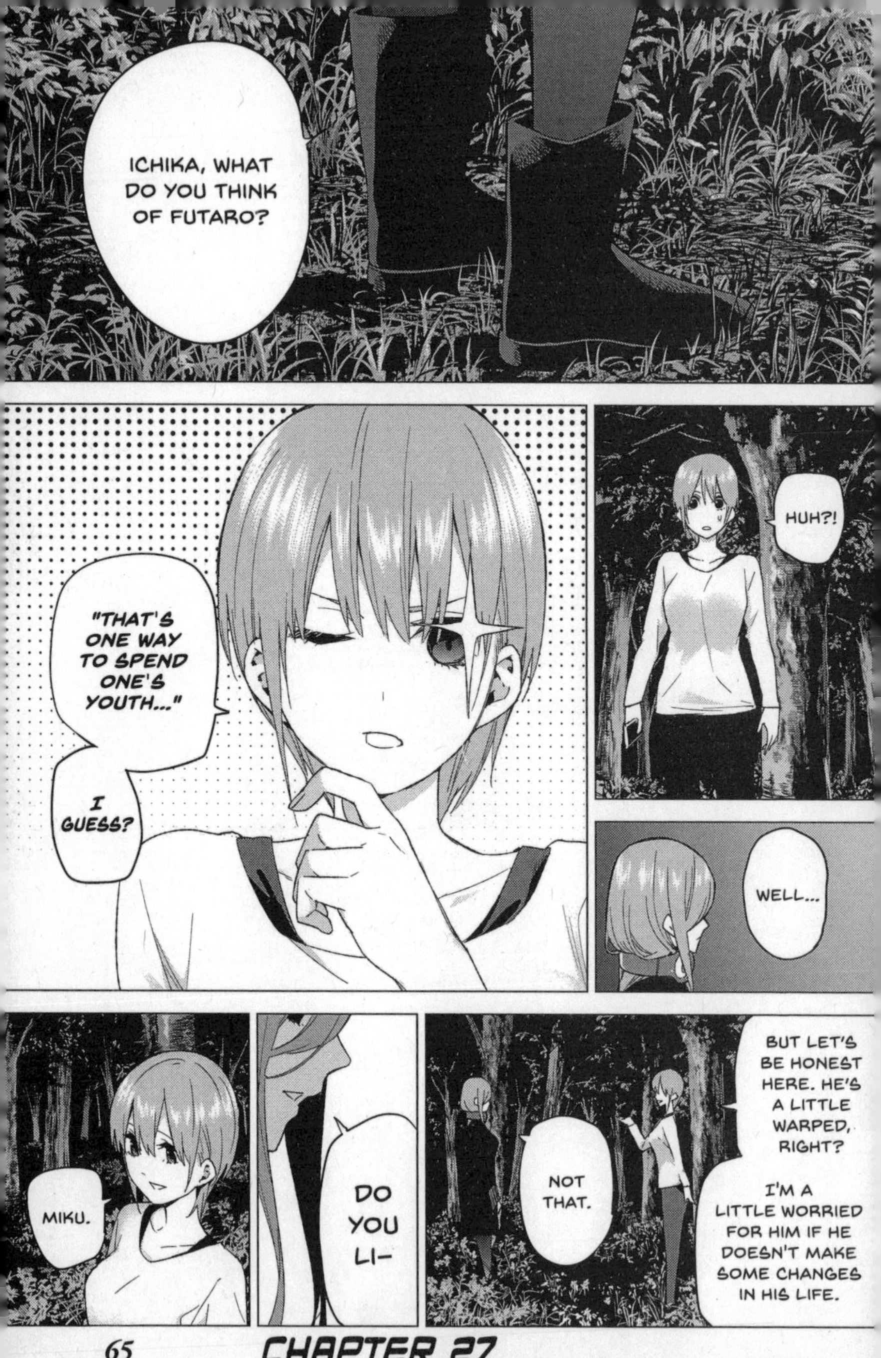
ICHIKA, WHAT DO YOU THINK OF FUTARO?
HUH?!
WELL...
"THAT'S ONE WAY TO SPEND ONE'S YOUTH..."
I GUESS?
BUT LET'S BE HONEST HERE. HE'S A LITTLE WARPED, RIGHT?
I'M A LITTLE WORRIED FOR HIM IF HE DOESN'T MAKE SOME CHANGES IN HIS LIFE.
NOT THAT.
DO YOU LI—
MIKU.

CHAPTER 27
THE BINDING LEGEND: DAY 2 ③

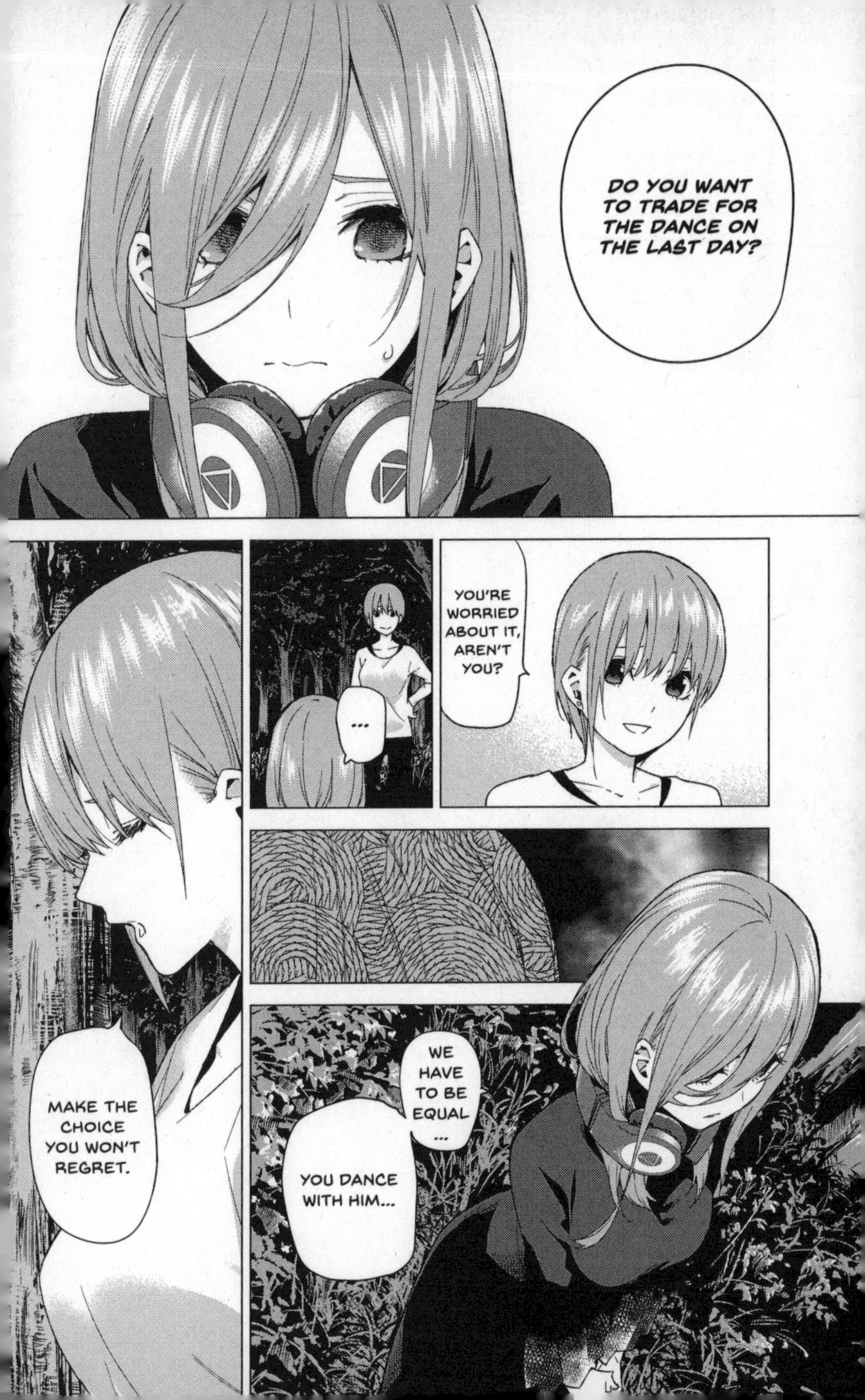
DO YOU WANT TO TRADE FOR THE DANCE ON THE LAST DAY?
YOU'RE WORRIED ABOUT IT, AREN'T YOU?
...
WE HAVE TO BE EQUAL...
YOU DANCE WITH HIM...
MAKE THE CHOICE YOU WON'T REGRET.

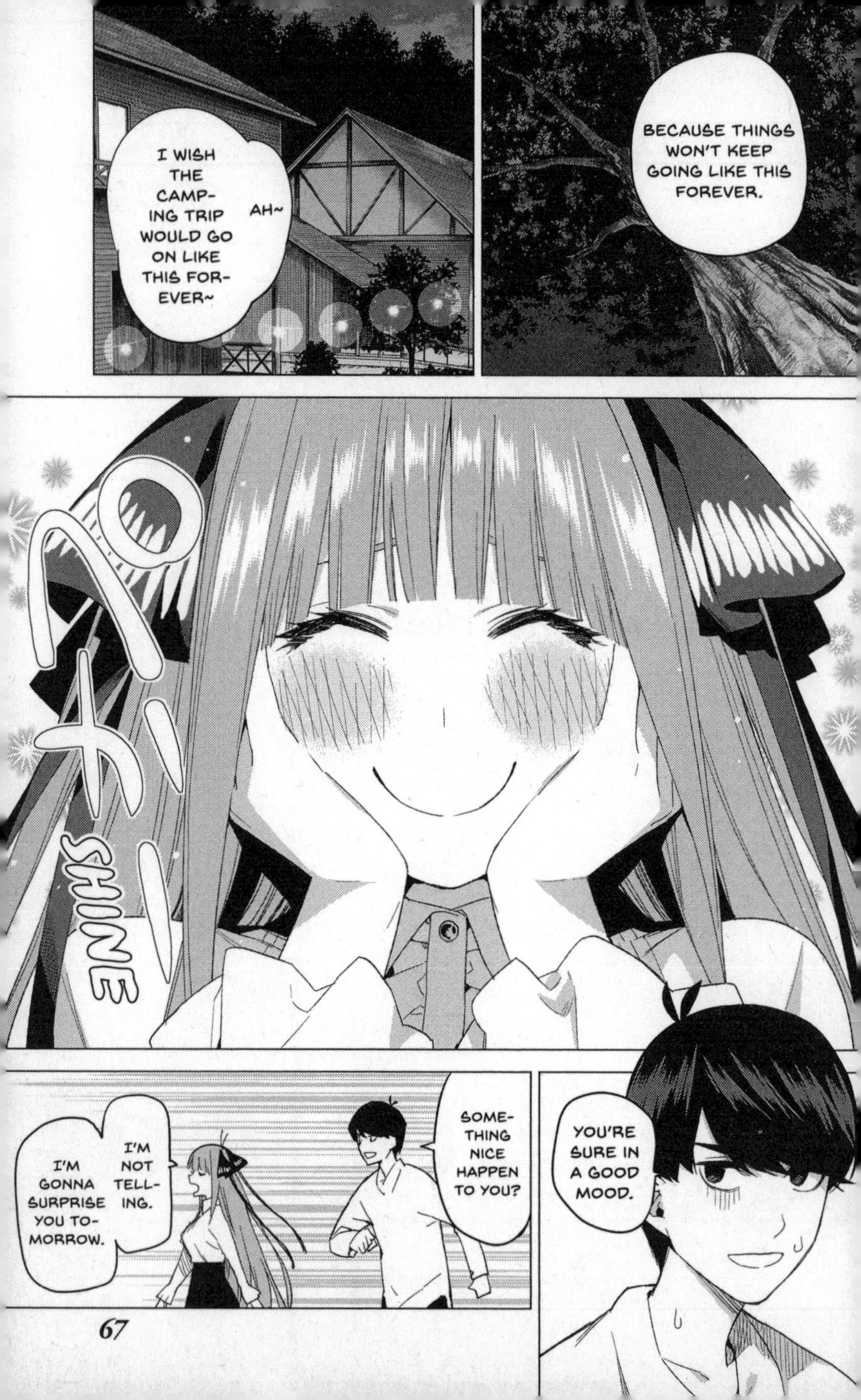
BECAUSE THINGS WON'T KEEP GOING LIKE THIS FOREVER.
AH~
I WISH THE CAMPING TRIP WOULD GO ON LIKE THIS FOREVER~
SHINE
YOU'RE SURE IN A GOOD MOOD.
SOMETHING NICE HAPPEN TO YOU?
I'M NOT TELLING.
I'M GONNA SURPRISE YOU TOMORROW.

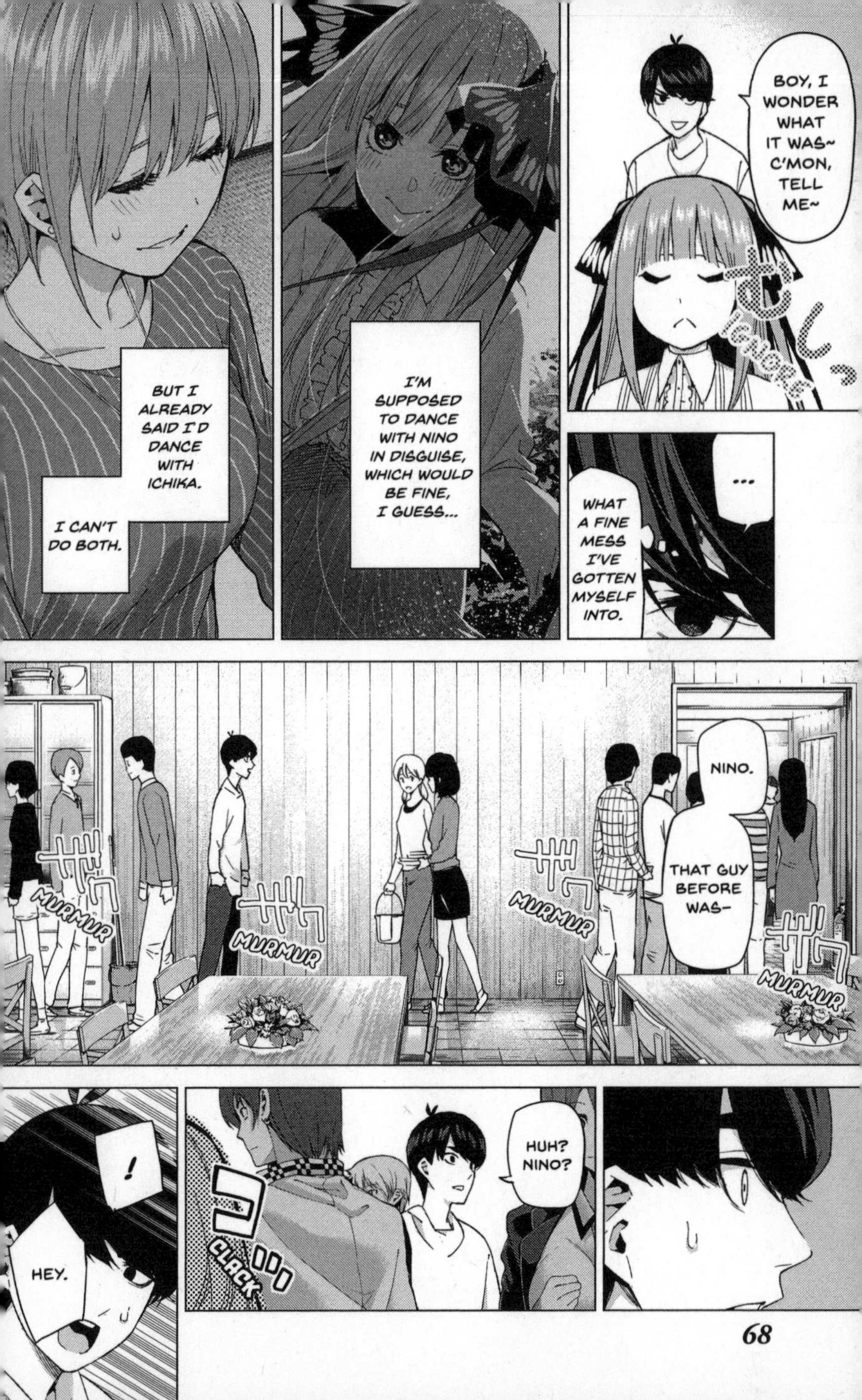

BOY, I WONDER WHAT IT WAS~ C'MON, TELL ME~
IGNORE
...
WHAT A FINE MESS I'VE GOTTEN MYSELF INTO.
I'M SUPPOSED TO DANCE WITH NINO IN DISGUISE, WHICH WOULD BE FINE, I GUESS...
BUT I ALREADY SAID I'D DANCE WITH ICHIKA.
I CAN'T DO BOTH.
NINO.
THAT GUY BEFORE WAS-
MURMUR
MURMUR
MURMUR
MURMUR
HUH? NINO?
CLACK
!
HEY.

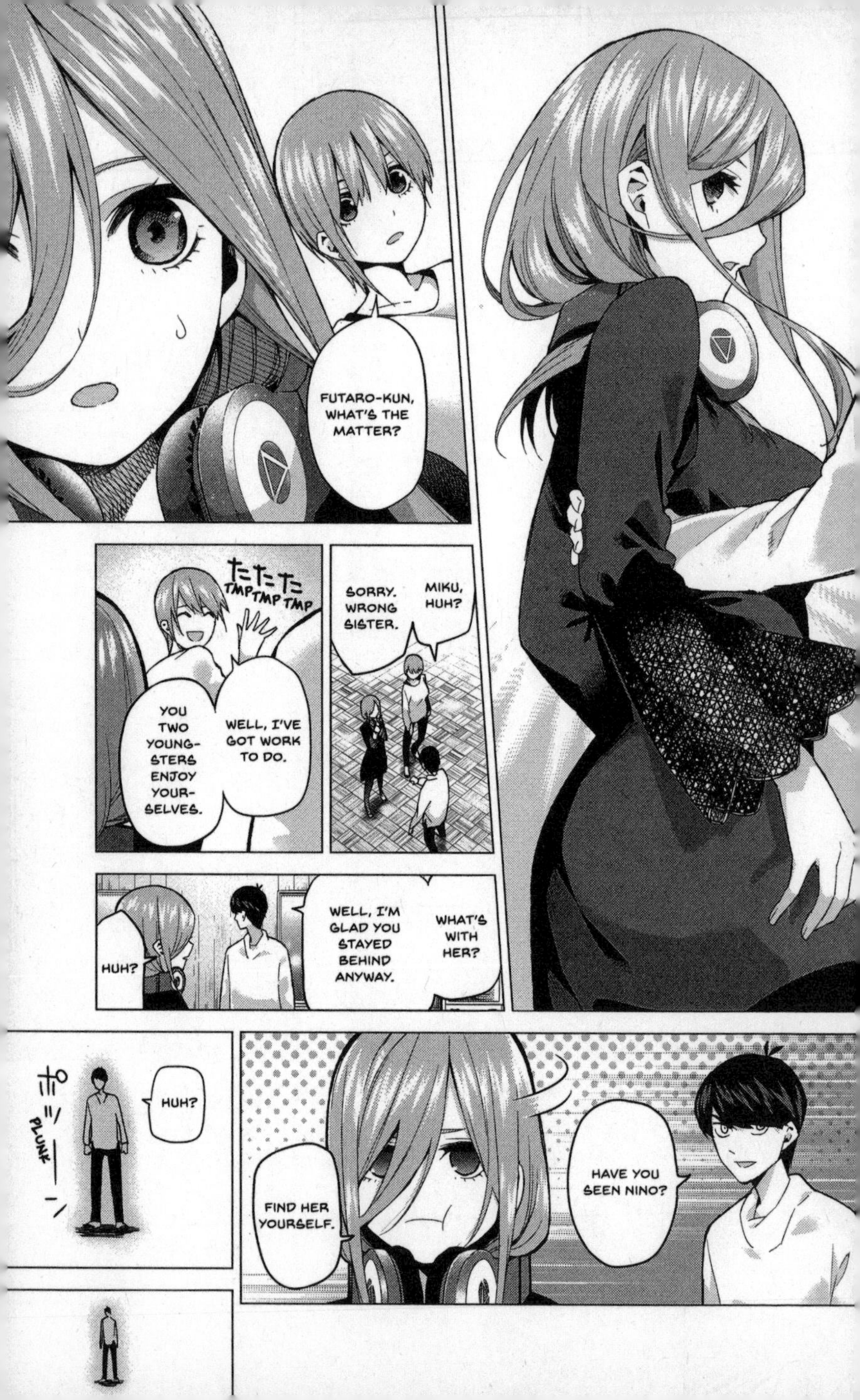
FUTARO-KUN, WHAT'S THE MATTER?
MIKU, HUH?
SORRY. WRONG SISTER.
たたたた
TMP TMP TMP
WELL, I'VE GOT WORK TO DO.
YOU TWO YOUNGSTERS ENJOY YOURSELVES.
WHAT'S WITH HER?
WELL, I'M GLAD YOU STAYED BEHIND ANYWAY.
HUH?
HAVE YOU SEEN NINO?
FIND HER YOURSELF.
HUH?
PLUNK

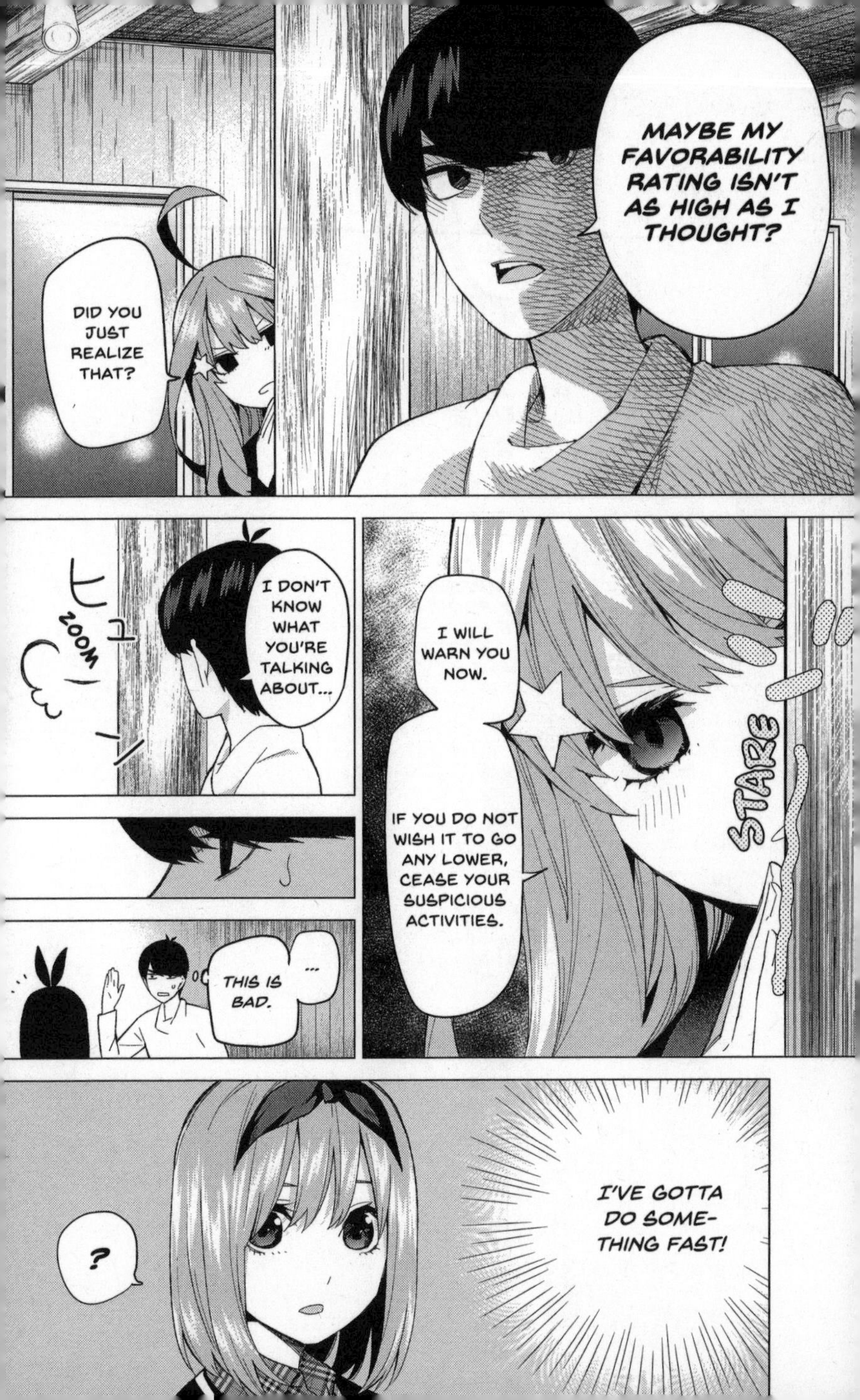
MAYBE MY FAVORABILITY RATING ISN'T AS HIGH AS I THOUGHT?
DID YOU JUST REALIZE THAT?
I WILL WARN YOU NOW.
IF YOU DO NOT WISH IT TO GO ANY LOWER, CEASE YOUR SUSPICIOUS ACTIVITIES.
STARE
I DON'T KNOW WHAT YOU'RE TALKING ABOUT...
ZOOM
...
THIS IS BAD.
I'VE GOTTA DO SOME-THING FAST!
?

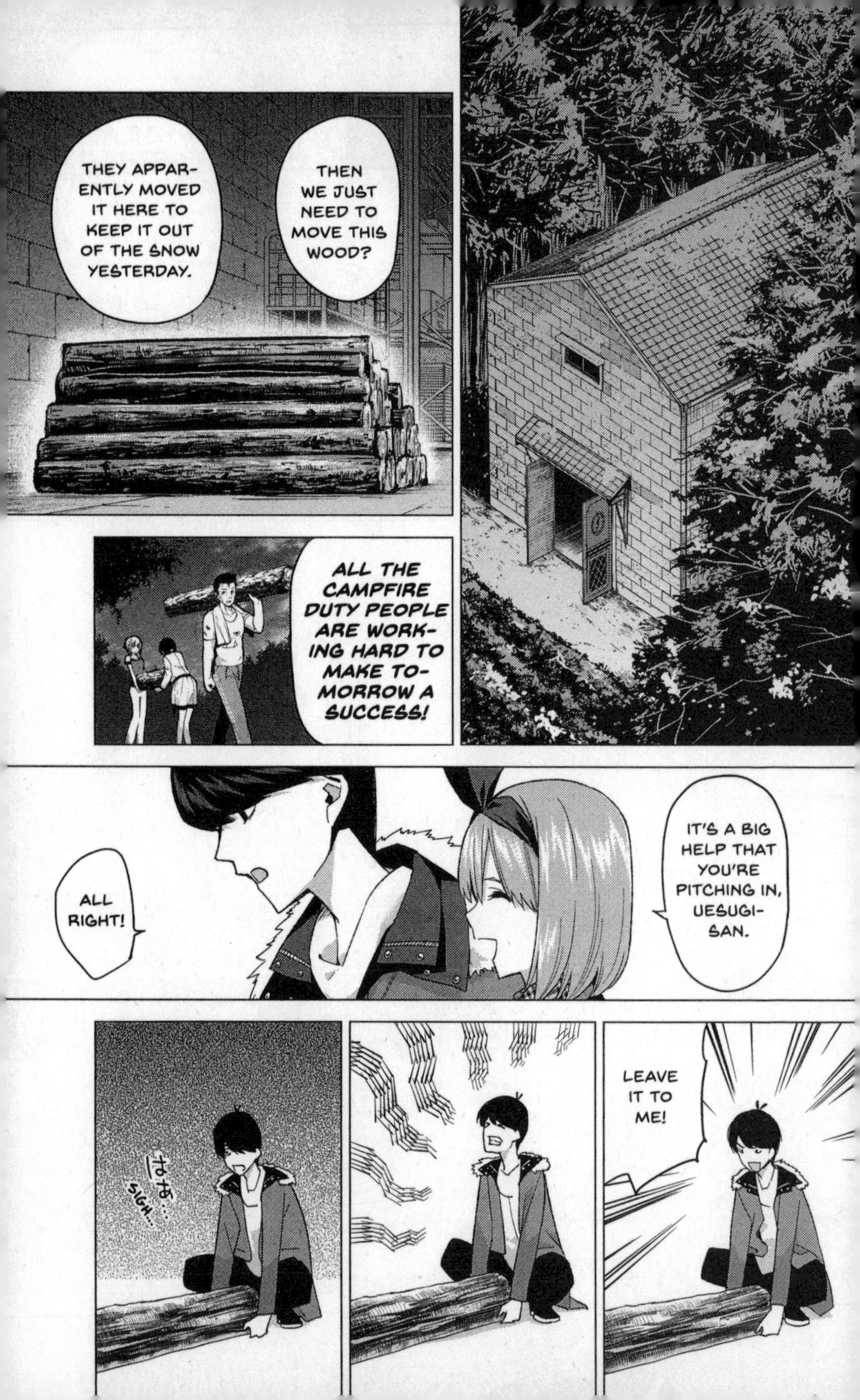
THEN WE JUST NEED TO MOVE THIS WOOD?
THEY APPAR-ENTLY MOVED IT HERE TO KEEP IT OUT OF THE SNOW YESTERDAY.
ALL THE CAMPFIRE DUTY PEOPLE ARE WORK-ING HARD TO MAKE TO-MORROW A SUCCESS!
IT'S A BIG HELP THAT YOU'RE PITCHING IN, UESUGI-SAN.
ALL RIGHT!
LEAVE IT TO ME!
はぁ…
SIGH...

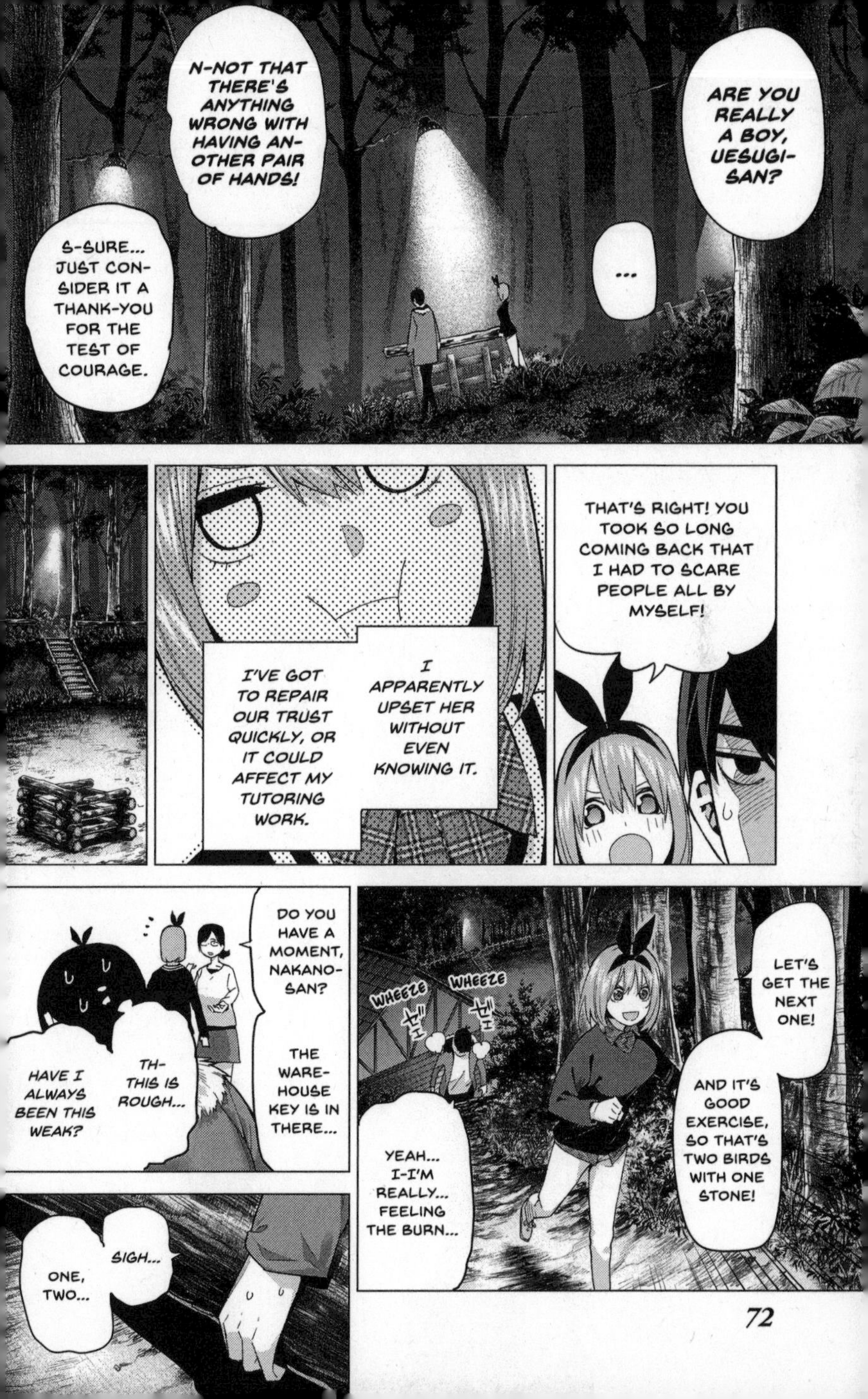
ARE YOU REALLY A BOY, UESUGI-SAN?
...
N-NOT THAT THERE'S ANYTHING WRONG WITH HAVING AN-OTHER PAIR OF HANDS!
S-SURE... JUST CON-SIDER IT A THANK-YOU FOR THE TEST OF COURAGE.
THAT'S RIGHT! YOU TOOK SO LONG COMING BACK THAT I HAD TO SCARE PEOPLE ALL BY MYSELF!
I APPARENTLY UPSET HER WITHOUT EVEN KNOWING IT.
I'VE GOT TO REPAIR OUR TRUST QUICKLY, OR IT COULD AFFECT MY TUTORING WORK.
LET'S GET THE NEXT ONE!
WHEEZE
WHEEZE
AND IT'S GOOD EXERCISE, SO THAT'S TWO BIRDS WITH ONE STONE!
YEAH... I-I'M REALLY... FEELING THE BURN...
DO YOU HAVE A MOMENT, NAKANO-SAN?
THE WARE-HOUSE KEY IS IN THERE...
TH-THIS IS ROUGH...
HAVE I ALWAYS BEEN THIS WEAK?
SIGH...
ONE, TWO...

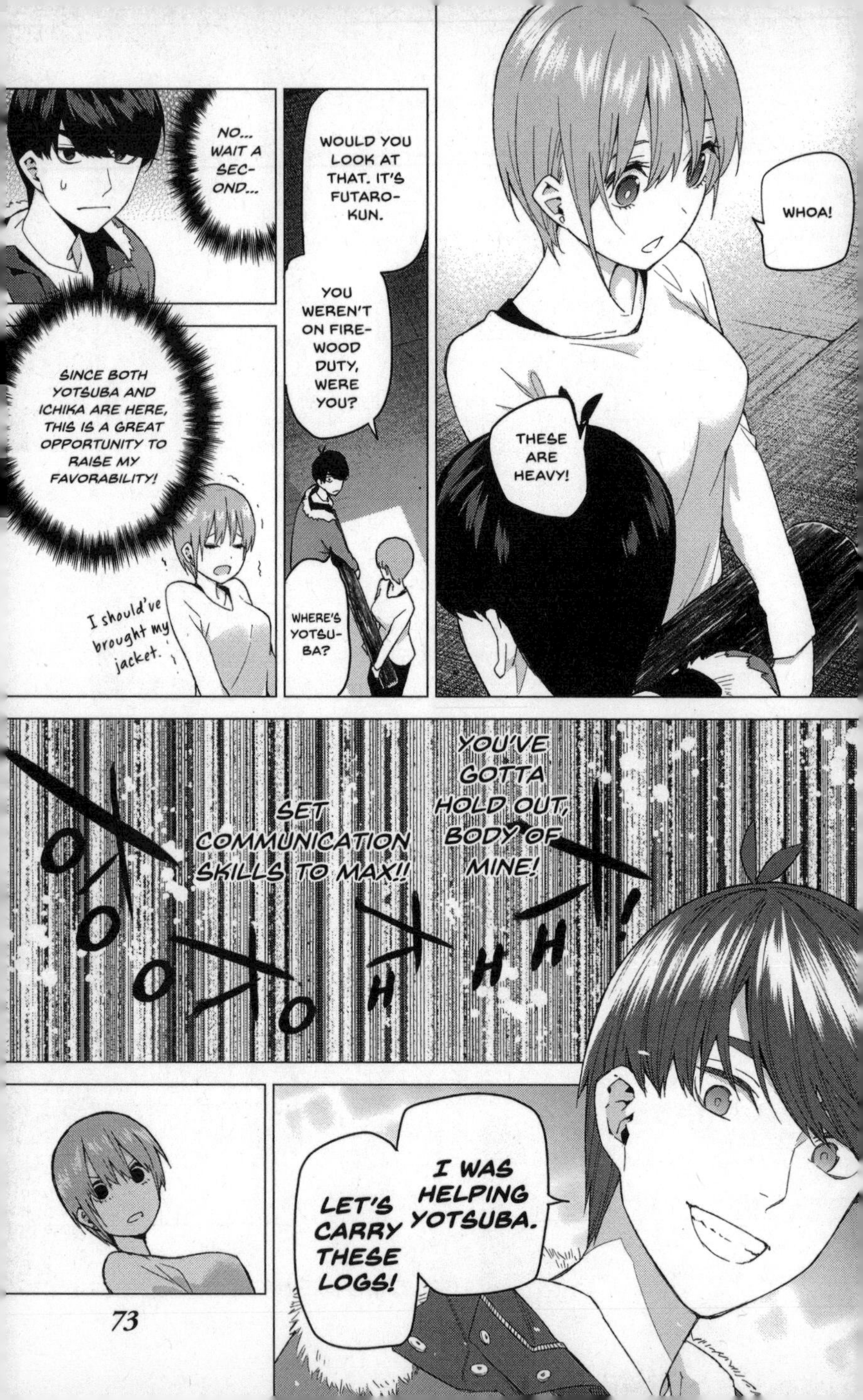
WHOA!
THESE ARE HEAVY!
WOULD YOU LOOK AT THAT. IT'S FUTARO-KUN.
YOU WEREN'T ON FIRE-WOOD DUTY, WERE YOU?
WHERE'S YOTSU-BA?
NO... WAIT A SEC-OND...
SINCE BOTH YOTSUBA AND ICHIKA ARE HERE, THIS IS A GREAT OPPORTUNITY TO RAISE MY FAVORABILITY!
I should've brought my jacket.
YOU'VE GOTTA HOLD OUT, BODY OF MINE!
SET COMMUNICATION SKILLS TO MAX!!
I WAS HELPING YOTSUBA.
LET'S CARRY THESE LOGS!

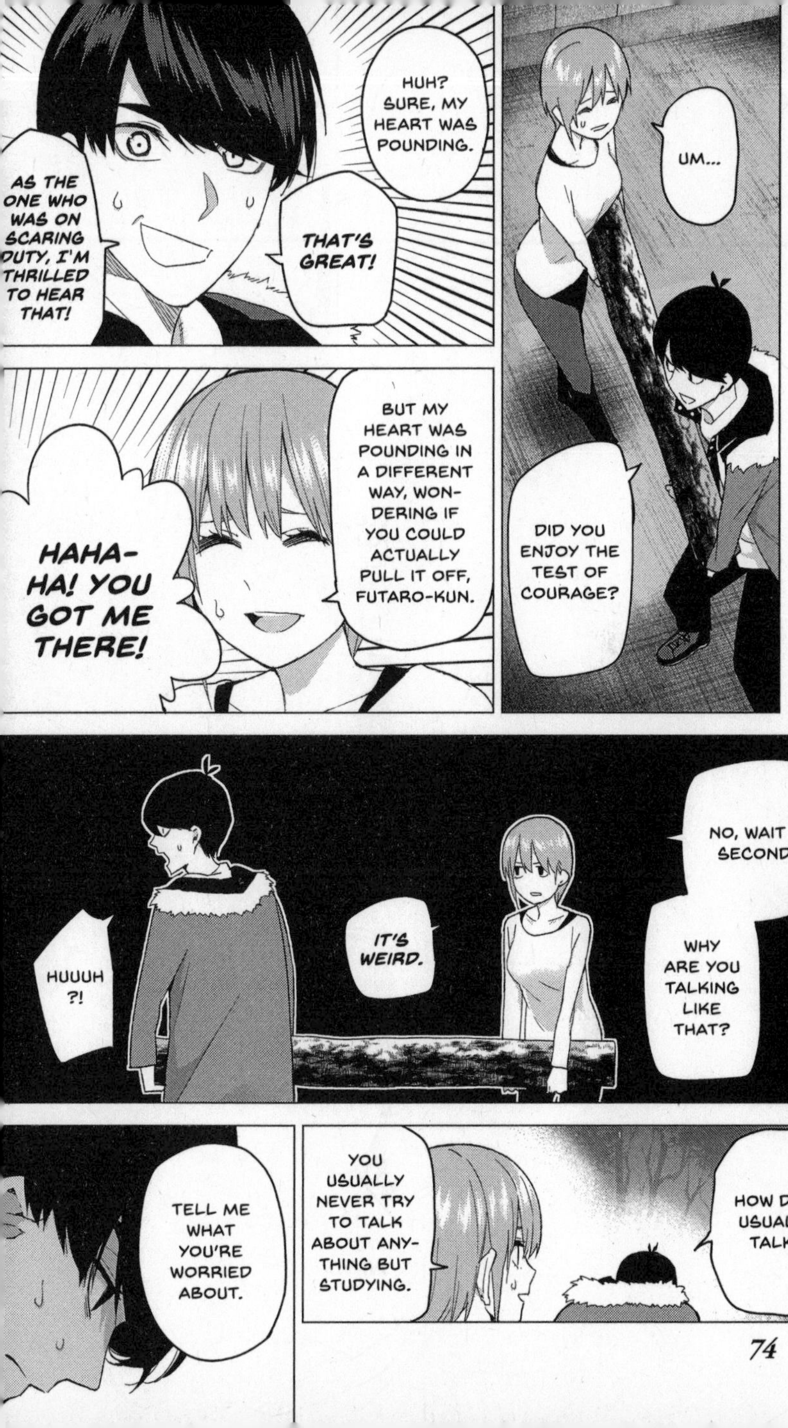
UM...
DID YOU ENJOY THE TEST OF COURAGE?
HUH? SURE, MY HEART WAS POUNDING.
THAT'S GREAT!
AS THE ONE WHO WAS ON SCARING DUTY, I'M THRILLED TO HEAR THAT!
BUT MY HEART WAS POUNDING IN A DIFFERENT WAY, WON-DERING IF YOU COULD ACTUALLY PULL IT OFF, FUTARO-KUN.
HAHA-HA! YOU GOT ME THERE!
NO, WAIT A SECOND.
WHY ARE YOU TALKING LIKE THAT?
IT'S WEIRD.
HUUUH ?!
HOW DO I USUALLY TALK?
YOU USUALLY NEVER TRY TO TALK ABOUT ANY-THING BUT STUDYING.
TELL ME WHAT YOU'RE WORRIED ABOUT.

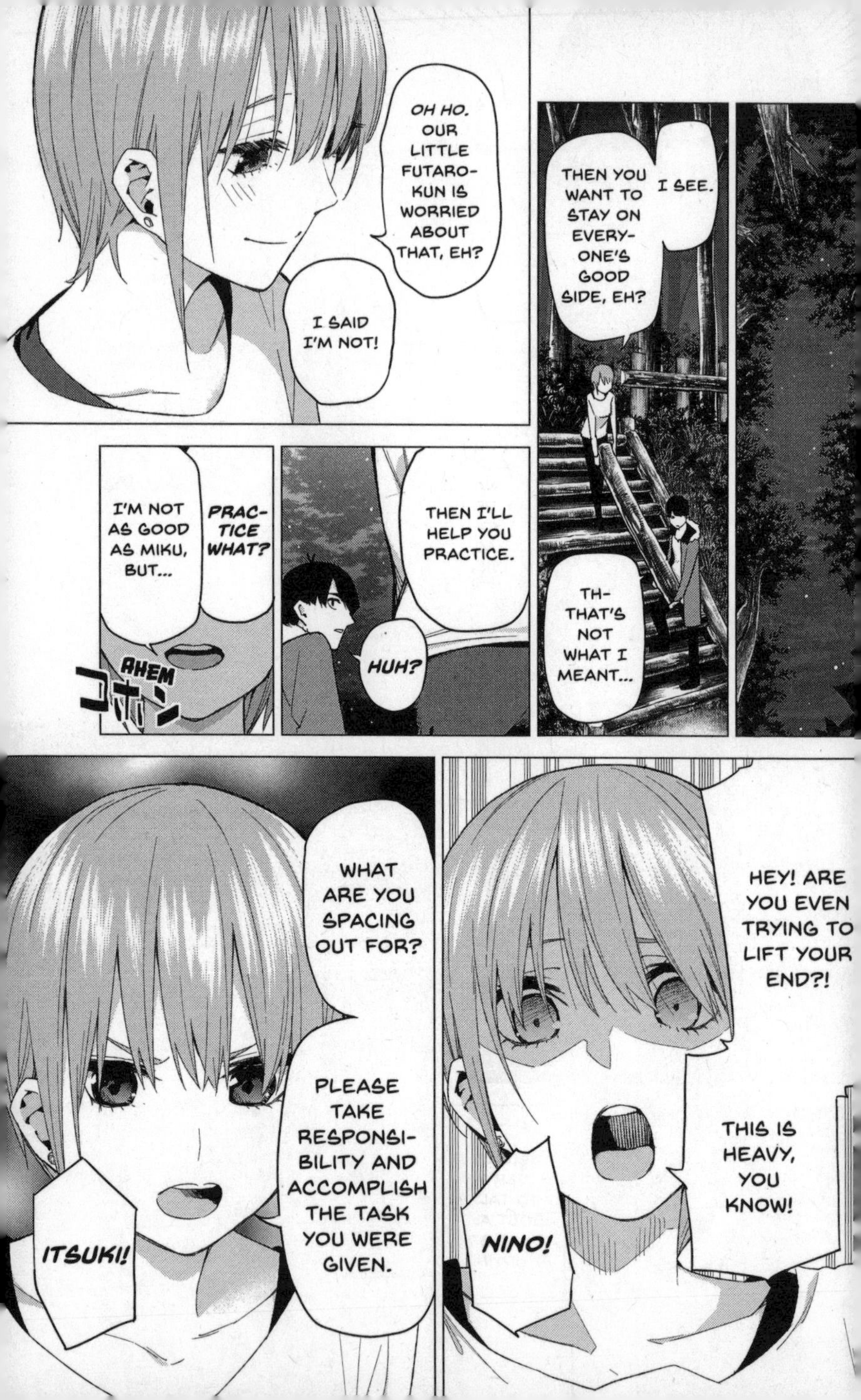
OH HO. OUR LITTLE FUTARO-KUN IS WORRIED ABOUT THAT, EH?
I SAID I'M NOT!
I SEE.
THEN YOU WANT TO STAY ON EVERY-ONE'S GOOD SIDE, EH?
TH-THAT'S NOT WHAT I MEANT...
THEN I'LL HELP YOU PRACTICE.
HUH?
PRAC-TICE WHAT?
I'M NOT AS GOOD AS MIKU, BUT...
AHEM
HEY! ARE YOU EVEN TRYING TO LIFT YOUR END?!
THIS IS HEAVY, YOU KNOW!
NINO!
WHAT ARE YOU SPACING OUT FOR?
PLEASE TAKE RESPONSI-BILITY AND ACCOMPLISH THE TASK YOU WERE GIVEN.
ITSUKI!

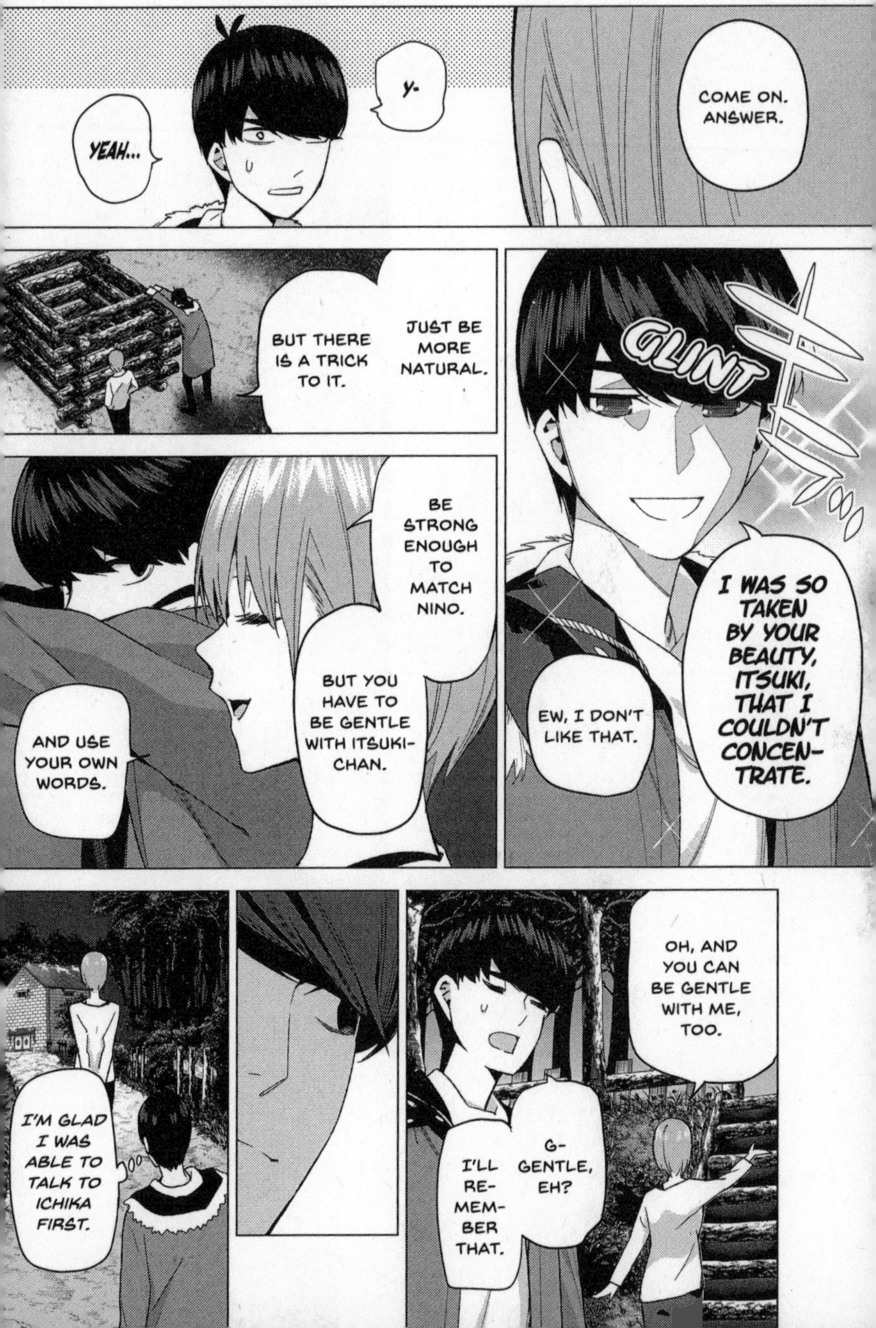
COME ON. ANSWER.
Y-
YEAH...
GLINT
I WAS SO TAKEN BY YOUR BEAUTY, ITSUKI, THAT I COULDN'T CONCENTRATE.
EW, I DON'T LIKE THAT.
JUST BE MORE NATURAL.
BUT THERE IS A TRICK TO IT.
BE STRONG ENOUGH TO MATCH NINO.
BUT YOU HAVE TO BE GENTLE WITH ITSUKI-CHAN.
AND USE YOUR OWN WORDS.
OH, AND YOU CAN BE GENTLE WITH ME, TOO.
G-GENTLE, EH?
I'LL RE-MEM-BER THAT.
I'M GLAD I WAS ABLE TO TALK TO ICHIKA FIRST.

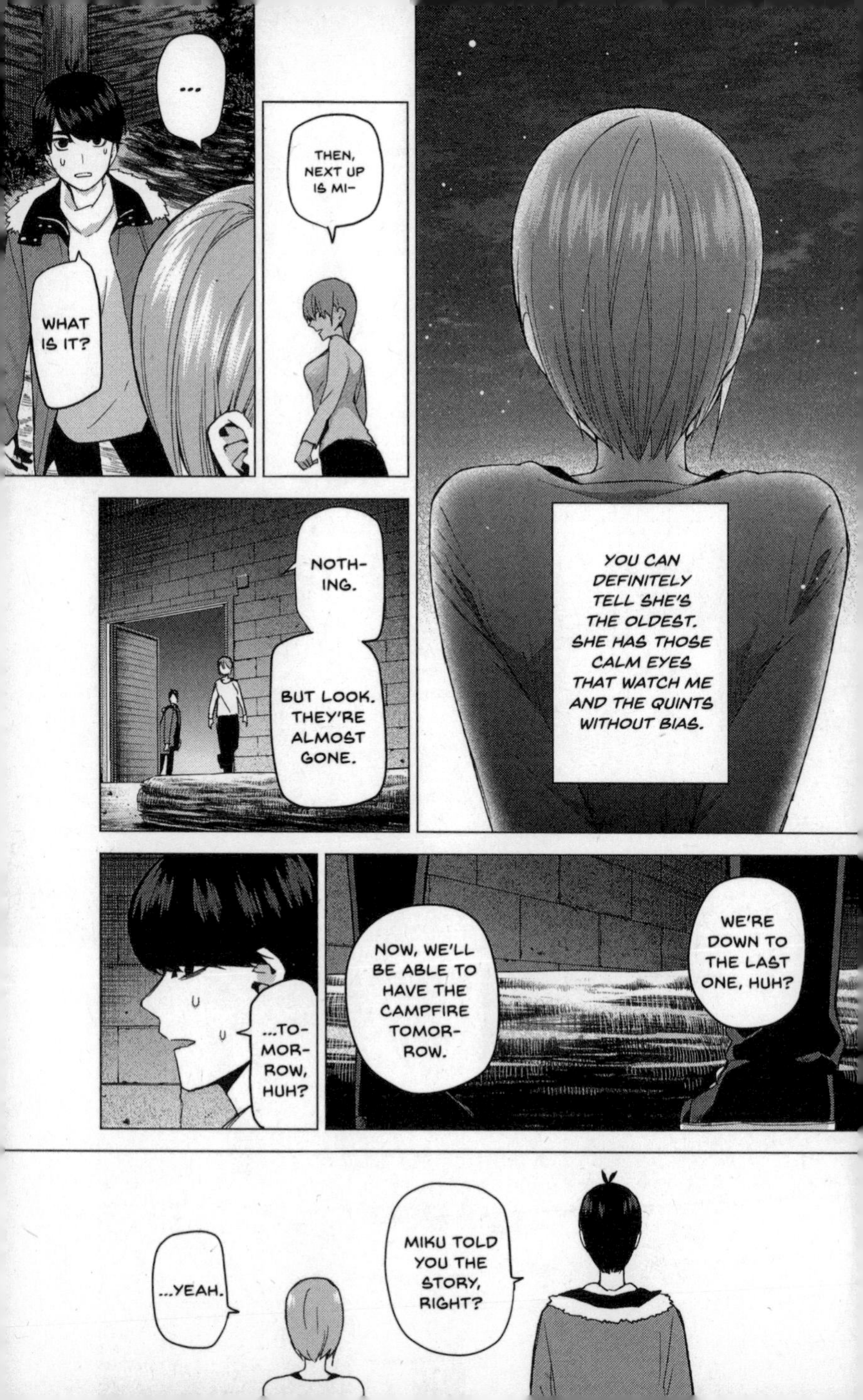
YOU CAN DEFINITELY TELL SHE'S THE OLDEST. SHE HAS THOSE CALM EYES THAT WATCH ME AND THE QUINTS WITHOUT BIAS.
THEN, NEXT UP IS MI-
...
WHAT IS IT?
NOTH-ING.
BUT LOOK. THEY'RE ALMOST GONE.
WE'RE DOWN TO THE LAST ONE, HUH?
NOW, WE'LL BE ABLE TO HAVE THE CAMPFIRE TOMOR-ROW.
...TO-MOR-ROW, HUH?
MIKU TOLD YOU THE STORY, RIGHT?
...YEAH.

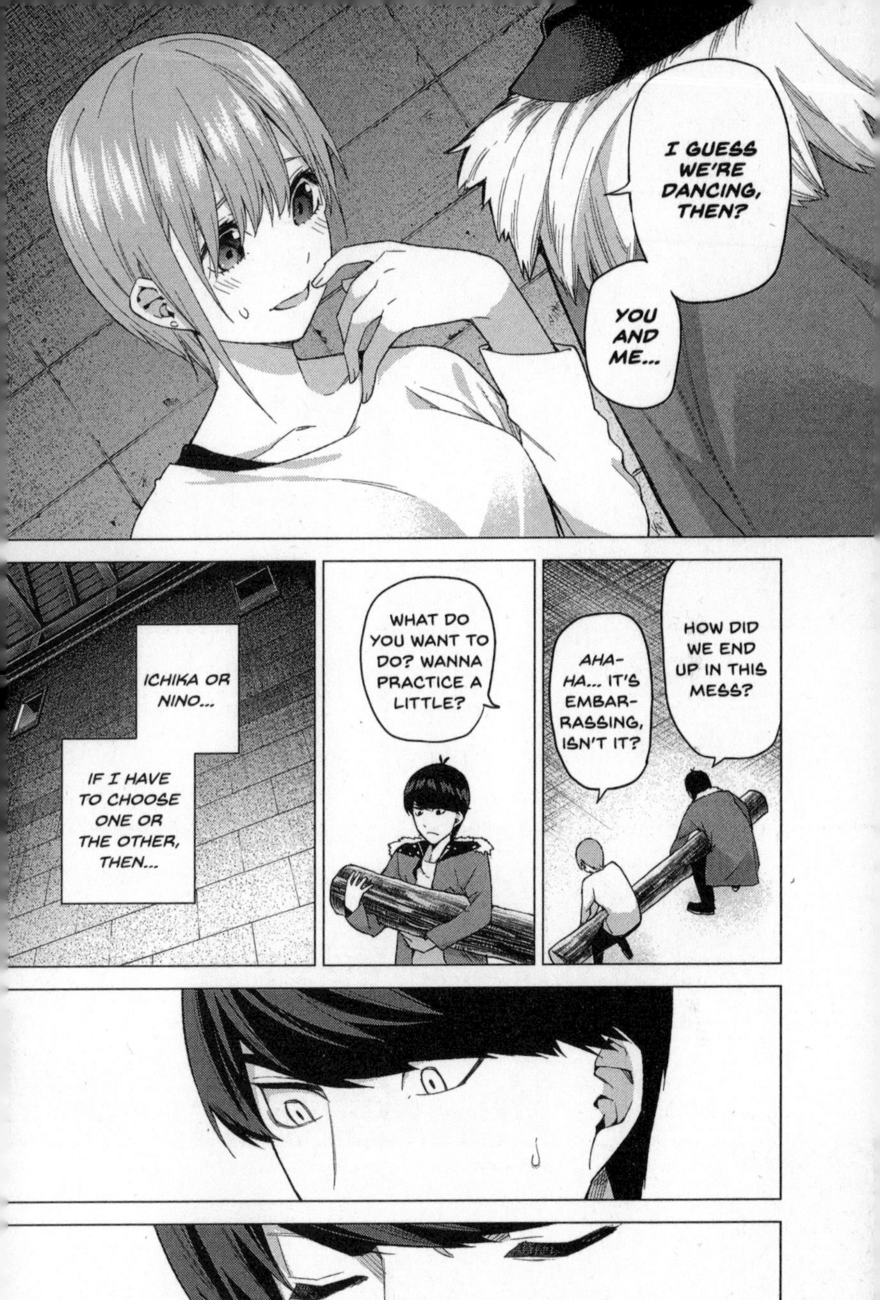
I GUESS WE'RE DANCING, THEN?
YOU AND ME...
HOW DID WE END UP IN THIS MESS?
AHA-HA... IT'S EMBARRASSING, ISN'T IT?
WHAT DO YOU WANT TO DO? WANNA PRACTICE A LITTLE?
ICHIKA OR NINO...
IF I HAVE TO CHOOSE ONE OR THE OTHER, THEN...

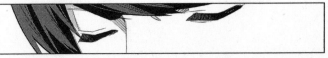

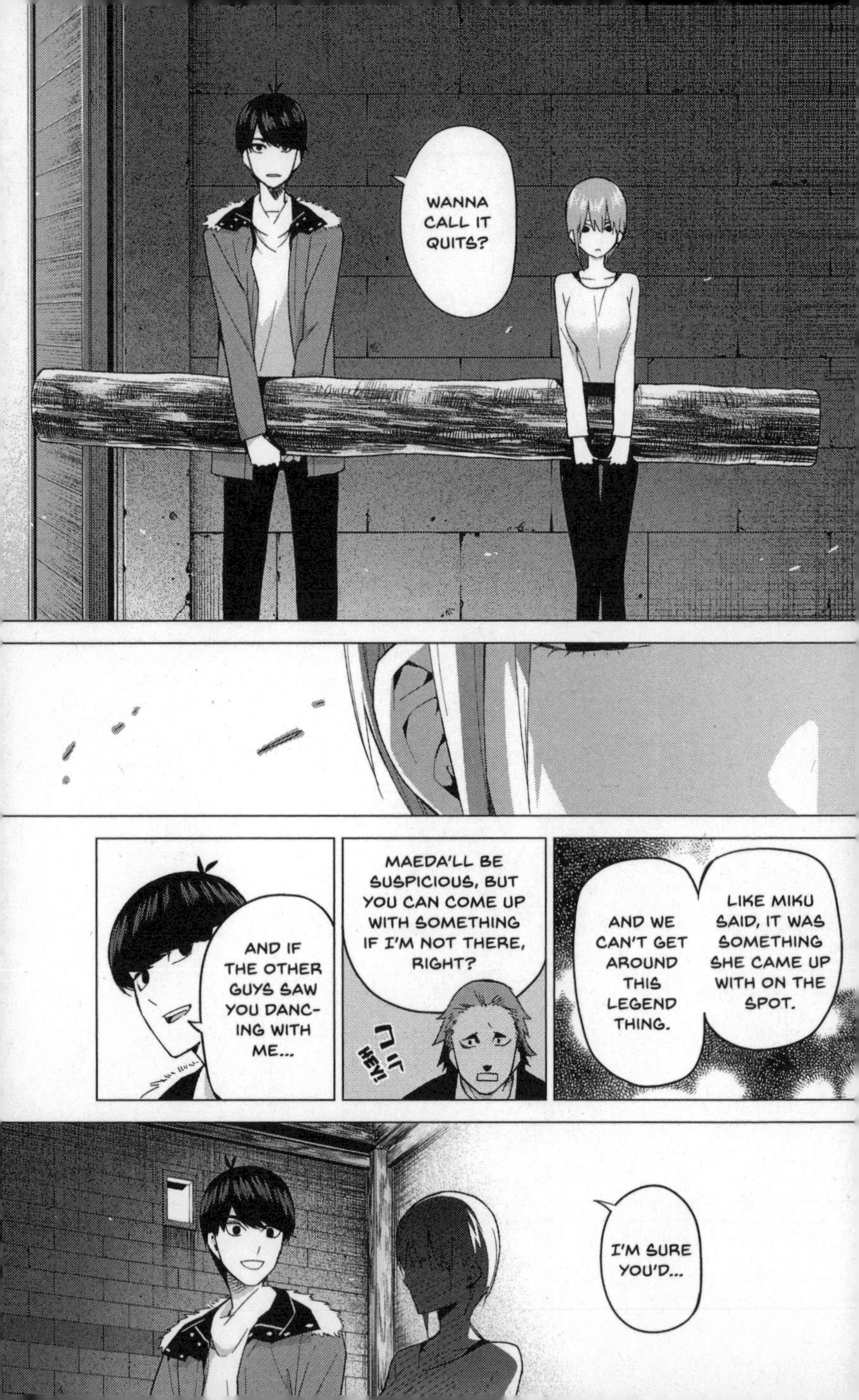
WANNA CALL IT QUITS?
LIKE MIKU SAID, IT WAS SOMETHING SHE CAME UP WITH ON THE SPOT.
AND WE CAN'T GET AROUND THIS LEGEND THING.
MAEDA'LL BE SUSPICIOUS, BUT YOU CAN COME UP WITH SOMETHING IF I'M NOT THERE, RIGHT?
HEY!
AND IF THE OTHER GUYS SAW YOU DANCING WITH ME...
I'M SURE YOU'D...

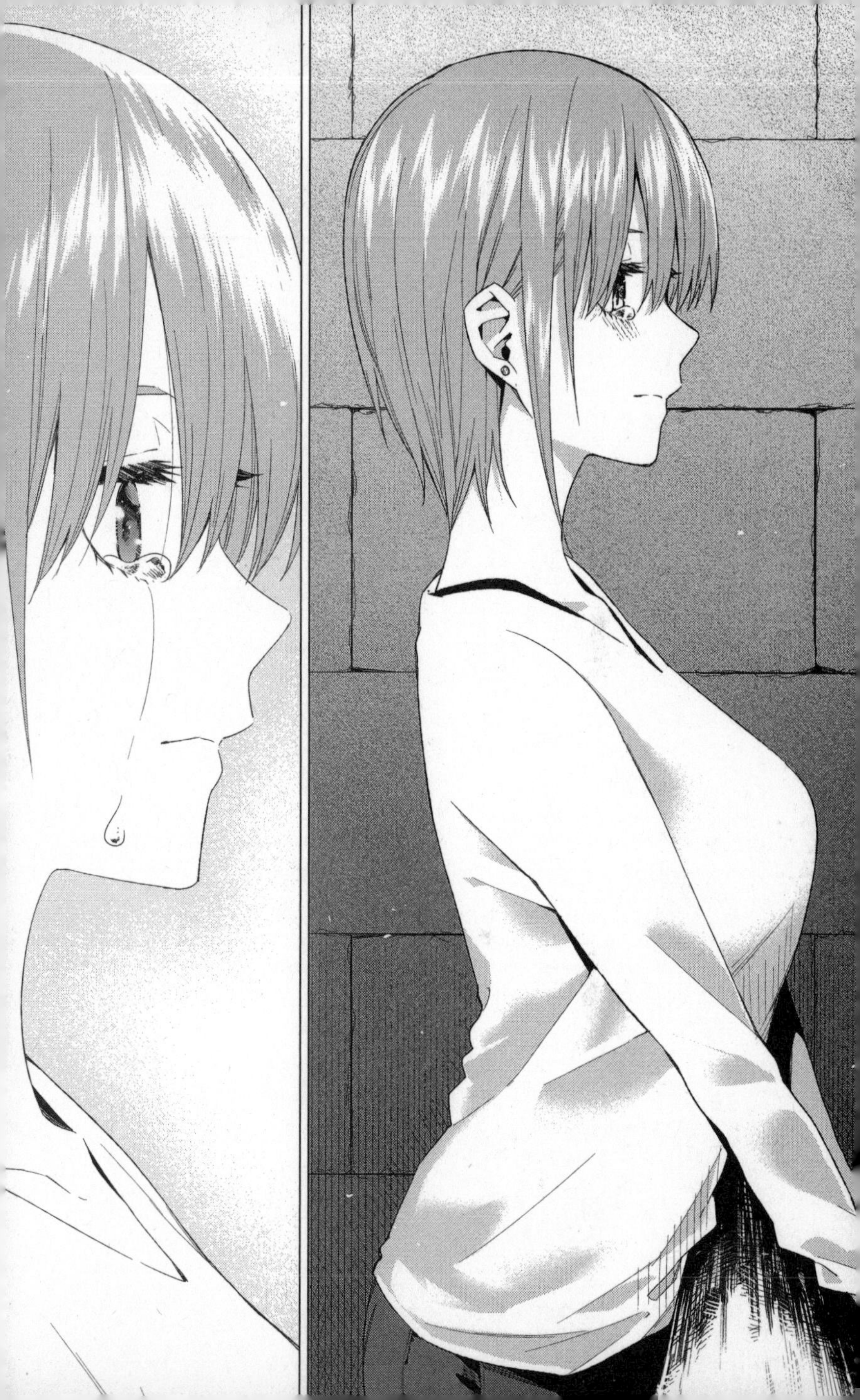

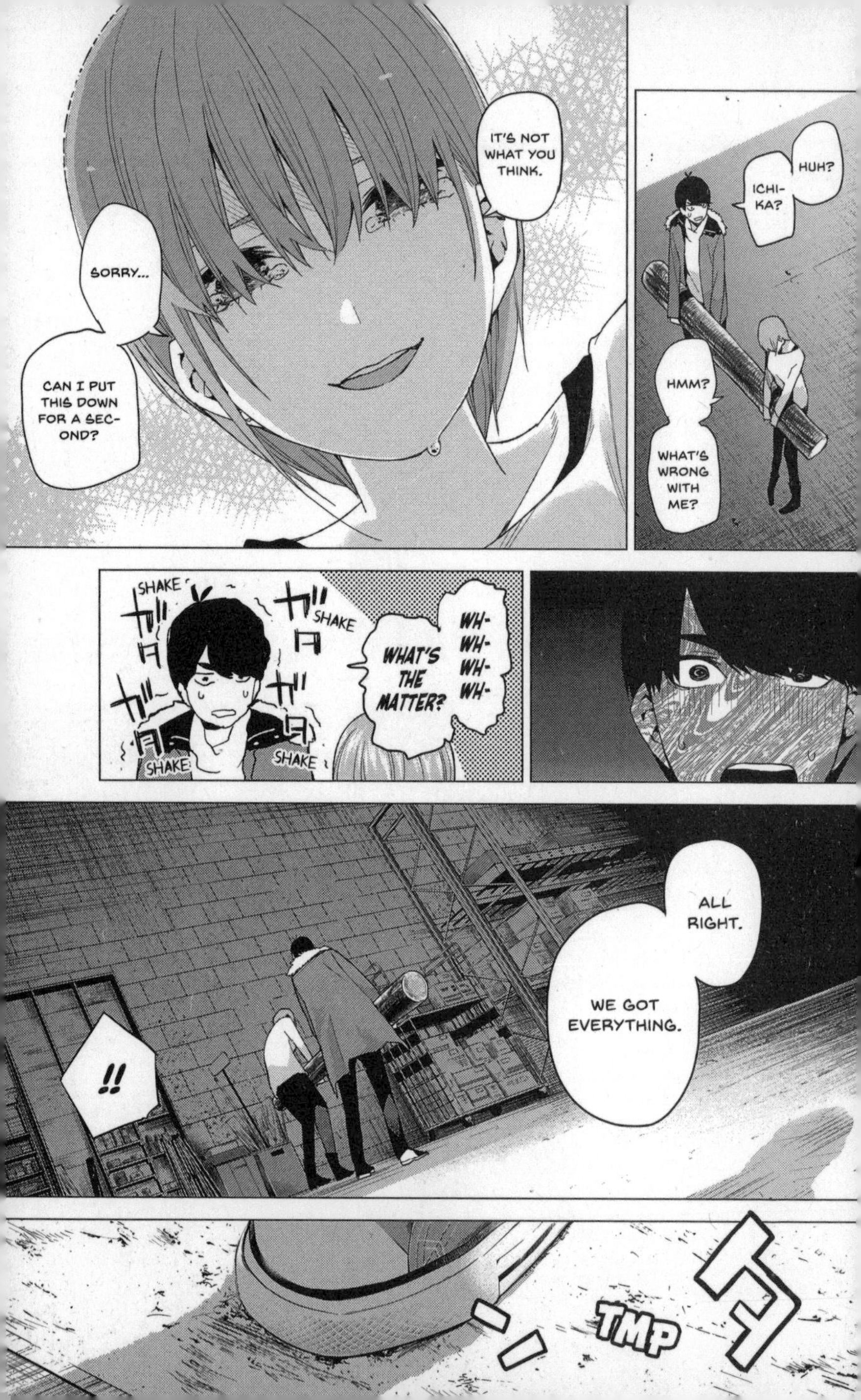
HUH?
ICHI-KA?
HMM?
WHAT'S WRONG WITH ME?
IT'S NOT WHAT YOU THINK.
SORRY...
CAN I PUT THIS DOWN FOR A SEC-OND?
WH-WH-WH-WH-
WHAT'S THE MATTER?
SHAKE
SHAKE
SHAKE
SHAKE
ALL RIGHT.
WE GOT EVERYTHING.
!!
TMP

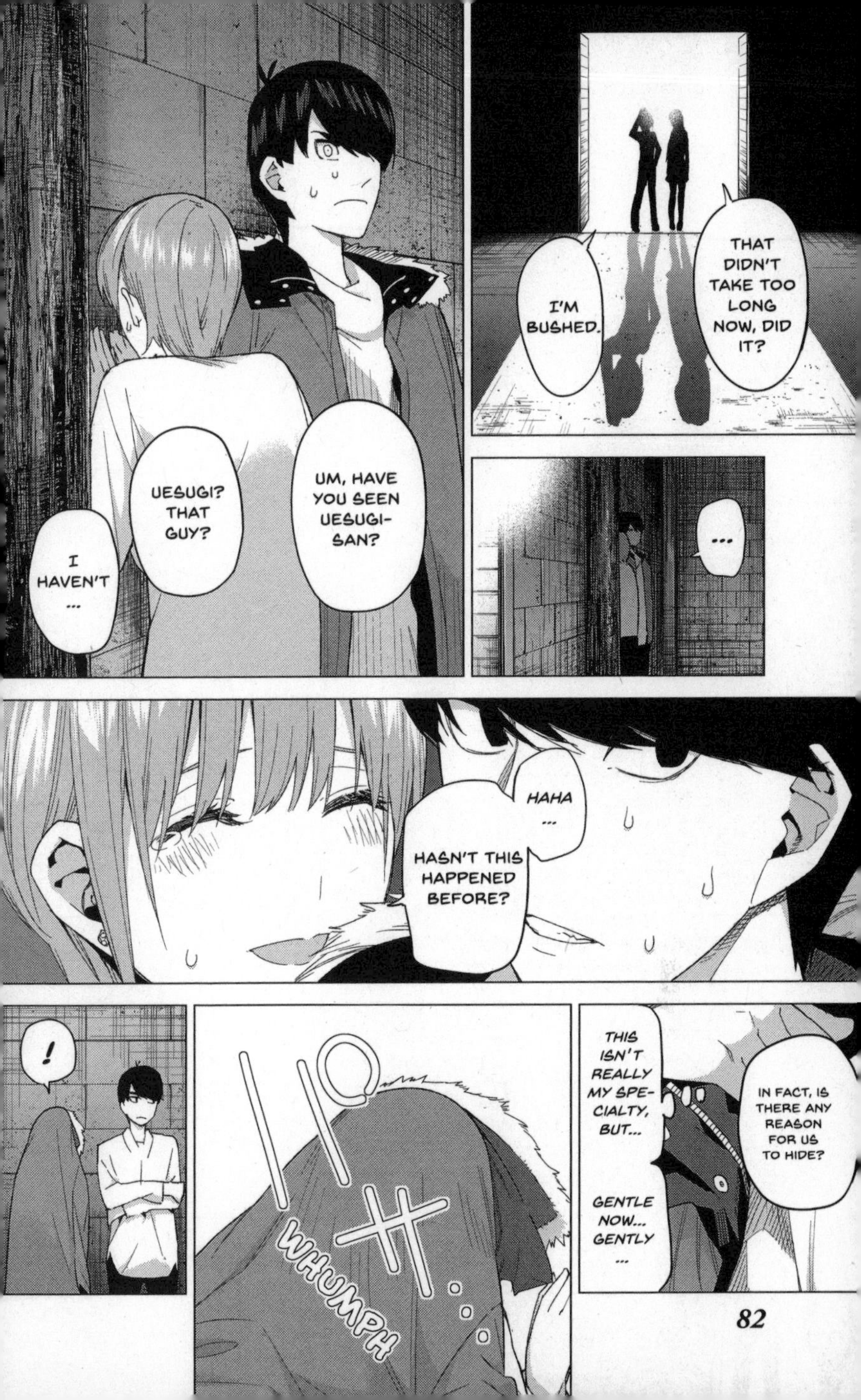
THAT DIDN'T TAKE TOO LONG NOW, DID IT?
I'M BUSHED.
...
UM, HAVE YOU SEEN UESUGI-SAN?
UESUGI? THAT GUY?
I HAVEN'T...
HAHA...
HASN'T THIS HAPPENED BEFORE?
IN FACT, IS THERE ANY REASON FOR US TO HIDE?
THIS ISN'T REALLY MY SPE-CIALTY, BUT...
GENTLE NOW... GENTLY...
WHUMPH
!

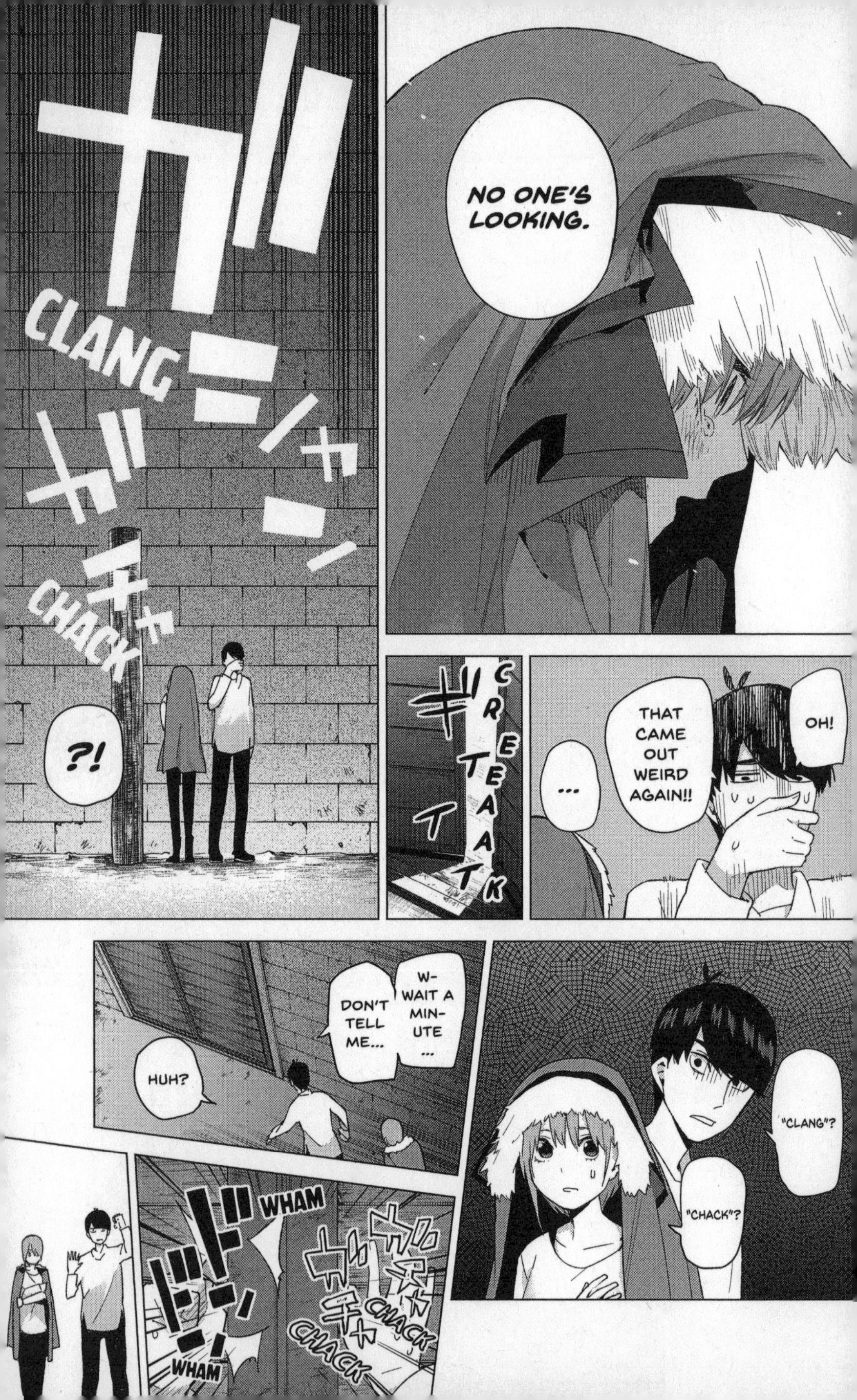
NO ONE'S LOOKING.
OH!
THAT CAME OUT WEIRD AGAIN!!
...
CREAK
CLANG
CHACK
?!
"CLANG"?
"CHACK"?
W-WAIT A MIN-UTE...
DON'T TELL ME...
HUH?
WHAM
CHACK
CHACK
WHAM

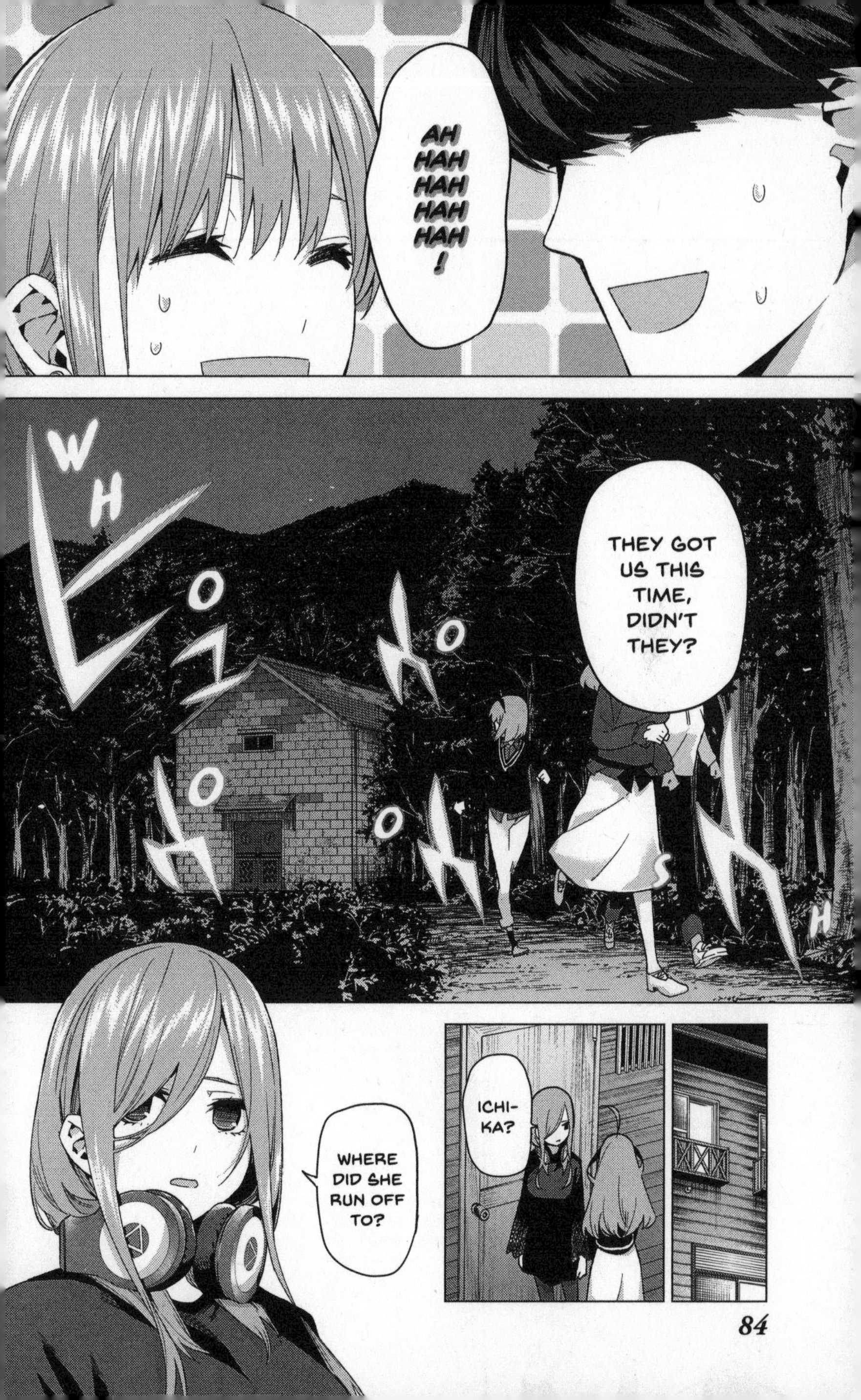
AH HAH HAH HAH HAH!
WHOOOOSH
THEY GOT US THIS TIME, DIDN'T THEY?
ICHI-KA?
WHERE DID SHE RUN OFF TO?

CHAPTER 28
THE BINDING LEGEND: DAY 2 ④

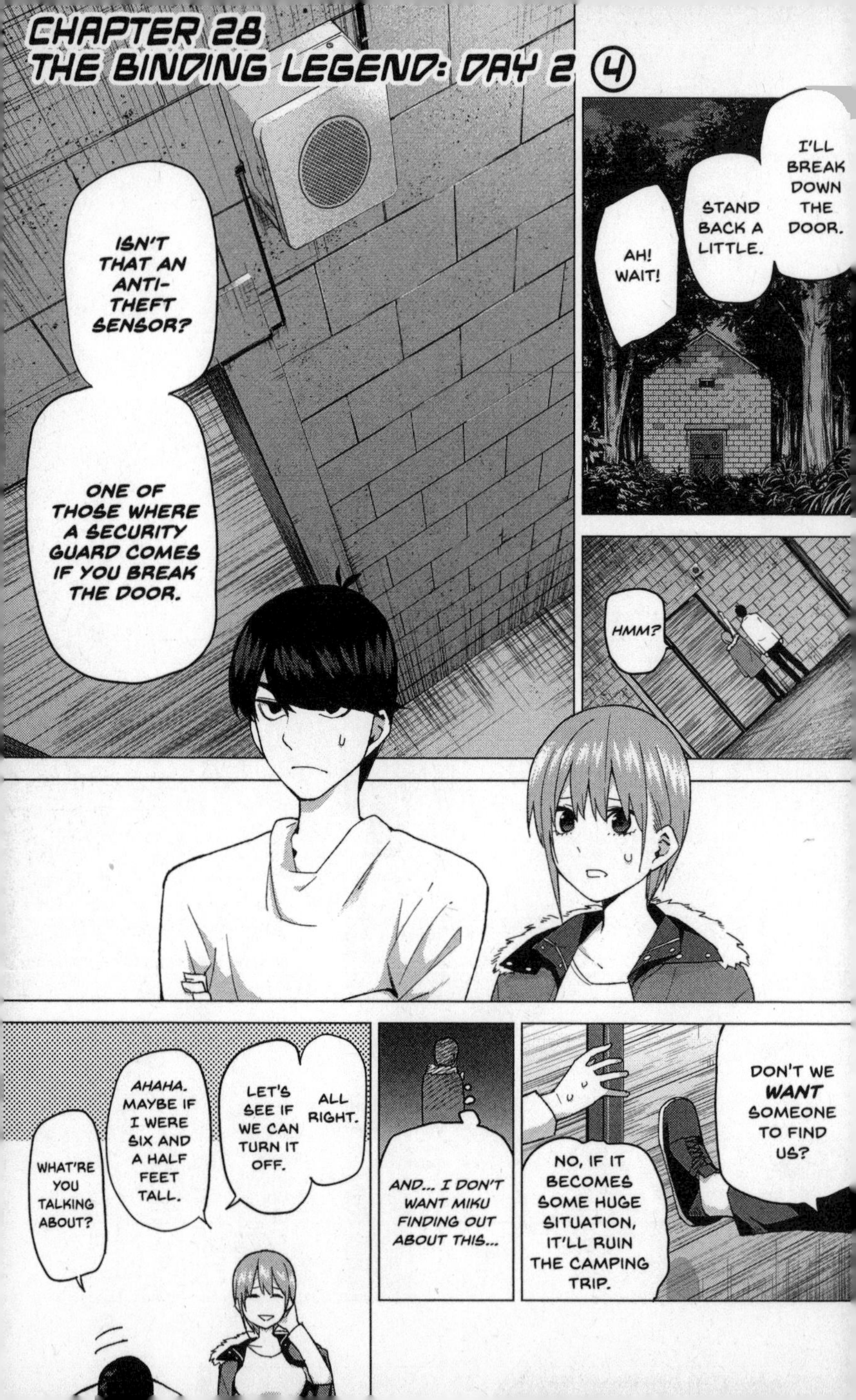
I'LL BREAK DOWN THE DOOR.
STAND BACK A LITTLE.
AH! WAIT!
HMM?
ISN'T THAT AN ANTI-THEFT SENSOR?
ONE OF THOSE WHERE A SECURITY GUARD COMES IF YOU BREAK THE DOOR.
DON'T WE WANT SOMEONE TO FIND US?
NO, IF IT BECOMES SOME HUGE SITUATION, IT'LL RUIN THE CAMPING TRIP.
AND... I DON'T WANT MIKU FINDING OUT ABOUT THIS...
ALL RIGHT.
LET'S SEE IF WE CAN TURN IT OFF.
AHAHA. MAYBE IF I WERE SIX AND A HALF FEET TALL.
WHAT'RE YOU TALKING ABOUT?

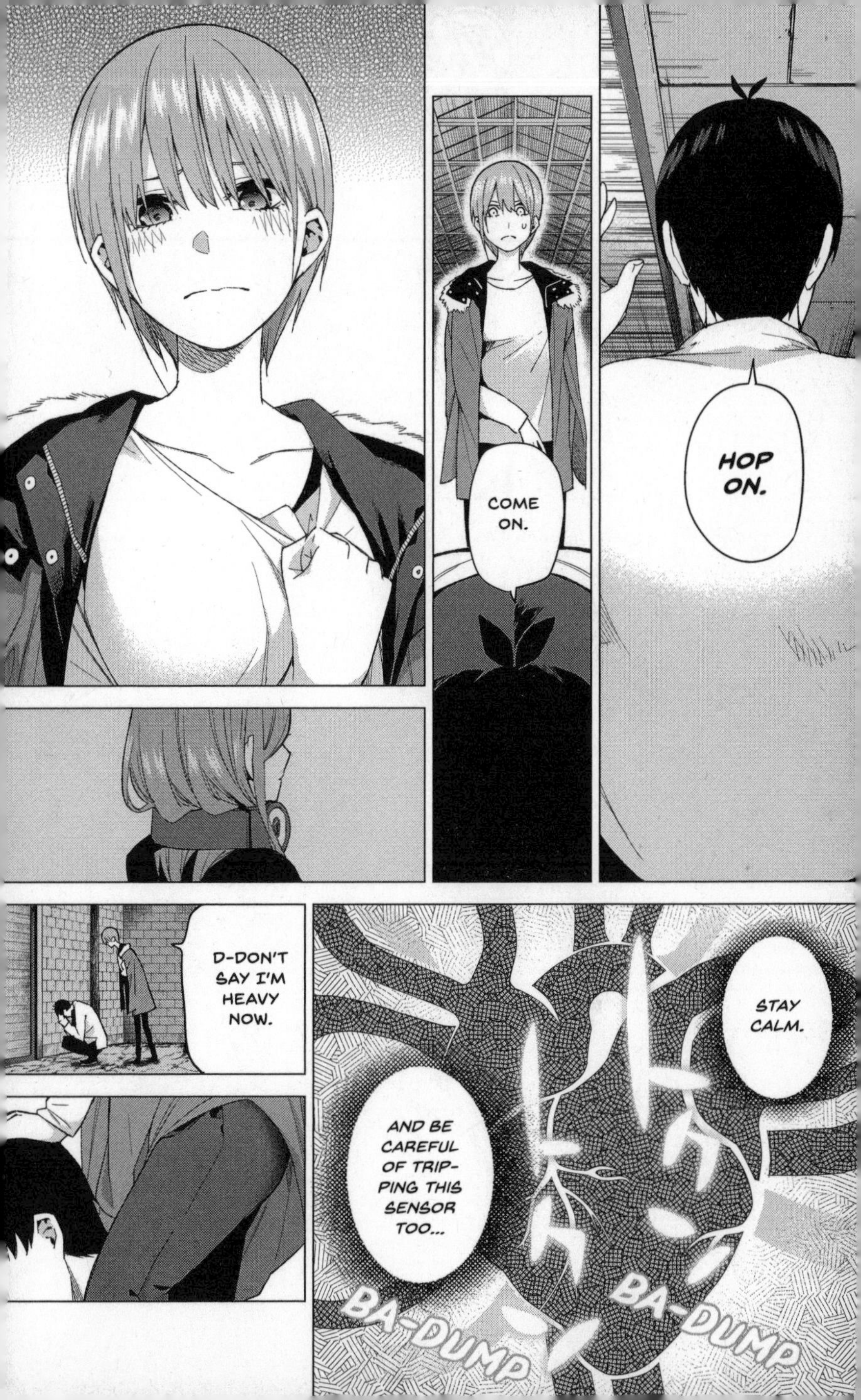
HOP ON.
COME ON.
STAY CALM.
AND BE CAREFUL OF TRIP-PING THIS SENSOR TOO...
BA-DUMP
BA-DUMP
D-DON'T SAY I'M HEAVY NOW.

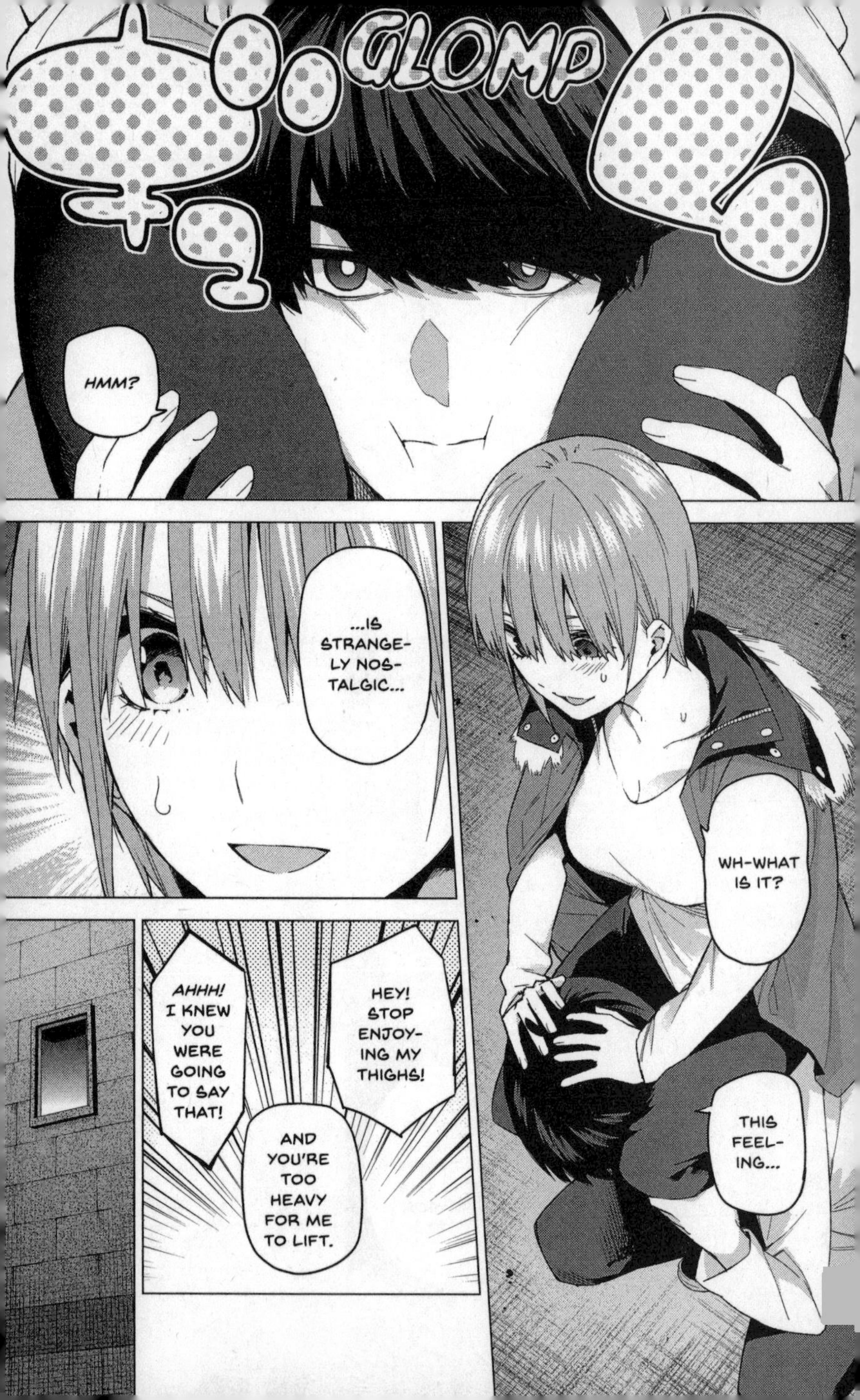
GLOMP
HMM?
WH-WHAT IS IT?
THIS FEELING...
...IS STRANGELY NOSTALGIC...
HEY! STOP ENJOYING MY THIGHS!
AHHH! I KNEW YOU WERE GOING TO SAY THAT!
AND YOU'RE TOO HEAVY FOR ME TO LIFT.

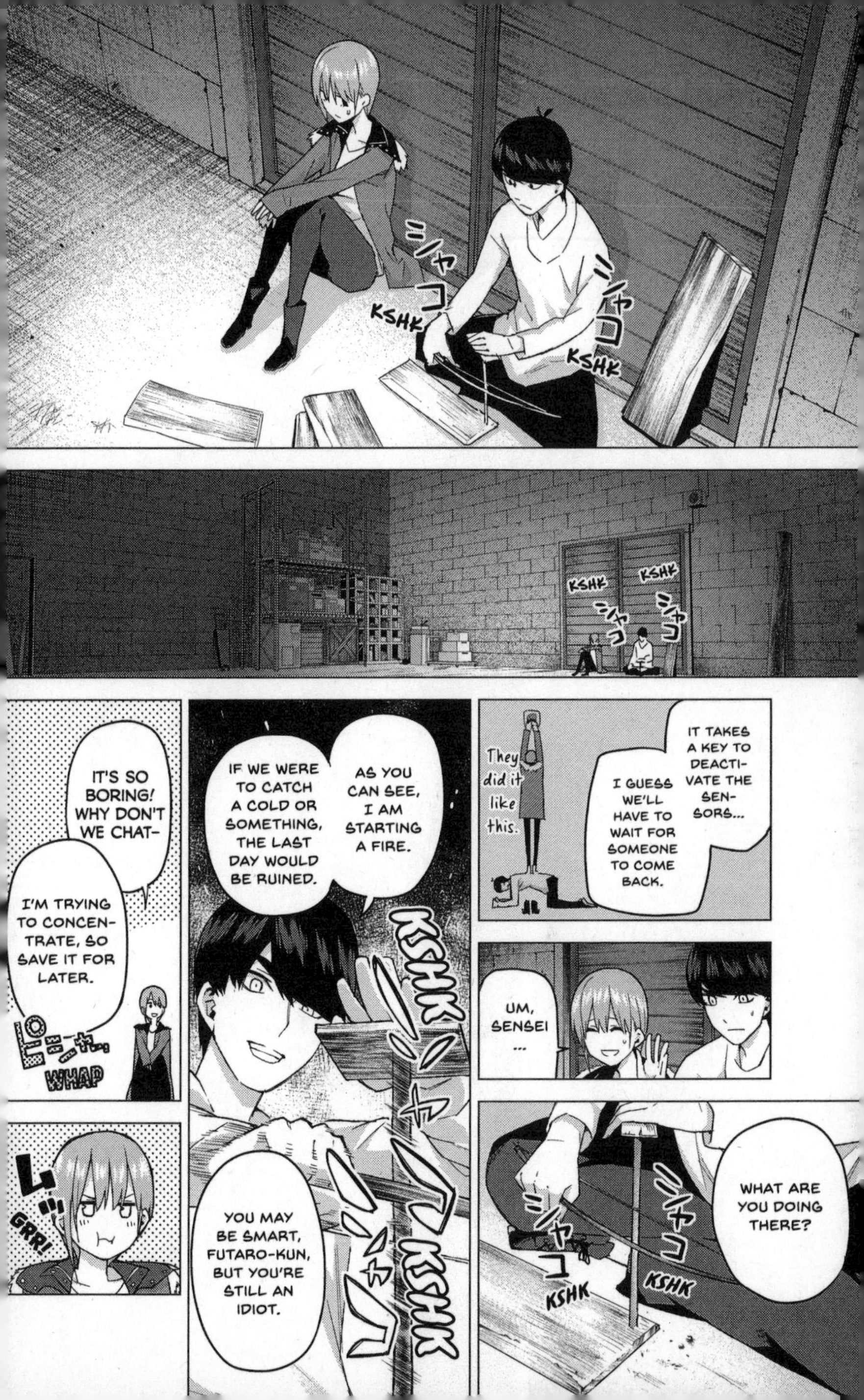

シャコ
KSHK
シャコ
KSHK
KSHK
シャコ
KSHK
シャコ
IT TAKES A KEY TO DEACTIVATE THE SENSORS...
I GUESS WE'LL HAVE TO WAIT FOR SOMEONE TO COME BACK.
They did it like this.
UM, SENSEI...
WHAT ARE YOU DOING THERE?
シャコ
KSHK
シャコ
KSHK
AS YOU CAN SEE, I AM STARTING A FIRE.
IF WE WERE TO CATCH A COLD OR SOMETHING, THE LAST DAY WOULD BE RUINED.
KSHK
KSHK
YOU MAY BE SMART, FUTARO-KUN, BUT YOU'RE STILL AN IDIOT.
IT'S SO BORING! WHY DON'T WE CHAT-
I'M TRYING TO CONCENTRATE, SO SAVE IT FOR LATER.
WHAP
GRR!

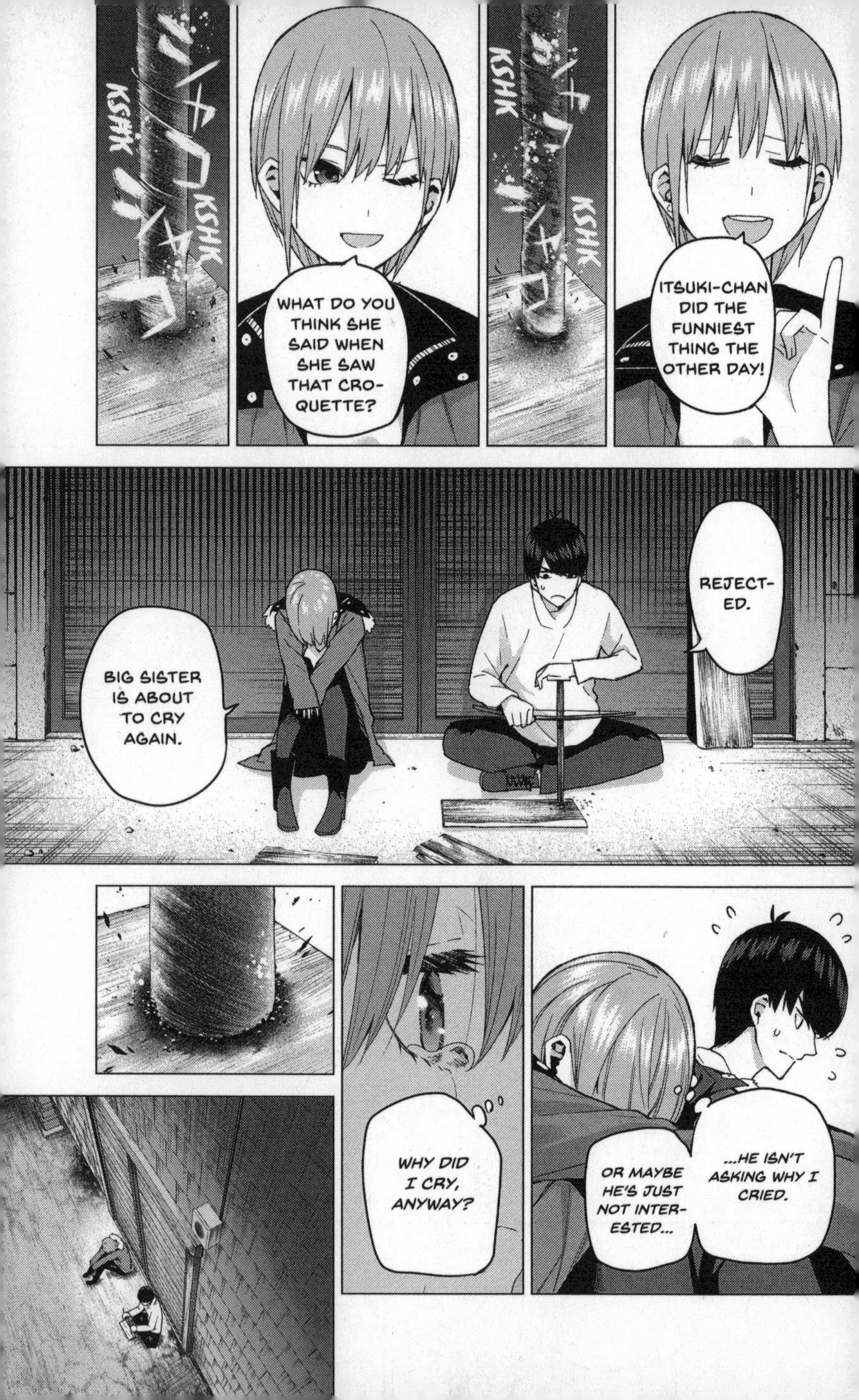

ITSUKI-CHAN DID THE FUNNIEST THING THE OTHER DAY!
KSHK
KSHK
WHAT DO YOU THINK SHE SAID WHEN SHE SAW THAT CROQUETTE?
KSHK
KSHK
REJECTED.
BIG SISTER IS ABOUT TO CRY AGAIN.
...HE ISN'T ASKING WHY I CRIED.
OR MAYBE HE'S JUST NOT INTERESTED...
WHY DID I CRY, ANYWAY?

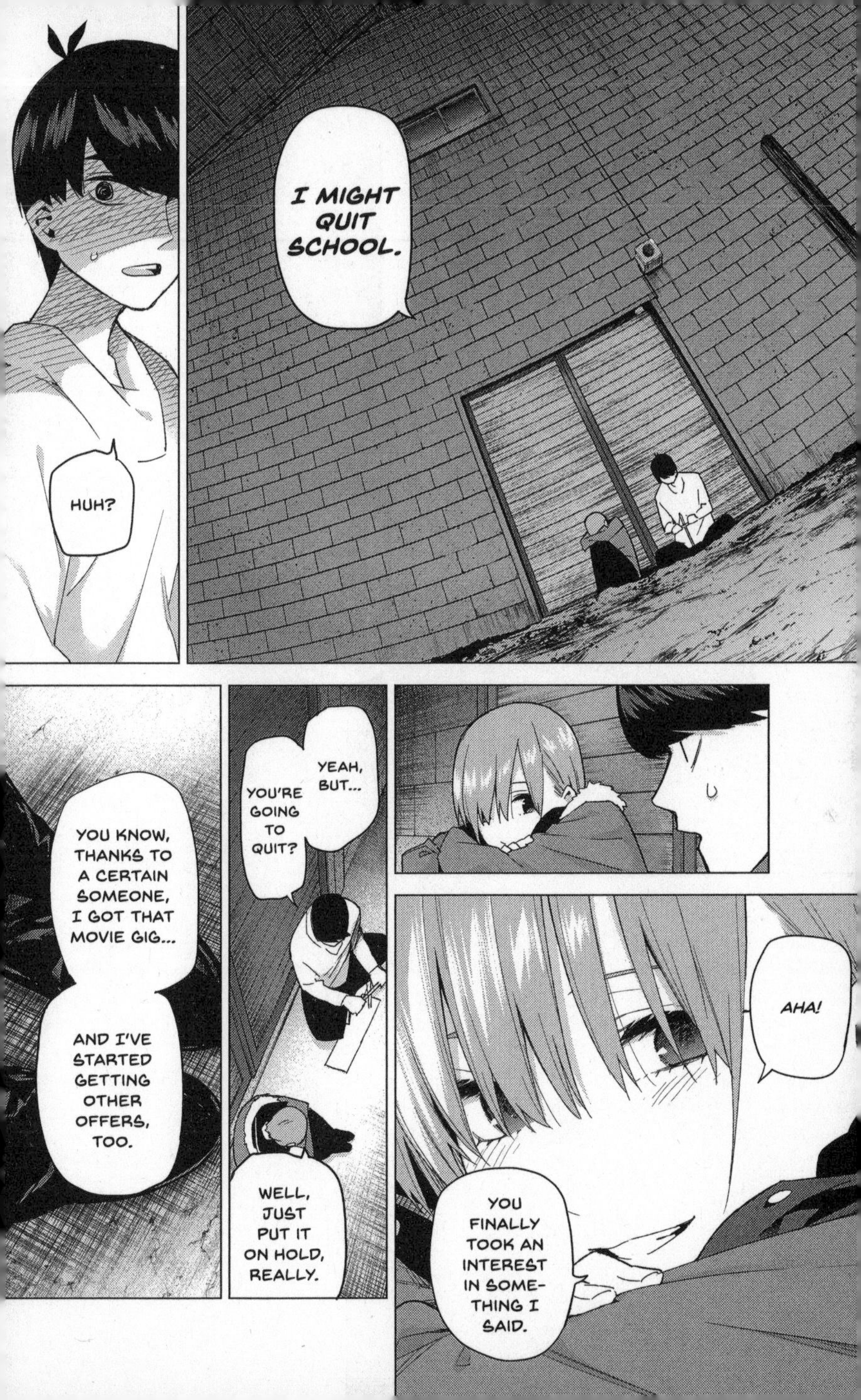
I MIGHT QUIT SCHOOL.
HUH?
AHA!
YOU FINALLY TOOK AN INTEREST IN SOME-THING I SAID.
YEAH, BUT...
YOU'RE GOING TO QUIT?
WELL, JUST PUT IT ON HOLD, REALLY.
YOU KNOW, THANKS TO A CERTAIN SOMEONE, I GOT THAT MOVIE GIG...
AND I'VE STARTED GETTING OTHER OFFERS, TOO.

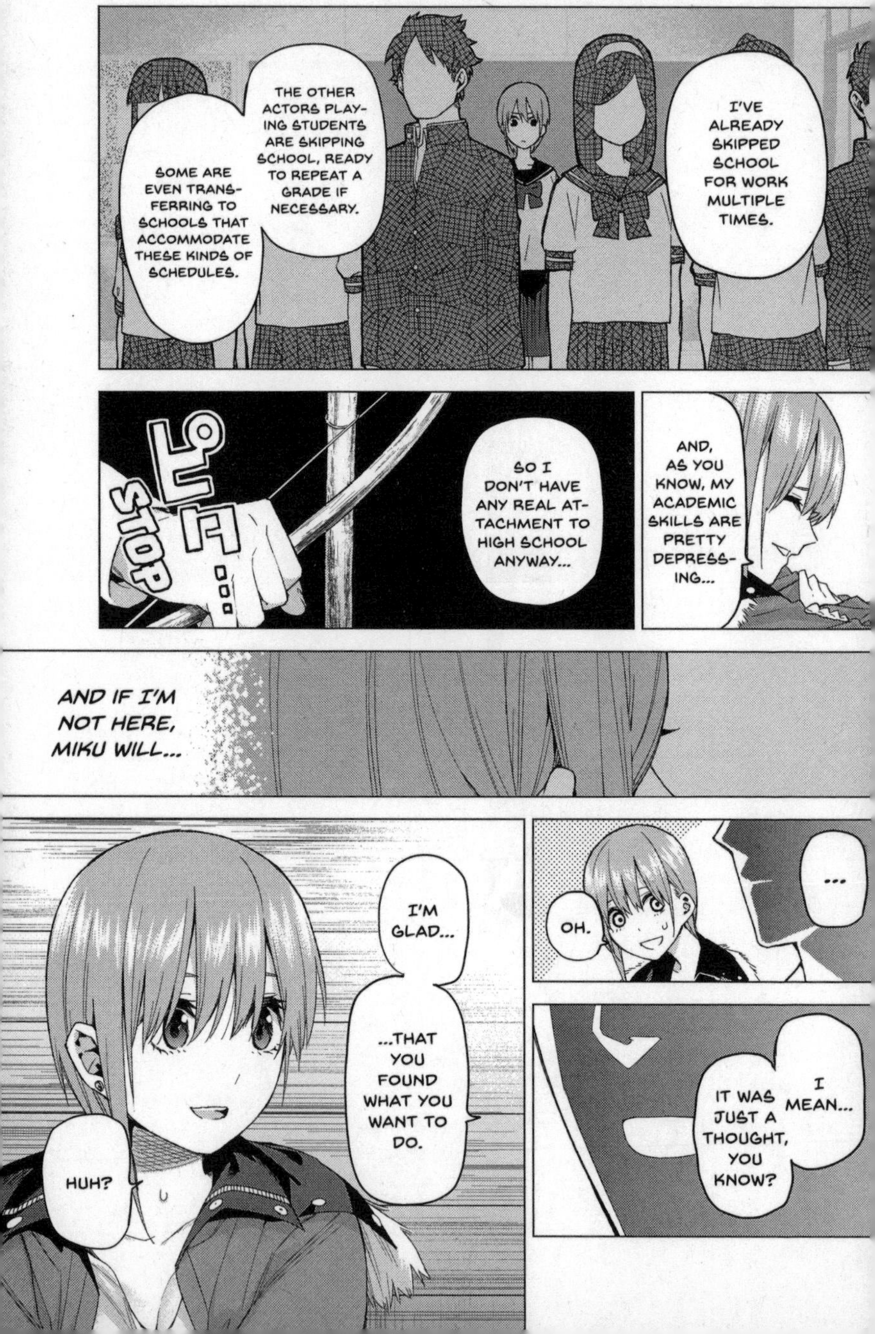
I'VE ALREADY SKIPPED SCHOOL FOR WORK MULTIPLE TIMES.
THE OTHER ACTORS PLAYING STUDENTS ARE SKIPPING SCHOOL, READY TO REPEAT A GRADE IF NECESSARY.
SOME ARE EVEN TRANSFERRING TO SCHOOLS THAT ACCOMMODATE THESE KINDS OF SCHEDULES.
AND, AS YOU KNOW, MY ACADEMIC SKILLS ARE PRETTY DEPRESSING...
SO I DON'T HAVE ANY REAL ATTACHMENT TO HIGH SCHOOL ANYWAY...
STOP...
AND IF I'M NOT HERE, MIKU WILL...
...
OH.
I MEAN...
IT WAS JUST A THOUGHT, YOU KNOW?
I'M GLAD...
...THAT YOU FOUND WHAT YOU WANT TO DO.
HUH?

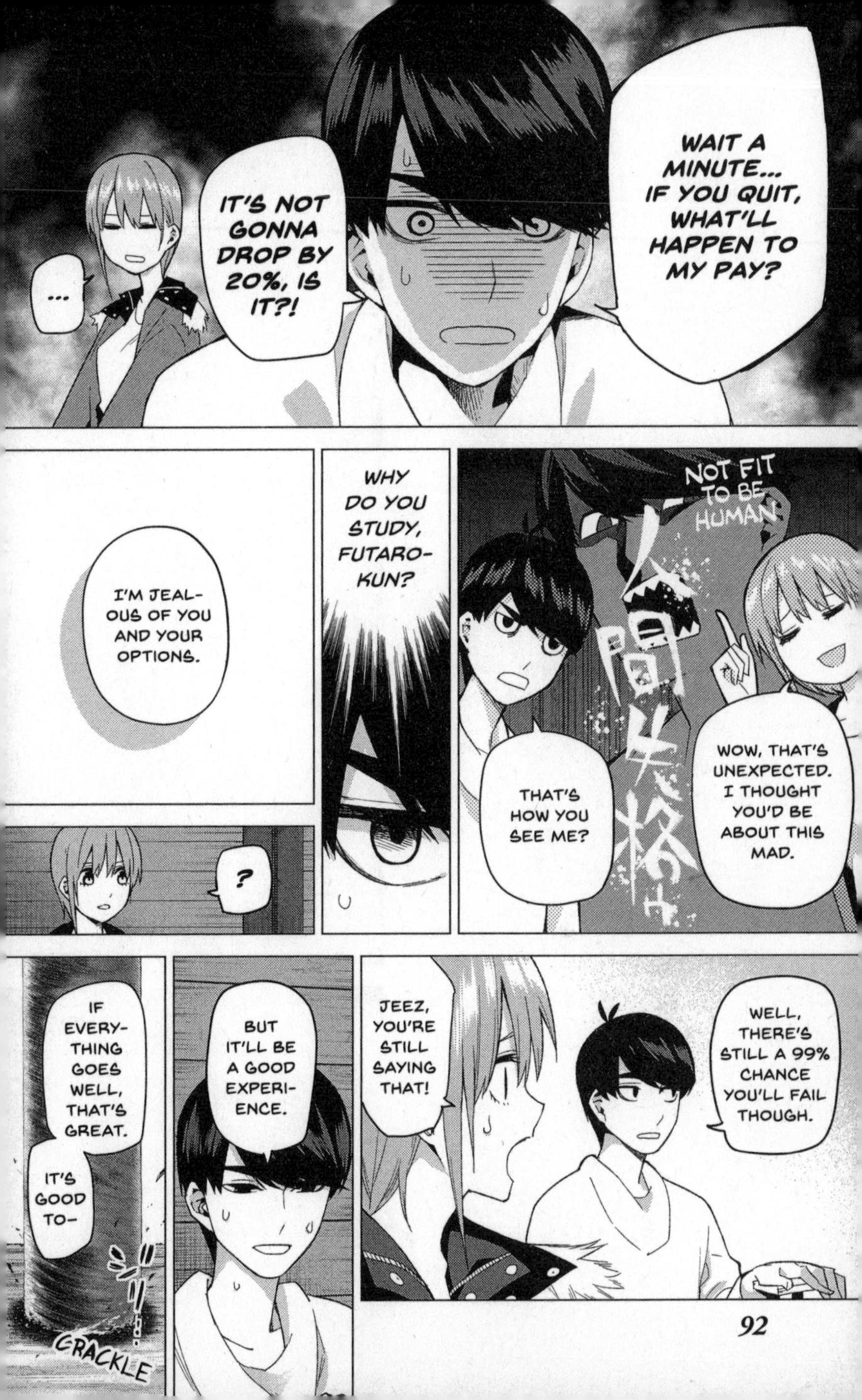
WAIT A MINUTE... IF YOU QUIT, WHAT'LL HAPPEN TO MY PAY?
IT'S NOT GONNA DROP BY 20%, IS IT?!
...
NOT FIT TO BE HUMAN
WOW, THAT'S UNEXPECTED. I THOUGHT YOU'D BE ABOUT THIS MAD.
THAT'S HOW YOU SEE ME?
WHY DO YOU STUDY, FUTARO-KUN?
I'M JEAL-OUS OF YOU AND YOUR OPTIONS.
?
WELL, THERE'S STILL A 99% CHANCE YOU'LL FAIL THOUGH.
JEEZ, YOU'RE STILL SAYING THAT!
BUT IT'LL BE A GOOD EXPERI-ENCE.
IF EVERY-THING GOES WELL, THAT'S GREAT.
IT'S GOOD TO-
CRACKLE

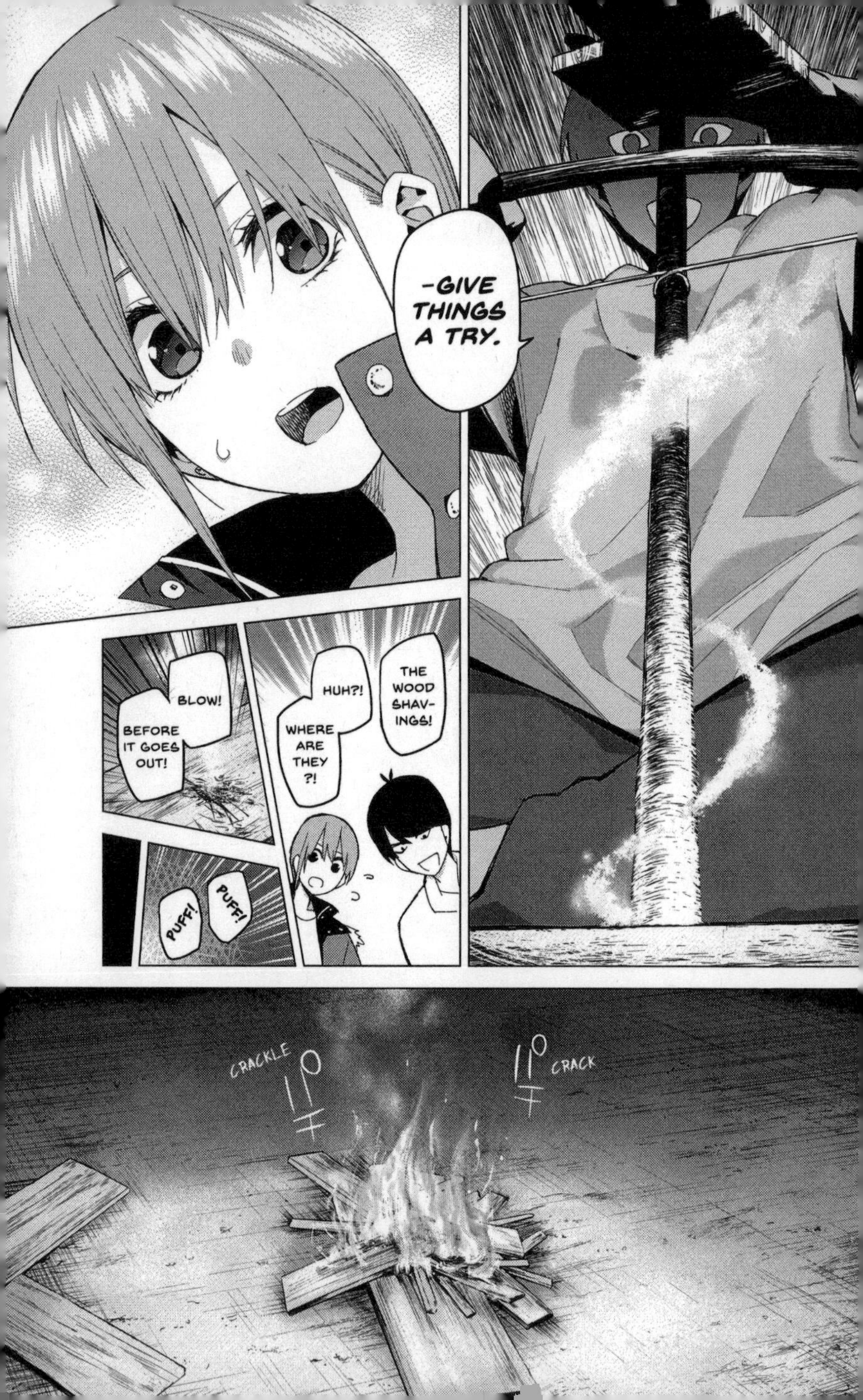
-GIVE THINGS A TRY.
THE WOOD SHAVINGS!
HUH?!
WHERE ARE THEY?!
BLOW!
BEFORE IT GOES OUT!
PUFF!
PUFF!
CRACK
CRACKLE

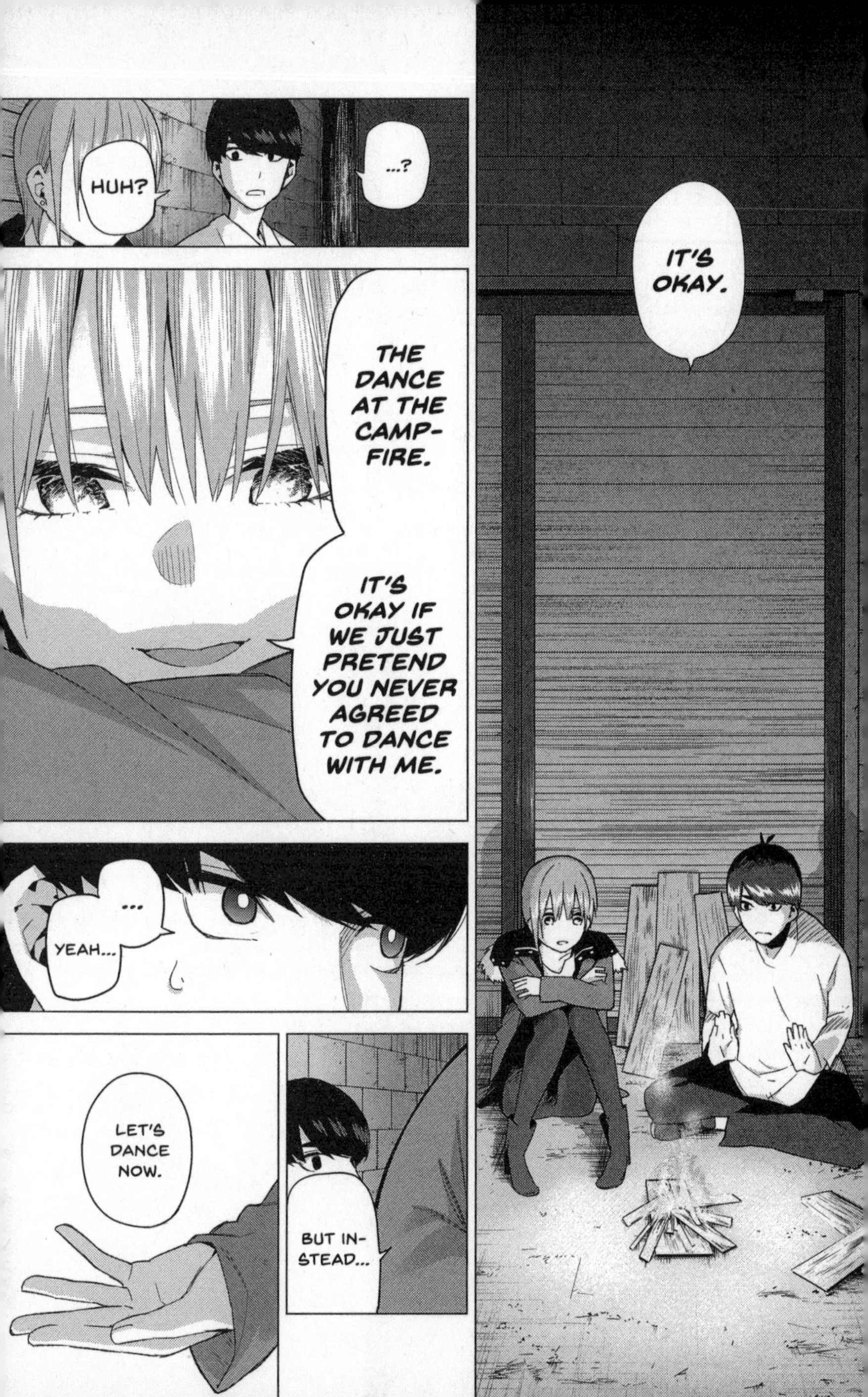
IT'S OKAY.
...?
HUH?
THE DANCE AT THE CAMP-FIRE.
IT'S OKAY IF WE JUST PRETEND YOU NEVER AGREED TO DANCE WITH ME.
... YEAH...
BUT IN-STEAD...
LET'S DANCE NOW.

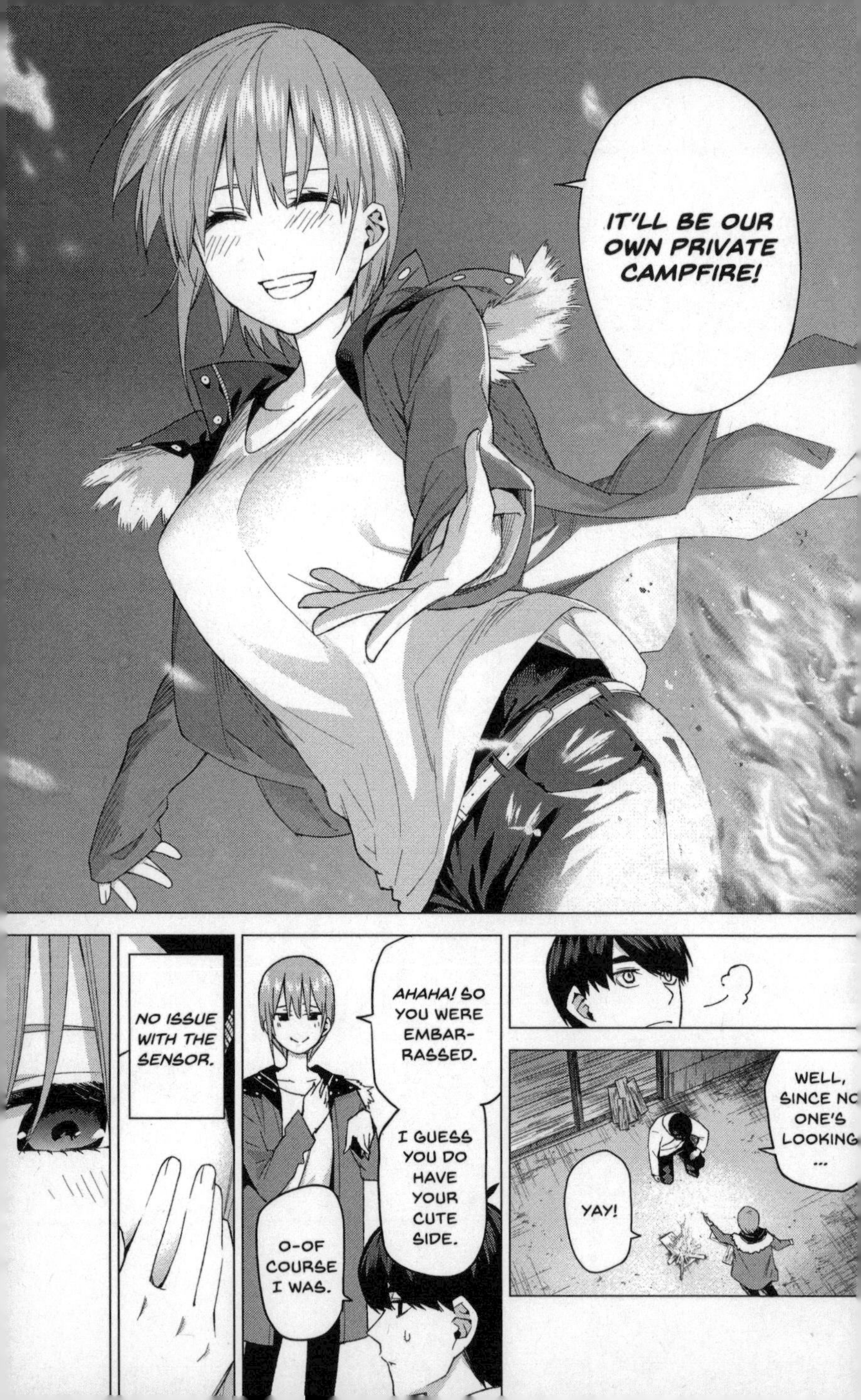
IT'LL BE OUR OWN PRIVATE CAMPFIRE!
WELL, SINCE NO ONE'S LOOKING ...
YAY!
AHAHA! SO YOU WERE EMBAR-RASSED.
I GUESS YOU DO HAVE YOUR CUTE SIDE.
O-OF COURSE I WAS.
NO ISSUE WITH THE SENSOR.

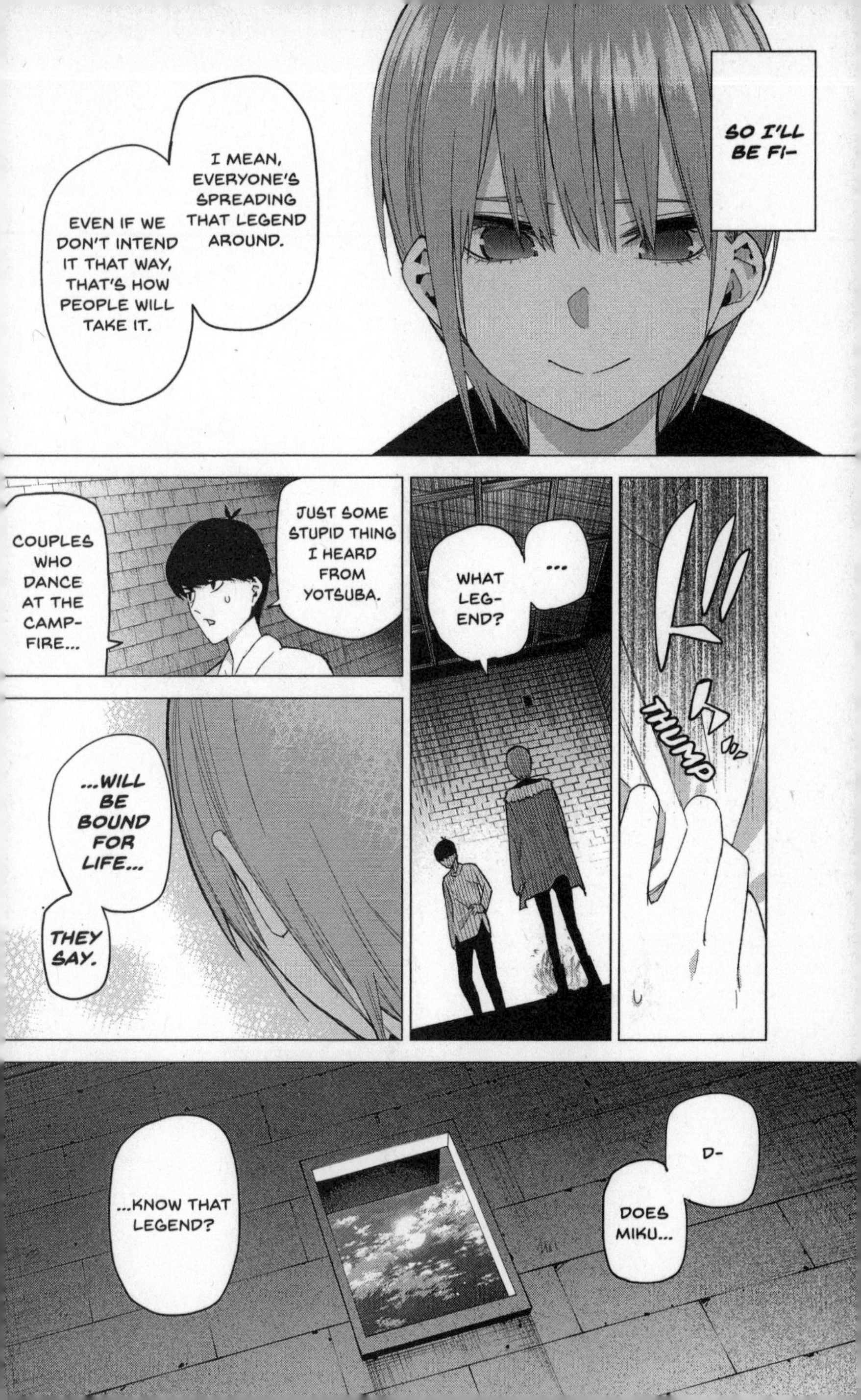
SO I'LL BE FI-
I MEAN, EVERYONE'S SPREADING THAT LEGEND AROUND.
EVEN IF WE DON'T INTEND IT THAT WAY, THAT'S HOW PEOPLE WILL TAKE IT.
THUMP
...
WHAT LEG-END?
JUST SOME STUPID THING I HEARD FROM YOTSUBA.
COUPLES WHO DANCE AT THE CAMP-FIRE...
...WILL BE BOUND FOR LIFE...
THEY SAY.
D-
DOES MIKU...
...KNOW THAT LEGEND?

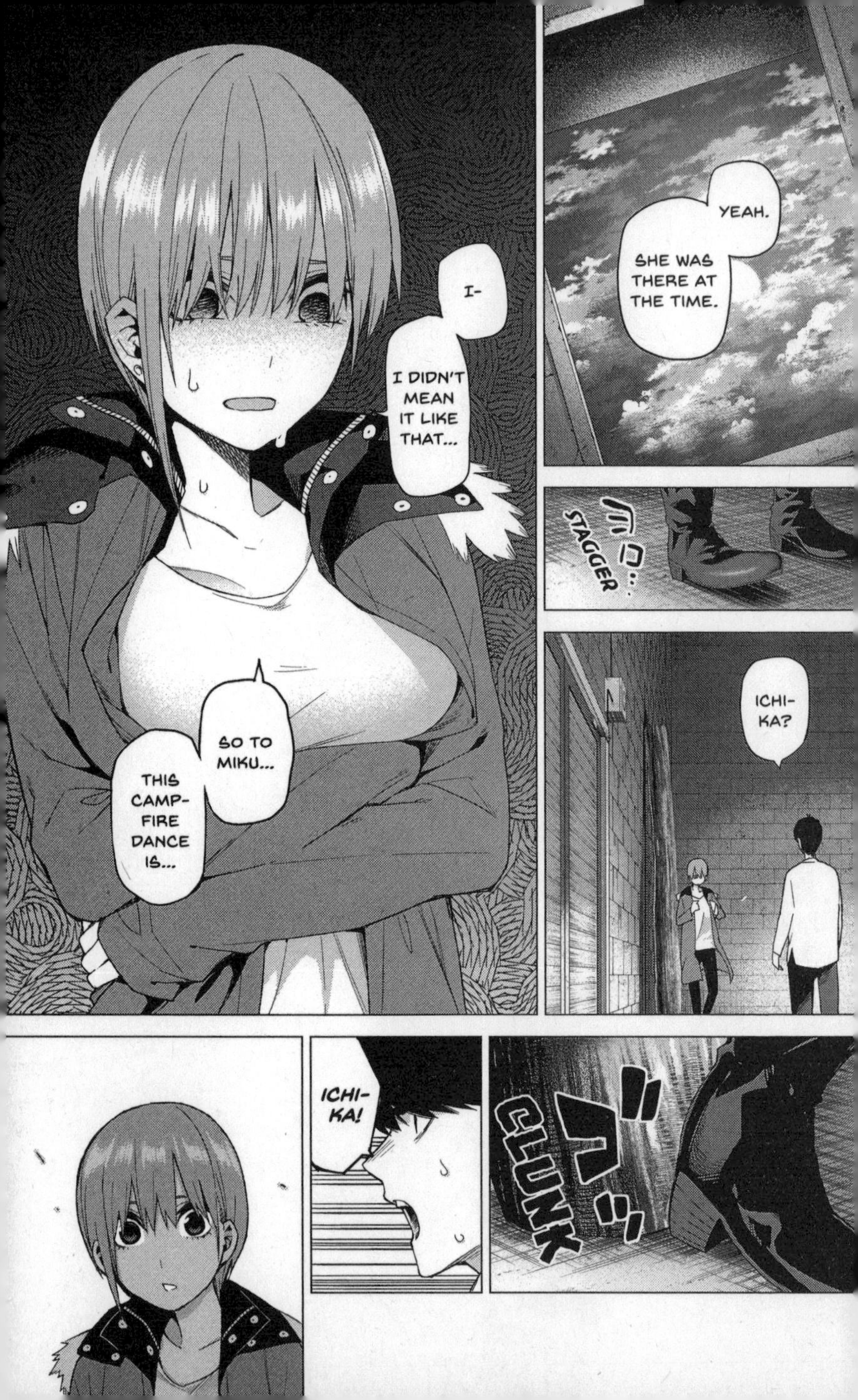
YEAH.
SHE WAS THERE AT THE TIME.
STAGGER
ICHI-KA?
I-
I DIDN'T MEAN IT LIKE THAT...
SO TO MIKU...
THIS CAMP-FIRE DANCE IS...
CLUNK
ICHI-KA!

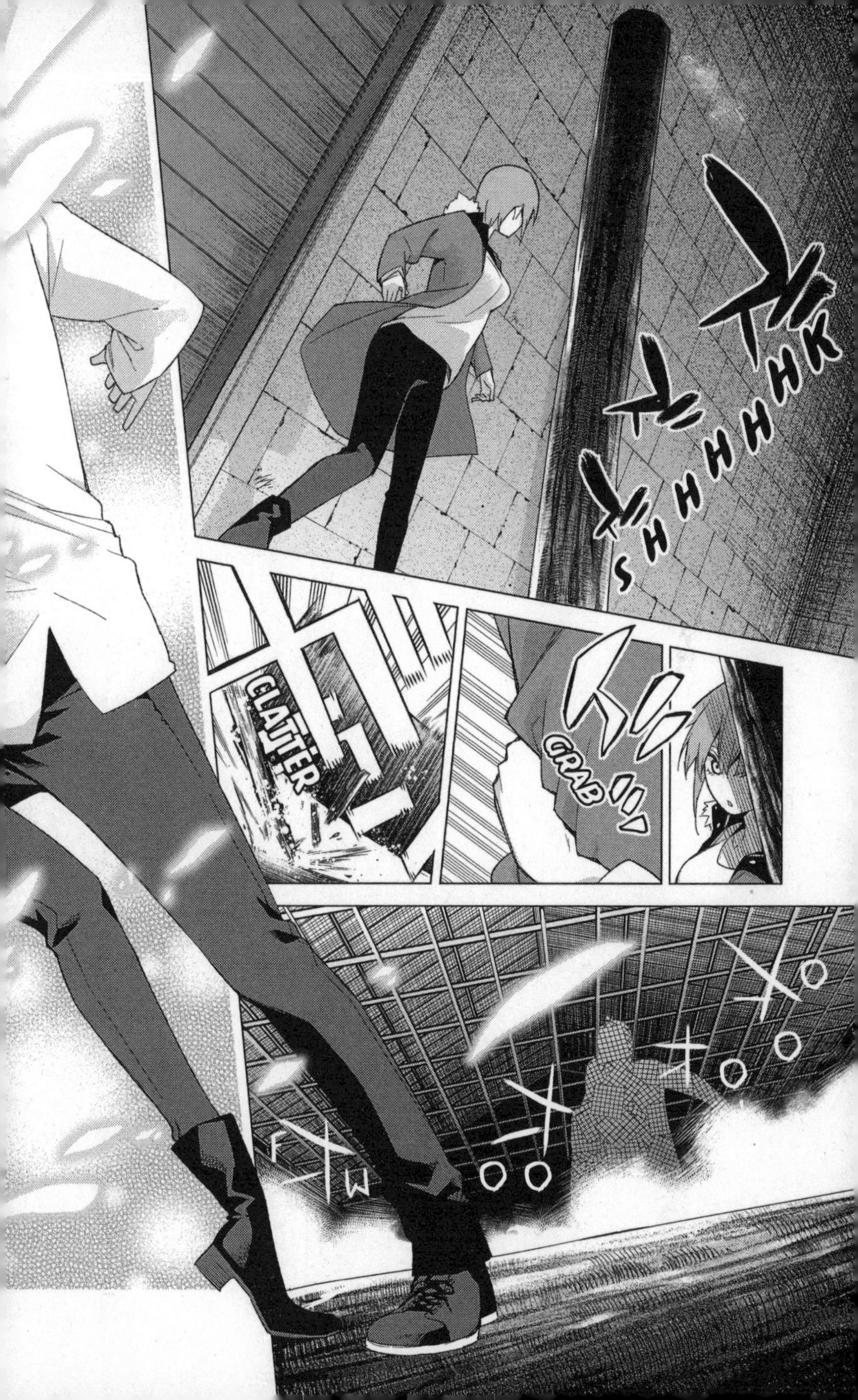
SHHHHHHK
GRAB
CLATTER

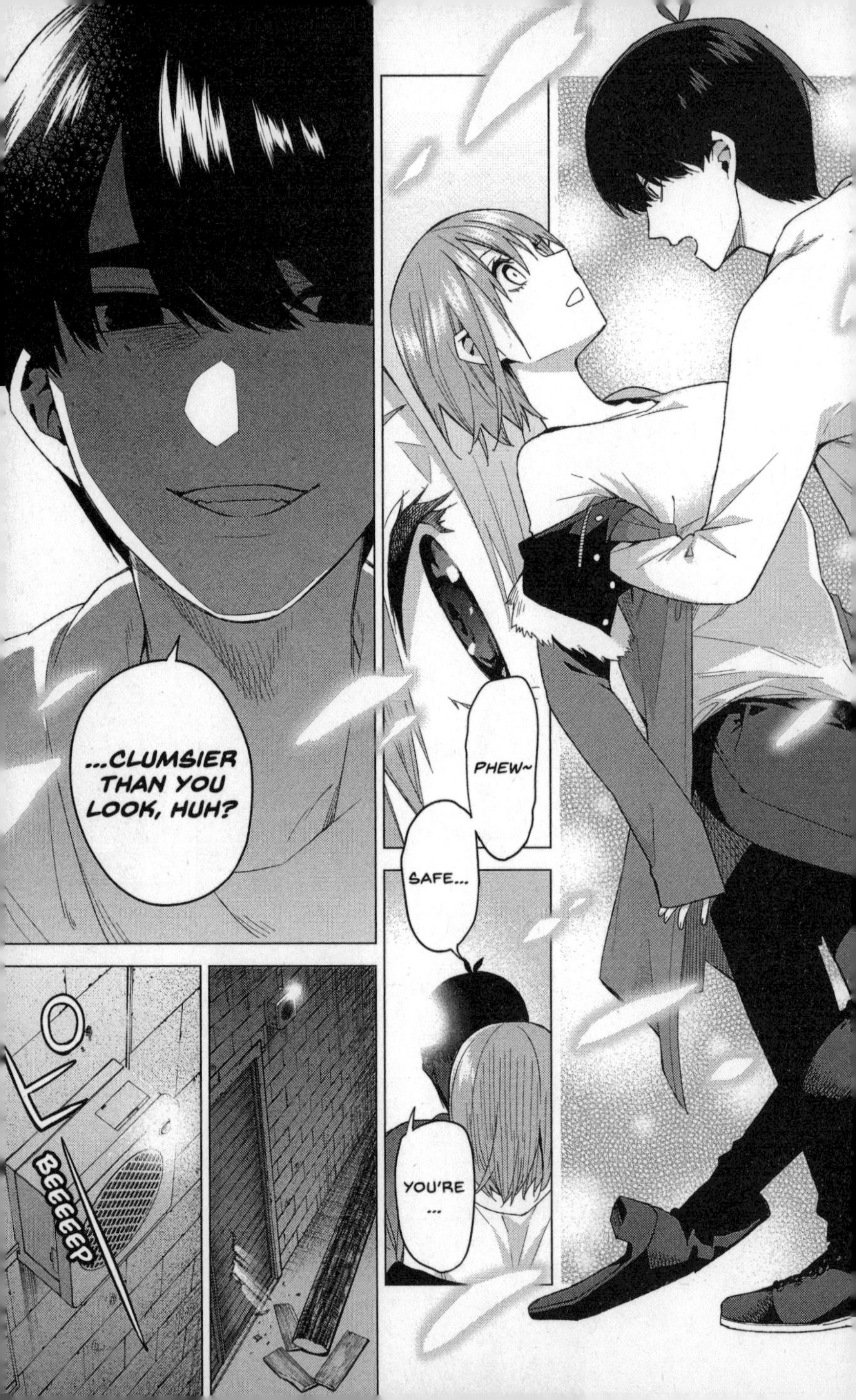
PHEW~
SAFE...
YOU'RE
...
...CLUMSIER THAN YOU LOOK, HUH?
BEEEEP

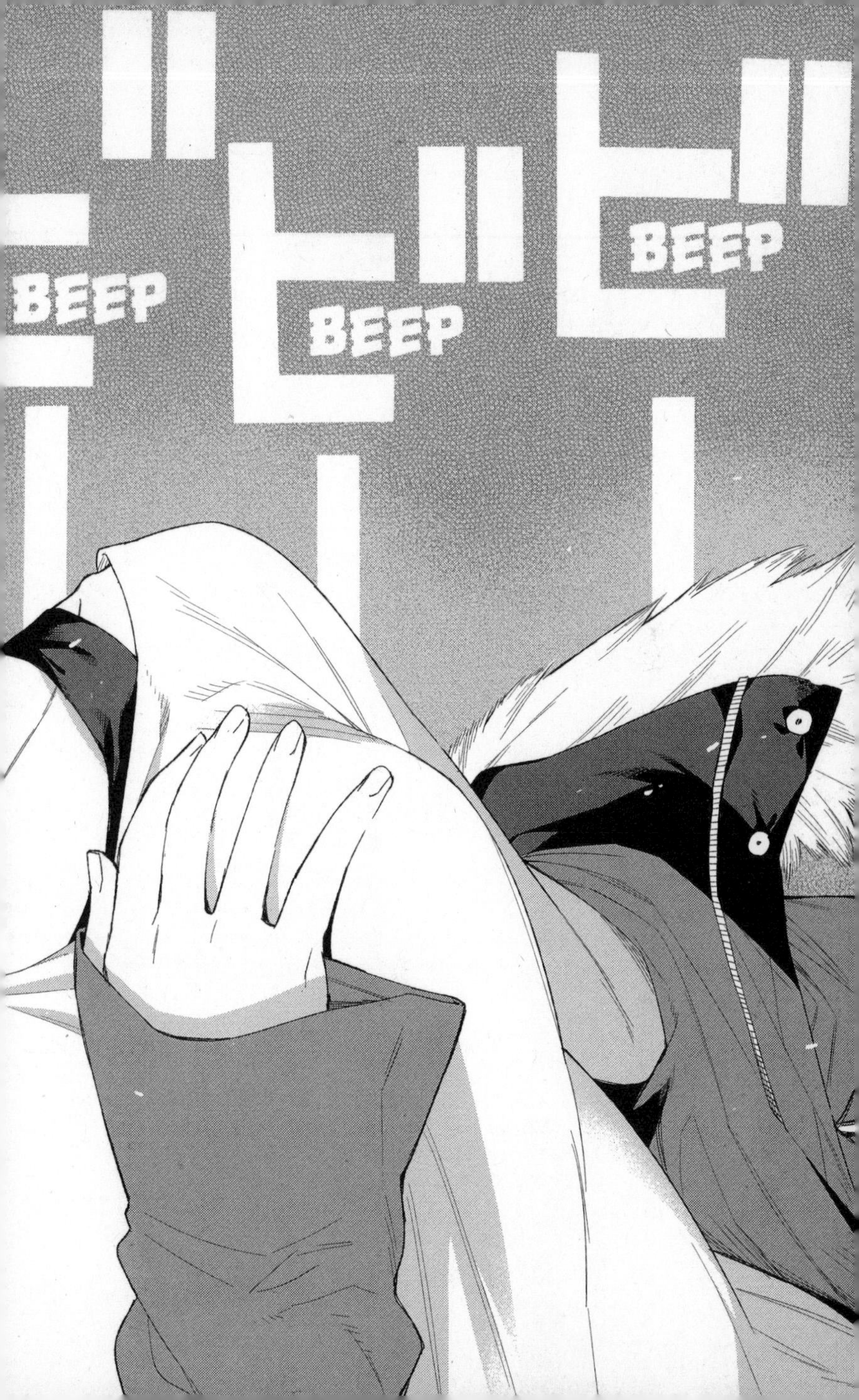
ビー
BEEP
ビー
BEEP
ビー
BEEP

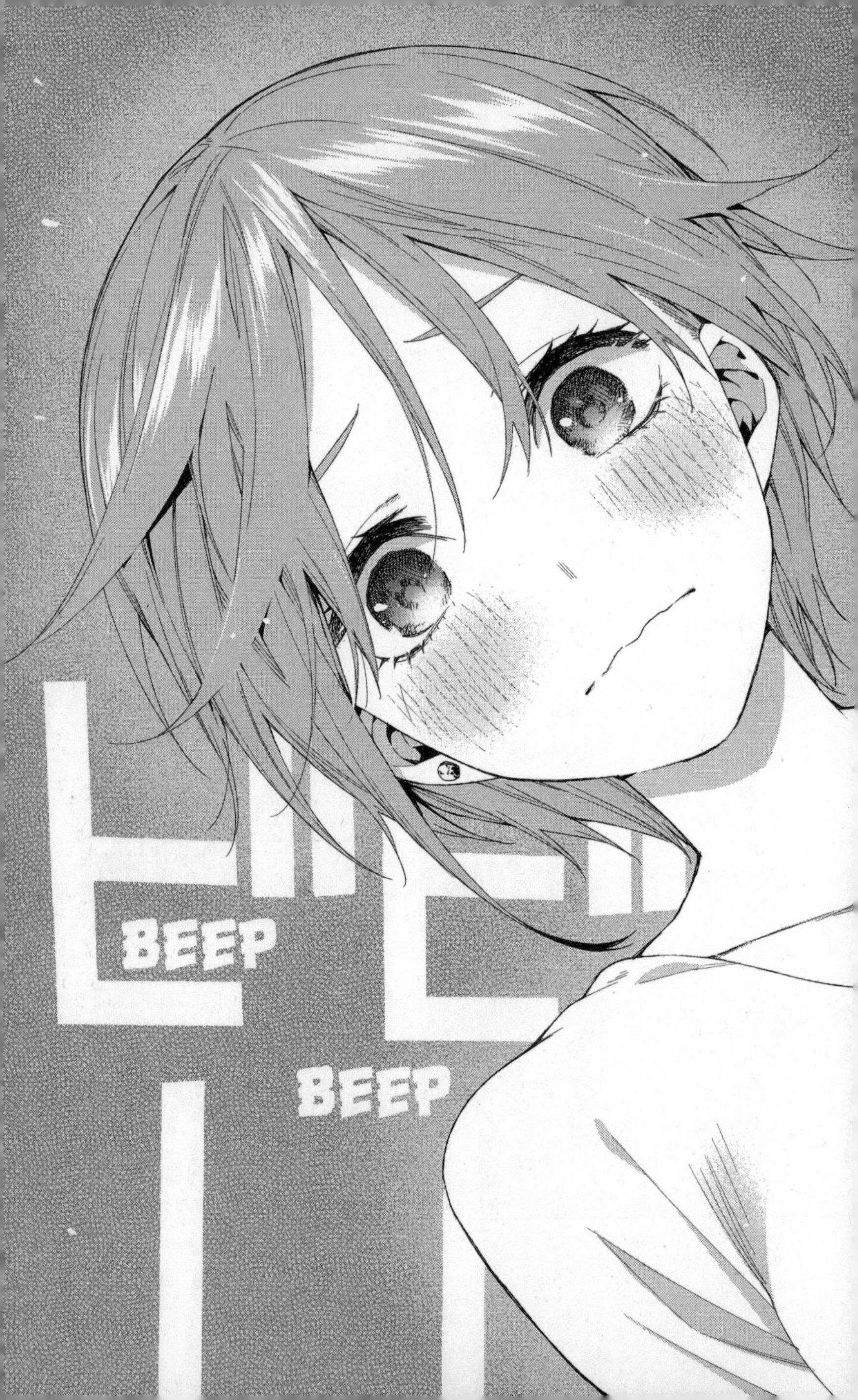
BEEP
BEEP

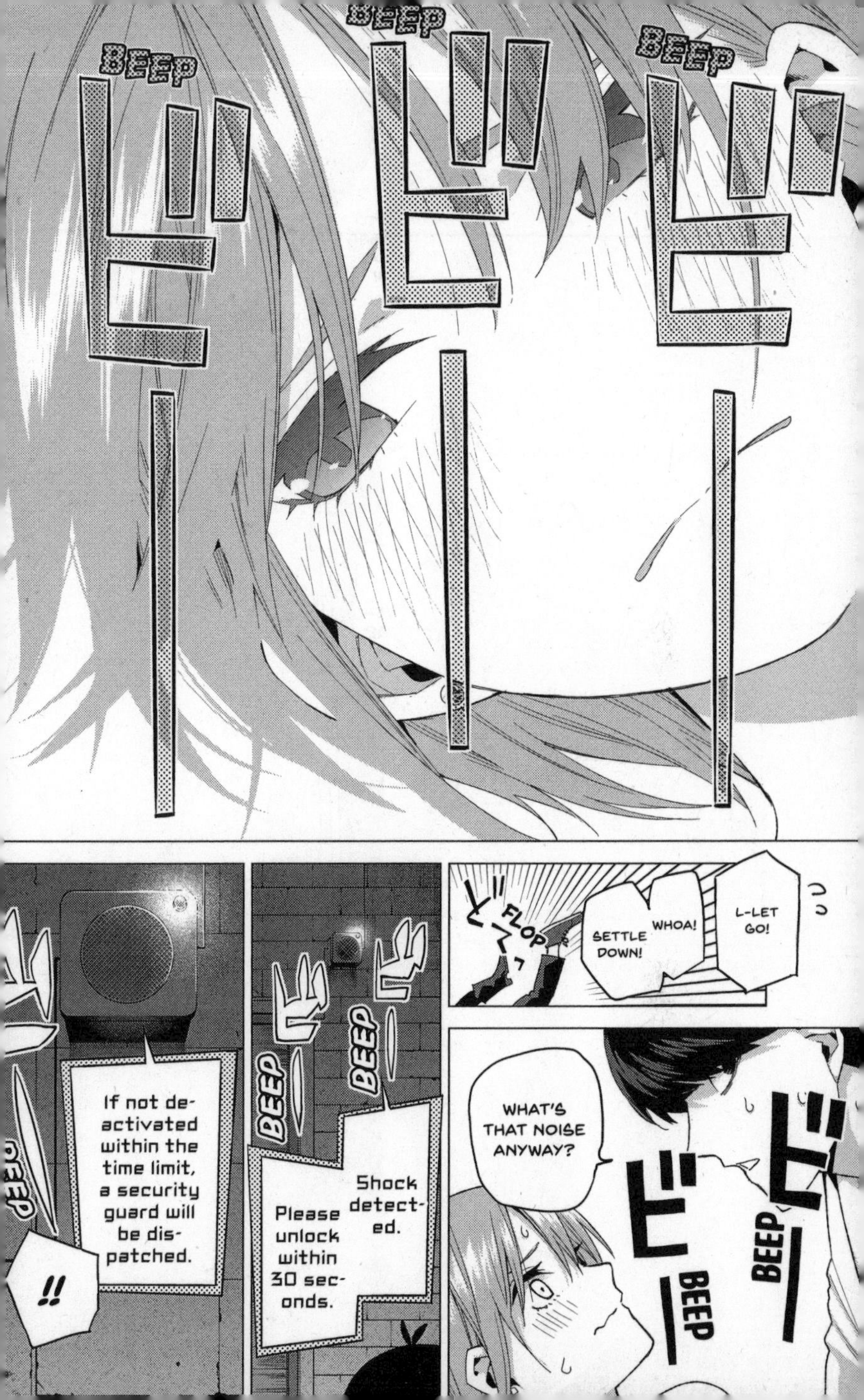
BEEP
BEEP
BEEP
L-LET GO!
WHOA!
SETTLE DOWN!
FLOP
WHAT'S THAT NOISE ANYWAY?
BEEP
BEEP
BEEP
BEEP
Shock detected.
Please unlock within 30 seconds.
If not de-activated within the time limit, a security guard will be dis-patched.
BEEP
!!

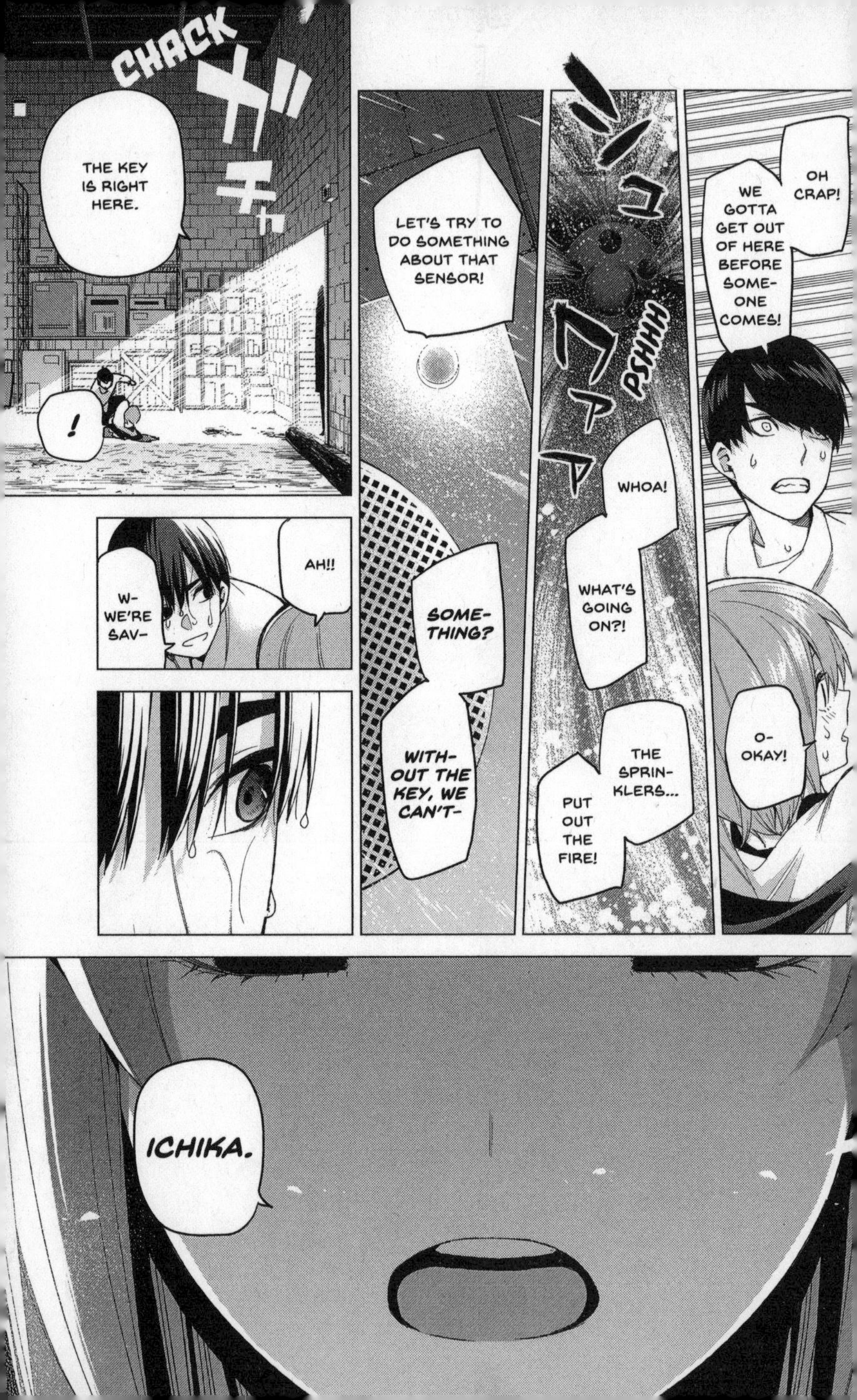
OH CRAP!
WE GOTTA GET OUT OF HERE BEFORE SOME-ONE COMES!
O-OKAY!
PSHHH
WHOA!
WHAT'S GOING ON?!
THE SPRINKLERS...
PUT OUT THE FIRE!
LET'S TRY TO DO SOMETHING ABOUT THAT SENSOR!
SOME-THING?
WITH-OUT THE KEY, WE CAN'T-
CHACK
THE KEY IS RIGHT HERE.
!
AH!!
W-WE'RE SAV-
ICHIKA.

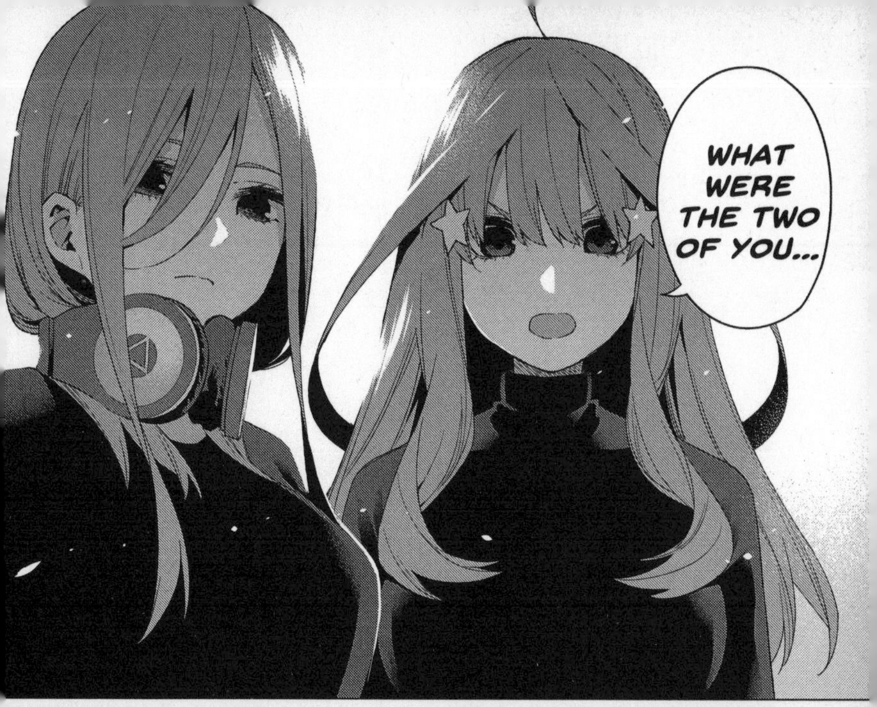
WHAT WERE THE TWO OF YOU...

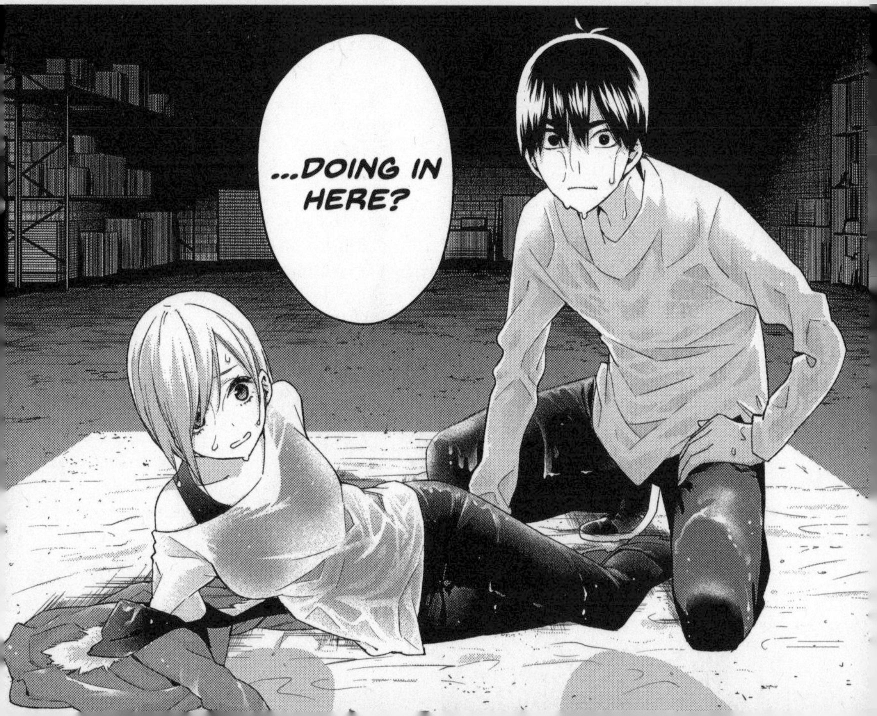
...DOING IN HERE?

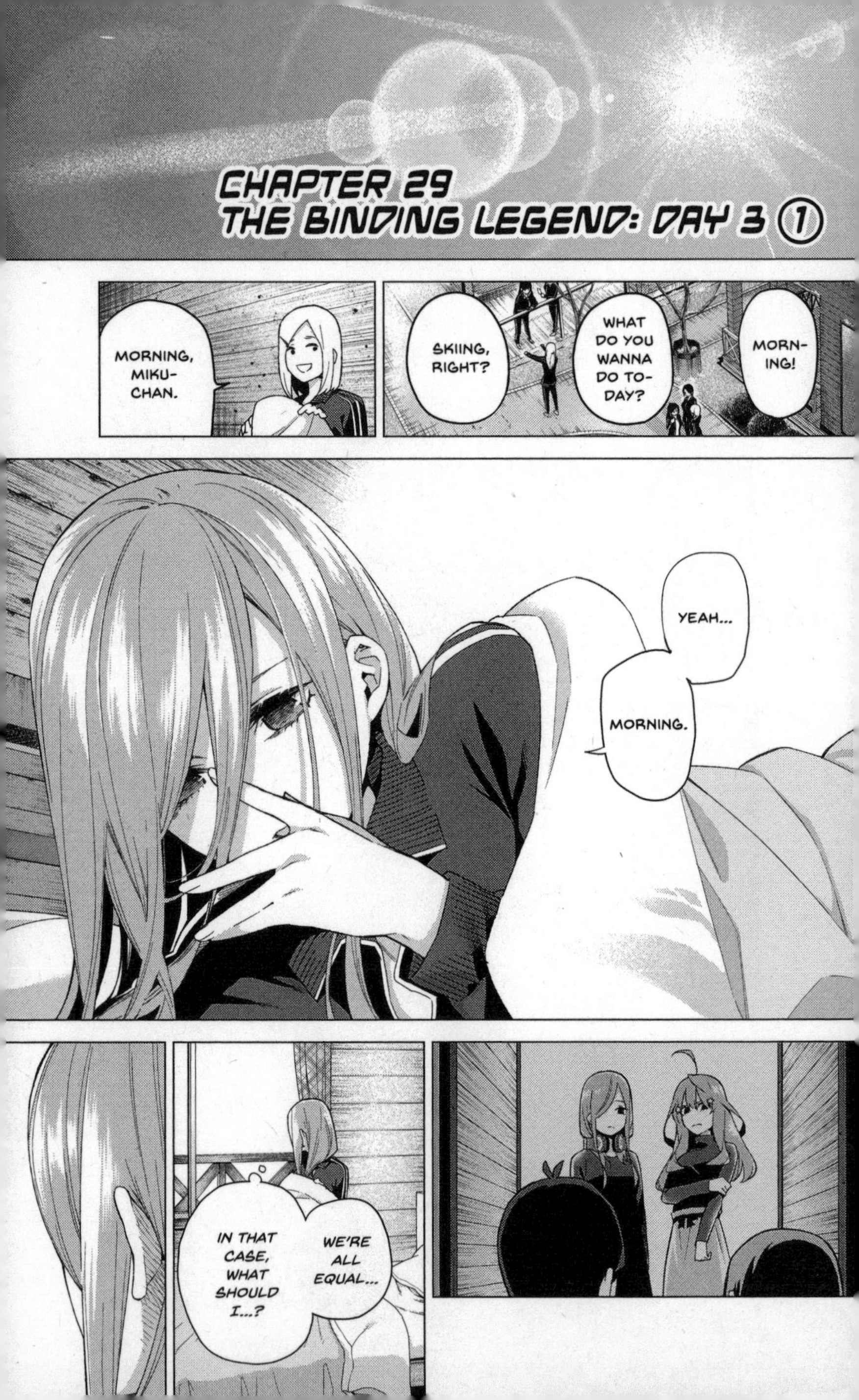
CHAPTER 29
THE BINDING LEGEND: DAY 3 ①
MORN-ING!
WHAT DO YOU WANNA DO TO-DAY?
SKIING, RIGHT?
MORNING, MIKU-CHAN.
YEAH...
MORNING.
WE'RE ALL EQUAL...
IN THAT CASE, WHAT SHOULD I...?

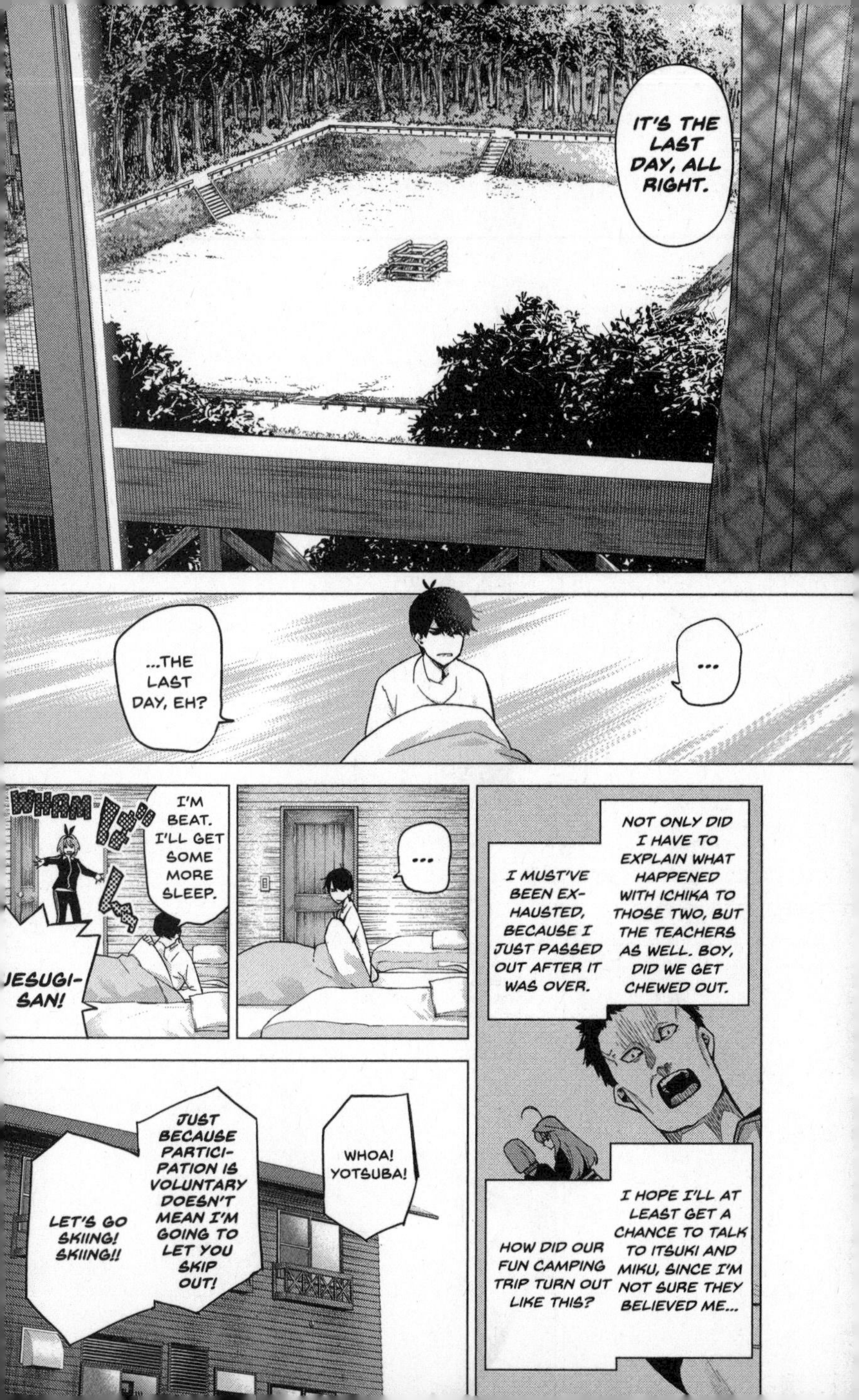
IT'S THE LAST DAY, ALL RIGHT.
...
...THE LAST DAY, EH?
NOT ONLY DID I HAVE TO EXPLAIN WHAT HAPPENED WITH ICHIKA TO THOSE TWO, BUT THE TEACHERS AS WELL. BOY, DID WE GET CHEWED OUT.
I MUST'VE BEEN EXHAUSTED, BECAUSE I JUST PASSED OUT AFTER IT WAS OVER.
I HOPE I'LL AT LEAST GET A CHANCE TO TALK TO ITSUKI AND MIKU, SINCE I'M NOT SURE THEY BELIEVED ME...
HOW DID OUR FUN CAMPING TRIP TURN OUT LIKE THIS?
...
I'M BEAT. I'LL GET SOME MORE SLEEP.
WHAM
!?
UESUGI-SAN!
WHOA! YOTSUBA!
JUST BECAUSE PARTICIPATION IS VOLUNTARY DOESN'T MEAN I'M GOING TO LET YOU SKIP OUT!
LET'S GO SKIING! SKIING!!

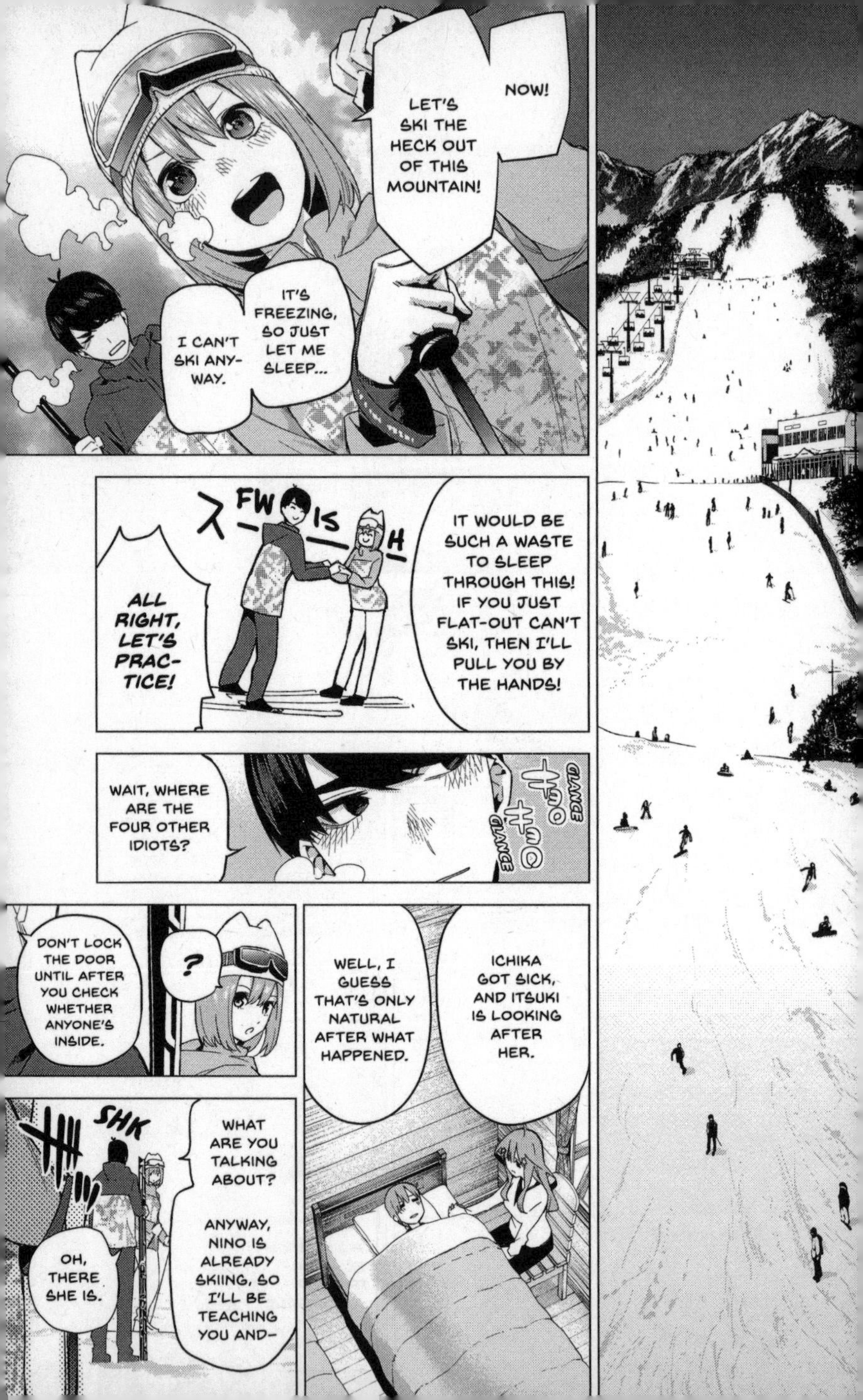
NOW!
LET'S SKI THE HECK OUT OF THIS MOUNTAIN!
IT'S FREEZING, SO JUST LET ME SLEEP...
I CAN'T SKI ANYWAY.
IT WOULD BE SUCH A WASTE TO SLEEP THROUGH THIS! IF YOU JUST FLAT-OUT CAN'T SKI, THEN I'LL PULL YOU BY THE HANDS!
FWISH
ALL RIGHT, LET'S PRACTICE!
GLANCE
GLANCE
WAIT, WHERE ARE THE FOUR OTHER IDIOTS?
ICHIKA GOT SICK, AND ITSUKI IS LOOKING AFTER HER.
WELL, I GUESS THAT'S ONLY NATURAL AFTER WHAT HAPPENED.
?
DON'T LOCK THE DOOR UNTIL AFTER YOU CHECK WHETHER ANYONE'S INSIDE.
SHK
WHAT ARE YOU TALKING ABOUT?
ANYWAY, NINO IS ALREADY SKIING, SO I'LL BE TEACHING YOU AND-
OH, THERE SHE IS.

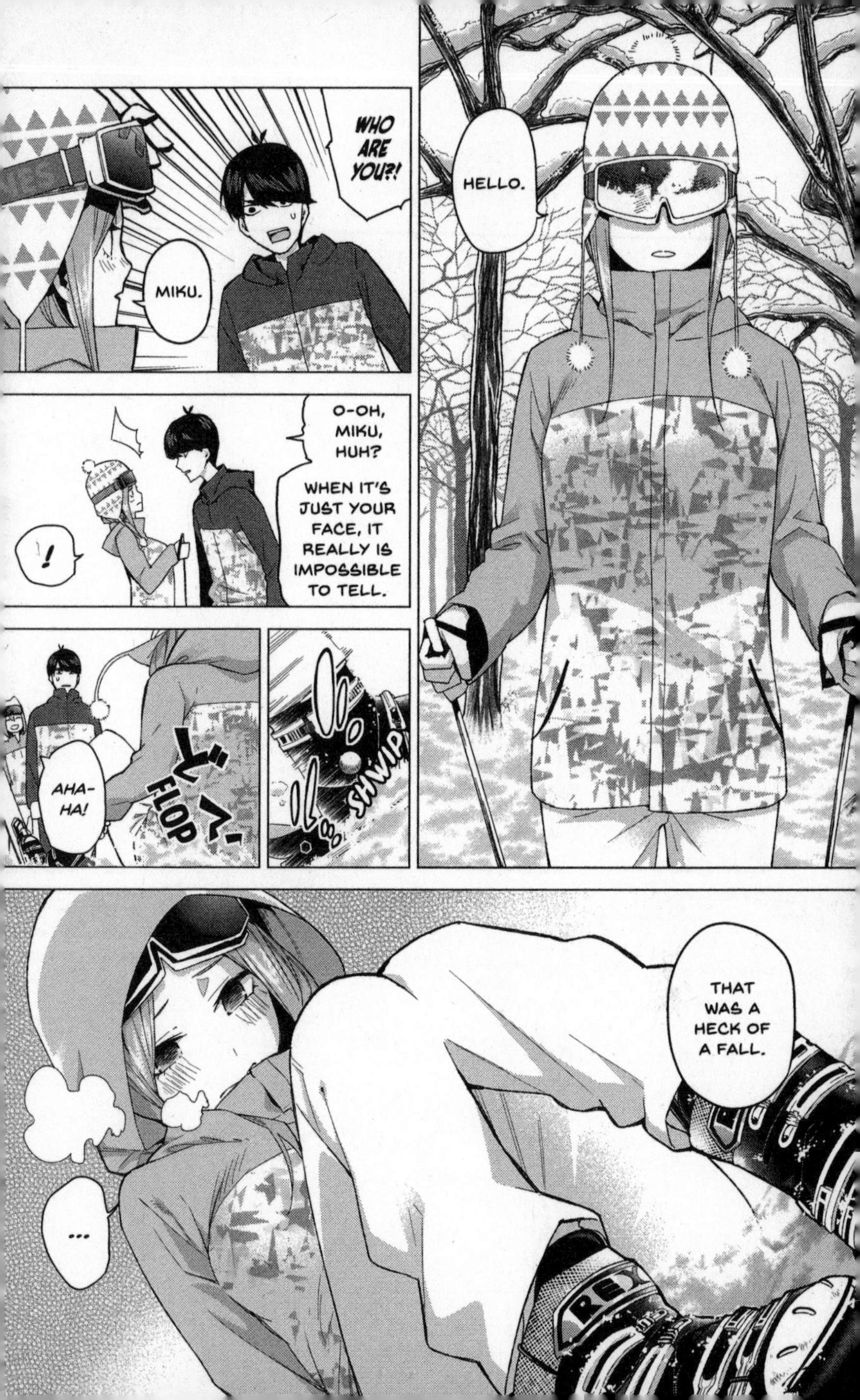
HELLO.
WHO ARE YOU?!
MIKU.
O-OH, MIKU, HUH?
WHEN IT'S JUST YOUR FACE, IT REALLY IS IMPOSSIBLE TO TELL.
!
SHWIP
FLOP
AHA-HA!
THAT WAS A HECK OF A FALL.
...

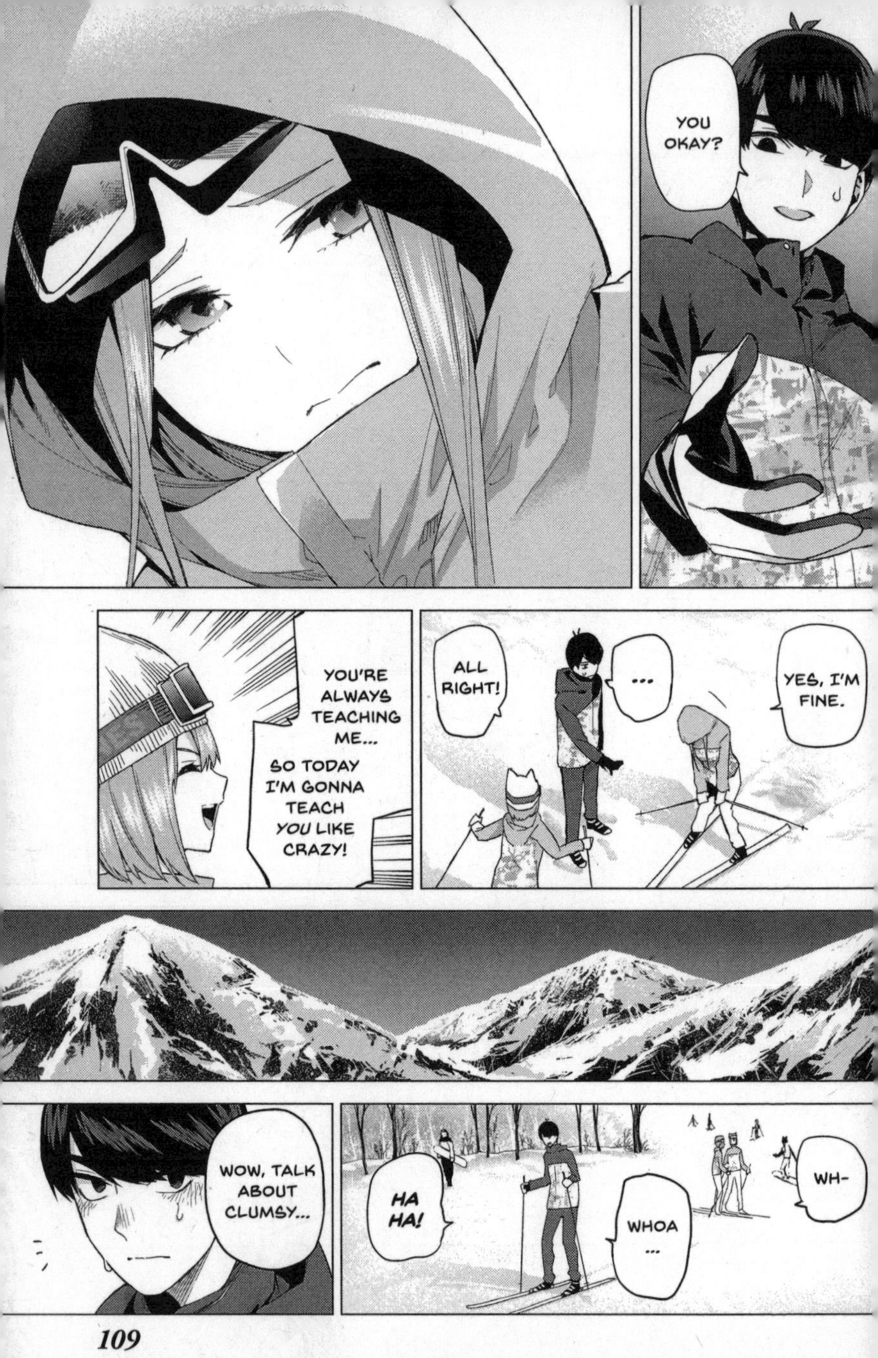
YOU OKAY?
YES, I'M FINE.
...
ALL RIGHT!
YOU'RE ALWAYS TEACHING ME...
SO TODAY I'M GONNA TEACH *YOU* LIKE CRAZY!
WH-
WHOA ...
HA HA!
WOW, TALK ABOUT CLUMSY...

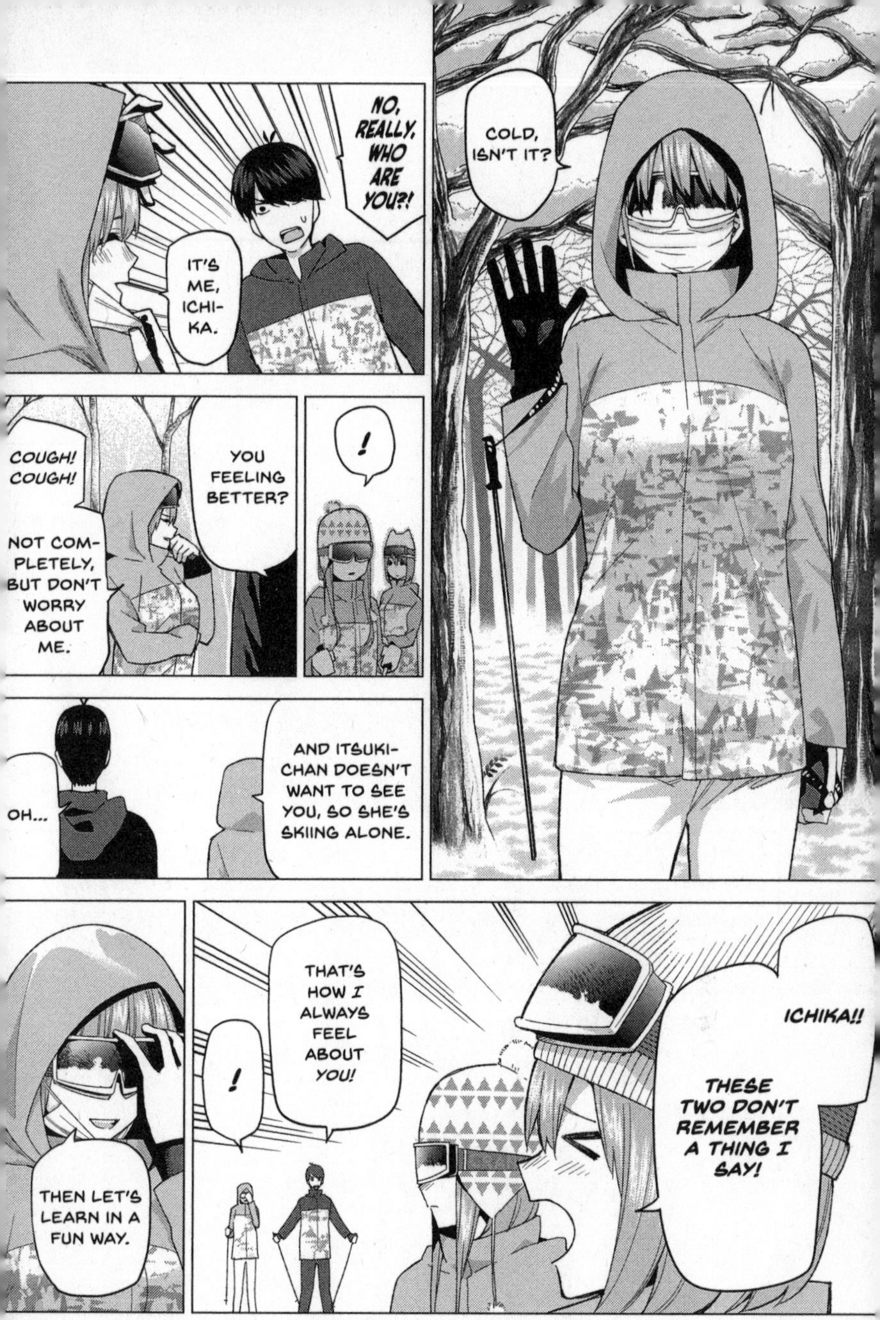
COLD, ISN'T IT?
NO, REALLY, WHO ARE YOU?!
IT'S ME, ICHIKA.
!
YOU FEELING BETTER?
COUGH! COUGH!
NOT COMPLETELY, BUT DON'T WORRY ABOUT ME.
AND ITSUKI-CHAN DOESN'T WANT TO SEE YOU, SO SHE'S SKIING ALONE.
OH...
ICHIKA!!
THESE TWO DON'T REMEMBER A THING I SAY!
THAT'S HOW I ALWAYS FEEL ABOUT YOU!
!
THEN LET'S LEARN IN A FUN WAY.

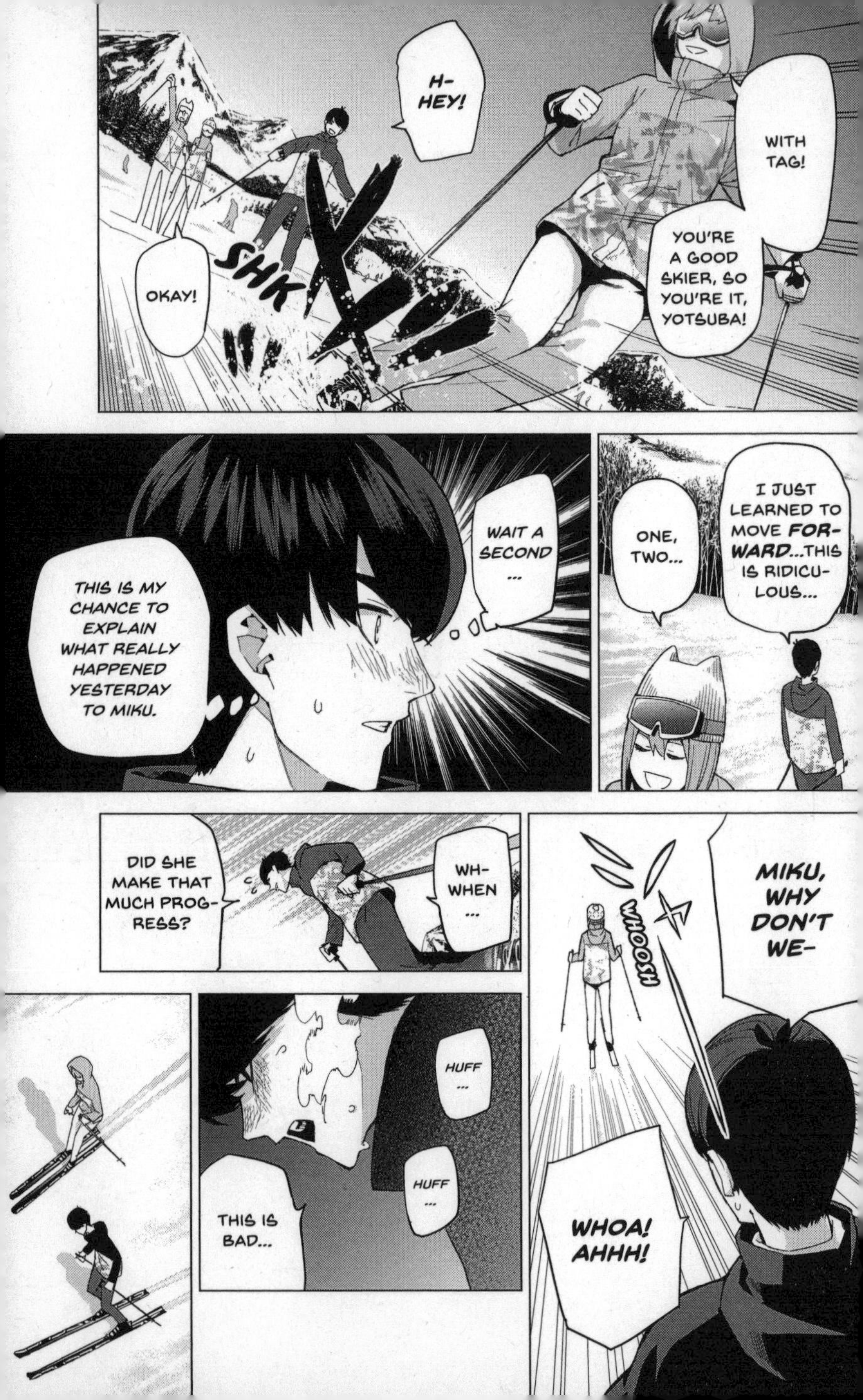
WITH TAG!
YOU'RE A GOOD SKIER, SO YOU'RE IT, YOTSUBA!
H-HEY!
SHK
OKAY!
I JUST LEARNED TO MOVE FORWARD...THIS IS RIDICULOUS...
ONE, TWO...
WAIT A SECOND ...
THIS IS MY CHANCE TO EXPLAIN WHAT REALLY HAPPENED YESTERDAY TO MIKU.
MIKU, WHY DON'T WE-
WHOOSH
WHOA! AHHH!
WH-WHEN ...
DID SHE MAKE THAT MUCH PROGRESS?
HUFF ...
HUFF ...
THIS IS BAD...

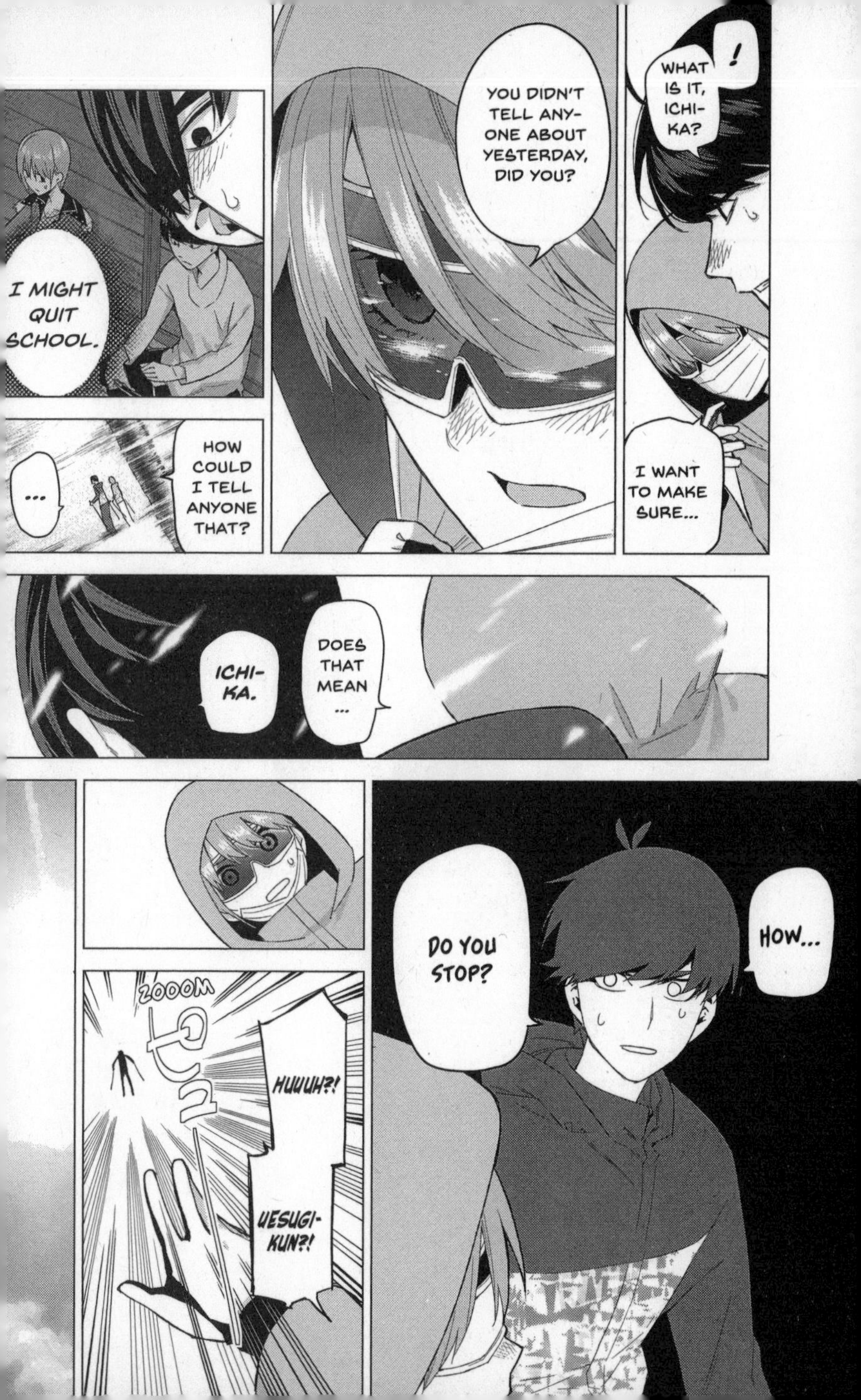

!
WHAT IS IT, ICHI-KA?
I WANT TO MAKE SURE...
YOU DIDN'T TELL ANY-ONE ABOUT YESTERDAY, DID YOU?
I MIGHT QUIT SCHOOL.
HOW COULD I TELL ANYONE THAT?
...
DOES THAT MEAN ...
ICHI-KA.
HOW...
DO YOU STOP?
ZOOOM
HUUUH?!
UESUGI-KUN?!

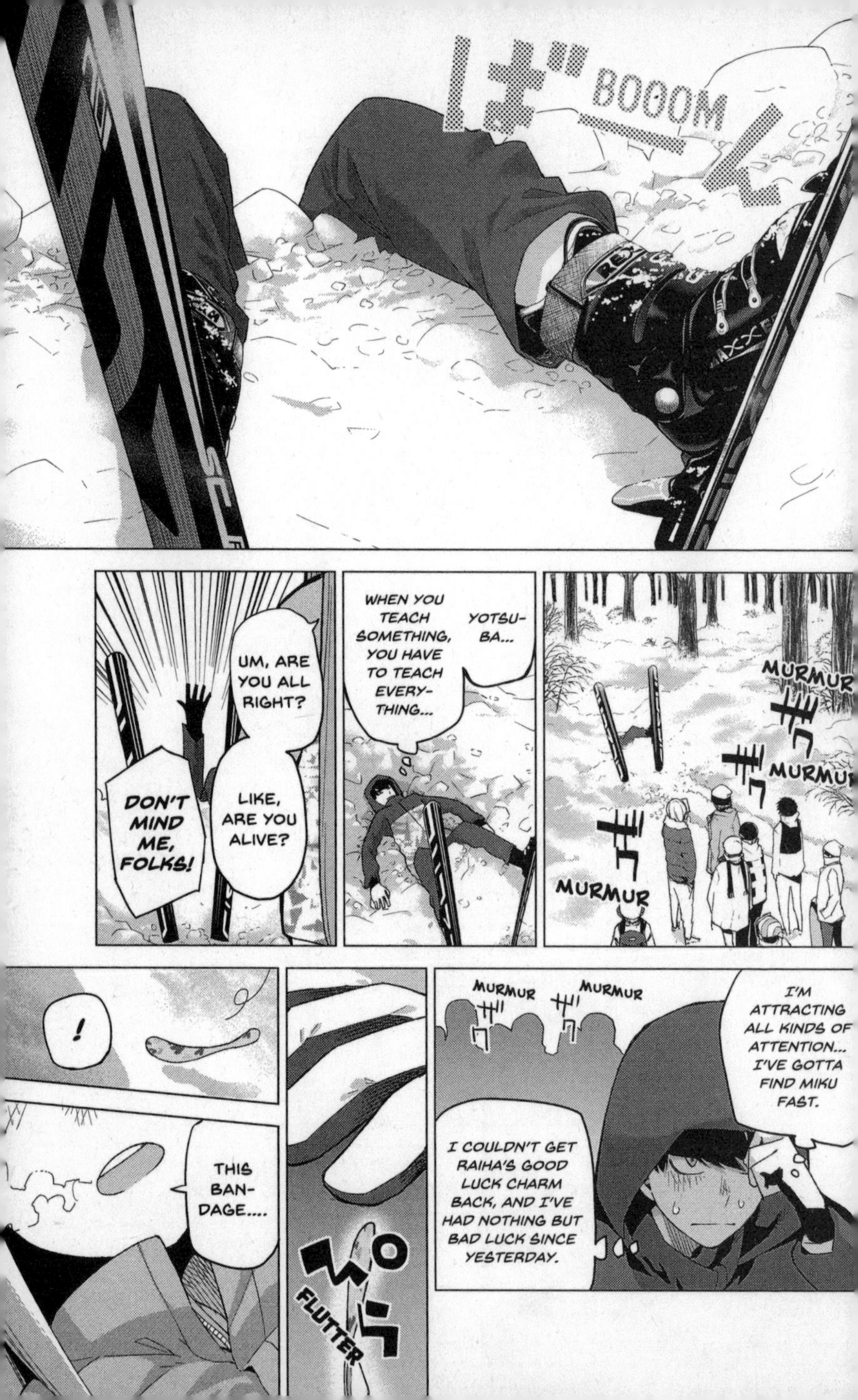
BOOOM
MURMUR
MURMUR
MURMUR
YOTSU-BA...
WHEN YOU TEACH SOMETHING, YOU HAVE TO TEACH EVERYTHING...
UM, ARE YOU ALL RIGHT?
LIKE, ARE YOU ALIVE?
DON'T MIND ME, FOLKS!
MURMUR
MURMUR
I'M ATTRACTING ALL KINDS OF ATTENTION... I'VE GOTTA FIND MIKU FAST.
I COULDN'T GET RAIHA'S GOOD LUCK CHARM BACK, AND I'VE HAD NOTHING BUT BAD LUCK SINCE YESTERDAY.
FLUTTER
!
THIS BANDAGE....

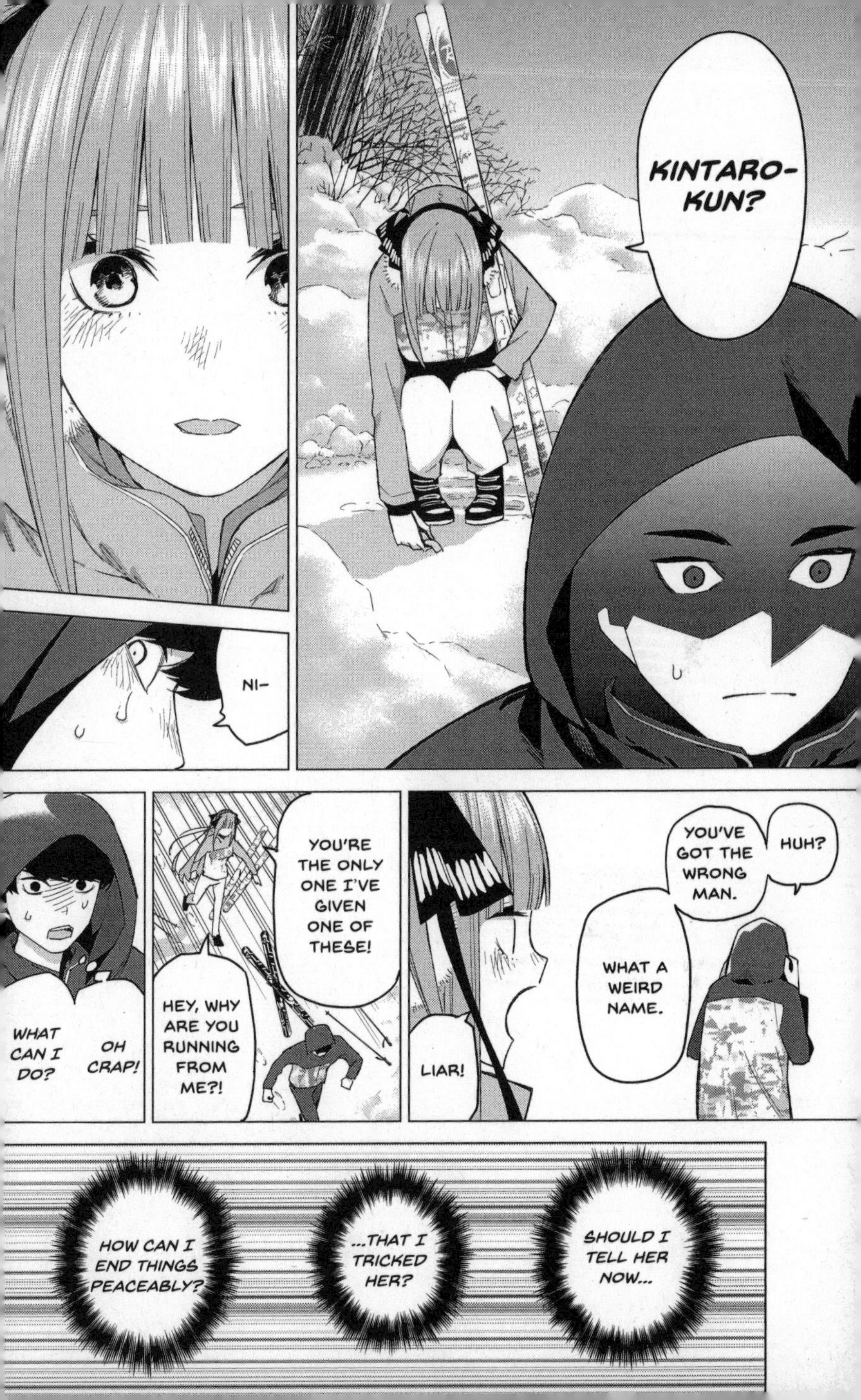
KINTARO-KUN?
NI-
YOU'VE GOT THE WRONG MAN.
HUH?
WHAT A WEIRD NAME.
LIAR!
YOU'RE THE ONLY ONE I'VE GIVEN ONE OF THESE!
HEY, WHY ARE YOU RUNNING FROM ME?!
OH CRAP!
WHAT CAN I DO?
SHOULD I TELL HER NOW...
...THAT I TRICKED HER?
HOW CAN I END THINGS PEACEABLY?

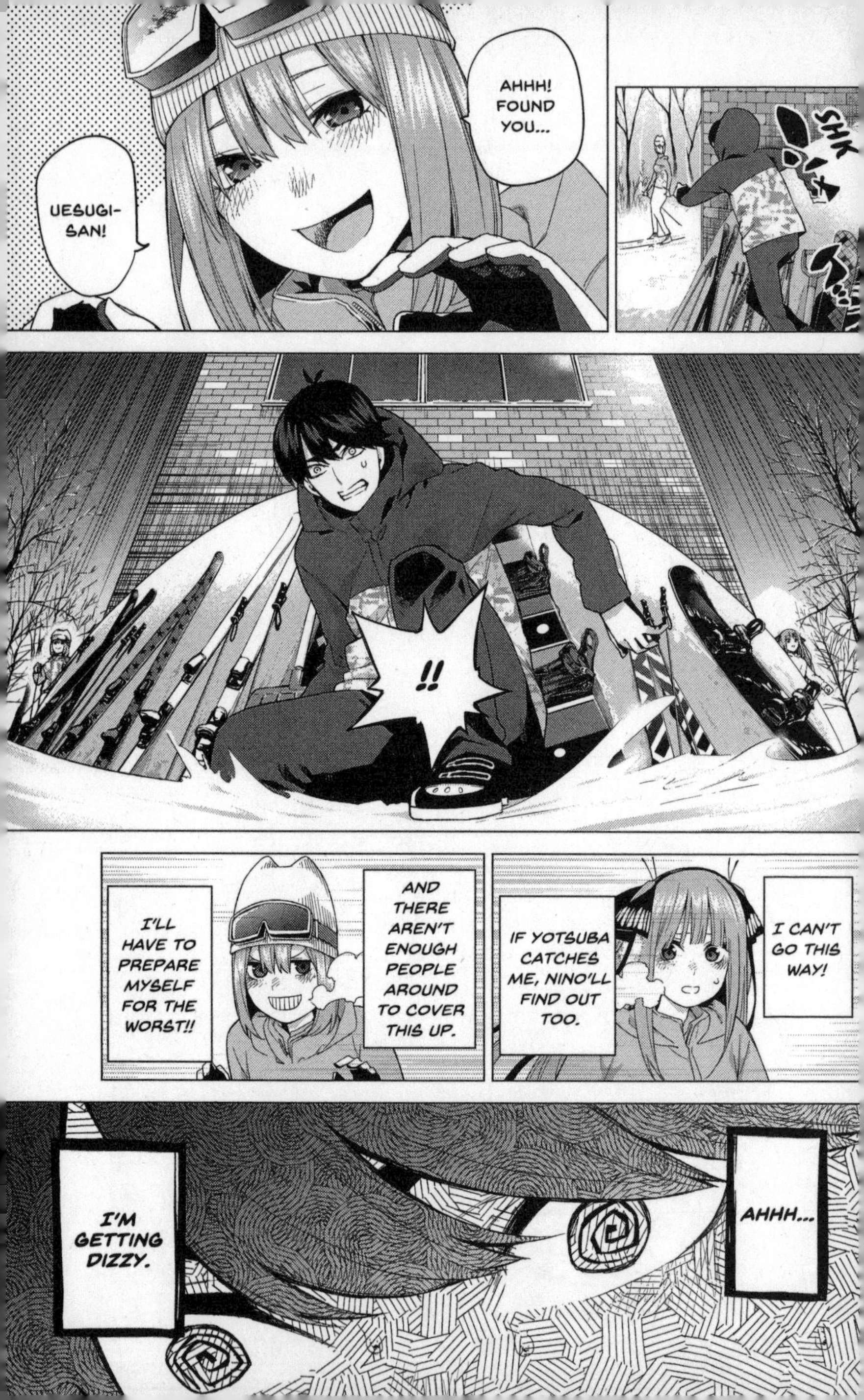
SHK
AHHH! FOUND YOU...
UESUGI-SAN!
!!
I CAN'T GO THIS WAY!
IF YOTSUBA CATCHES ME, NINO'LL FIND OUT TOO.
AND THERE AREN'T ENOUGH PEOPLE AROUND TO COVER THIS UP.
I'LL HAVE TO PREPARE MYSELF FOR THE WORST!!
AHHH...
I'M GETTING DIZZY.

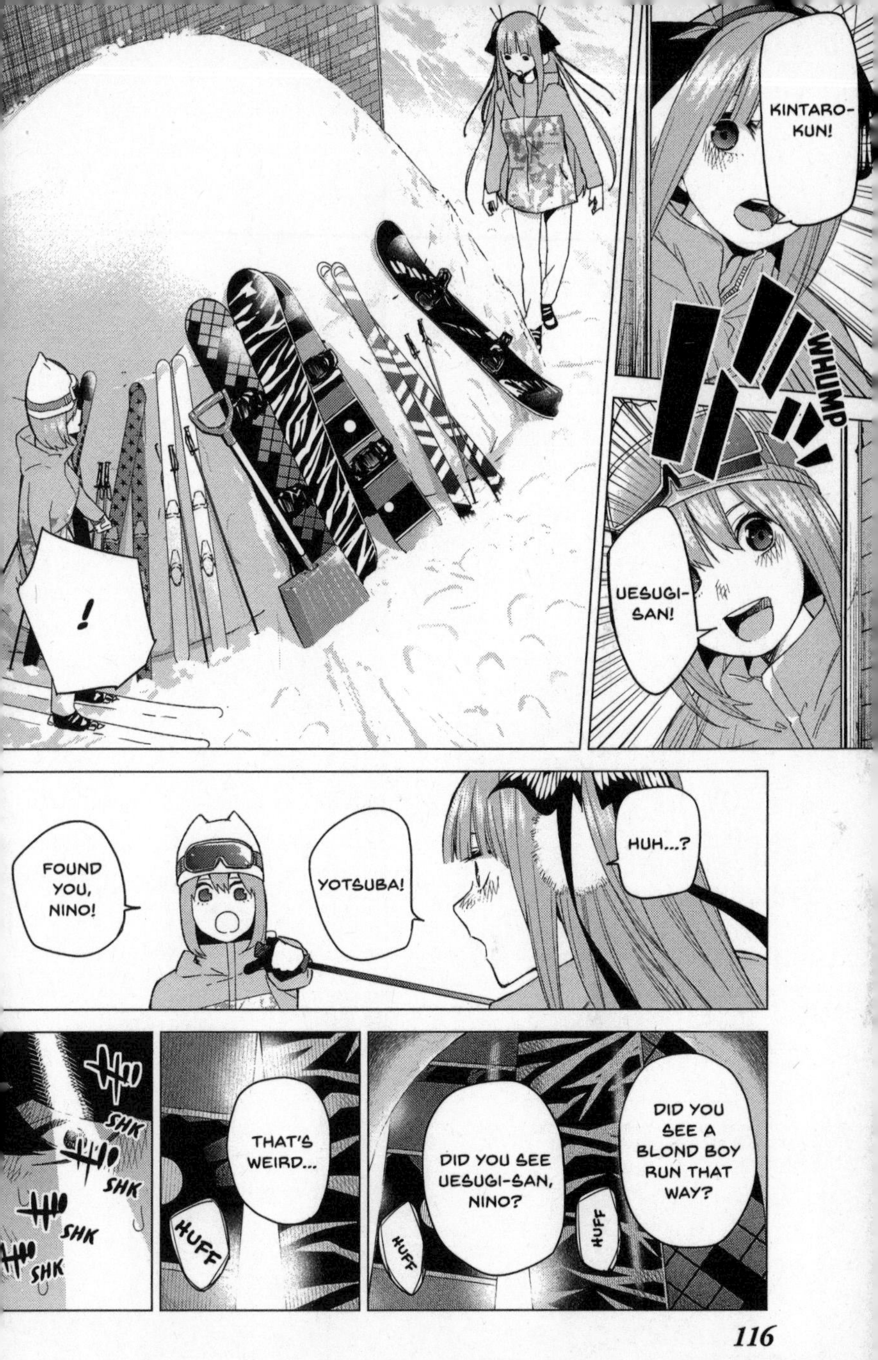
KINTARO-KUN!
WHUMP
UESUGI-SAN!
!
HUH...?
YOTSUBA!
FOUND YOU, NINO!
DID YOU SEE A BLOND BOY RUN THAT WAY?
HUFF
DID YOU SEE UESUGI-SAN, NINO?
HUFF
THAT'S WEIRD...
HUFF
SHK
SHK
SHK
SHK

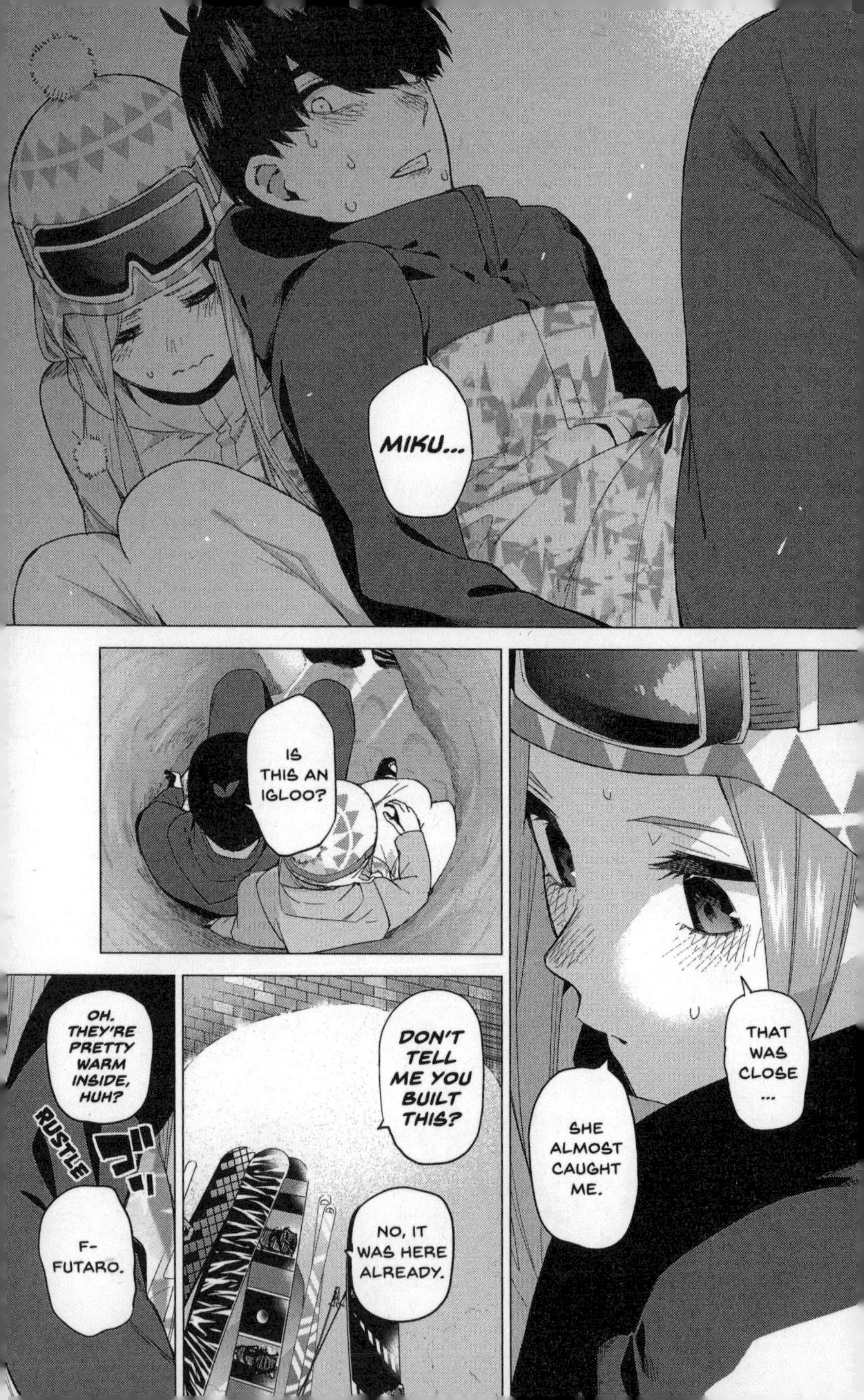
MIKU...
THAT WAS CLOSE...
SHE ALMOST CAUGHT ME.
IS THIS AN IGLOO?
DON'T TELL ME YOU BUILT THIS?
NO, IT WAS HERE ALREADY.
OH. THEY'RE PRETTY WARM INSIDE, HUH?
RUSTLE
F-FUTARO.

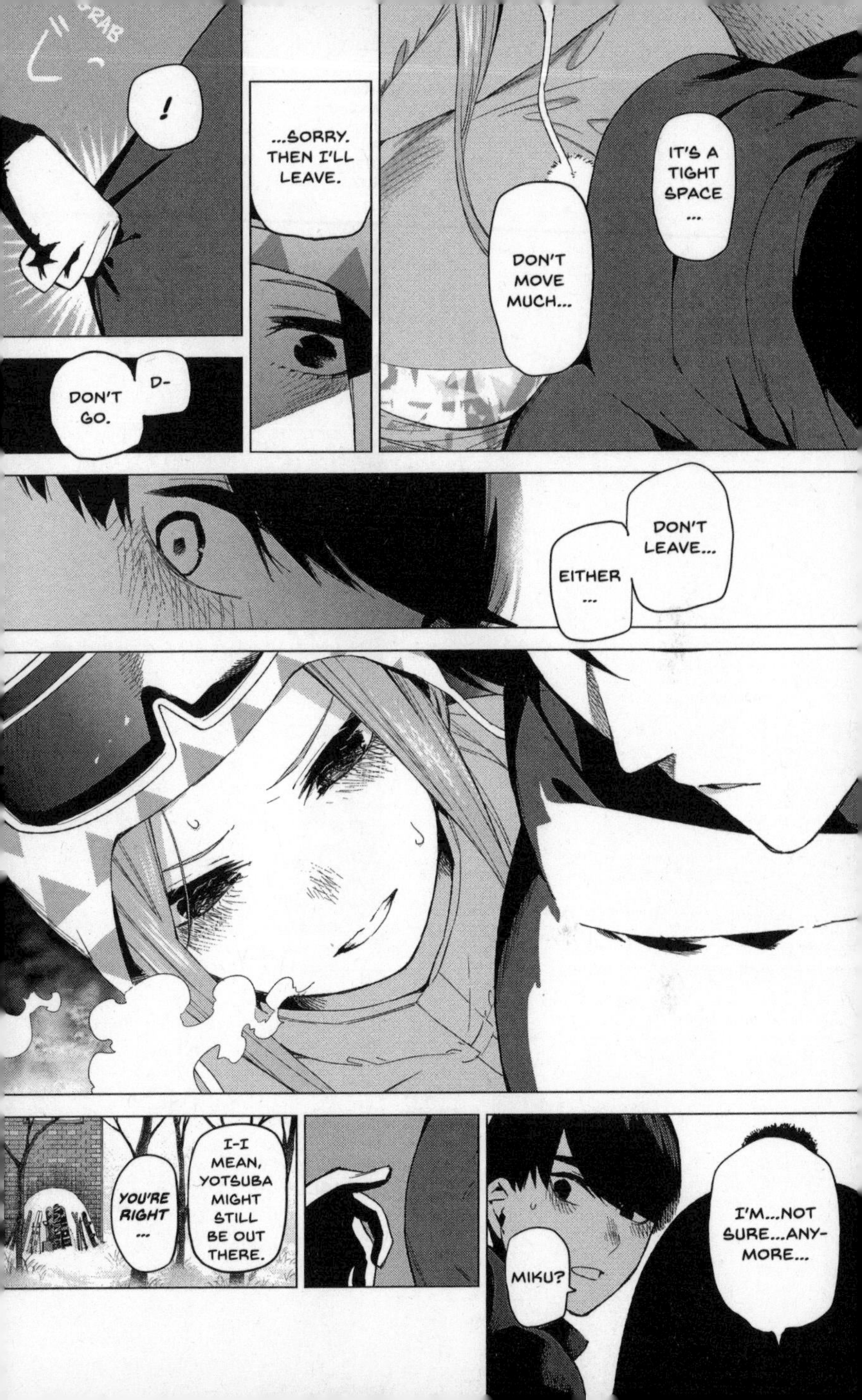
IT'S A TIGHT SPACE ...
DON'T MOVE MUCH...
...SORRY. THEN I'LL LEAVE.
GRAB
!
D- DON'T GO.
DON'T LEAVE... EITHER ...
I'M...NOT SURE...ANY-MORE...
MIKU?
I-I MEAN, YOTSUBA MIGHT STILL BE OUT THERE.
YOU'RE RIGHT ...

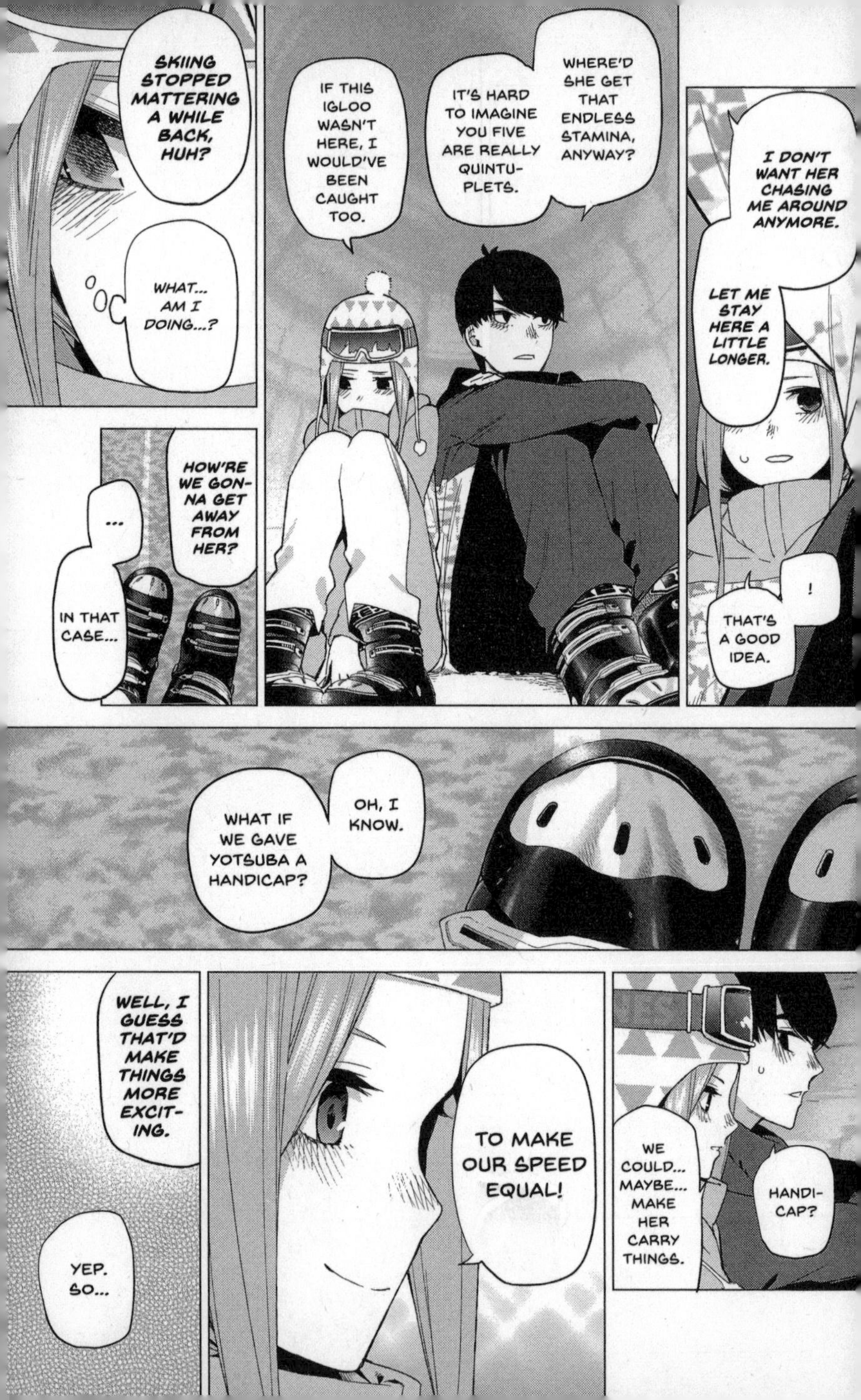
I DON'T WANT HER CHASING ME AROUND ANYMORE.
LET ME STAY HERE A LITTLE LONGER.
!
THAT'S A GOOD IDEA.
WHERE'D SHE GET THAT ENDLESS STAMINA, ANYWAY?
IT'S HARD TO IMAGINE YOU FIVE ARE REALLY QUINTU-PLETS.
IF THIS IGLOO WASN'T HERE, I WOULD'VE BEEN CAUGHT TOO.
SKIING STOPPED MATTERING A WHILE BACK, HUH?
WHAT... AM I DOING...?
HOW'RE WE GON-NA GET AWAY FROM HER?
...
IN THAT CASE...
OH, I KNOW.
WHAT IF WE GAVE YOTSUBA A HANDICAP?
HANDI-CAP?
WE COULD... MAYBE... MAKE HER CARRY THINGS.
TO MAKE OUR SPEED EQUAL!
WELL, I GUESS THAT'D MAKE THINGS MORE EXCIT-ING.
YEP. SO...

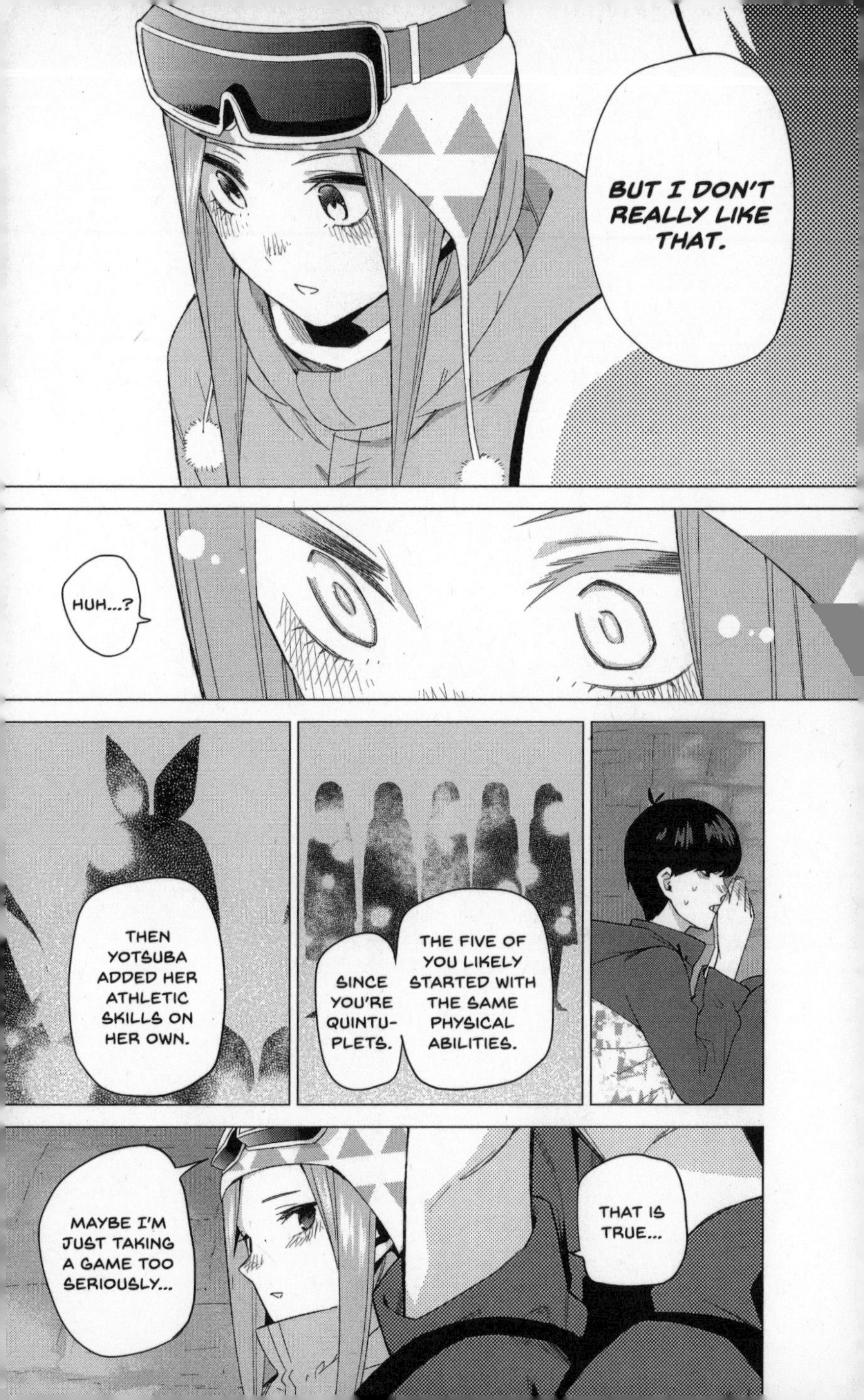
BUT I DON'T REALLY LIKE THAT.
HUH...?
THE FIVE OF YOU LIKELY STARTED WITH THE SAME PHYSICAL ABILITIES.
SINCE YOU'RE QUINTU-PLETS.
THEN YOTSUBA ADDED HER ATHLETIC SKILLS ON HER OWN.
THAT IS TRUE...
MAYBE I'M JUST TAKING A GAME TOO SERIOUSLY...

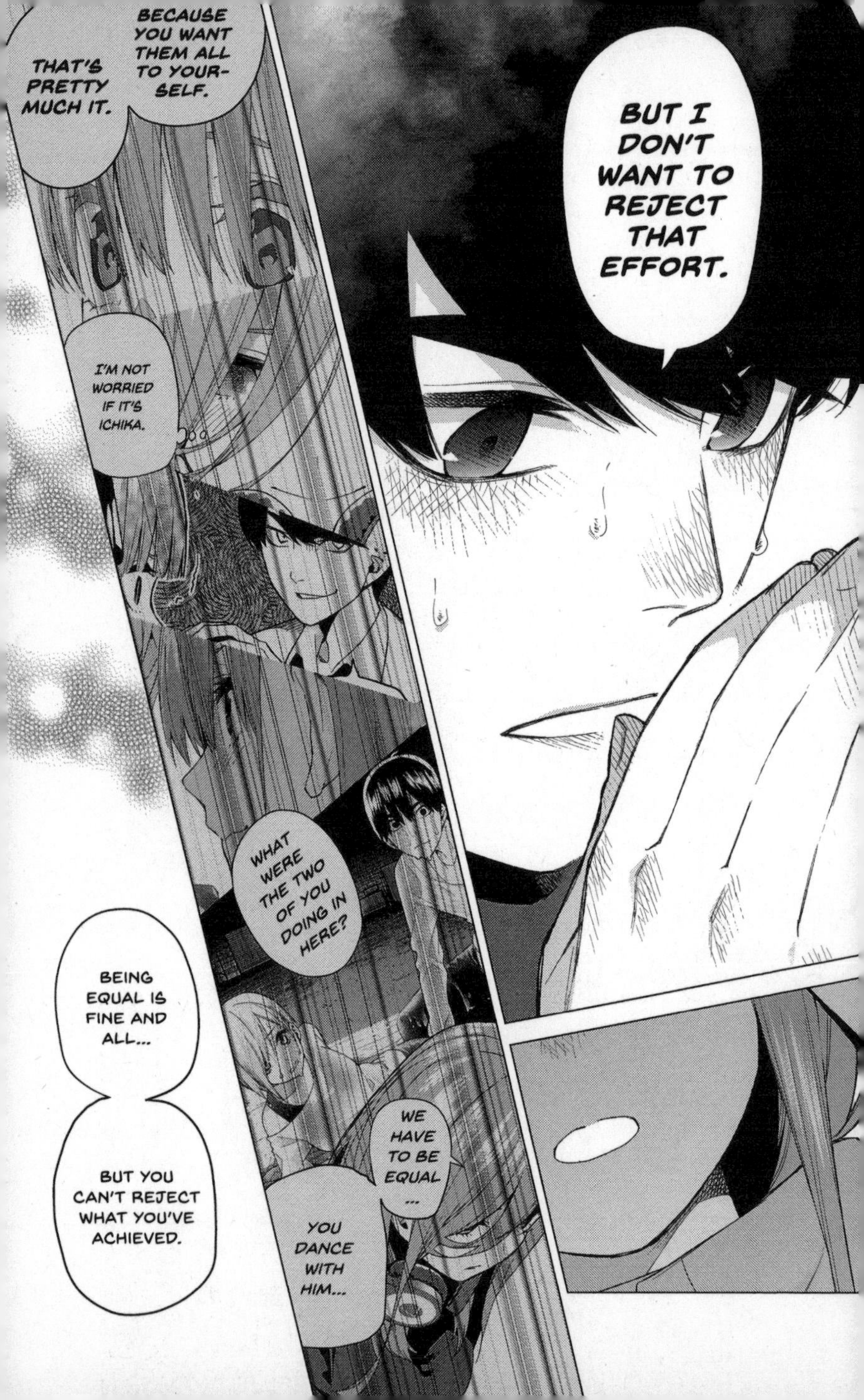
BUT I DON'T WANT TO REJECT THAT EFFORT.
BECAUSE YOU WANT THEM ALL TO YOUR-SELF.
THAT'S PRETTY MUCH IT.
I'M NOT WORRIED IF IT'S ICHIKA.
WHAT WERE THE TWO OF YOU DOING IN HERE?
WE HAVE TO BE EQUAL...
YOU DANCE WITH HIM...
BEING EQUAL IS FINE AND ALL...
BUT YOU CAN'T REJECT WHAT YOU'VE ACHIEVED.

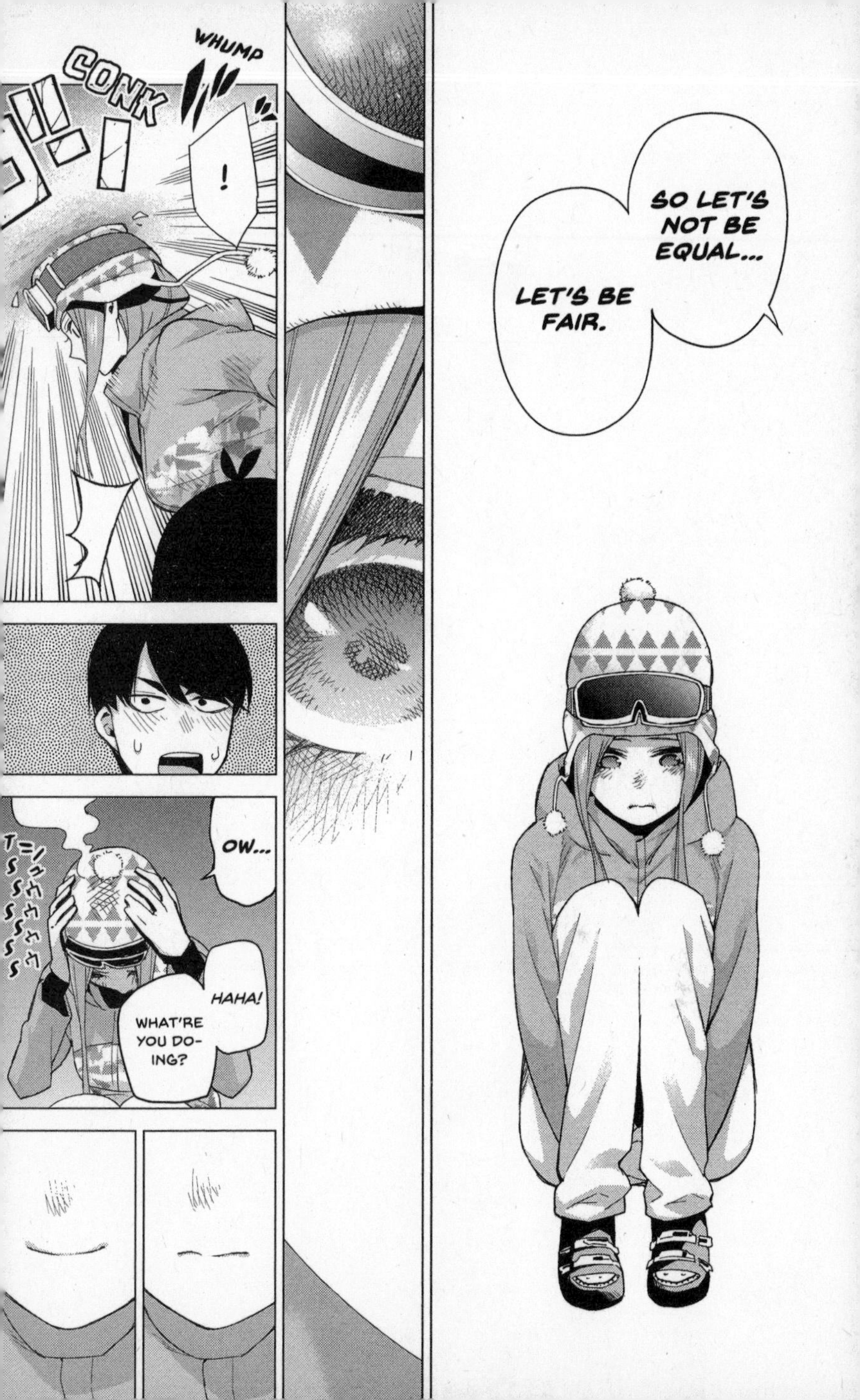
SO LET'S NOT BE EQUAL...
LET'S BE FAIR.
WHUMP
CONK
!
OW...
HAHA!
WHAT'RE YOU DO-ING?
TSSSSSS

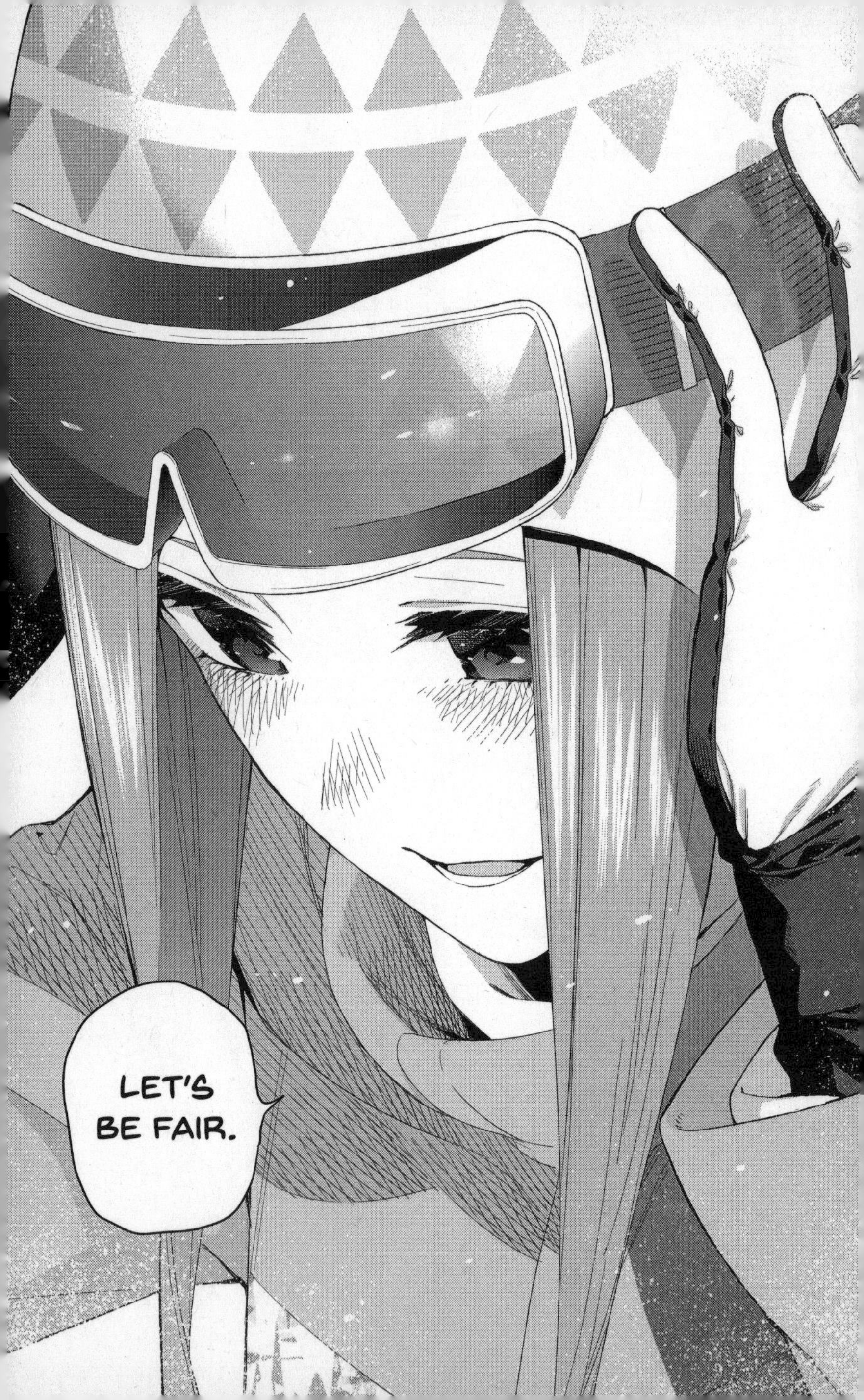
LET'S BE FAIR.

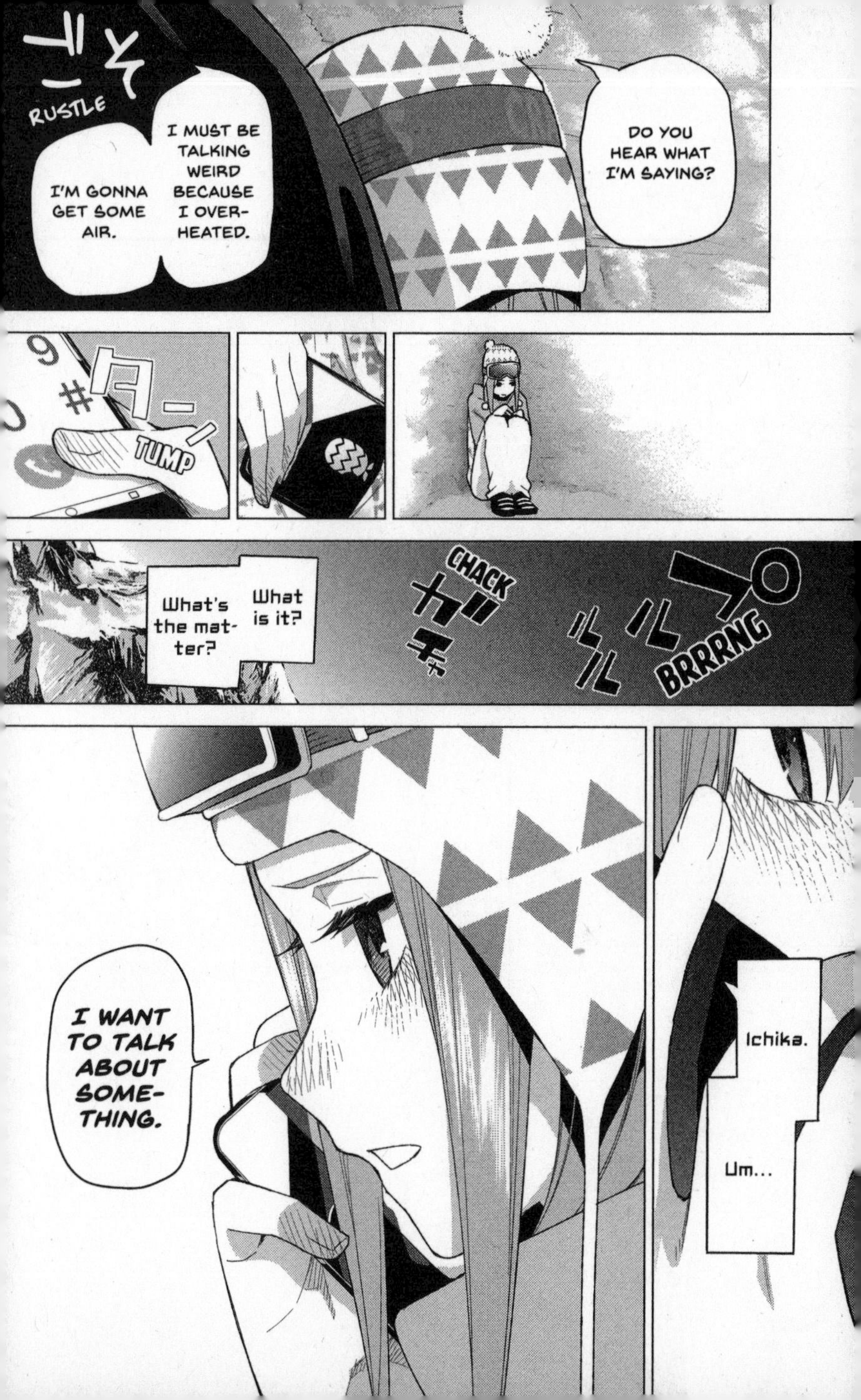
DO YOU HEAR WHAT I'M SAYING?
I MUST BE TALKING WEIRD BECAUSE I OVER-HEATED.
I'M GONNA GET SOME AIR.
RUSTLE
TUMP
BRRRNG
CHACK
What is it?
What's the mat-ter?
Ichika.
Um...
I WANT TO TALK ABOUT SOME-THING.

CHAPTER 30
THE BINDING LEGEND: DAY 3 ②

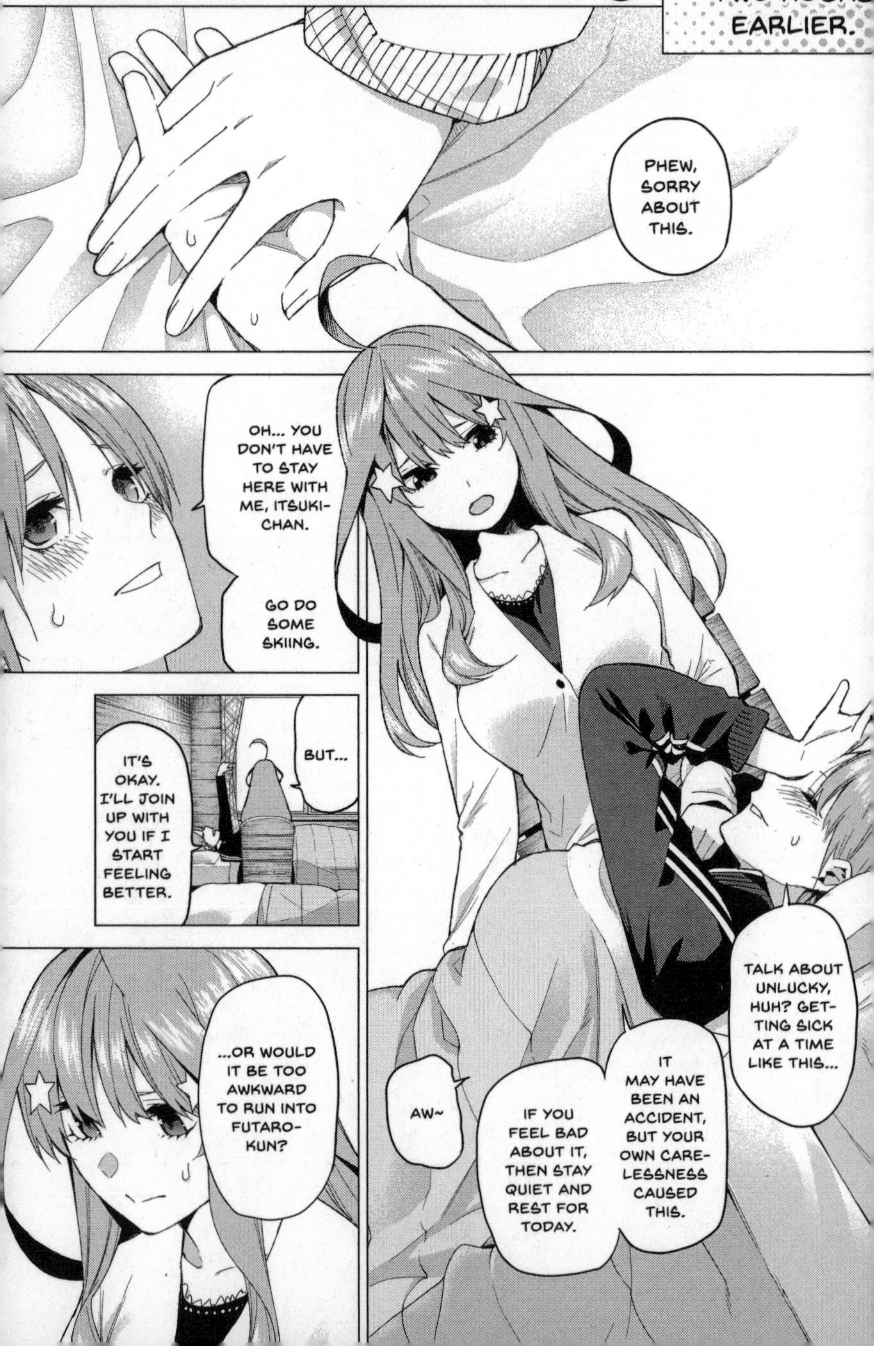

TWO HOURS EARLIER.
PHEW, SORRY ABOUT THIS.
TALK ABOUT UNLUCKY, HUH? GETTING SICK AT A TIME LIKE THIS...
IT MAY HAVE BEEN AN ACCIDENT, BUT YOUR OWN CARELESSNESS CAUSED THIS.
IF YOU FEEL BAD ABOUT IT, THEN STAY QUIET AND REST FOR TODAY.
AW~
OH... YOU DON'T HAVE TO STAY HERE WITH ME, ITSUKI-CHAN.
GO DO SOME SKIING.
BUT...
IT'S OKAY. I'LL JOIN UP WITH YOU IF I START FEELING BETTER.
...OR WOULD IT BE TOO AWKWARD TO RUN INTO FUTARO-KUN?

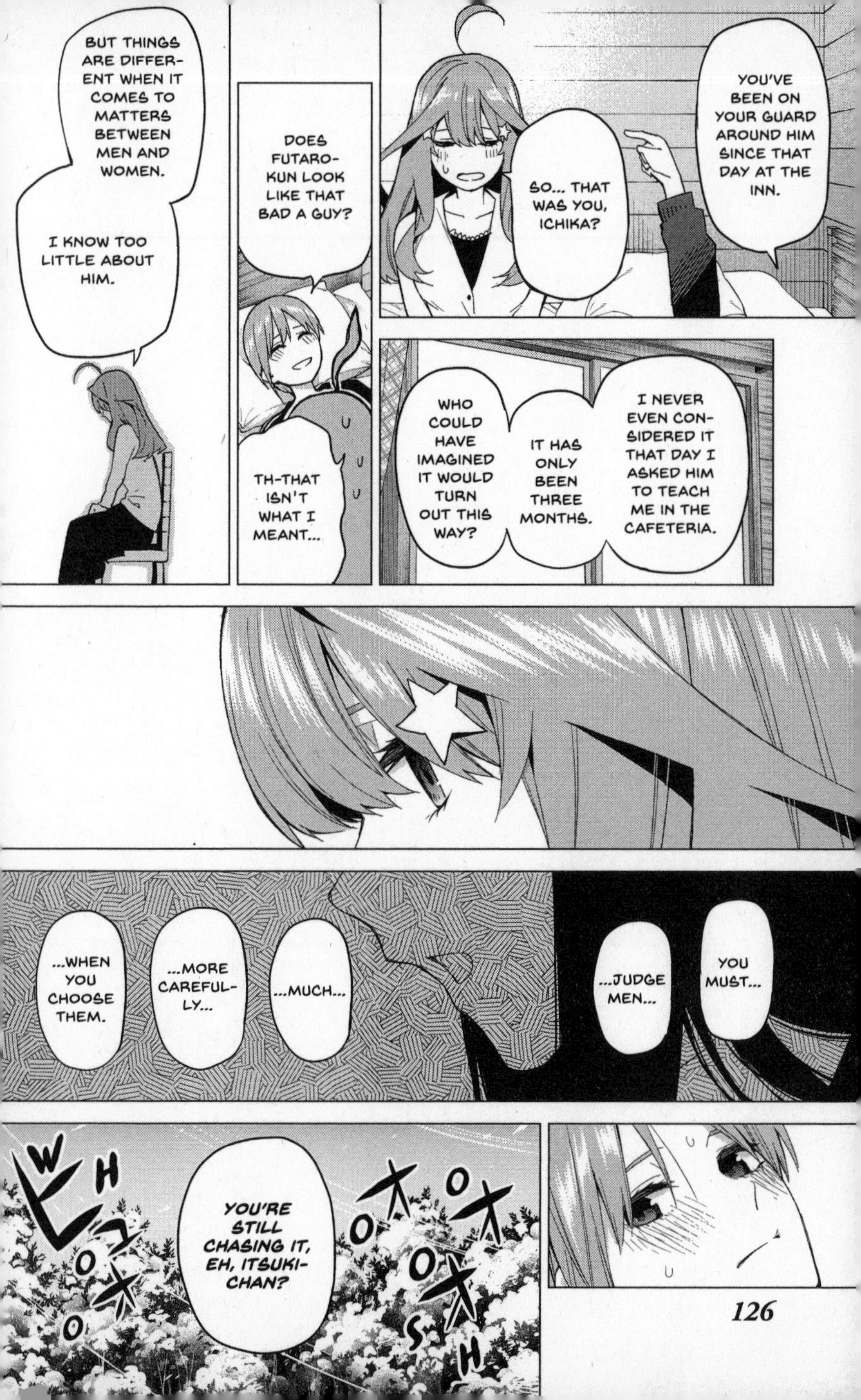
YOU'VE BEEN ON YOUR GUARD AROUND HIM SINCE THAT DAY AT THE INN.
SO... THAT WAS YOU, ICHIKA?
I NEVER EVEN CONSIDERED IT THAT DAY I ASKED HIM TO TEACH ME IN THE CAFETERIA.
IT HAS ONLY BEEN THREE MONTHS.
WHO COULD HAVE IMAGINED IT WOULD TURN OUT THIS WAY?
DOES FUTARO-KUN LOOK LIKE THAT BAD A GUY?
TH-THAT ISN'T WHAT I MEANT...
BUT THINGS ARE DIFFERENT WHEN IT COMES TO MATTERS BETWEEN MEN AND WOMEN.
I KNOW TOO LITTLE ABOUT HIM.
YOU MUST...
...JUDGE MEN...
...MUCH...
...MORE CAREFULLY...
...WHEN YOU CHOOSE THEM.
OOOOOSH
YOU'RE STILL CHASING IT, EH, ITSUKI-CHAN?
WHOO

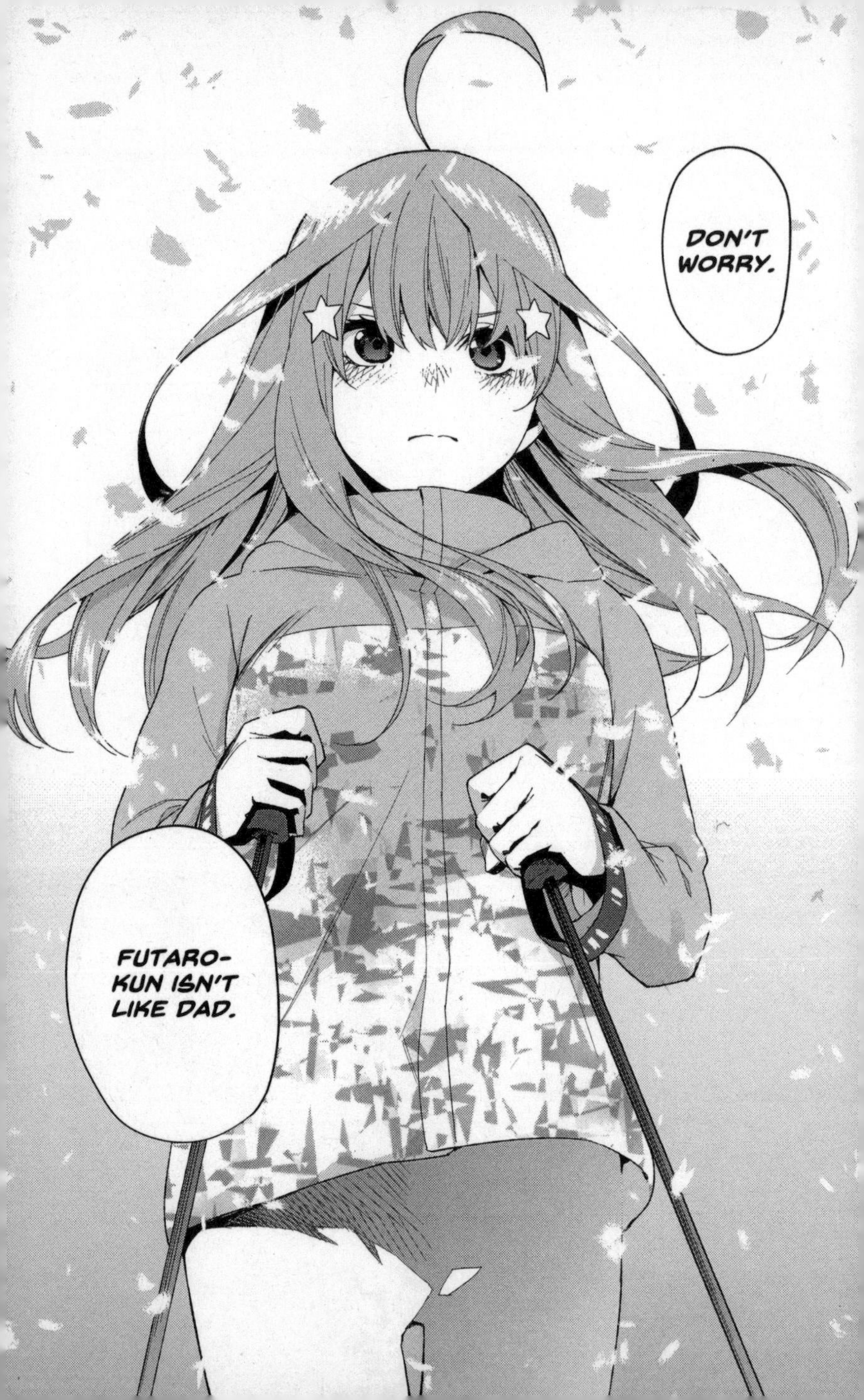
DON'T WORRY.
FUTARO-KUN ISN'T LIKE DAD.

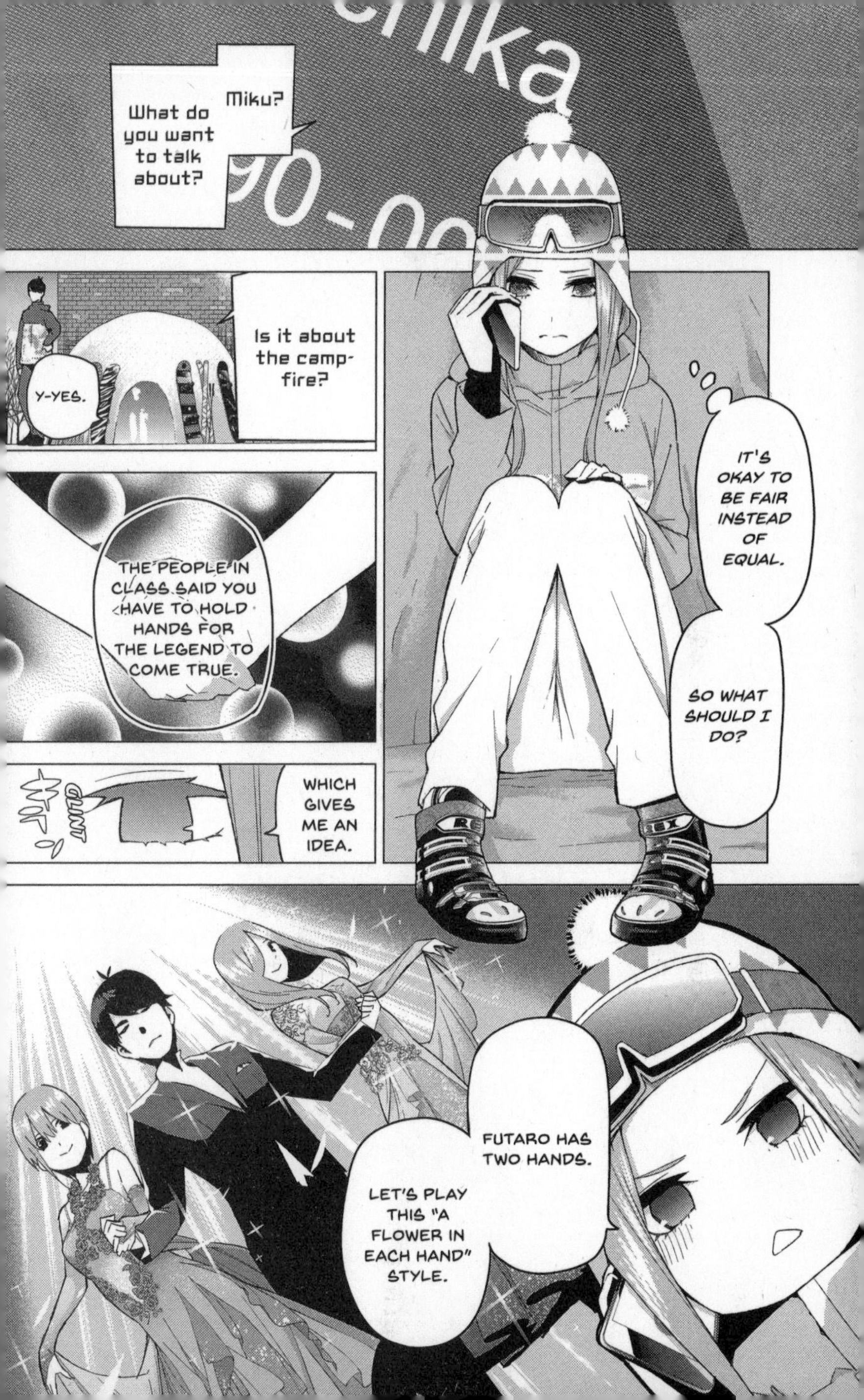
Miku?
What do you want to talk about?
IT'S OKAY TO BE FAIR INSTEAD OF EQUAL.
SO WHAT SHOULD I DO?
Is it about the camp-fire?
Y-YES.
THE PEOPLE IN CLASS SAID YOU HAVE TO HOLD HANDS FOR THE LEGEND TO COME TRUE.
WHICH GIVES ME AN IDEA.
CLINT
FUTARO HAS TWO HANDS.
LET'S PLAY THIS "A FLOWER IN EACH HAND" STYLE.

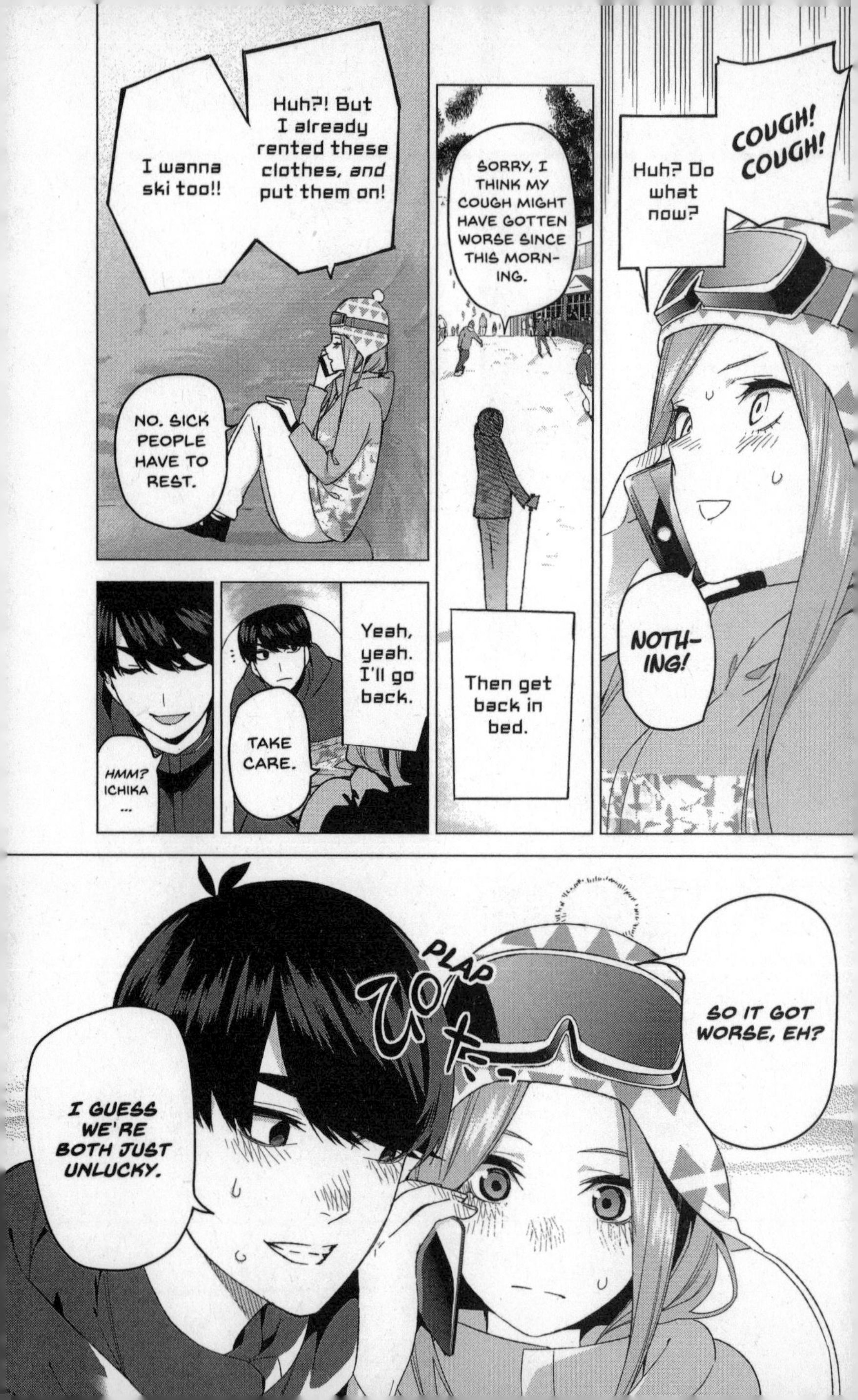
COUGH! COUGH!
Huh? Do what now?
NOTH-ING!
SORRY, I THINK MY COUGH MIGHT HAVE GOTTEN WORSE SINCE THIS MORN-ING.
Then get back in bed.
Huh?! But I already rented these clothes, *and* put them on!
I wanna ski too!!
NO. SICK PEOPLE HAVE TO REST.
Yeah, yeah. I'll go back.
TAKE CARE.
HMM? ICHIKA ...
SO IT GOT WORSE, EH?
PLAP
I GUESS WE'RE BOTH JUST UNLUCKY.

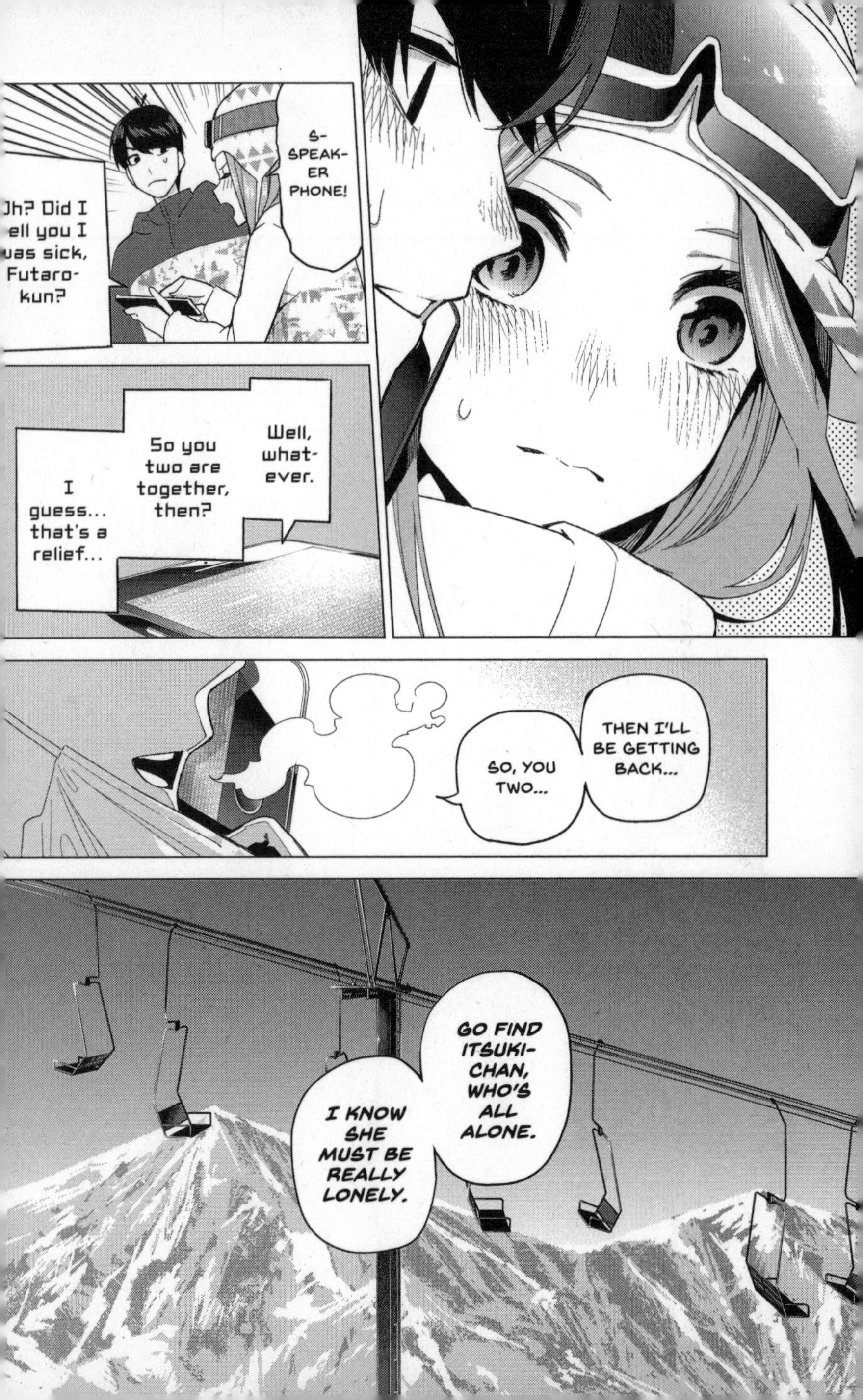
S-SPEAKER-PHONE!
h? Did I ell you I as sick, Futaro-kun?
Well, whatever.
So you two are together, then?
I guess... that's a relief...
THEN I'LL BE GETTING BACK...
SO, YOU TWO...
GO FIND ITSUKI-CHAN, WHO'S ALL ALONE.
I KNOW SHE MUST BE REALLY LONELY.

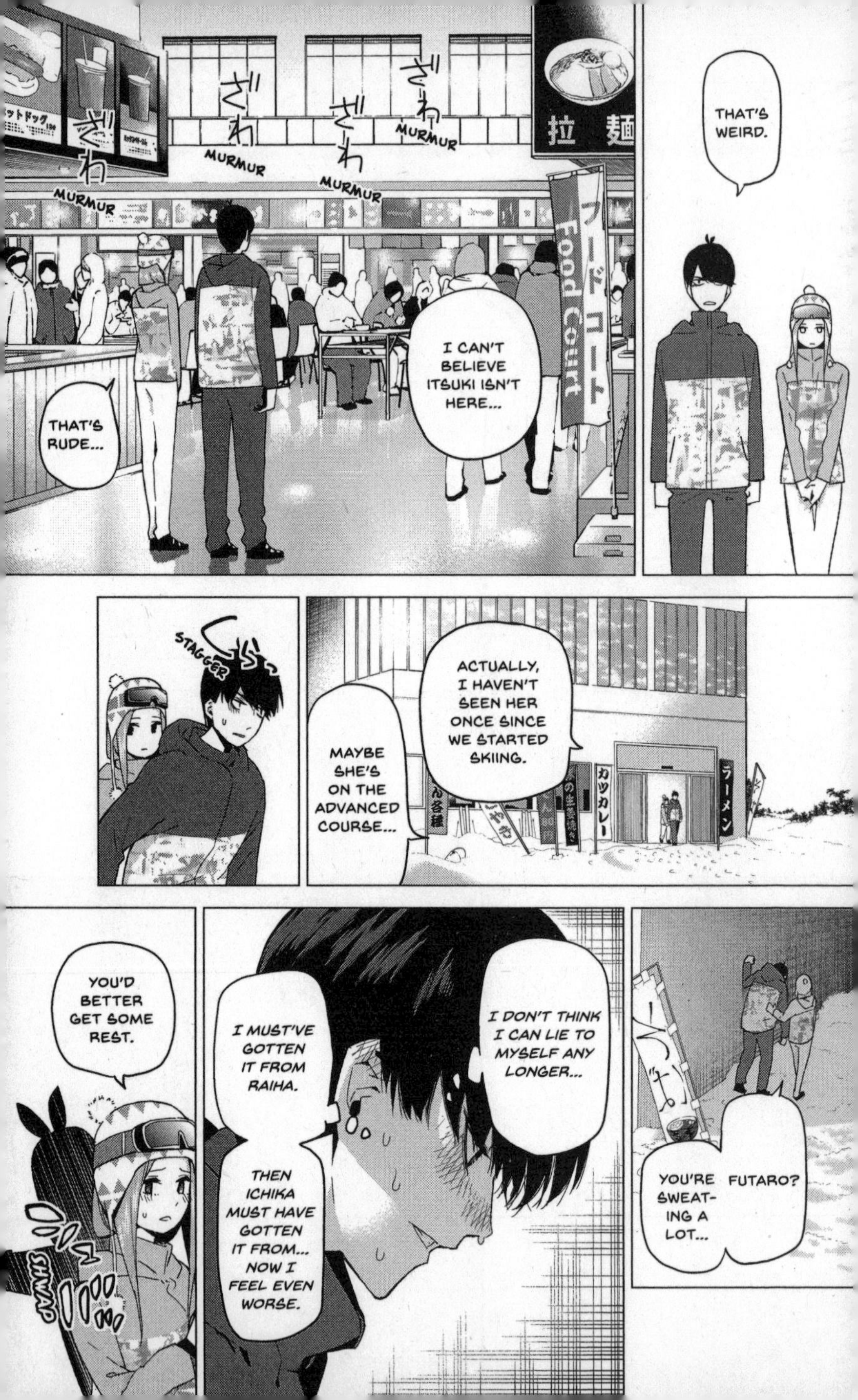
THAT'S WEIRD.
拉麺
ざわ
MURMUR
ざわ
MURMUR
ざわ
MURMUR
ざわ
MURMUR
フードコート
Food Court
I CAN'T BELIEVE ITSUKI ISN'T HERE...
THAT'S RUDE...
ACTUALLY, I HAVEN'T SEEN HER ONCE SINCE WE STARTED SKIING.
MAYBE SHE'S ON THE ADVANCED COURSE...
ラーメン
カツカレー
STAGGER
FUTARO?
YOU'RE SWEAT-ING A LOT...
I DON'T THINK I CAN LIE TO MYSELF ANY LONGER...
I MUST'VE GOTTEN IT FROM RAIHA.
THEN ICHIKA MUST HAVE GOTTEN IT FROM... NOW I FEEL EVEN WORSE.
YOU'D BETTER GET SOME REST.
SHWAP

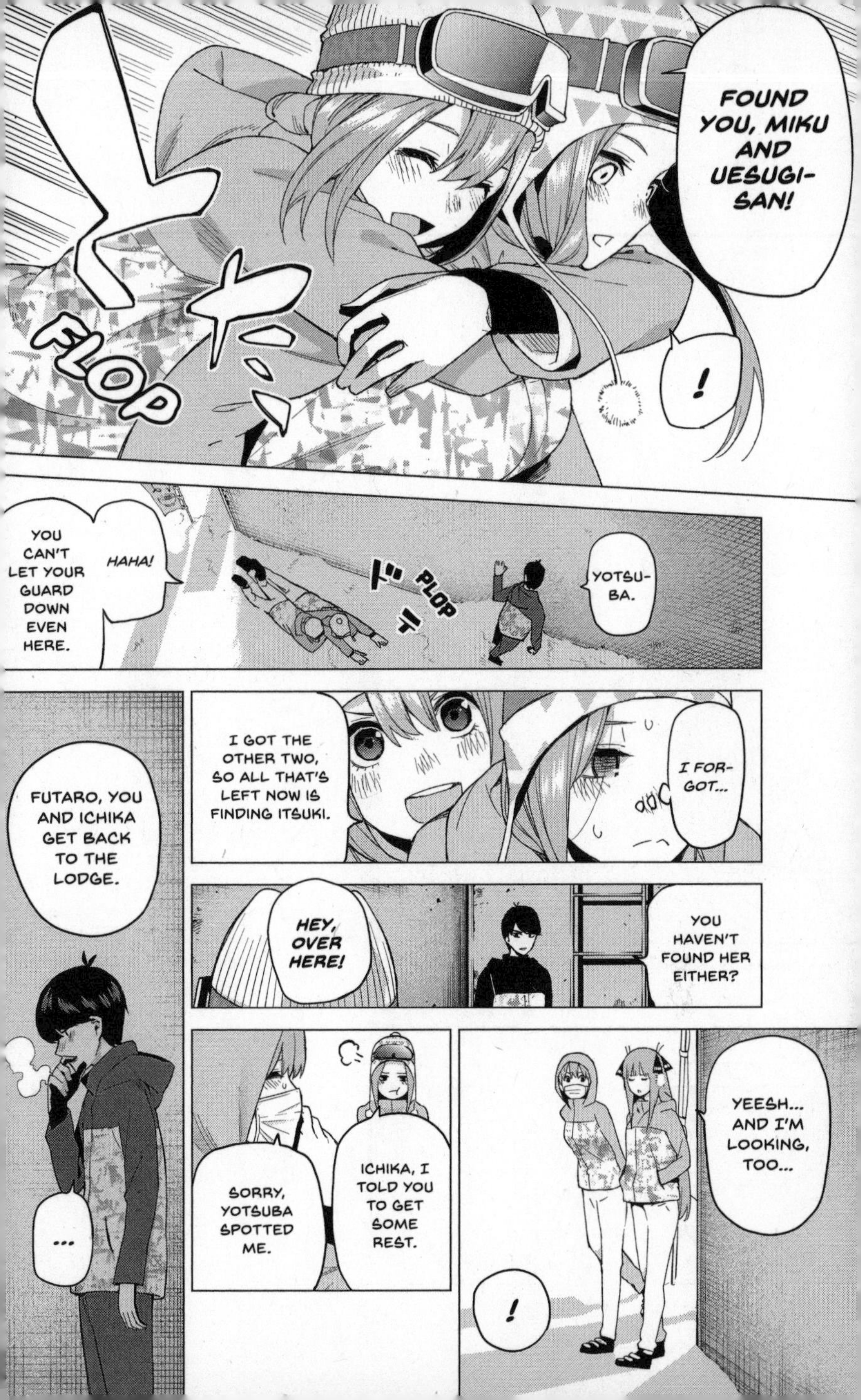
FOUND YOU, MIKU AND UESUGI-SAN!
!
FLOP
YOTSU-BA.
PLOP
HAHA!
YOU CAN'T LET YOUR GUARD DOWN EVEN HERE.
I FOR-GOT...
I GOT THE OTHER TWO, SO ALL THAT'S LEFT NOW IS FINDING ITSUKI.
YOU HAVEN'T FOUND HER EITHER?
HEY, OVER HERE!
YEESH... AND I'M LOOKING, TOO...
!
ICHIKA, I TOLD YOU TO GET SOME REST.
SORRY, YOTSUBA SPOTTED ME.
FUTARO, YOU AND ICHIKA GET BACK TO THE LODGE.
...

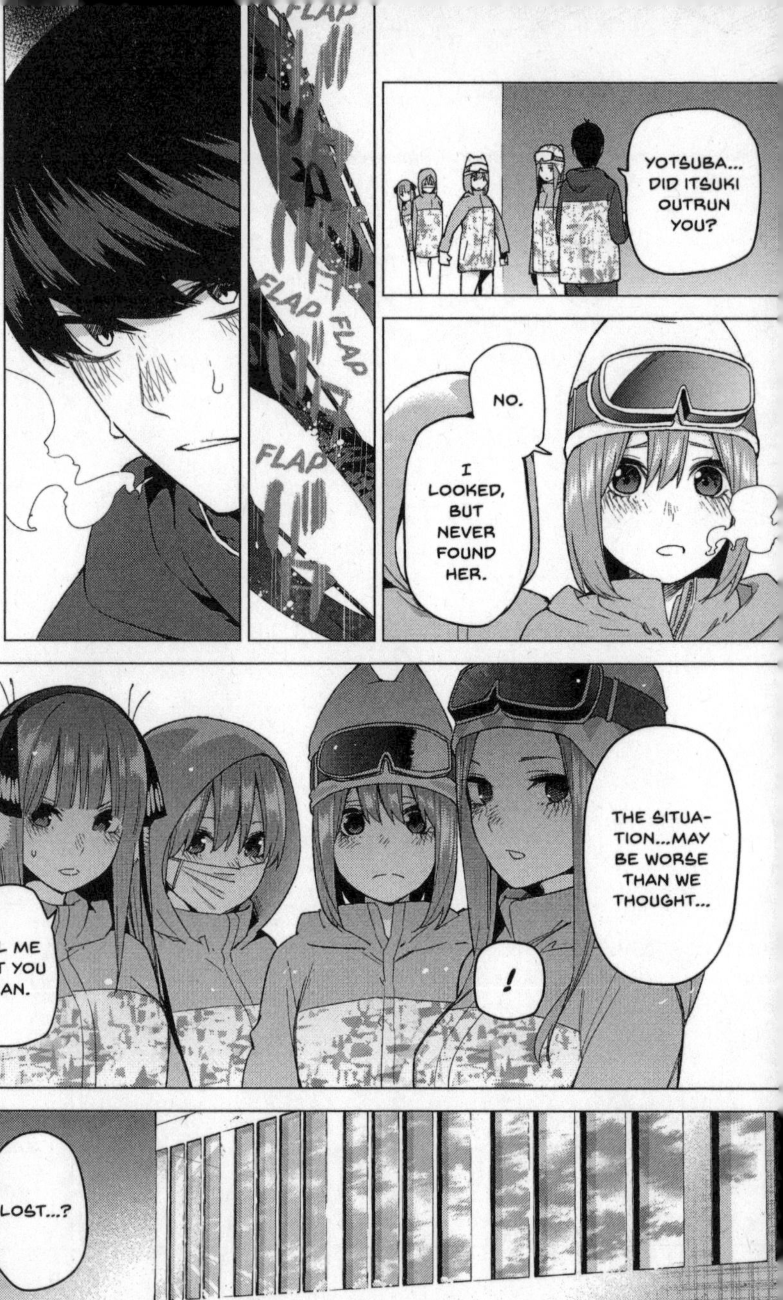
YOTSUBA... DID ITSUKI OUTRUN YOU?
NO.
I LOOKED, BUT NEVER FOUND HER.
FLAP
FLAP
FLAP
FLAP
THE SITUA-TION...MAY BE WORSE THAN WE THOUGHT...
!
TELL ME WHAT YOU MEAN.
LOST...?

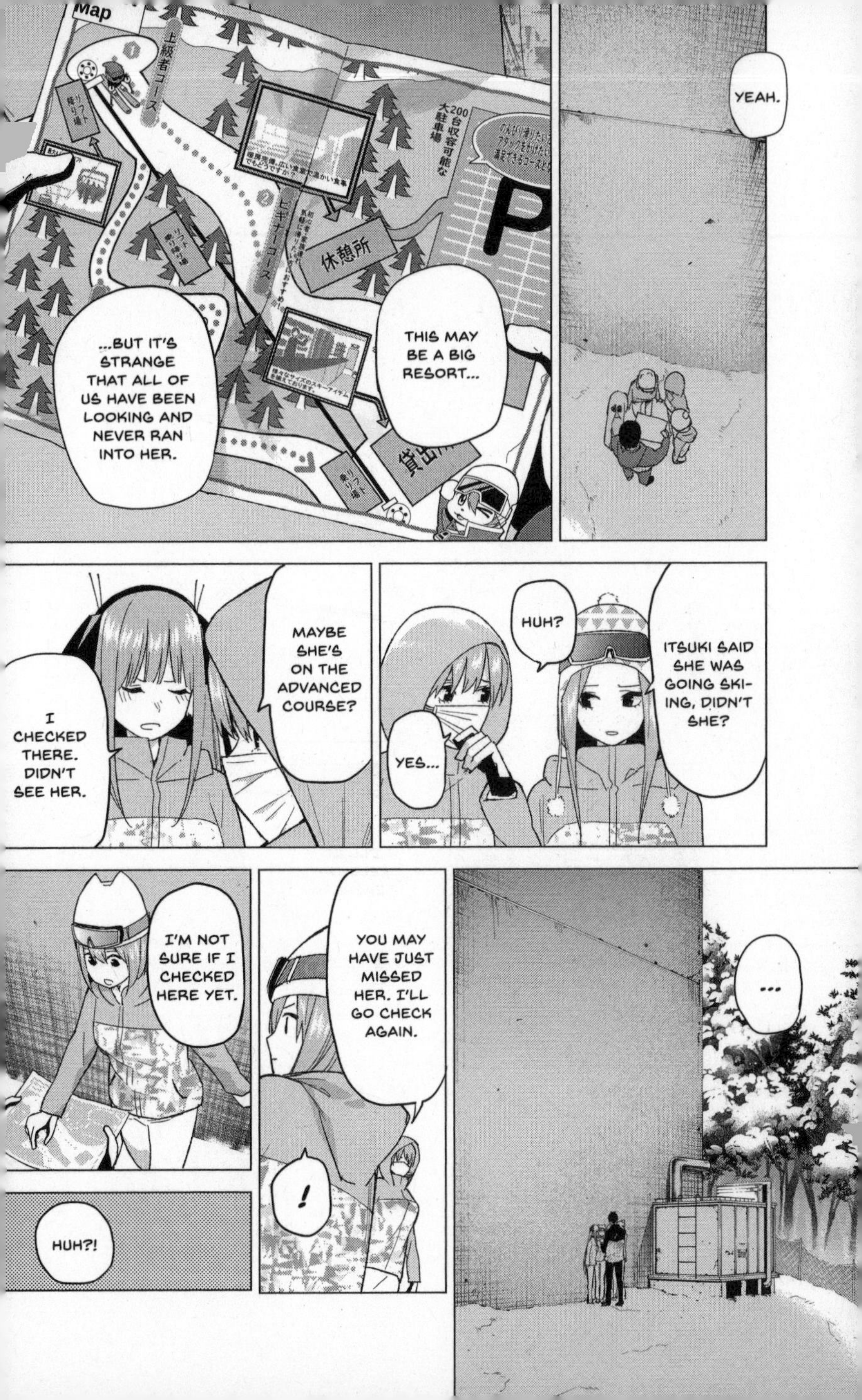
YEAH.
Map
上級者コース
200台収容可能大駐車場
休憩所
ビギナーコース
P
THIS MAY BE A BIG RESORT...
...BUT IT'S STRANGE THAT ALL OF US HAVE BEEN LOOKING AND NEVER RAN INTO HER.
ITSUKI SAID SHE WAS GOING SKI-ING, DIDN'T SHE?
HUH?
YES...
MAYBE SHE'S ON THE ADVANCED COURSE?
I CHECKED THERE. DIDN'T SEE HER.
...
YOU MAY HAVE JUST MISSED HER. I'LL GO CHECK AGAIN.
!
I'M NOT SURE IF I CHECKED HERE YET.
HUH?!

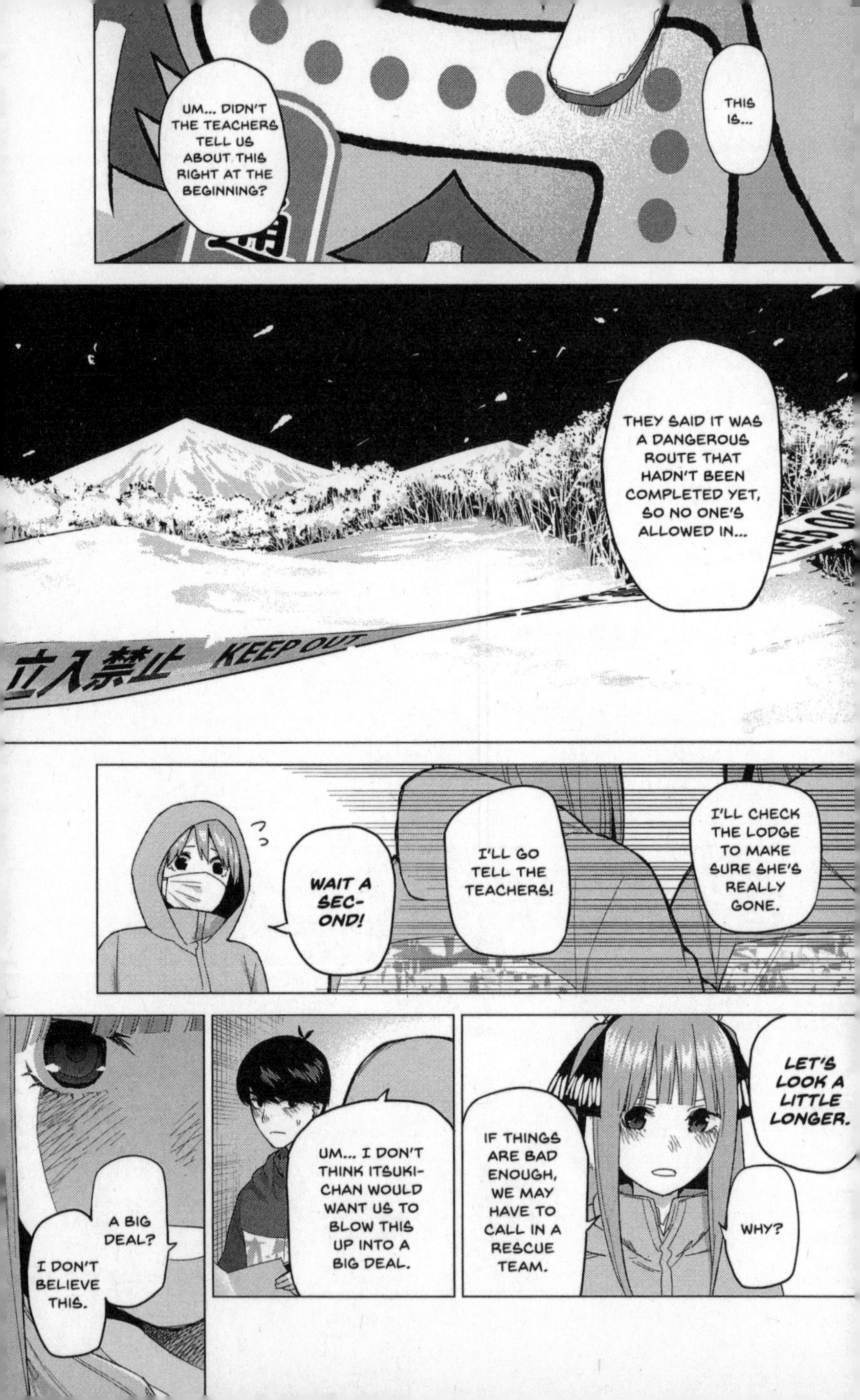
THIS IS...
UM... DIDN'T THE TEACHERS TELL US ABOUT THIS RIGHT AT THE BEGINNING?
THEY SAID IT WAS A DANGEROUS ROUTE THAT HADN'T BEEN COMPLETED YET, SO NO ONE'S ALLOWED IN...
立入禁止 KEEP OUT
I'LL CHECK THE LODGE TO MAKE SURE SHE'S REALLY GONE.
I'LL GO TELL THE TEACHERS!
WAIT A SEC-OND!
LET'S LOOK A LITTLE LONGER.
WHY?
IF THINGS ARE BAD ENOUGH, WE MAY HAVE TO CALL IN A RESCUE TEAM.
UM... I DON'T THINK ITSUKI-CHAN WOULD WANT US TO BLOW THIS UP INTO A BIG DEAL.
A BIG DEAL?
I DON'T BELIEVE THIS.

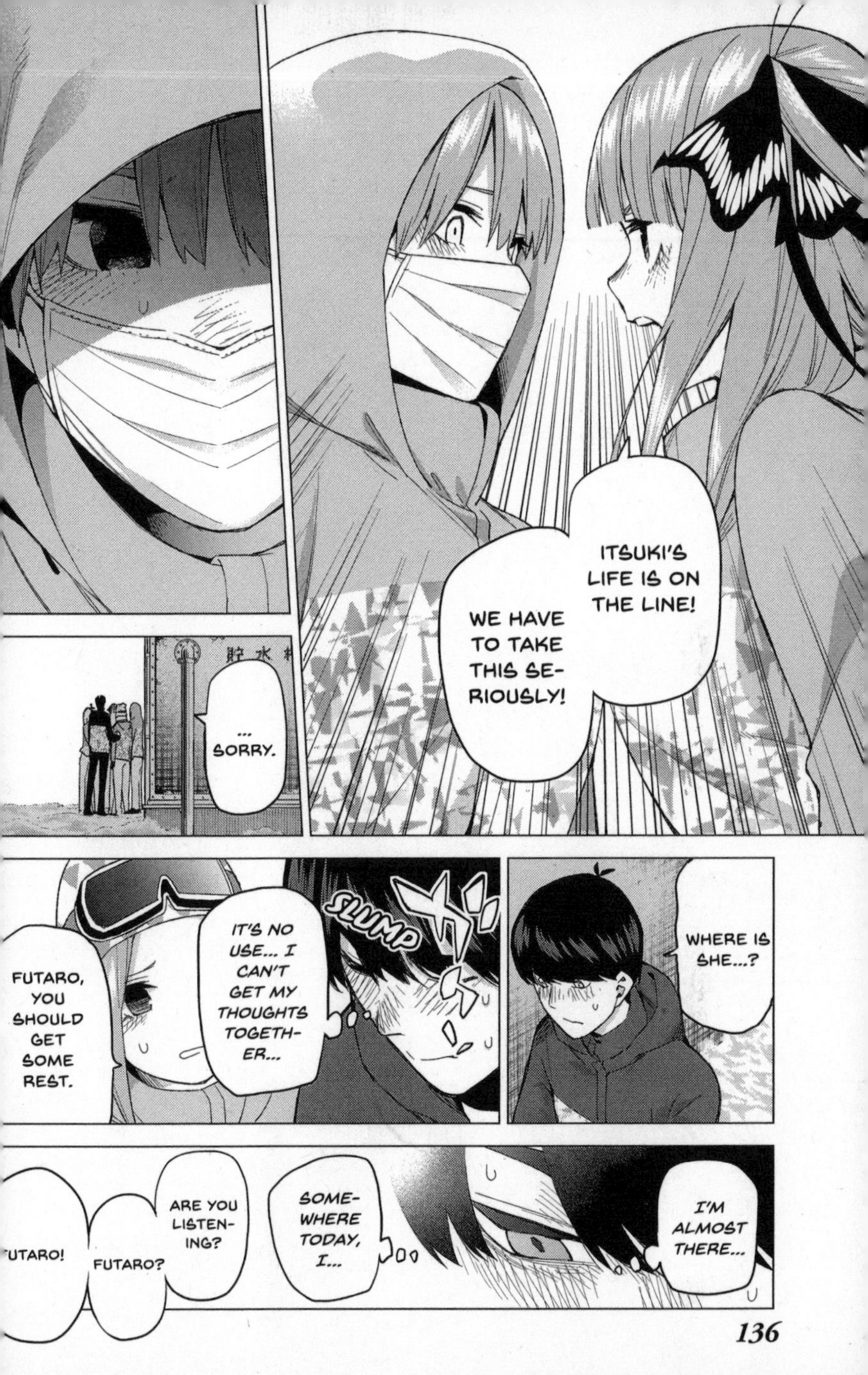
ITSUKI'S LIFE IS ON THE LINE!
WE HAVE TO TAKE THIS SE-RIOUSLY!
... SORRY.
WHERE IS SHE...?
IT'S NO USE... I CAN'T GET MY THOUGHTS TOGETH-ER...
SLUMP
FUTARO, YOU SHOULD GET SOME REST.
I'M ALMOST THERE...
SOME-WHERE TODAY, I...
ARE YOU LISTEN-ING?
FUTARO?
FUTARO!

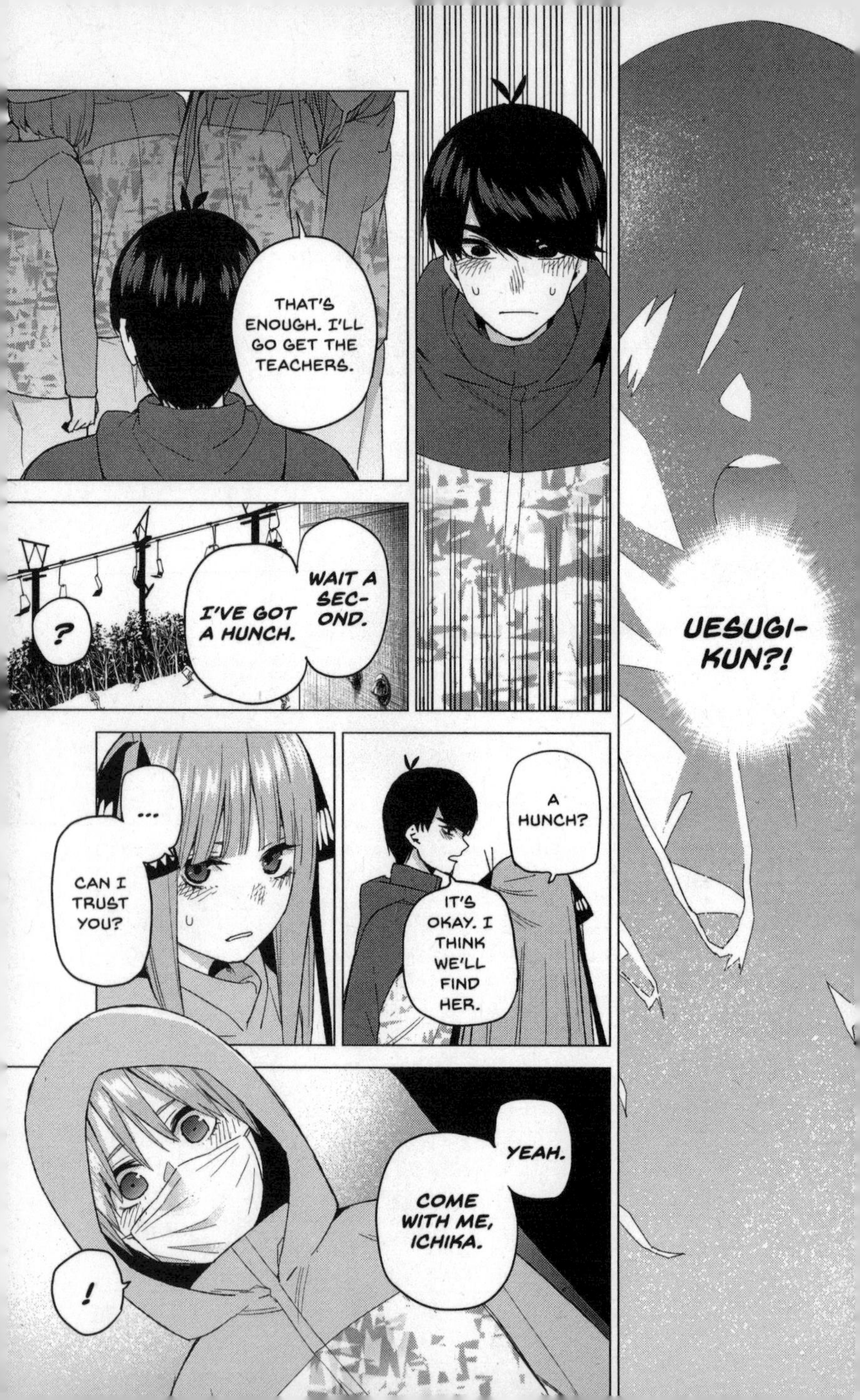
UESUGI-KUN?!
THAT'S ENOUGH. I'LL GO GET THE TEACHERS.
WAIT A SEC-OND.
I'VE GOT A HUNCH.
?
A HUNCH?
IT'S OKAY. I THINK WE'LL FIND HER.
...
CAN I TRUST YOU?
YEAH.
COME WITH ME, ICHIKA.
!

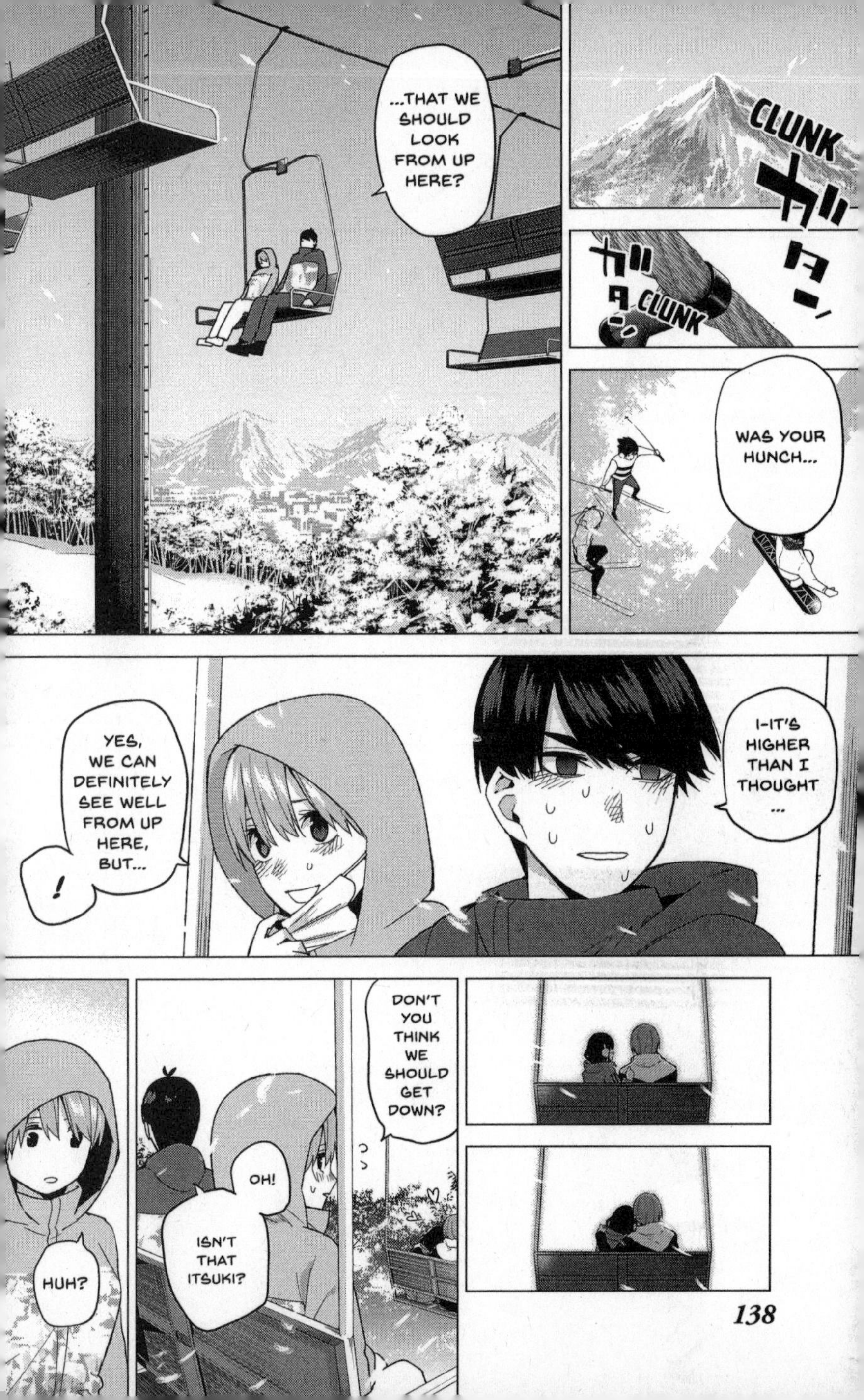
CLUNK
CLUNK
WAS YOUR HUNCH...
...THAT WE SHOULD LOOK FROM UP HERE?
I-IT'S HIGHER THAN I THOUGHT...
YES, WE CAN DEFINITELY SEE WELL FROM UP HERE, BUT...
!
DON'T YOU THINK WE SHOULD GET DOWN?
OH!
ISN'T THAT ITSUKI?
HUH?

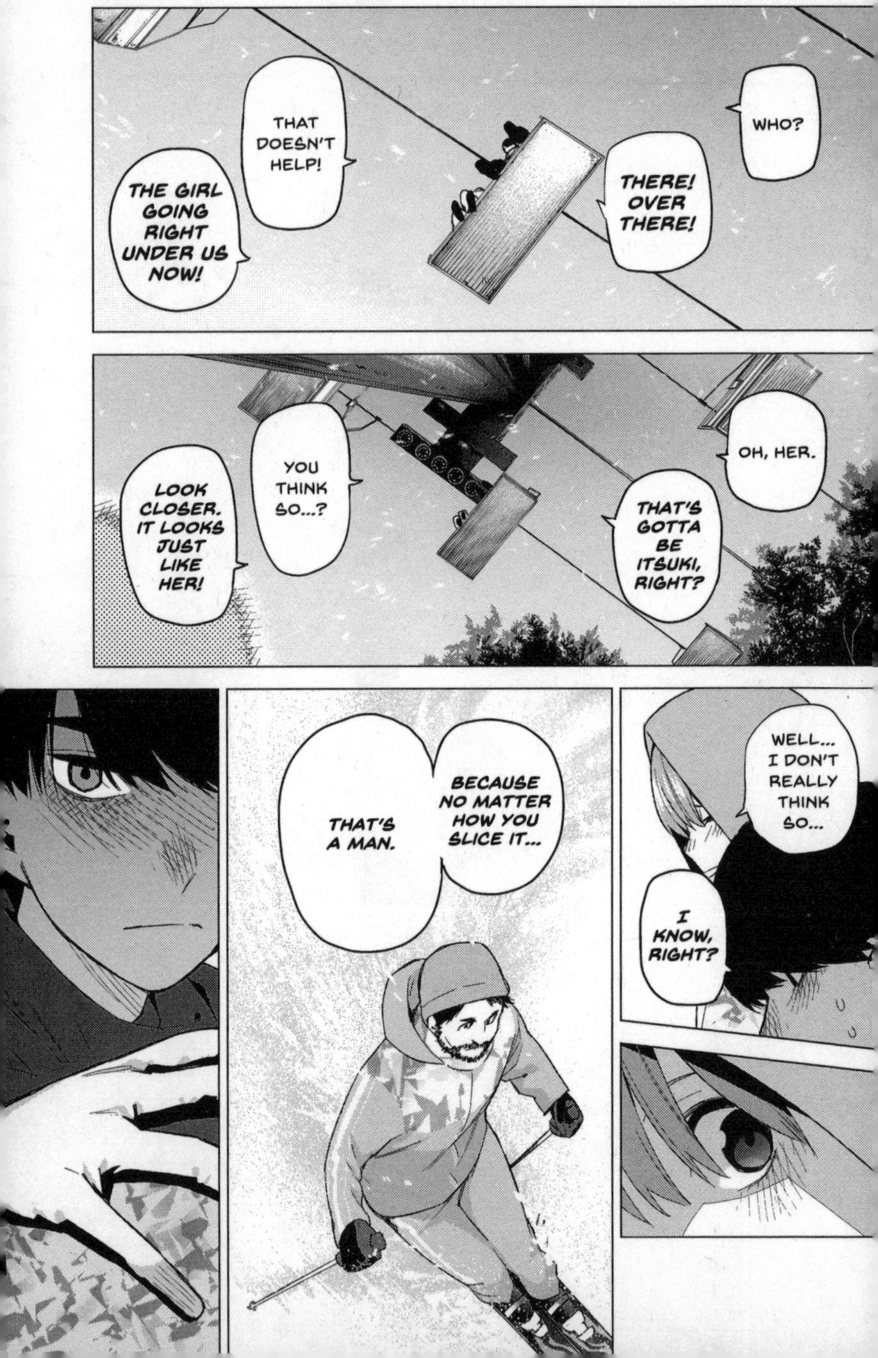
WHO?
THERE! OVER THERE!
THAT DOESN'T HELP!
THE GIRL GOING RIGHT UNDER US NOW!
OH, HER.
THAT'S GOTTA BE ITSUKI, RIGHT?
YOU THINK SO...?
LOOK CLOSER. IT LOOKS JUST LIKE HER!
WELL... I DON'T REALLY THINK SO...
I KNOW, RIGHT?
BECAUSE NO MATTER HOW YOU SLICE IT...
THAT'S A MAN.

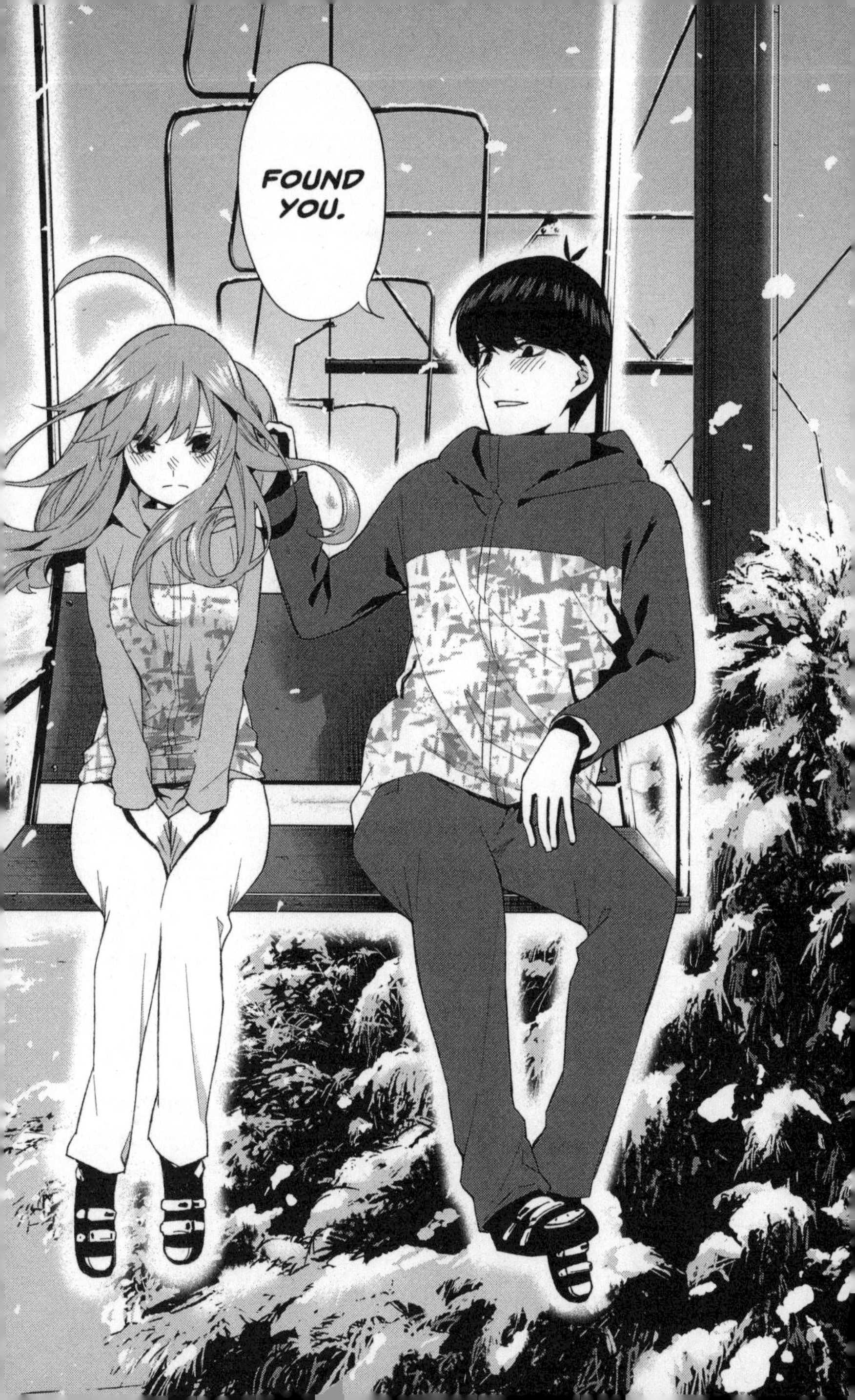
FOUND YOU.

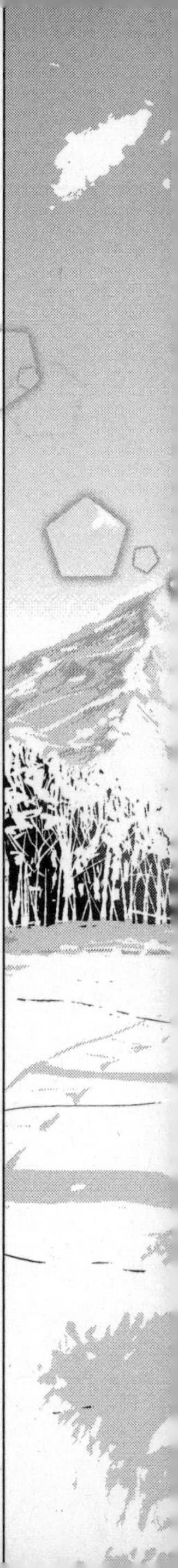

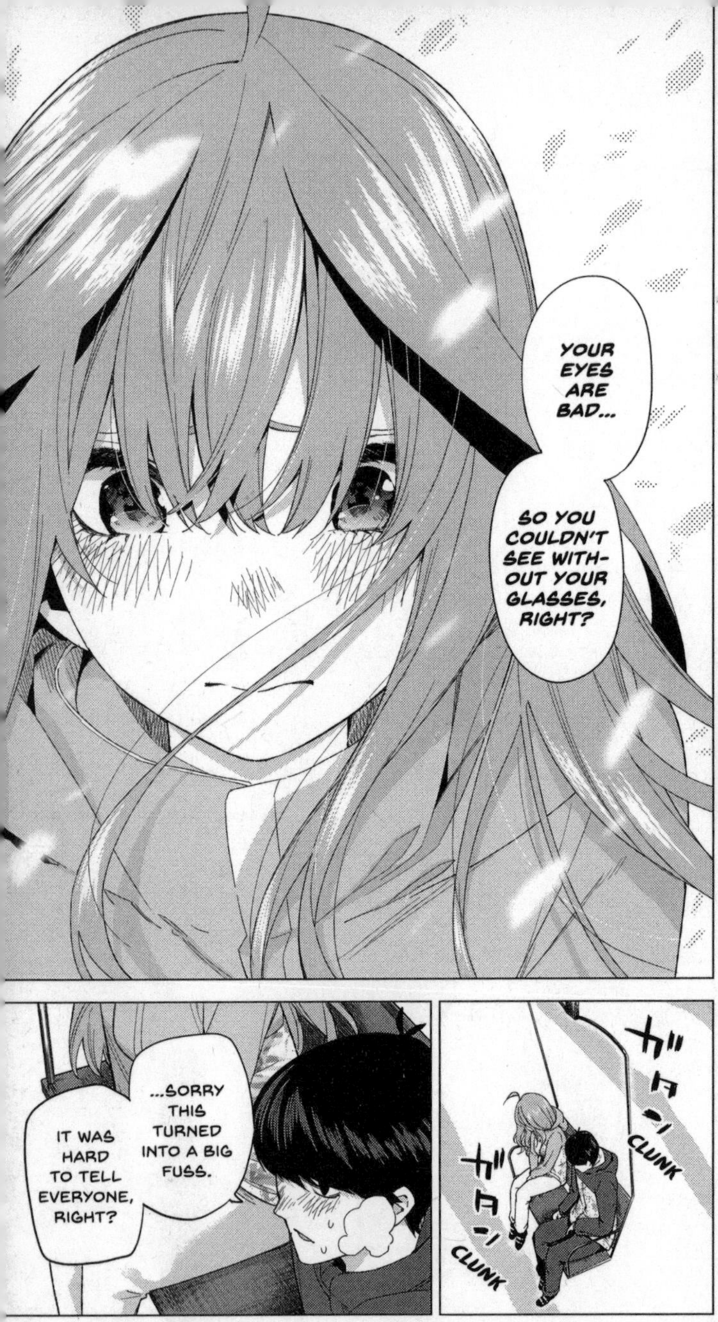
YOUR EYES ARE BAD...
SO YOU COULDN'T SEE WITH-OUT YOUR GLASSES, RIGHT?
ガタッ
CLUNK
ガタッ
CLUNK
...SORRY THIS TURNED INTO A BIG FUSS.
IT WAS HARD TO TELL EVERYONE, RIGHT?

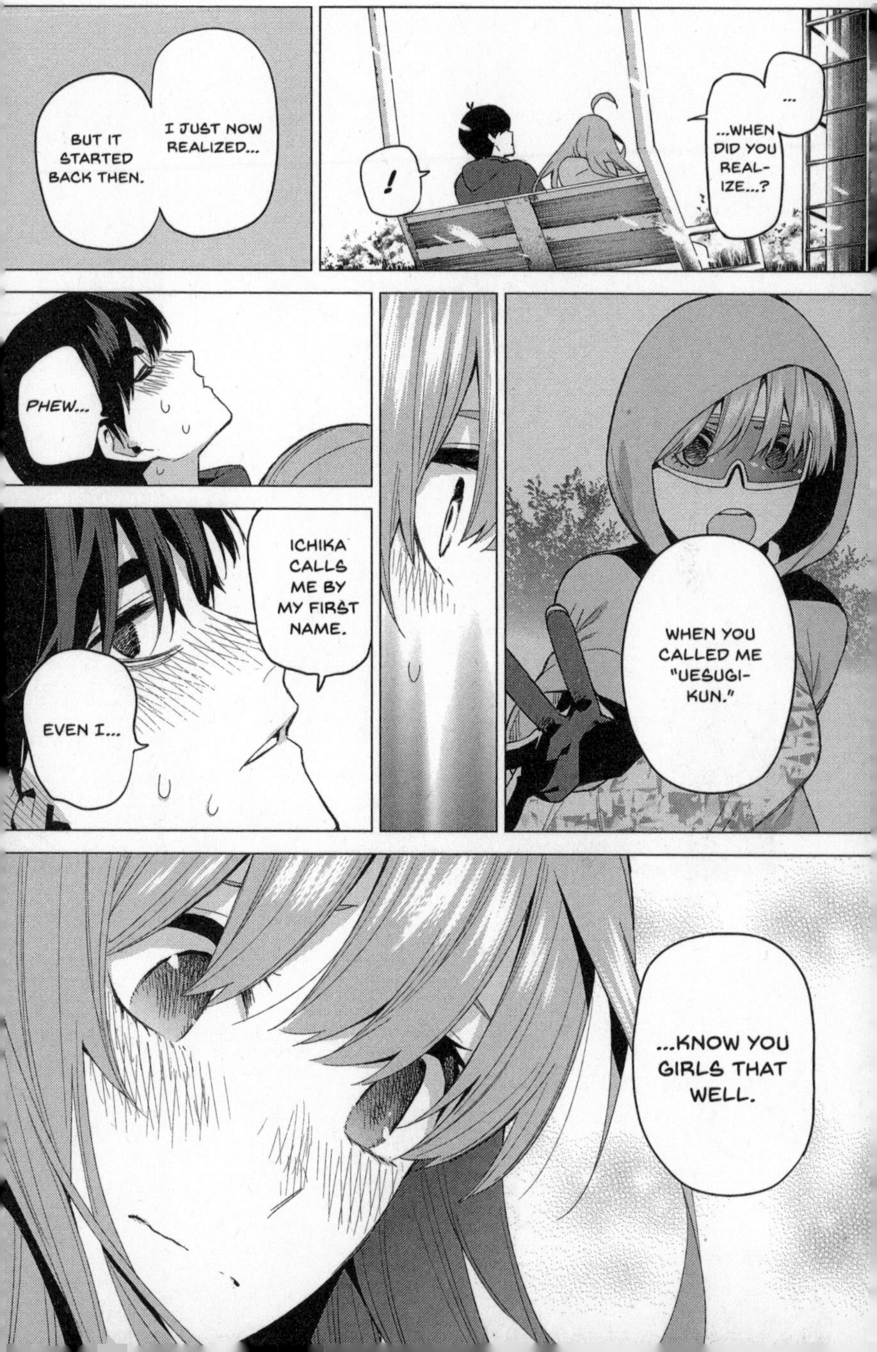
...
...WHEN DID YOU REAL-IZE...?
!
I JUST NOW REALIZED...
BUT IT STARTED BACK THEN.
WHEN YOU CALLED ME "UESUGI-KUN."
PHEW...
ICHIKA CALLS ME BY MY FIRST NAME.
EVEN I...
...KNOW YOU GIRLS THAT WELL.

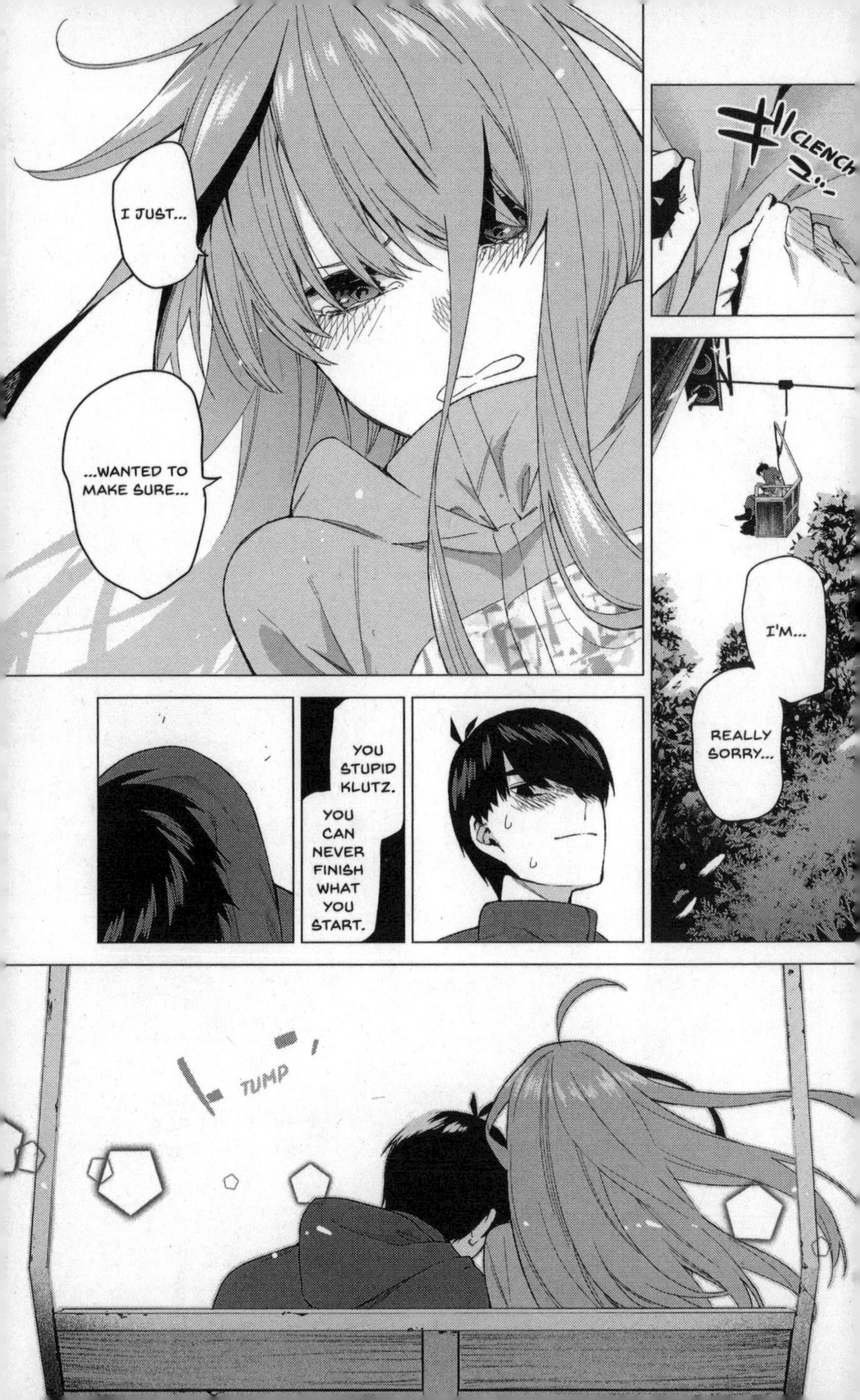
CLENCH
I JUST...
...WANTED TO MAKE SURE...
I'M...
REALLY SORRY...
YOU STUPID KLUTZ.
YOU CAN NEVER FINISH WHAT YOU START.
TUMP

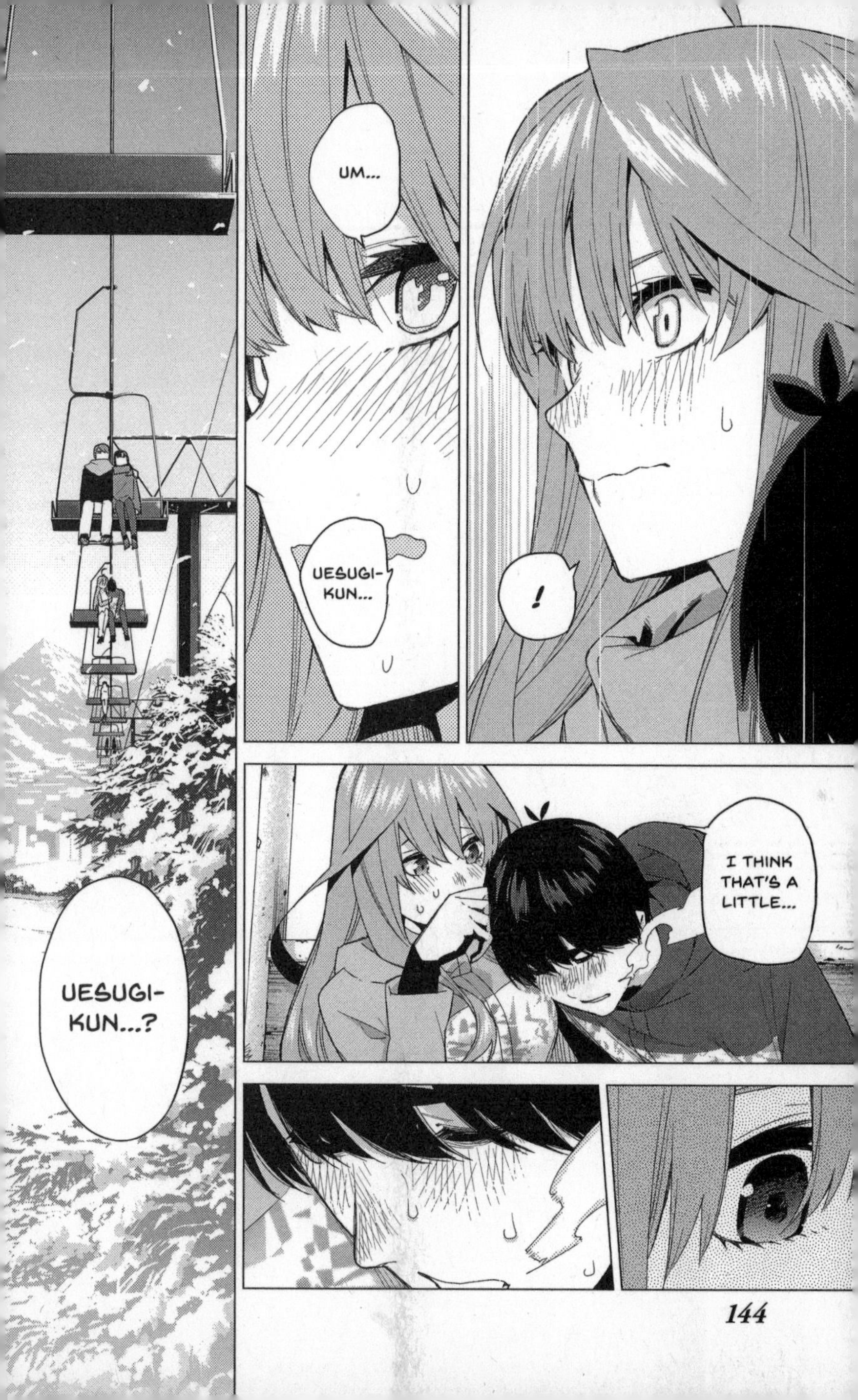
!
UM...
UESUGI-KUN...
I THINK THAT'S A LITTLE...
UESUGI-KUN...?

CHAPTER 31
THE BINDING LEGEND: DAY 3 ③

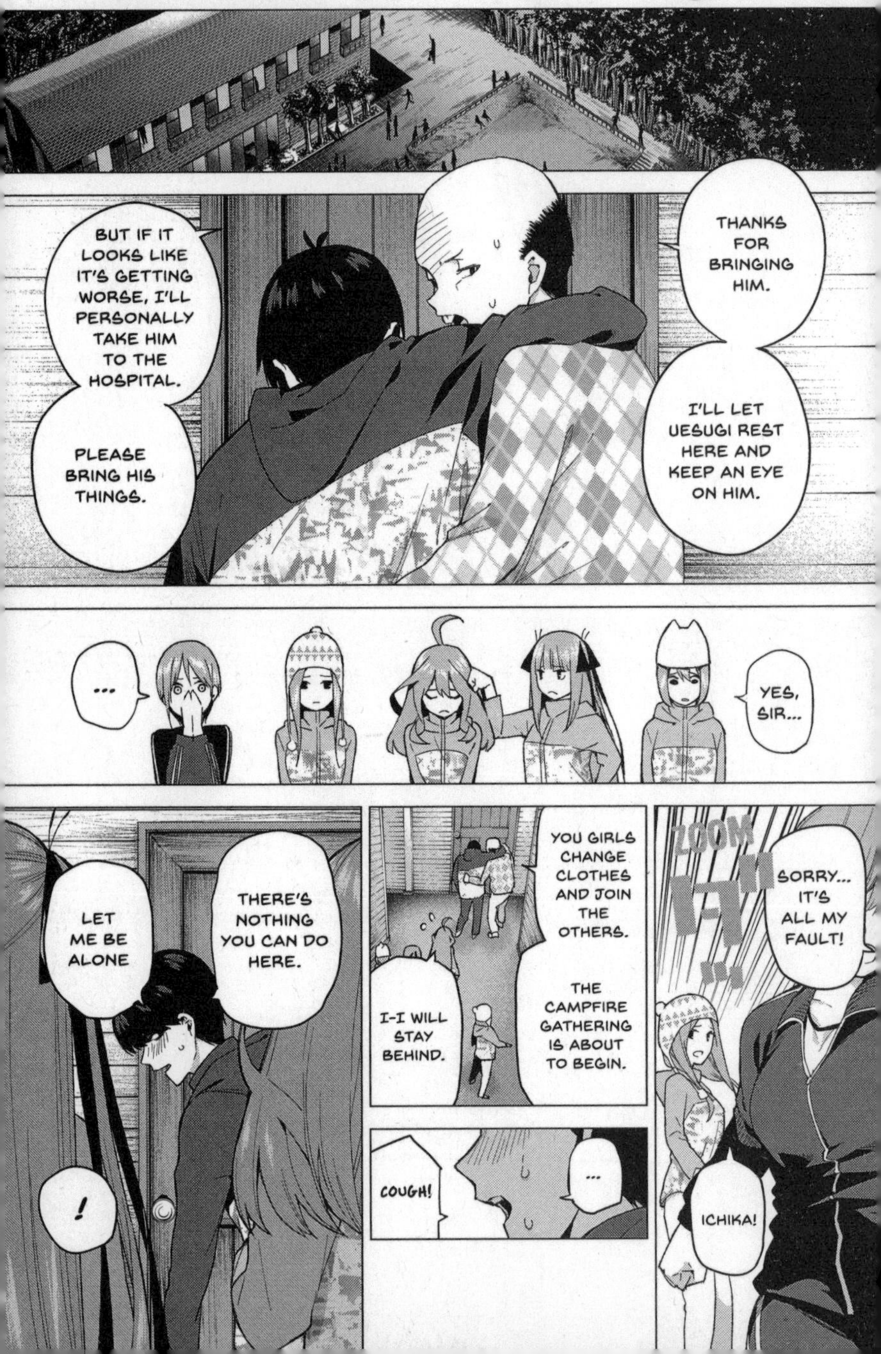
THANKS FOR BRINGING HIM.
I'LL LET UESUGI REST HERE AND KEEP AN EYE ON HIM.
BUT IF IT LOOKS LIKE IT'S GETTING WORSE, I'LL PERSONALLY TAKE HIM TO THE HOSPITAL.
PLEASE BRING HIS THINGS.
YES, SIR...
...
ZOOM
SORRY... IT'S ALL MY FAULT!
ICHIKA!
YOU GIRLS CHANGE CLOTHES AND JOIN THE OTHERS.
THE CAMPFIRE GATHERING IS ABOUT TO BEGIN.
I-I WILL STAY BEHIND.
...
COUGH!
THERE'S NOTHING YOU CAN DO HERE.
LET ME BE ALONE
!

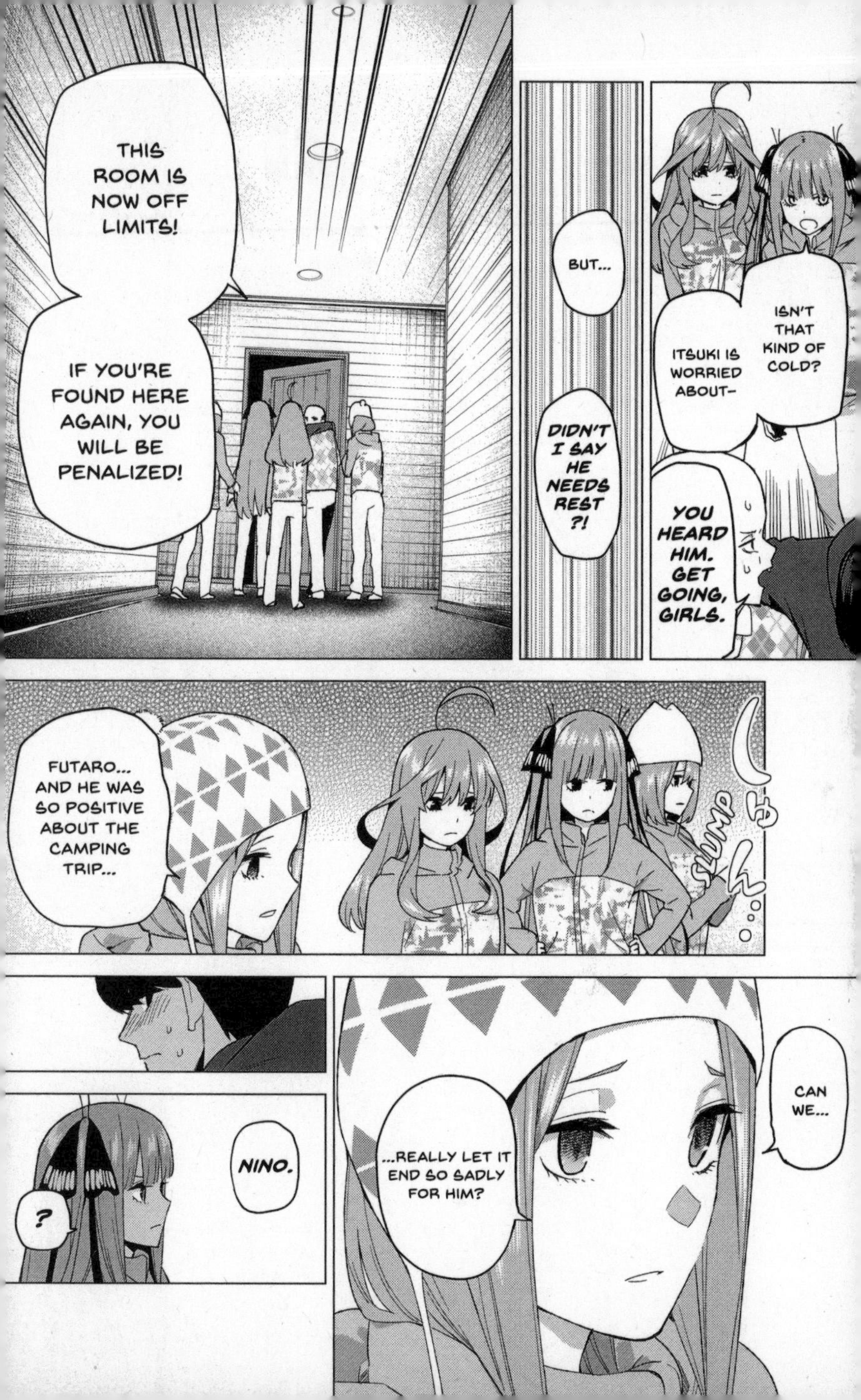
ISN'T THAT KIND OF COLD?
ITSUKI IS WORRIED ABOUT-
YOU HEARD HIM. GET GOING, GIRLS.
BUT...
DIDN'T I SAY HE NEEDS REST?!
THIS ROOM IS NOW OFF LIMITS!
IF YOU'RE FOUND HERE AGAIN, YOU WILL BE PENALIZED!
SLUMP
FUTARO... AND HE WAS SO POSITIVE ABOUT THE CAMPING TRIP...
CAN WE...
...REALLY LET IT END SO SADLY FOR HIM?
NINO.
?

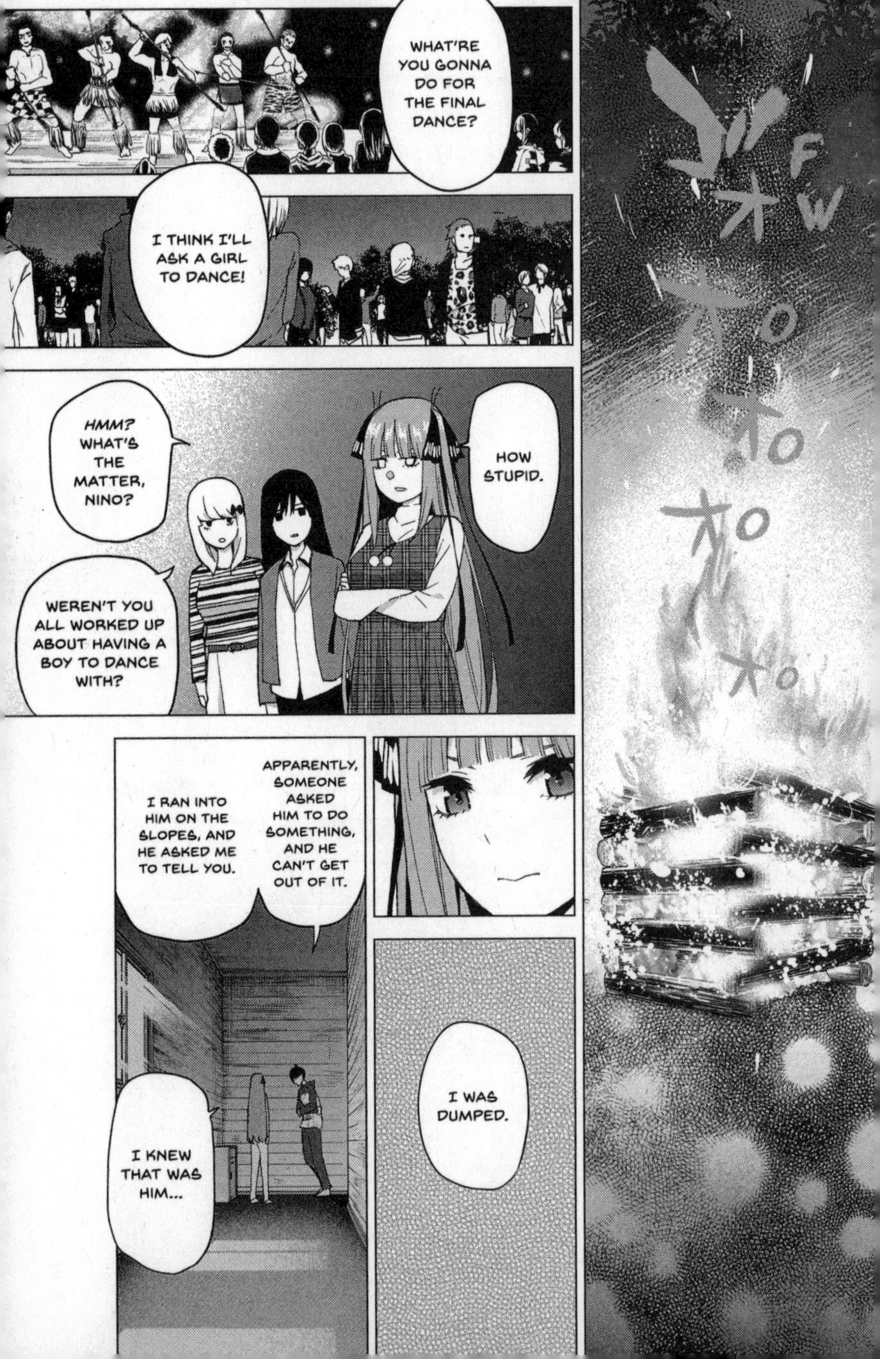
FW
WHAT'RE YOU GONNA DO FOR THE FINAL DANCE?
I THINK I'LL ASK A GIRL TO DANCE!
HOW STUPID.
HMM? WHAT'S THE MATTER, NINO?
WEREN'T YOU ALL WORKED UP ABOUT HAVING A BOY TO DANCE WITH?
I WAS DUMPED.
APPARENTLY, SOMEONE ASKED HIM TO DO SOMETHING, AND HE CAN'T GET OUT OF IT.
I RAN INTO HIM ON THE SLOPES, AND HE ASKED ME TO TELL YOU.
I KNEW THAT WAS HIM...

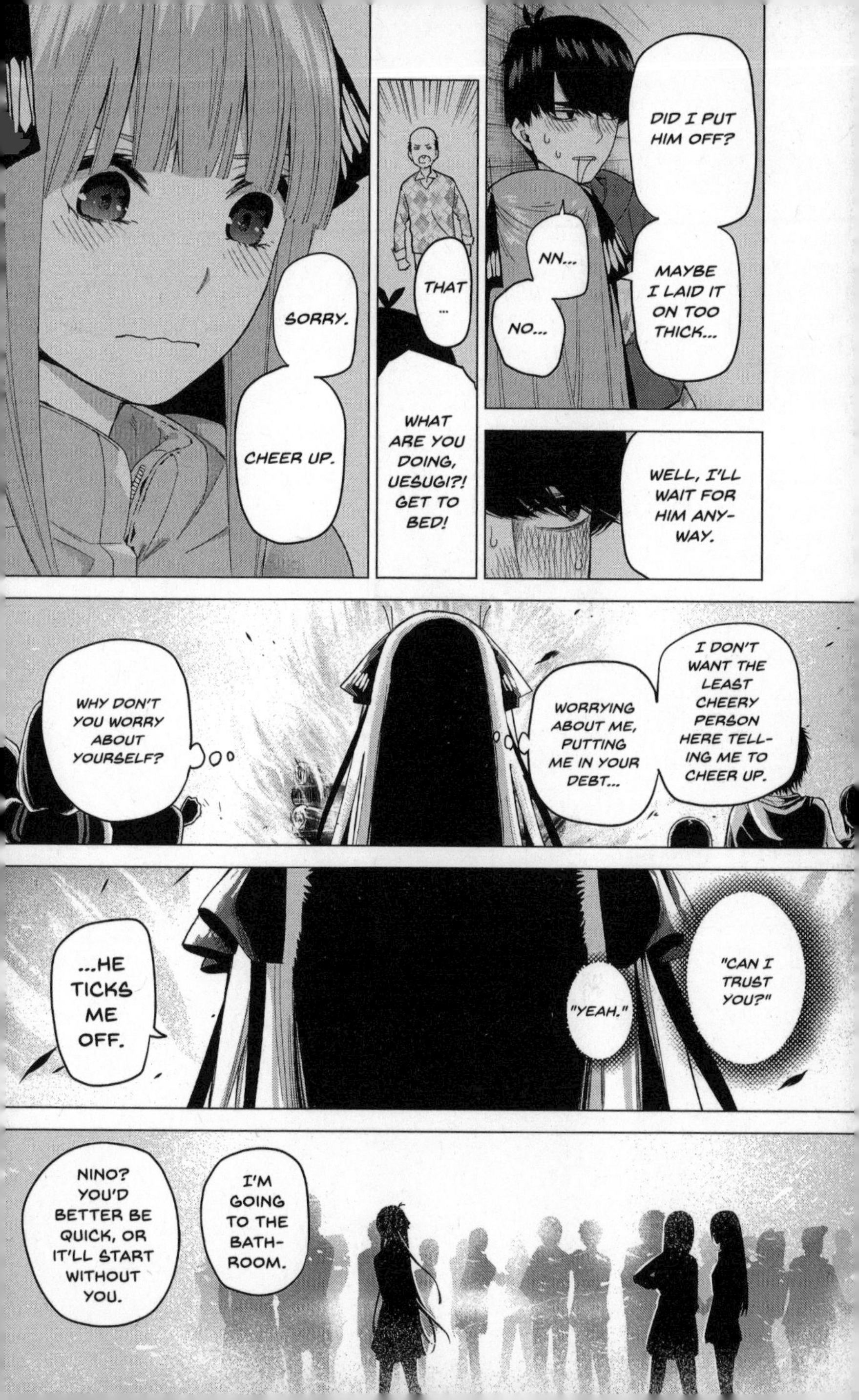
DID I PUT HIM OFF?
MAYBE I LAID IT ON TOO THICK...
NN... NO...
WELL, I'LL WAIT FOR HIM ANYWAY.
THAT ...
WHAT ARE YOU DOING, UESUGI?! GET TO BED!
SORRY.
CHEER UP.
I DON'T WANT THE LEAST CHEERY PERSON HERE TELLING ME TO CHEER UP.
WORRYING ABOUT ME, PUTTING ME IN YOUR DEBT...
WHY DON'T YOU WORRY ABOUT YOURSELF?
"CAN I TRUST YOU?"
"YEAH."
...HE TICKS ME OFF.
I'M GOING TO THE BATHROOM.
NINO? YOU'D BETTER BE QUICK, OR IT'LL START WITHOUT YOU.

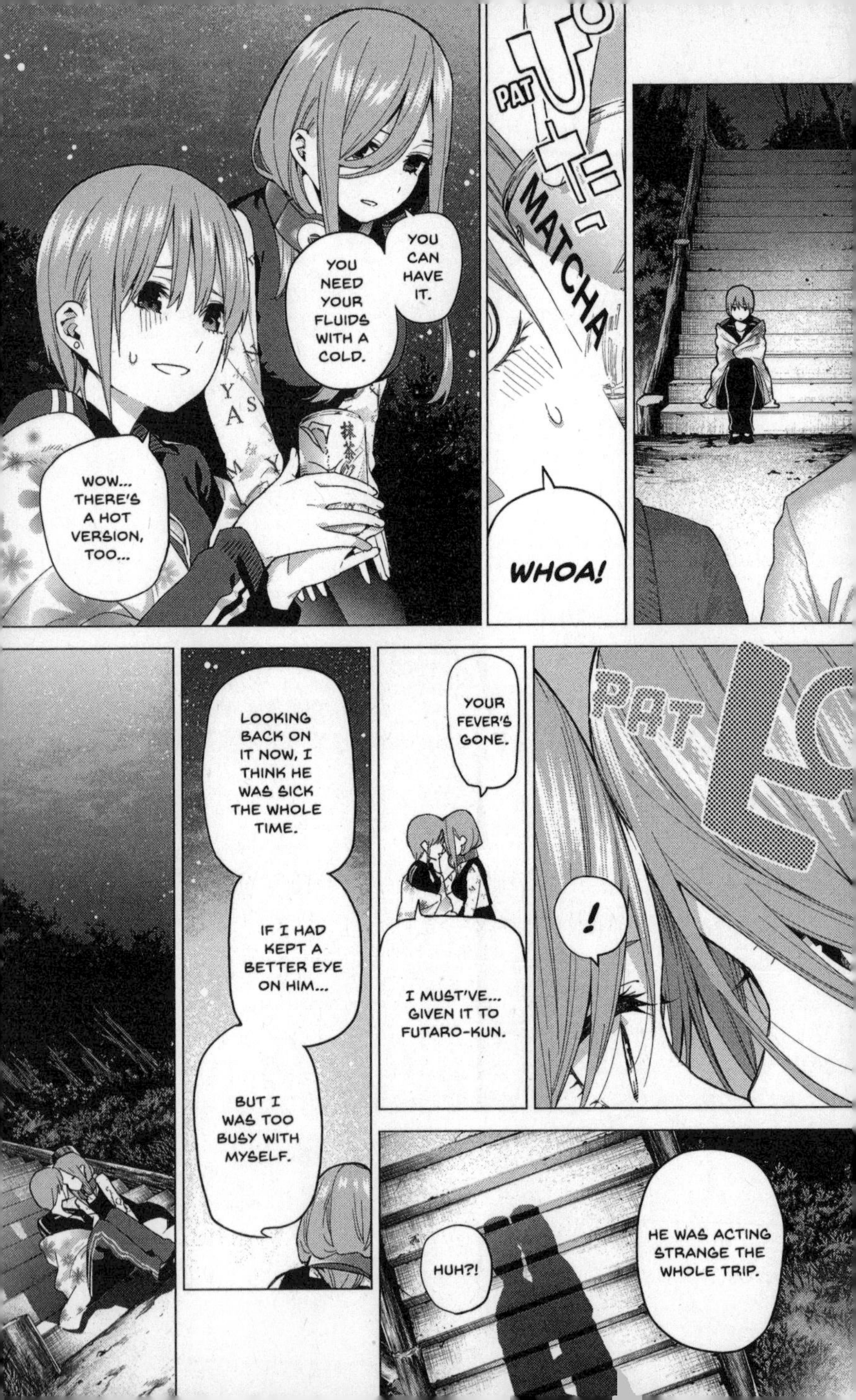
PAT
MATCHA
WHOA!
YOU CAN HAVE IT.
YOU NEED YOUR FLUIDS WITH A COLD.
WOW... THERE'S A HOT VERSION, TOO...
PAT
!
YOUR FEVER'S GONE.
I MUST'VE... GIVEN IT TO FUTARO-KUN.
HE WAS ACTING STRANGE THE WHOLE TRIP.
HUH?!
LOOKING BACK ON IT NOW, I THINK HE WAS SICK THE WHOLE TIME.
IF I HAD KEPT A BETTER EYE ON HIM...
BUT I WAS TOO BUSY WITH MYSELF.

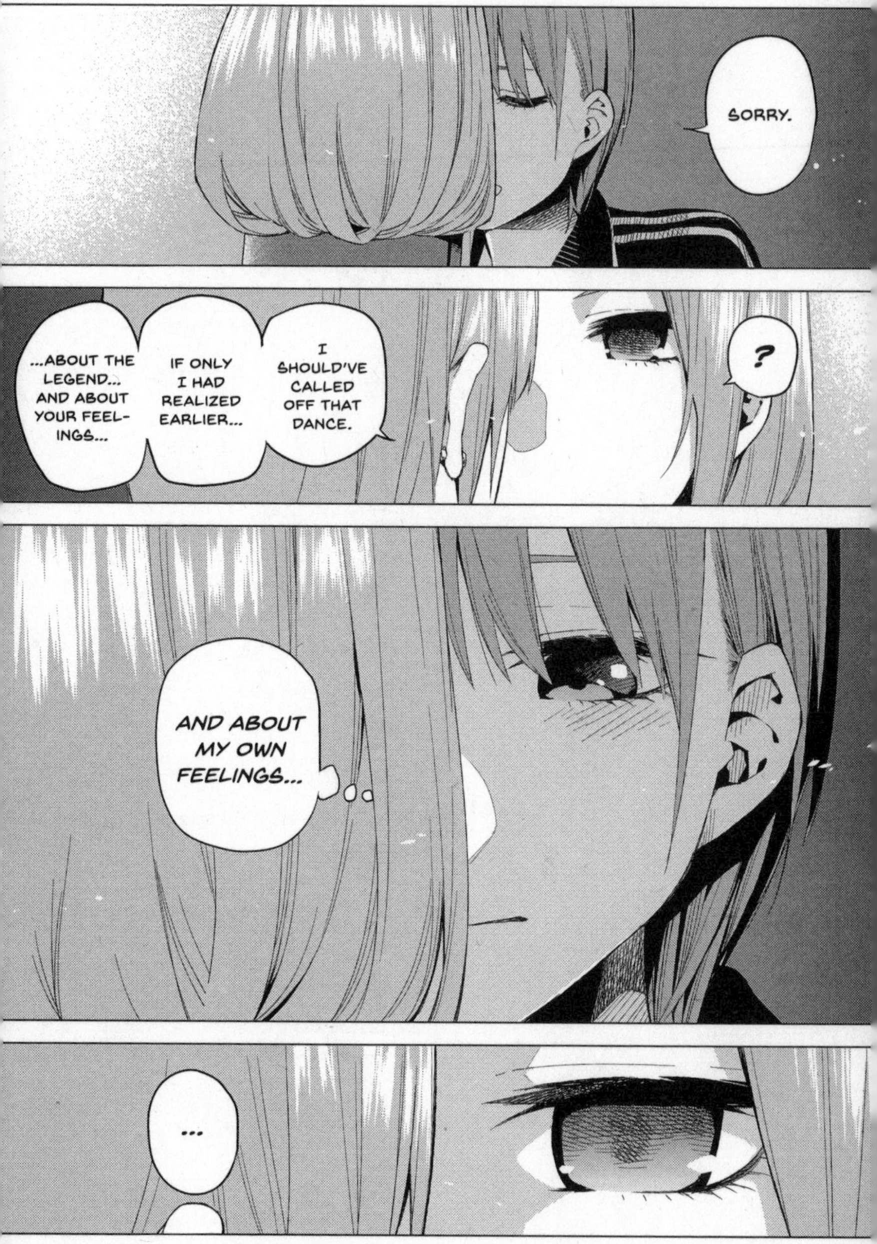
SORRY.
?
I SHOULD'VE CALLED OFF THAT DANCE.
IF ONLY I HAD REALIZED EARLIER...
...ABOUT THE LEGEND... AND ABOUT YOUR FEEL- INGS...
AND ABOUT MY OWN FEELINGS...
...

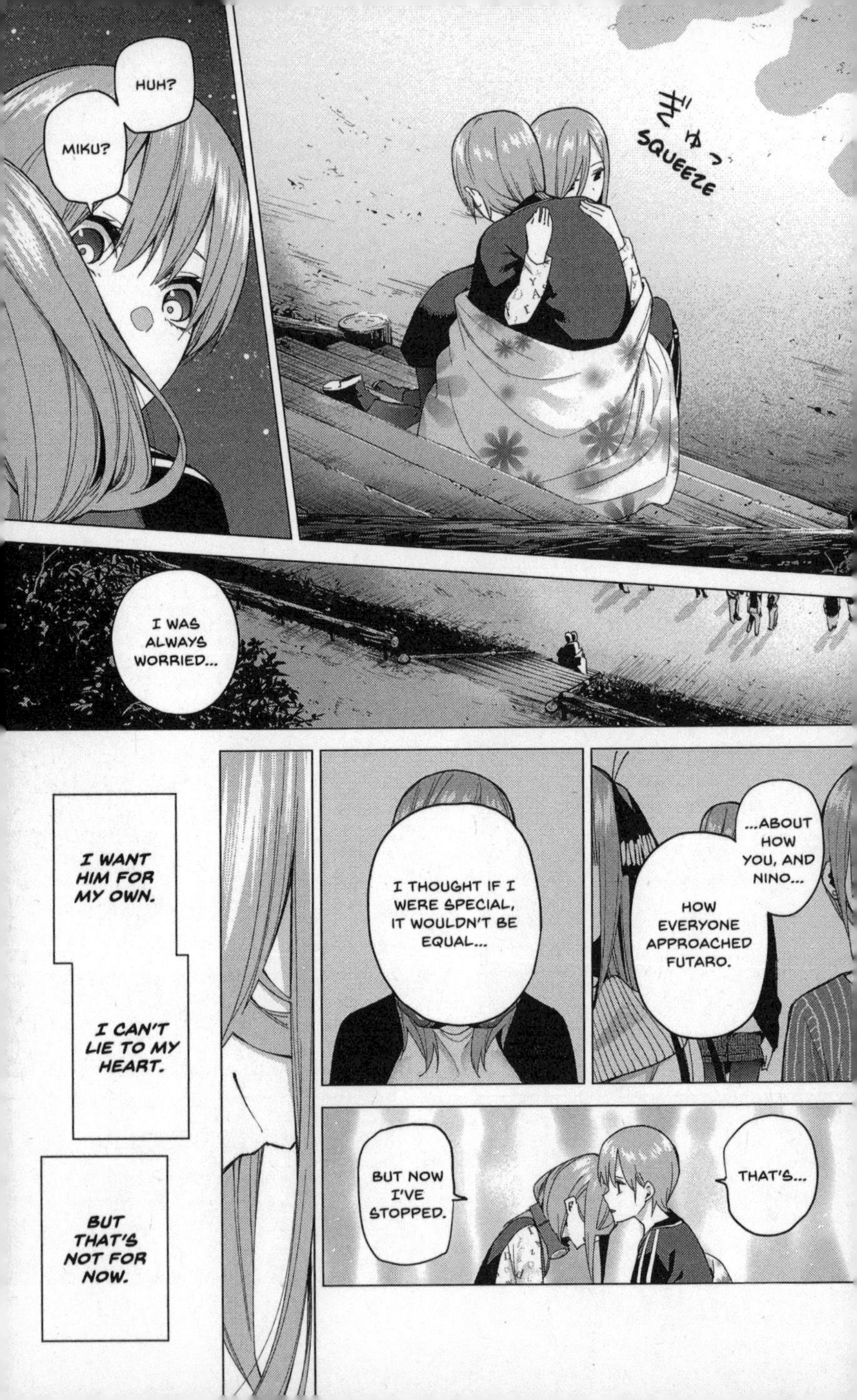
ぎゅっ
SQUEEZE
HUH?
MIKU?
I WAS ALWAYS WORRIED...
...ABOUT HOW YOU, AND NINO...
HOW EVERYONE APPROACHED FUTARO.
I THOUGHT IF I WERE SPECIAL, IT WOULDN'T BE EQUAL...
THAT'S...
BUT NOW I'VE STOPPED.
I WANT HIM FOR MY OWN.
I CAN'T LIE TO MY HEART.
BUT THAT'S NOT FOR NOW.

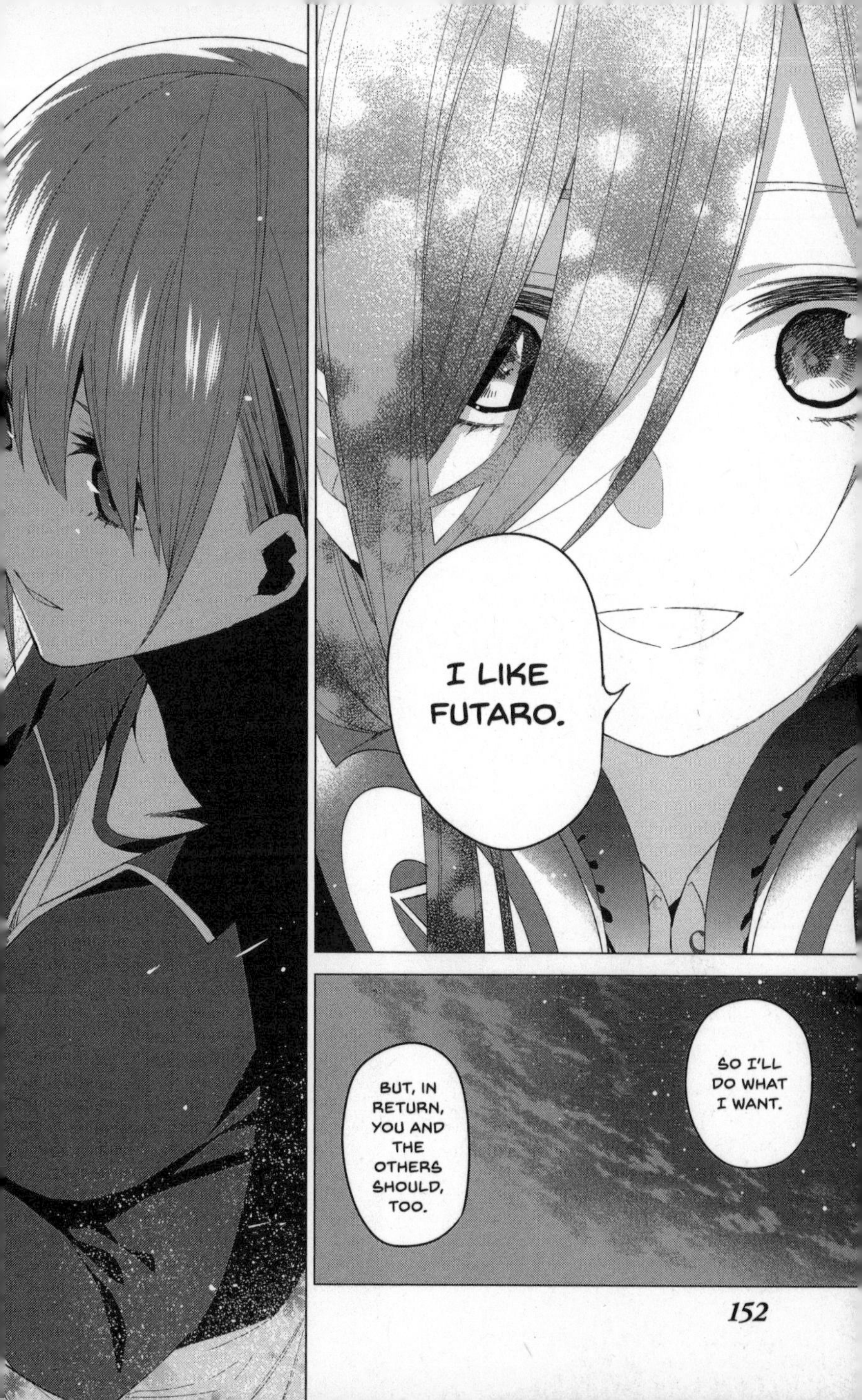
I LIKE FUTARO.
SO I'LL DO WHAT I WANT.
BUT, IN RETURN, YOU AND THE OTHERS SHOULD, TOO.

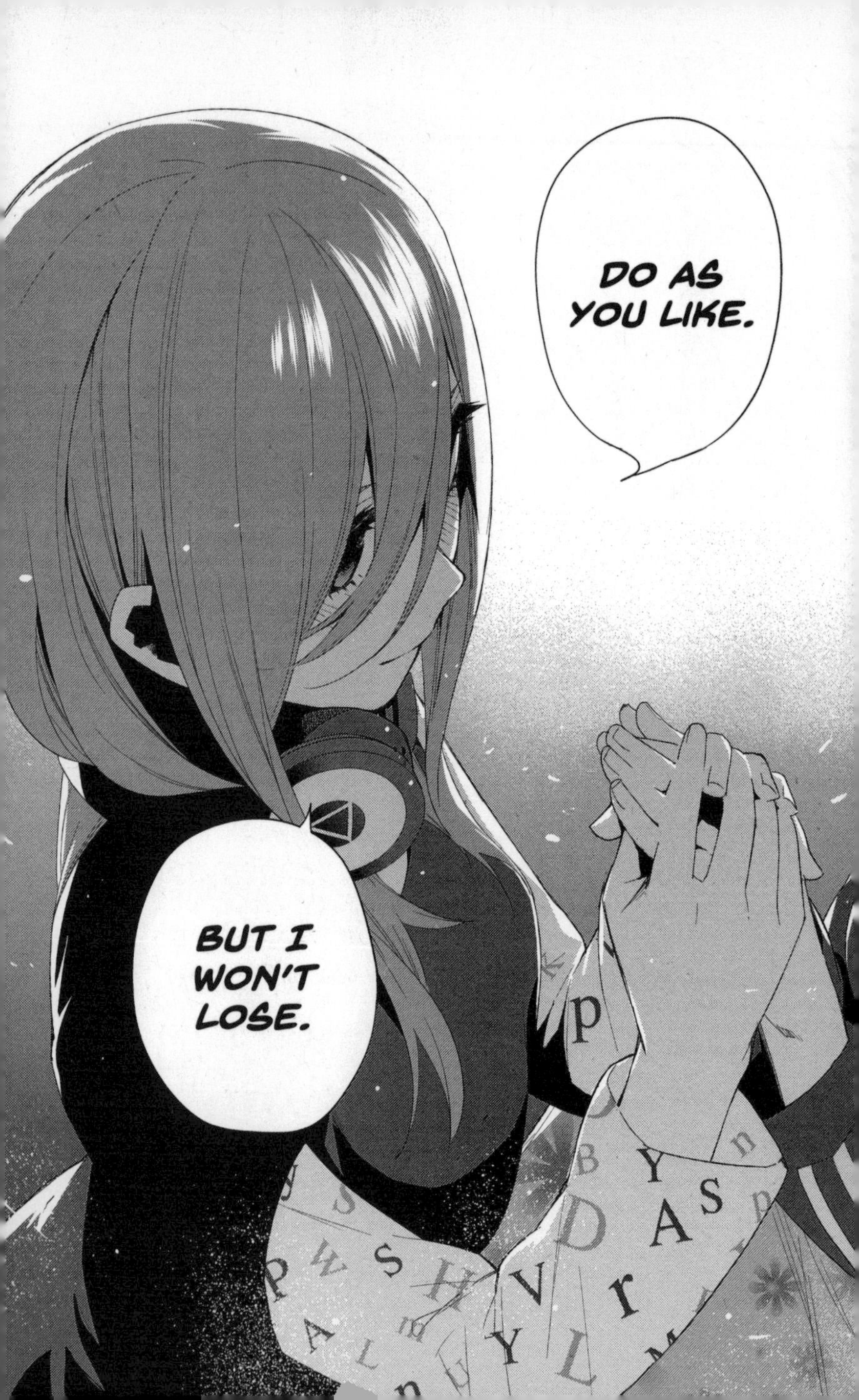
DO AS YOU LIKE.
BUT I WON'T LOSE.

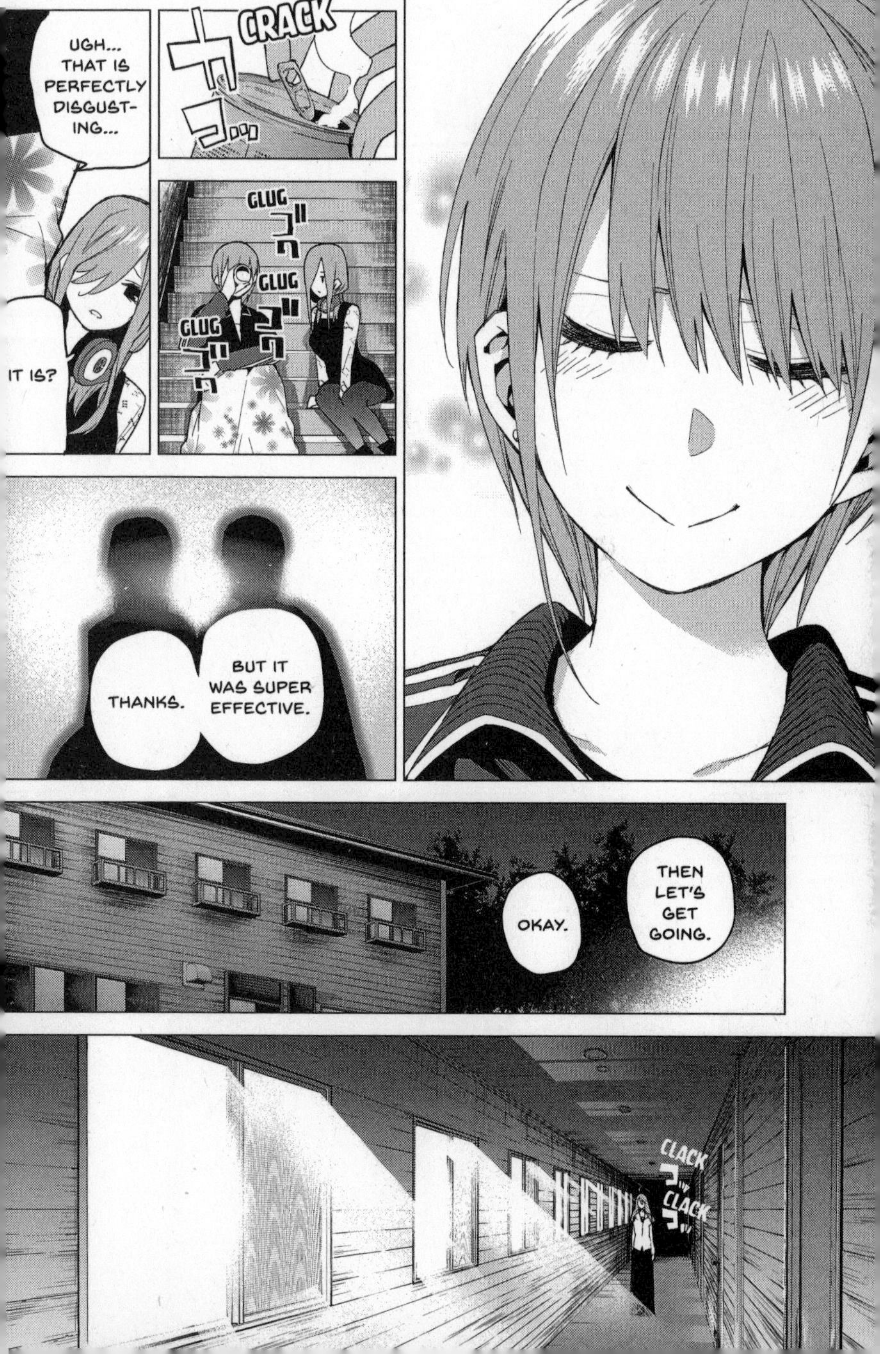
CRACK
UGH... THAT IS PERFECTLY DISGUSTING...
GLUG
GLUG
GLUG
IT IS?
BUT IT WAS SUPER EFFECTIVE.
THANKS.
THEN LET'S GET GOING.
OKAY.
CLACK
CLACK

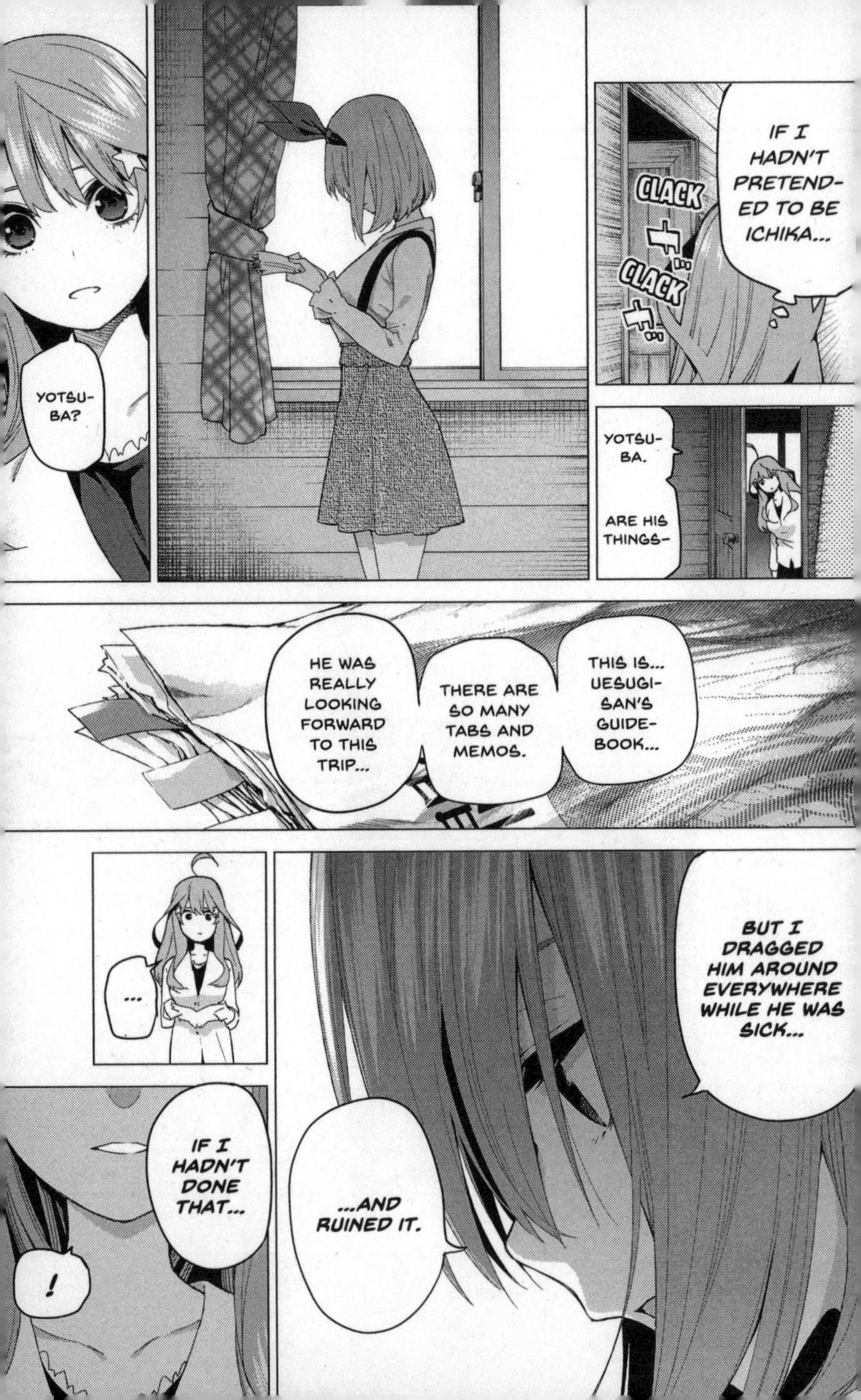
IF I HADN'T PRETEND-ED TO BE ICHIKA...
CLACK
CLACK
YOTSU-BA.
ARE HIS THINGS-
YOTSU-BA?
THIS IS... UESUGI-SAN'S GUIDE-BOOK...
THERE ARE SO MANY TABS AND MEMOS.
HE WAS REALLY LOOKING FORWARD TO THIS TRIP...
BUT I DRAGGED HIM AROUND EVERYWHERE WHILE HE WAS SICK...
...AND RUINED IT.
...
IF I HADN'T DONE THAT...
!

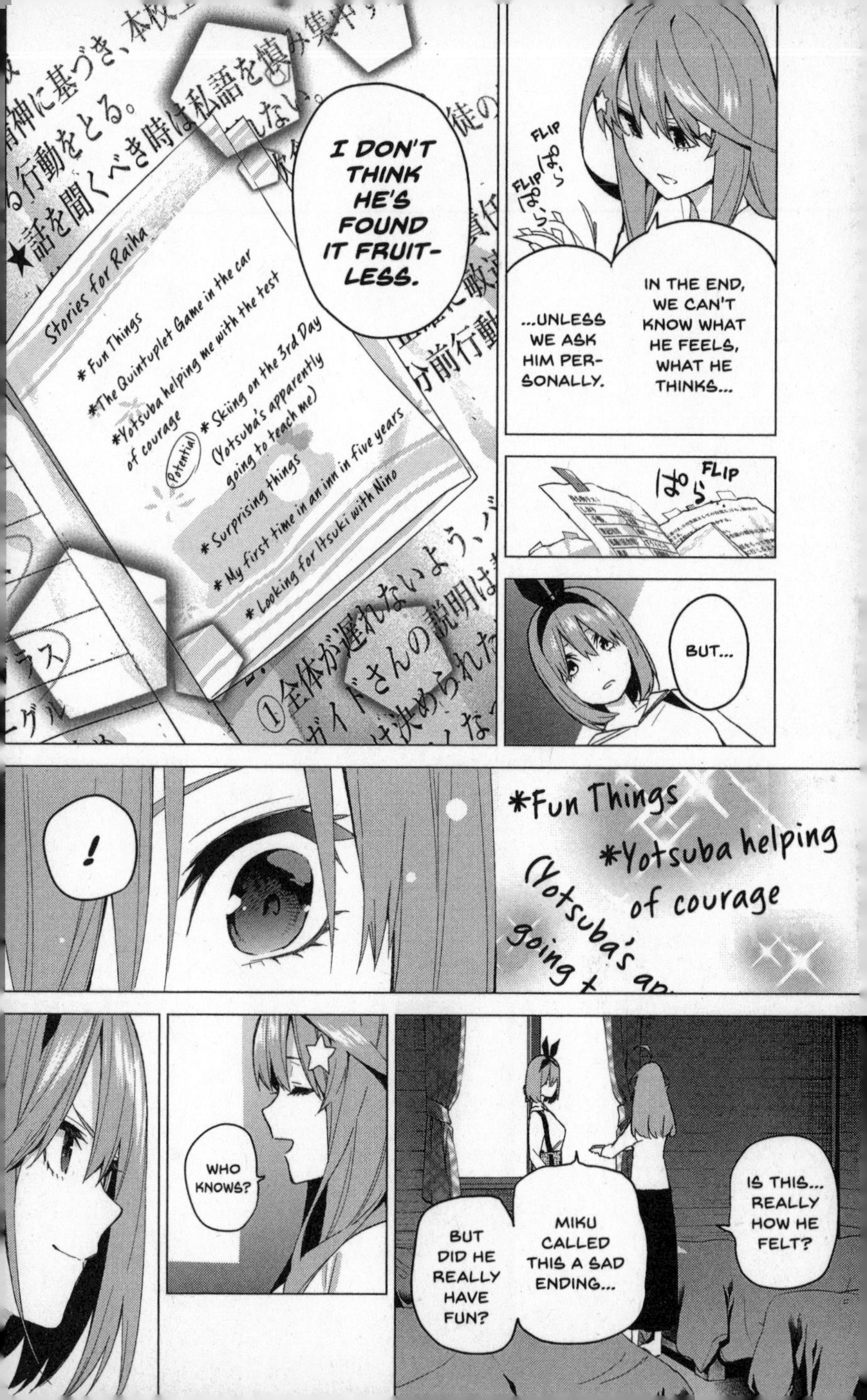
FLIP ぱら
FLIP ぱら
IN THE END, WE CAN'T KNOW WHAT HE FEELS, WHAT HE THINKS...
...UNLESS WE ASK HIM PERSONALLY.
ぱら FLIP
BUT...
Stories for Raiha
* Fun Things
* The Quintuplet Game in the car
* Yotsuba helping me with the test of courage
Potential * Skiing on the 3rd Day (Yotsuba's apparently going to teach me)
* Surprising things
* My first time in an inn in five years
* Looking for Itsuki with Nino
I DON'T THINK HE'S FOUND IT FRUITLESS.
*Fun Things
*Yotsuba helping
of courage
!
IS THIS... REALLY HOW HE FELT?
MIKU CALLED THIS A SAD ENDING...
BUT DID HE REALLY HAVE FUN?
WHO KNOWS?

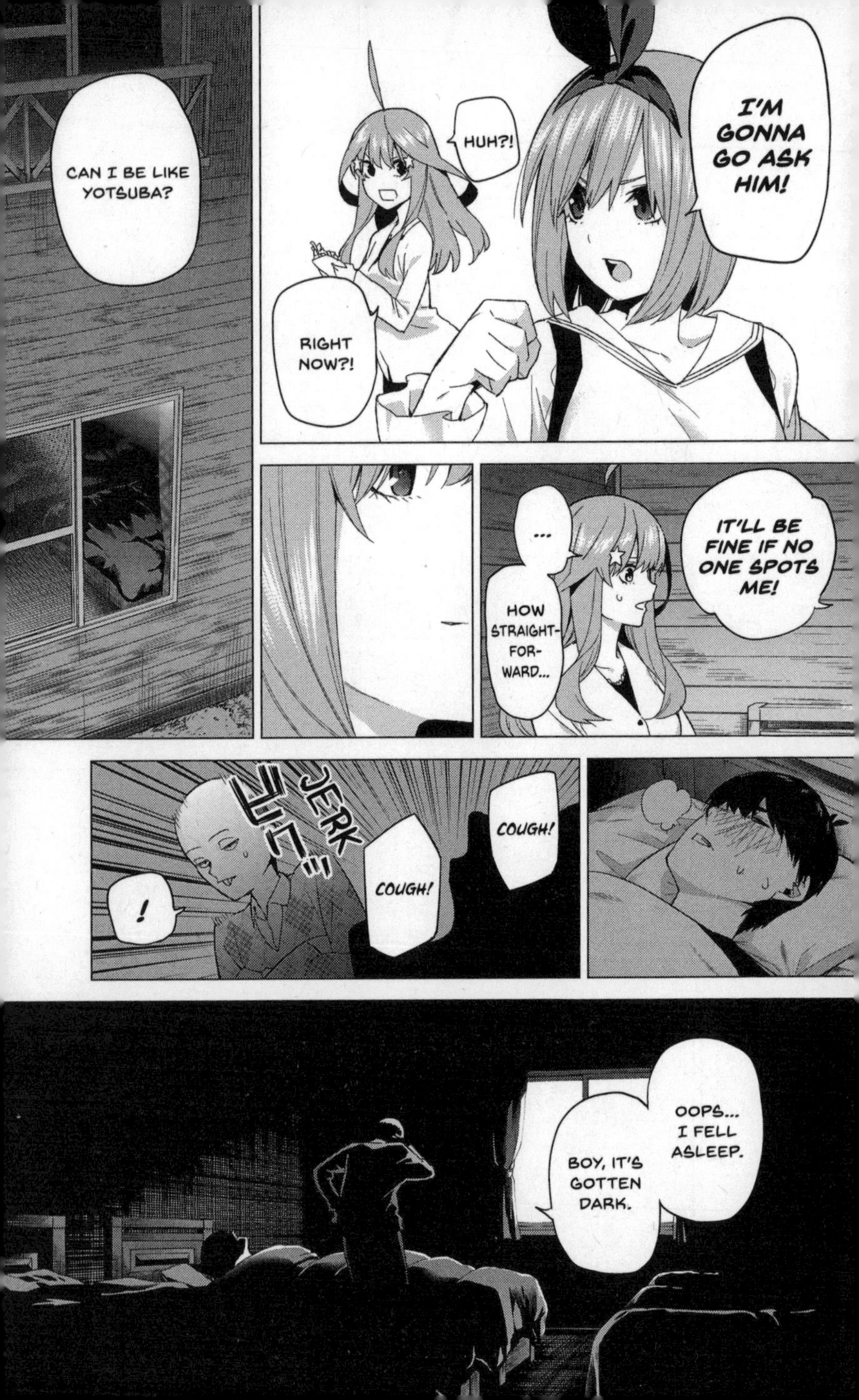
I'M GONNA GO ASK HIM!
HUH?!
RIGHT NOW?!
IT'LL BE FINE IF NO ONE SPOTS ME!
...
HOW STRAIGHT-FOR-WARD...
CAN I BE LIKE YOTSUBA?
COUGH!
COUGH!
JERK
!
OOPS... I FELL ASLEEP.
BOY, IT'S GOTTEN DARK.

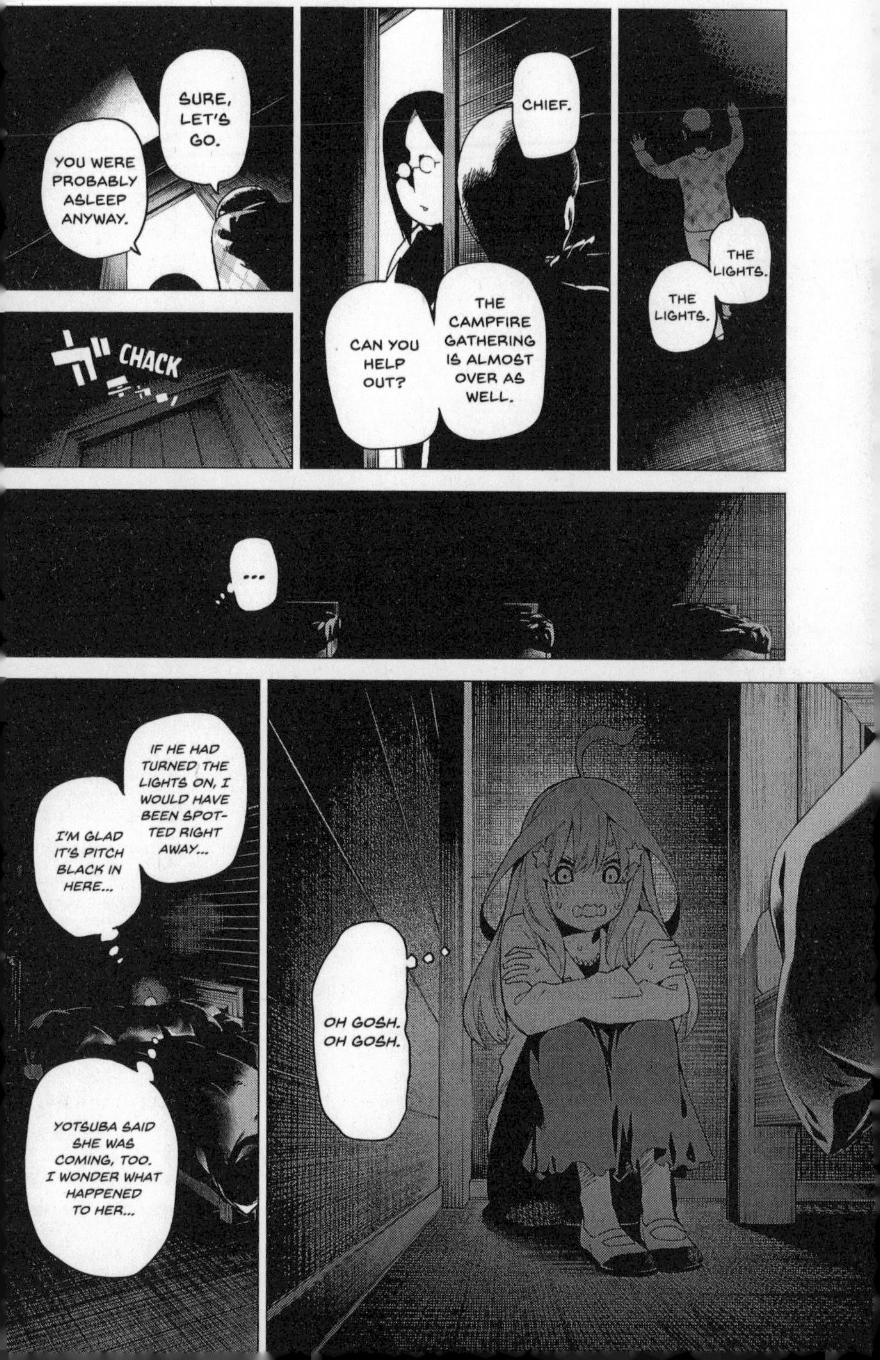

THE LIGHTS.
THE LIGHTS.
CHIEF.
THE CAMPFIRE GATHERING IS ALMOST OVER AS WELL.
CAN YOU HELP OUT?
SURE, LET'S GO.
YOU WERE PROBABLY ASLEEP ANYWAY.
CHACK
...
OH GOSH. OH GOSH.
IF HE HAD TURNED THE LIGHTS ON, I WOULD HAVE BEEN SPOTTED RIGHT AWAY...
I'M GLAD IT'S PITCH BLACK IN HERE...
YOTSUBA SAID SHE WAS COMING, TOO. I WONDER WHAT HAPPENED TO HER...

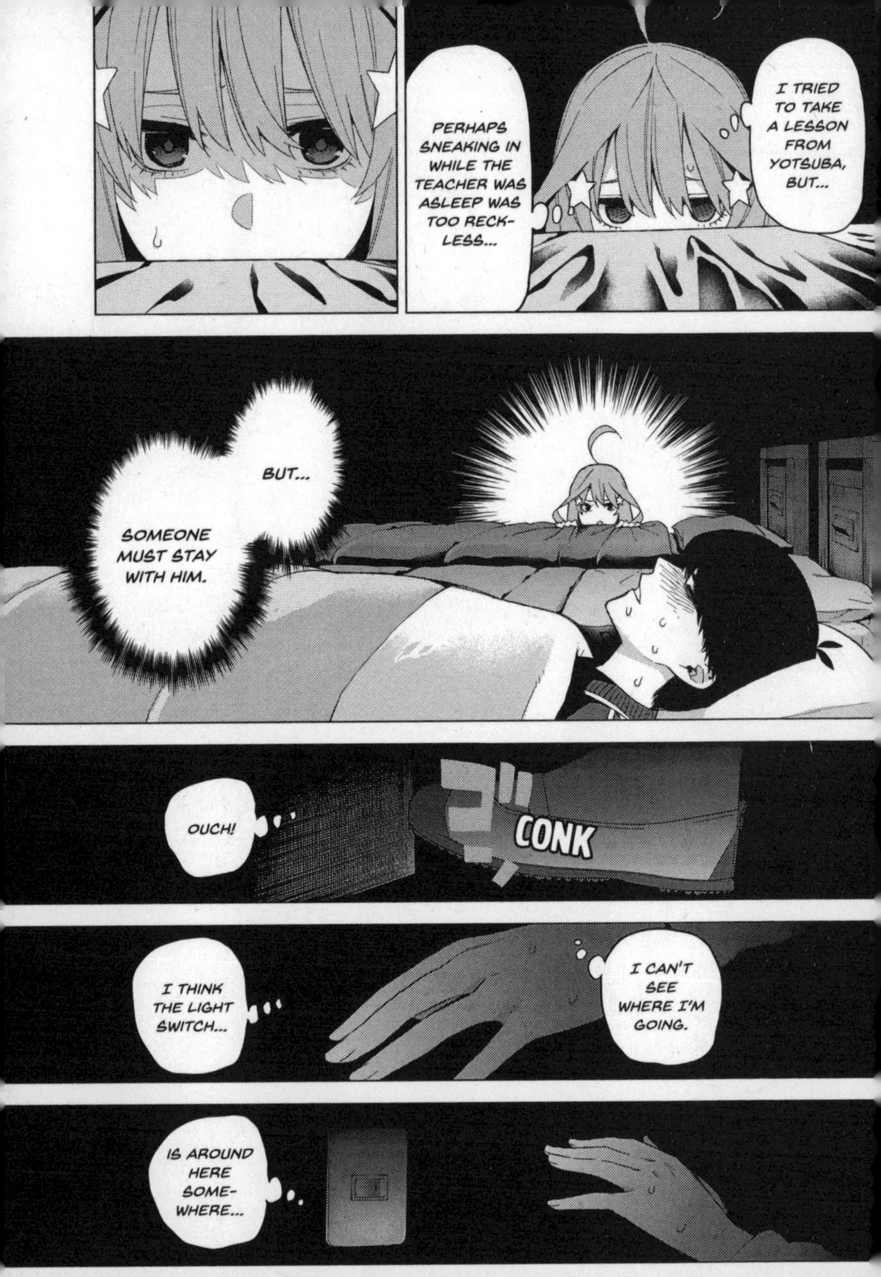
I TRIED TO TAKE A LESSON FROM YOTSUBA, BUT...
PERHAPS SNEAKING IN WHILE THE TEACHER WAS ASLEEP WAS TOO RECK-LESS...
BUT...
SOMEONE MUST STAY WITH HIM.
CONK
OUCH!
I CAN'T SEE WHERE I'M GOING.
I THINK THE LIGHT SWITCH...
IS AROUND HERE SOME-WHERE...

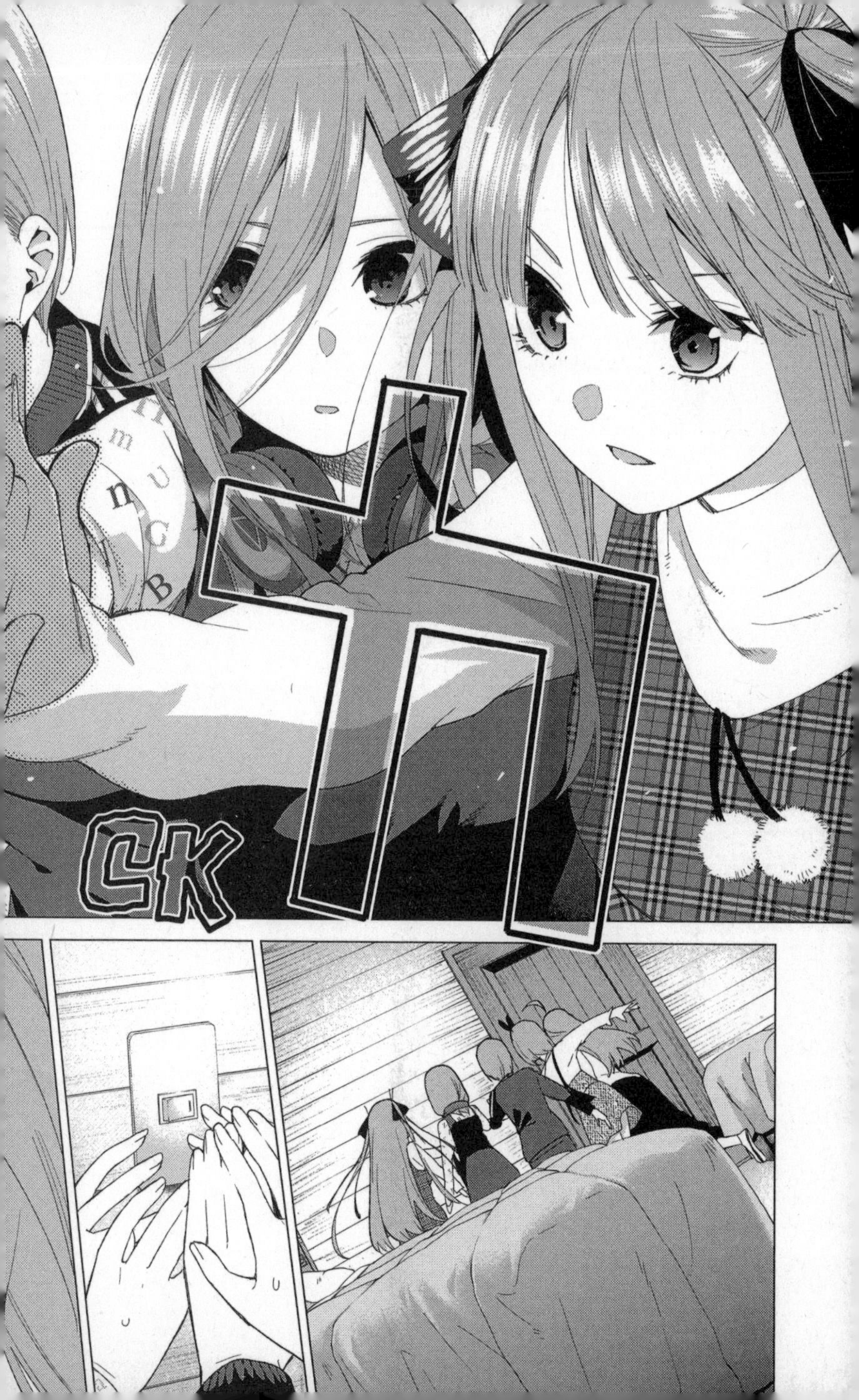
カ
CK

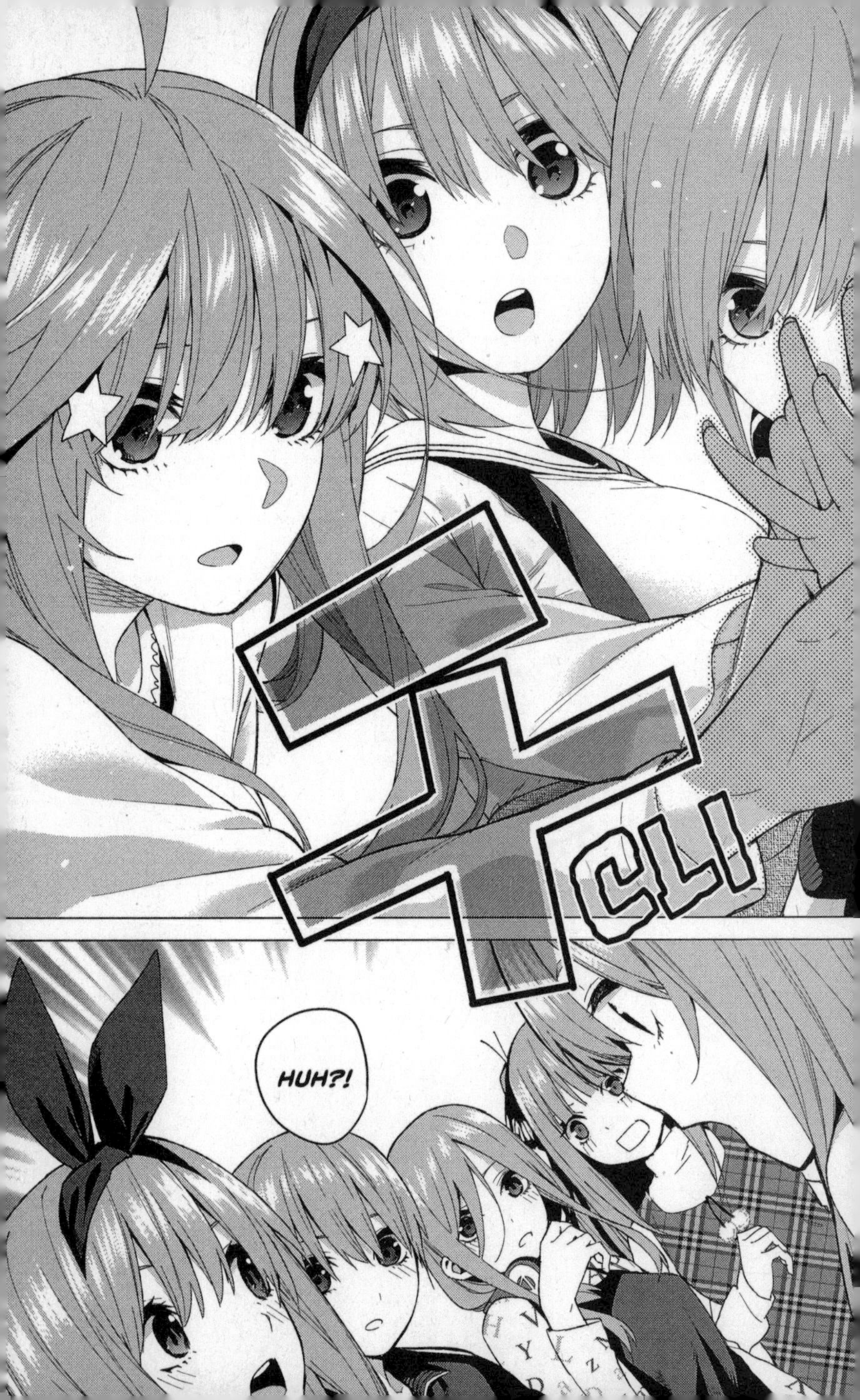
CLI
HUH?!

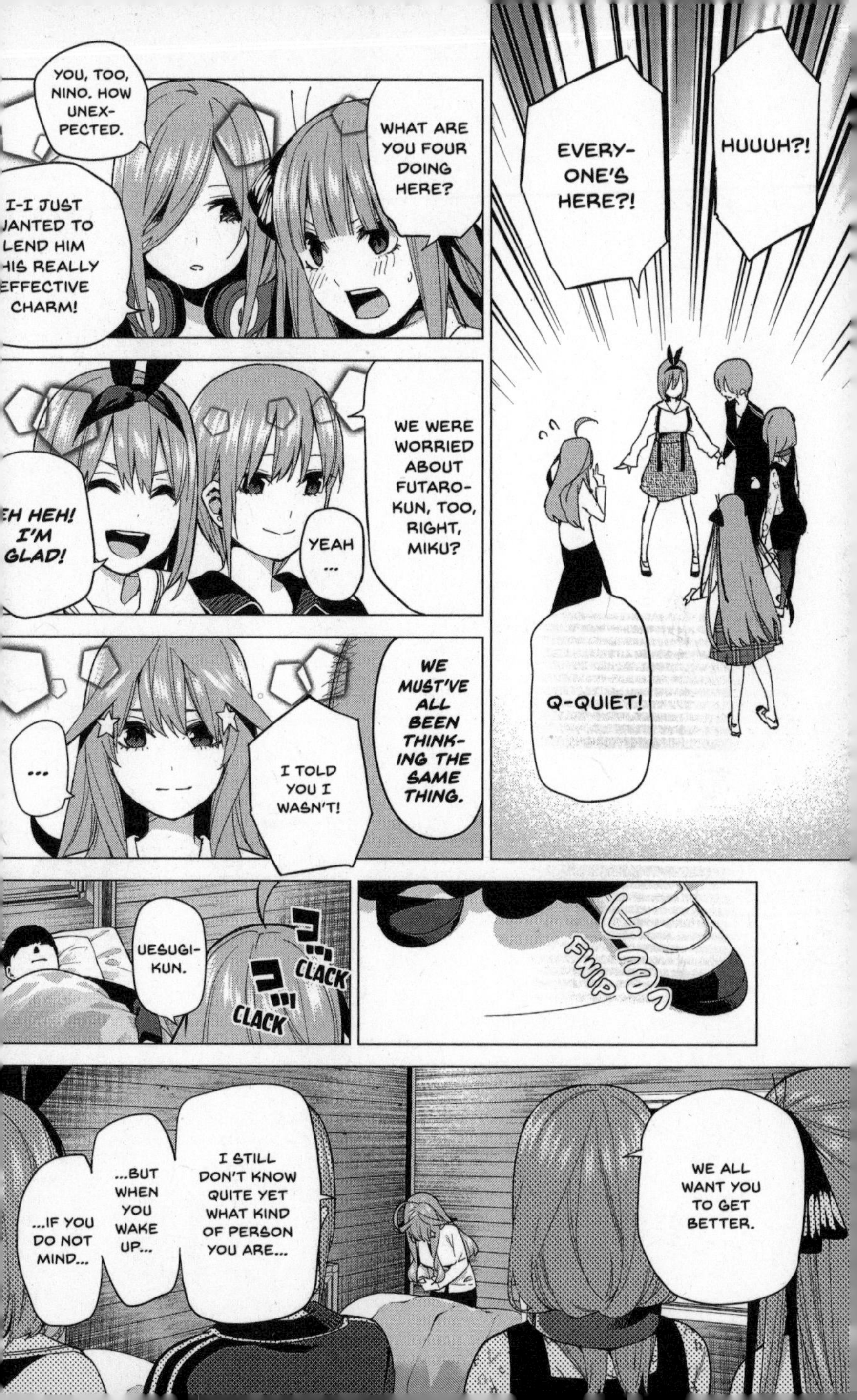
HUUUH?!
EVERY-ONE'S HERE?!
Q-QUIET!
WHAT ARE YOU FOUR DOING HERE?
YOU, TOO, NINO. HOW UNEX-PECTED.
I-I JUST WANTED TO LEND HIM HIS REALLY EFFECTIVE CHARM!
WE WERE WORRIED ABOUT FUTARO-KUN, TOO, RIGHT, MIKU?
YEAH ...
EH HEH! I'M GLAD!
WE MUST'VE ALL BEEN THINK-ING THE SAME THING.
I TOLD YOU I WASN'T!
...
FWIP
UESUGI-KUN.
CLACK
CLACK
WE ALL WANT YOU TO GET BETTER.
I STILL DON'T KNOW QUITE YET WHAT KIND OF PERSON YOU ARE...
...BUT WHEN YOU WAKE UP...
...IF YOU DO NOT MIND...

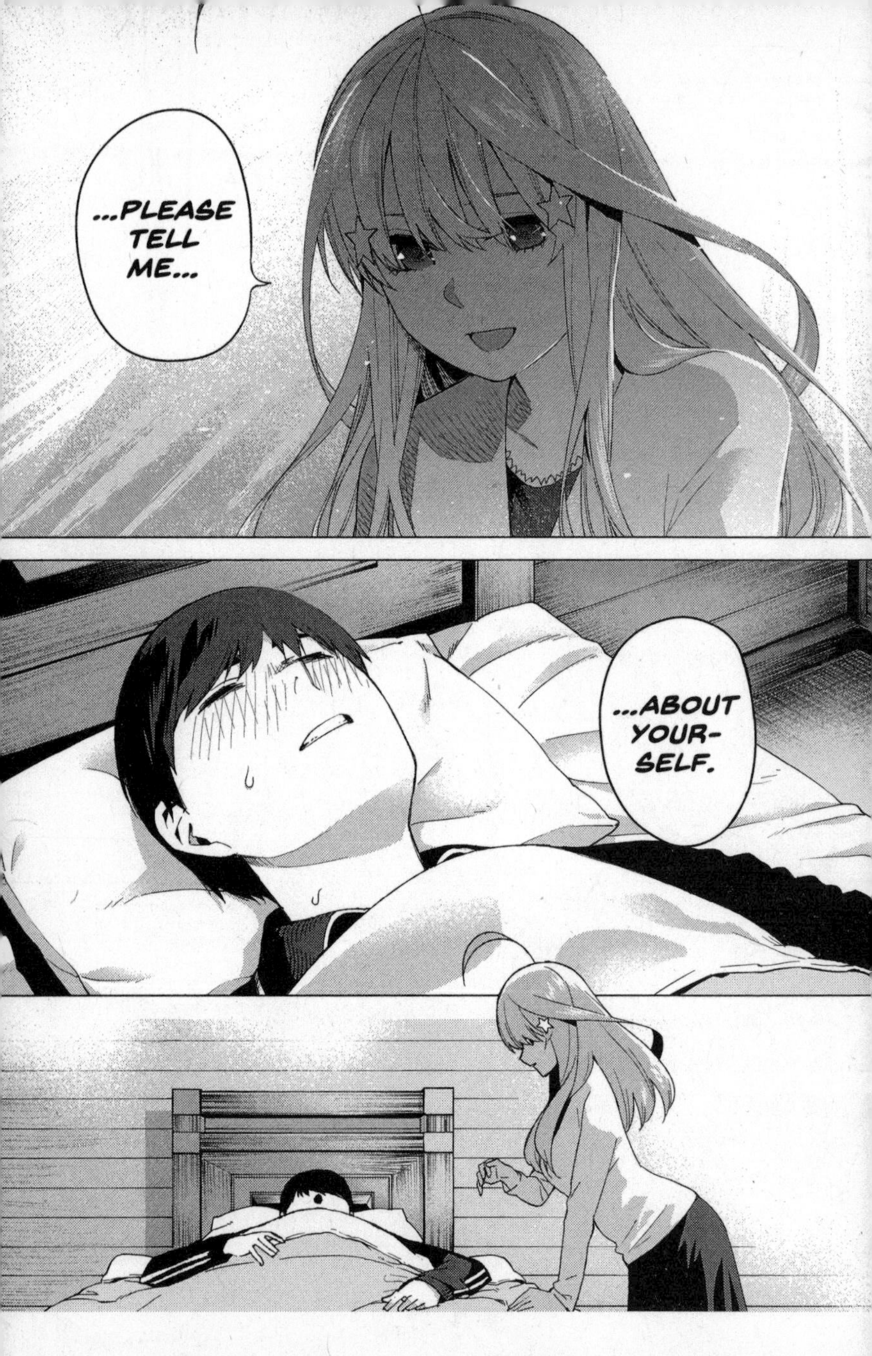
...PLEASE TELL ME...
...ABOUT YOURSELF.

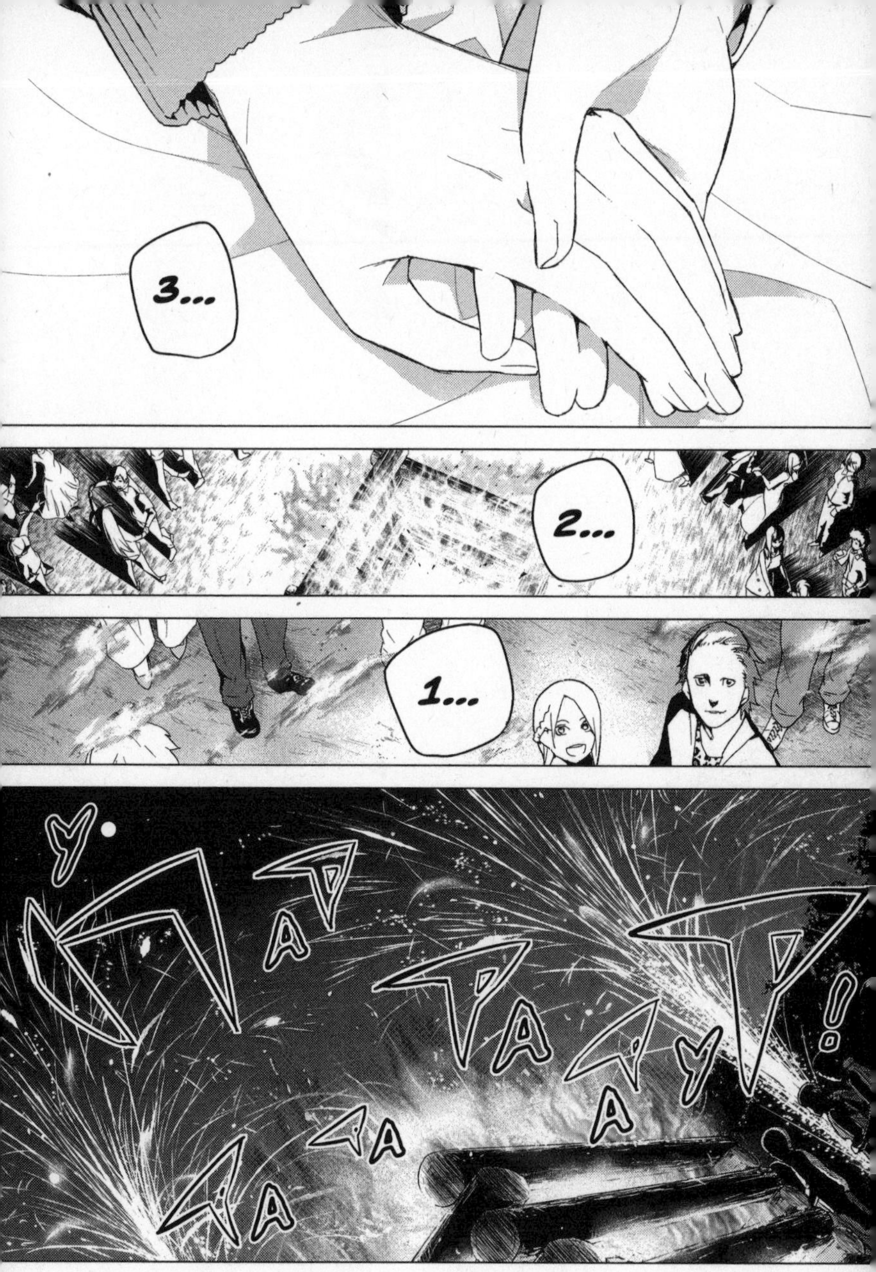
3...
2...
1...
YAAAAAAY!

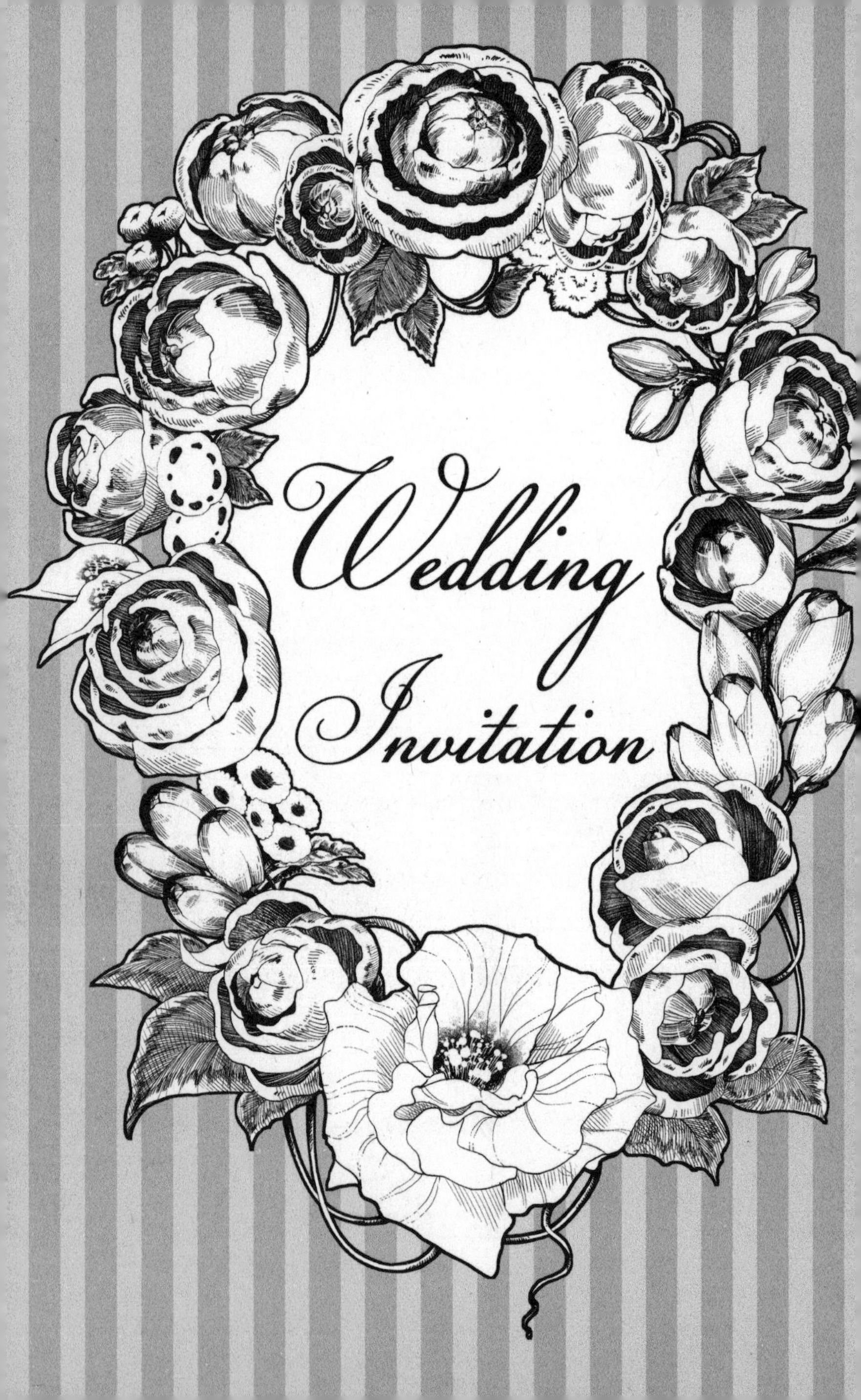
Wedding
Invitation

Please circle one.

Attending

Not Attending

Name
_____

Address
_____

_____

Phone
_____

Message
_____

_____

If you have food or drink allergies or other dietary needs, please
include details below.

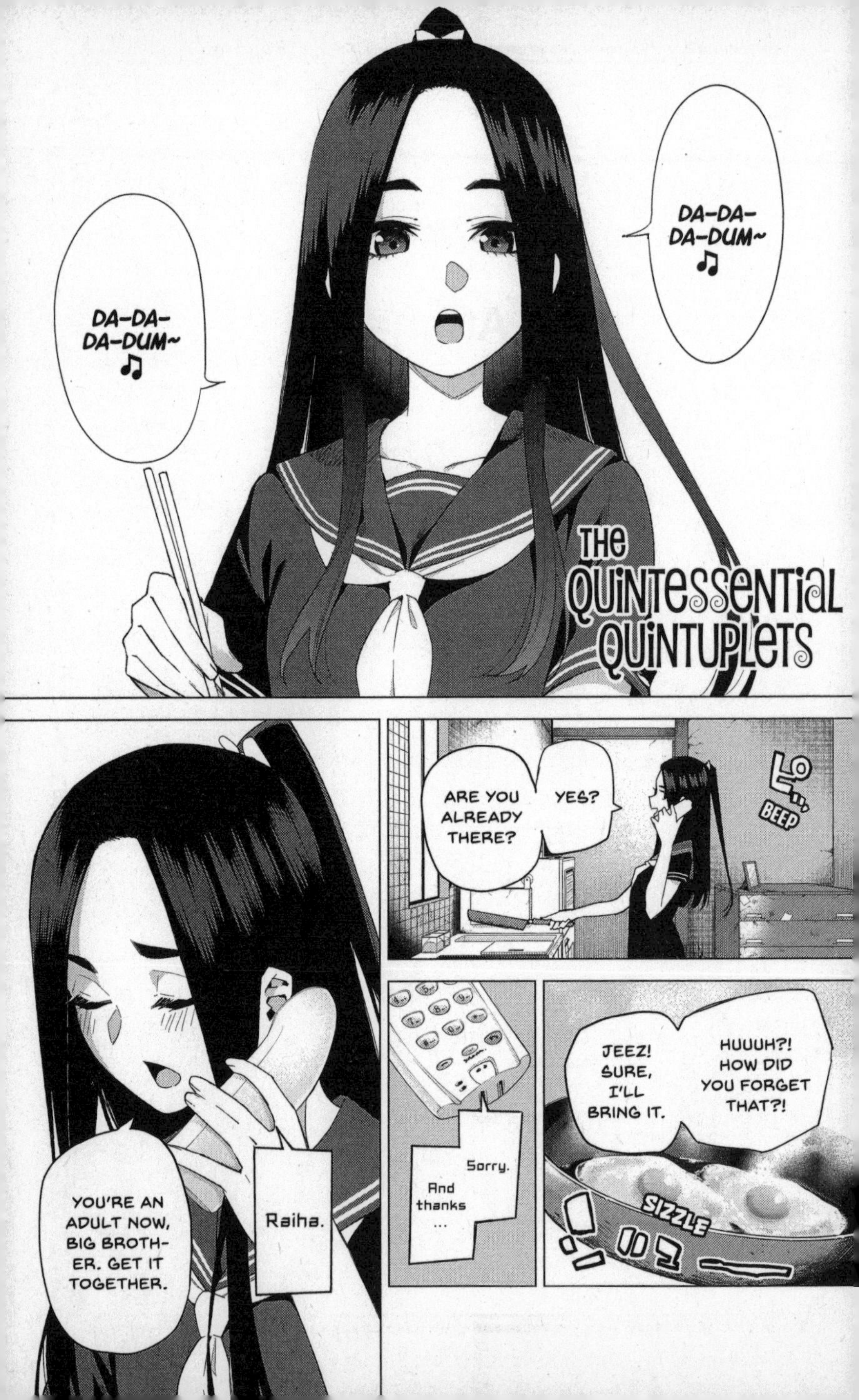
DA-DA-DA-DUM~ ♫
THE QUINTESSENTIAL QUINTUPLETS
DA-DA-DA-DUM~ ♫
BEEP
YES?
ARE YOU ALREADY THERE?
HUUUH?! HOW DID YOU FORGET THAT?!
JEEZ! SURE, I'LL BRING IT.
SIZZLE
Sorry.
And thanks...
Raiha.
YOU'RE AN ADULT NOW, BIG BROTH-ER. GET IT TOGETHER.

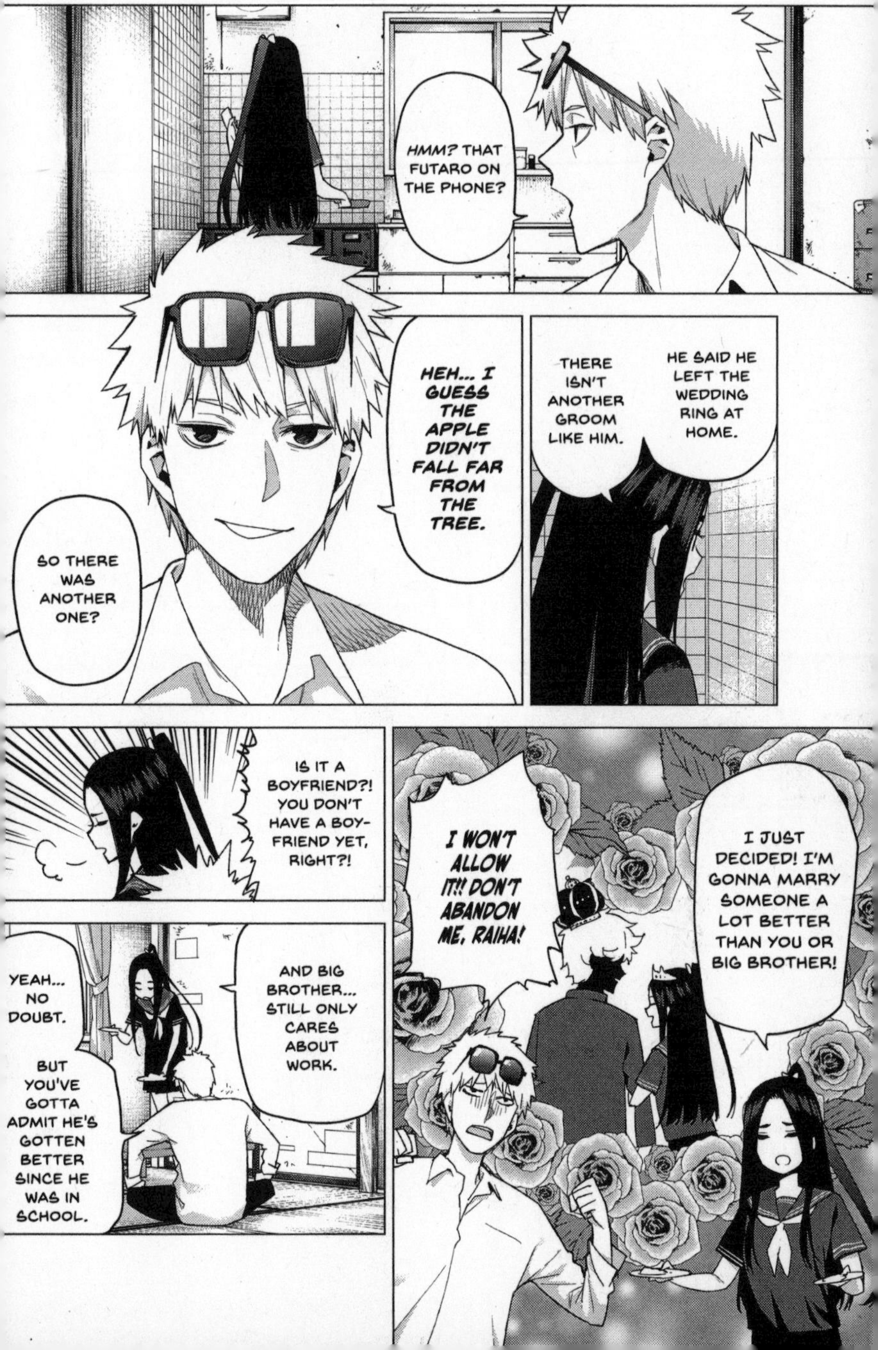
HMM? THAT FUTARO ON THE PHONE?
HE SAID HE LEFT THE WEDDING RING AT HOME.
THERE ISN'T ANOTHER GROOM LIKE HIM.
HEH... I GUESS THE APPLE DIDN'T FALL FAR FROM THE TREE.
SO THERE WAS ANOTHER ONE?
I JUST DECIDED! I'M GONNA MARRY SOMEONE A LOT BETTER THAN YOU OR BIG BROTHER!
I WON'T ALLOW IT!! DON'T ABANDON ME, RAIHA!
IS IT A BOYFRIEND?! YOU DON'T HAVE A BOY-FRIEND YET, RIGHT?!
AND BIG BROTHER... STILL ONLY CARES ABOUT WORK.
YEAH... NO DOUBT.
BUT YOU'VE GOTTA ADMIT HE'S GOTTEN BETTER SINCE HE WAS IN SCHOOL.

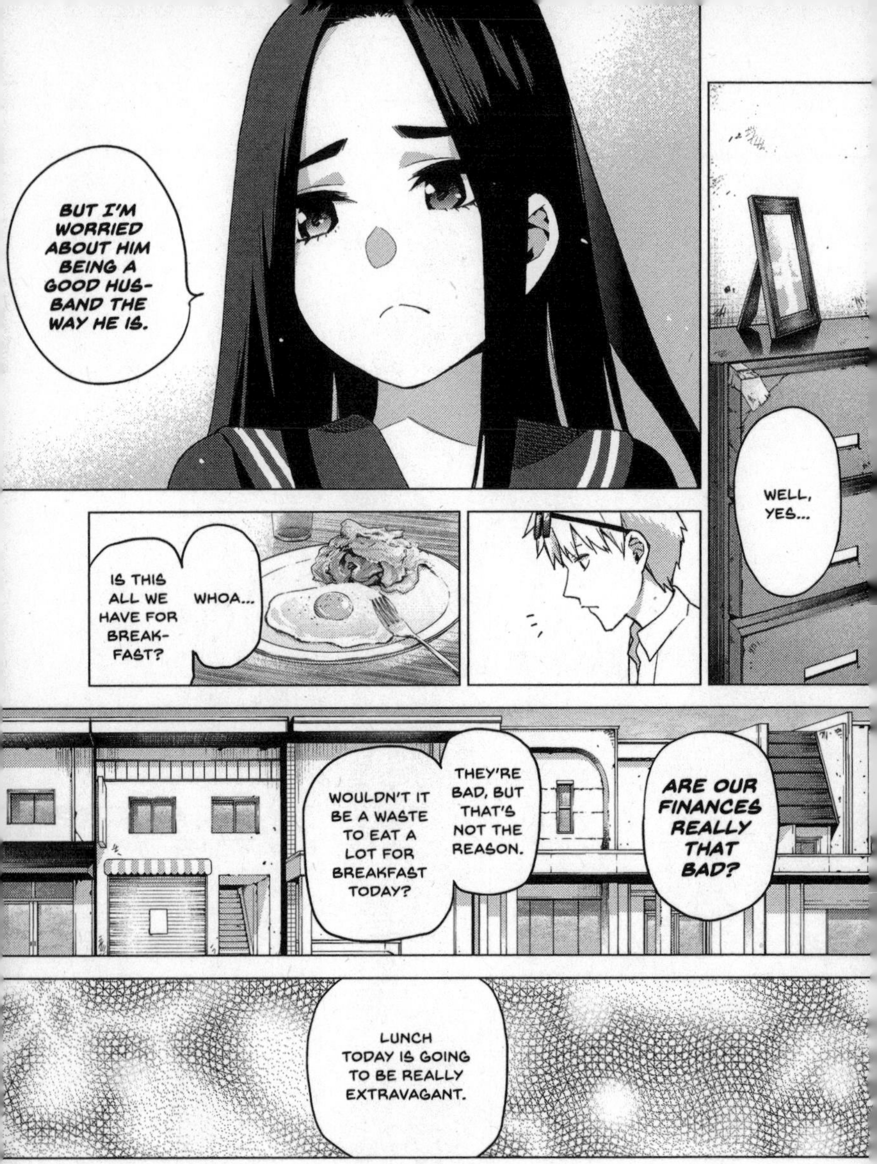
WELL, YES...
BUT I'M WORRIED ABOUT HIM BEING A GOOD HUS-BAND THE WAY HE IS.
WHOA...
IS THIS ALL WE HAVE FOR BREAK-FAST?
ARE OUR FINANCES REALLY THAT BAD?
THEY'RE BAD, BUT THAT'S NOT THE REASON.
WOULDN'T IT BE A WASTE TO EAT A LOT FOR BREAKFAST TODAY?
LUNCH TODAY IS GOING TO BE REALLY EXTRAVAGANT.

CHAPTER 32

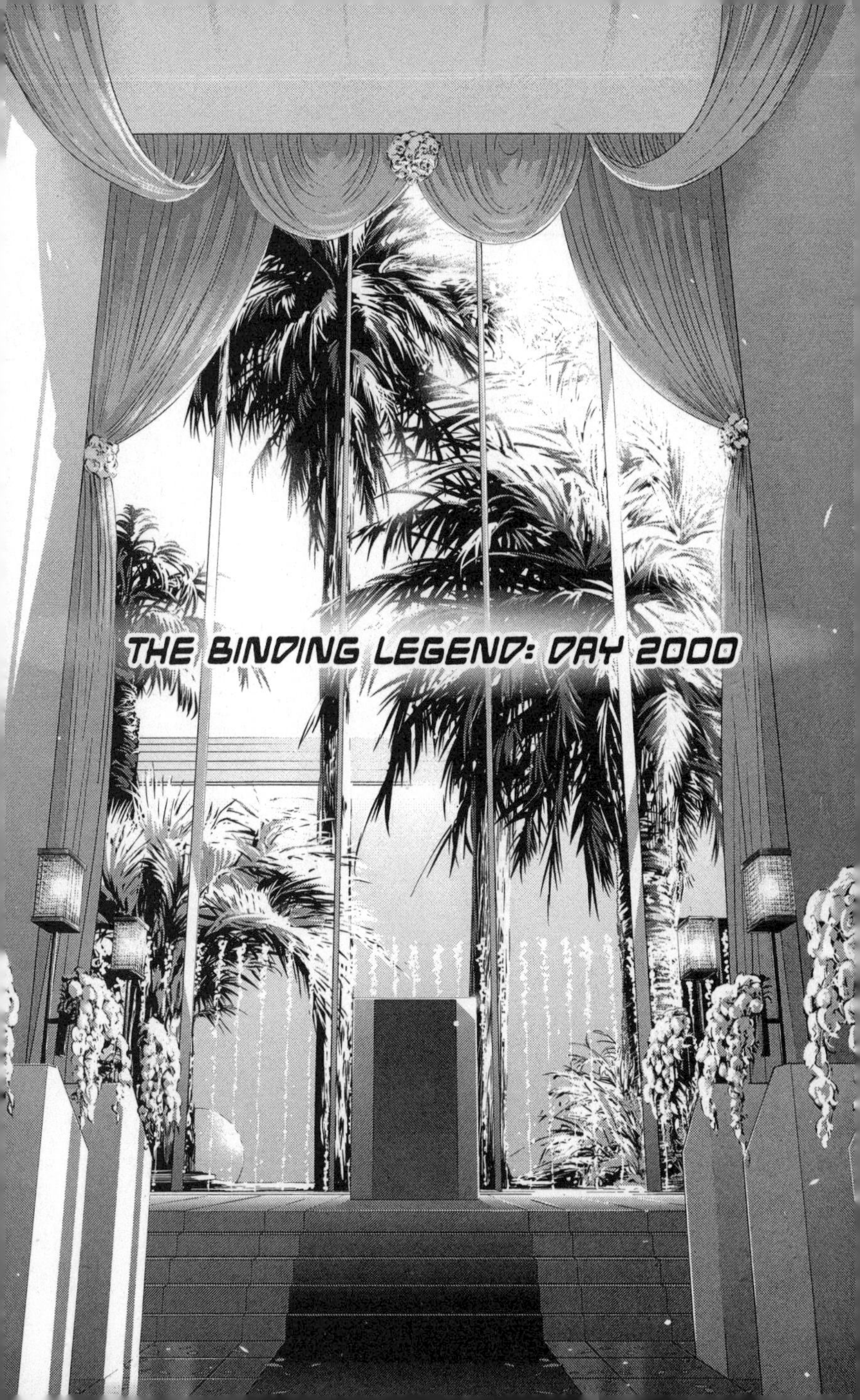
THE BINDING LEGEND: DAY 2000

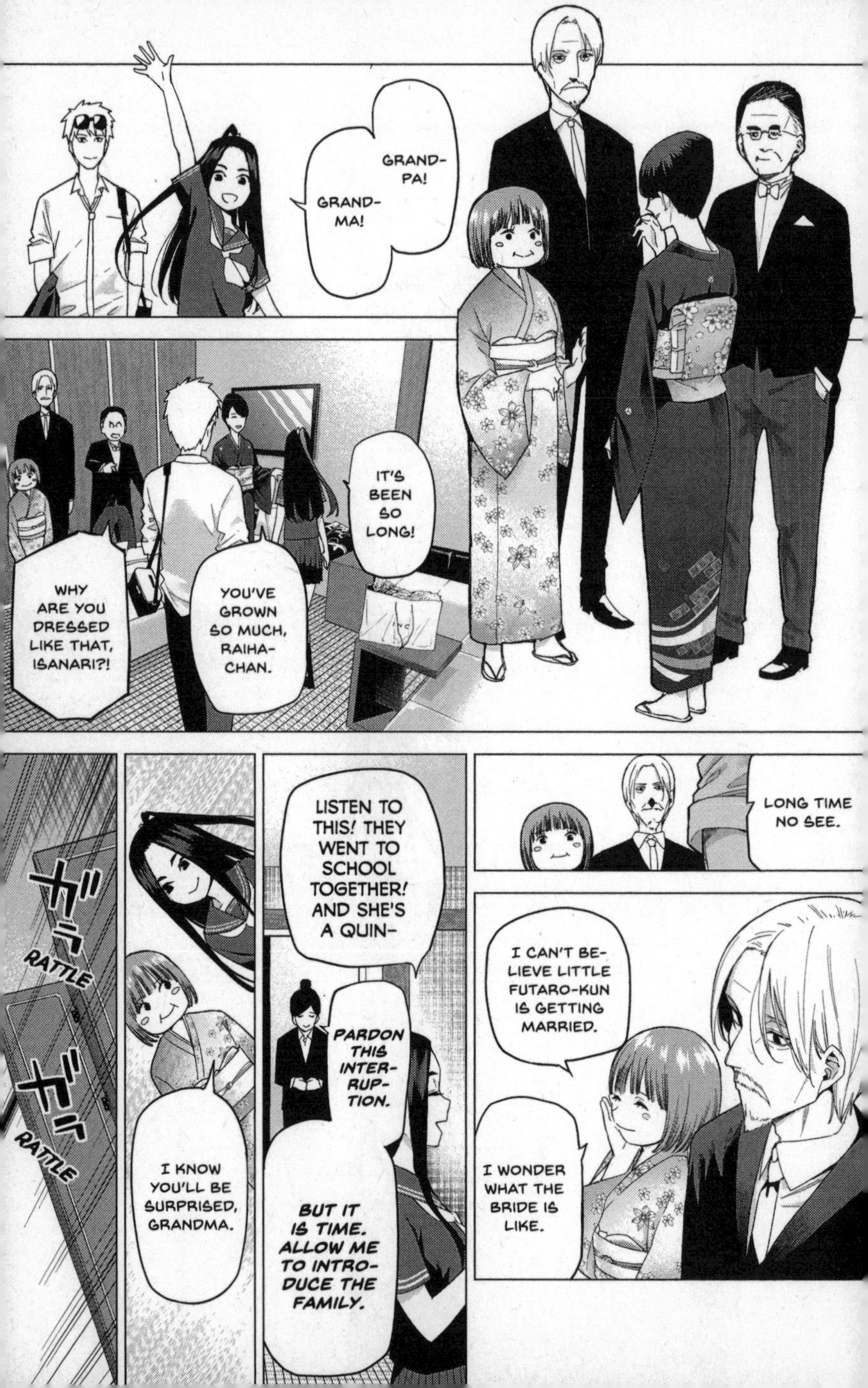
GRAND-PA!
GRAND-MA!
IT'S BEEN SO LONG!
YOU'VE GROWN SO MUCH, RAIHA-CHAN.
WHY ARE YOU DRESSED LIKE THAT, ISANARI?!
LONG TIME NO SEE.
I CAN'T BE-LIEVE LITTLE FUTARO-KUN IS GETTING MARRIED.
I WONDER WHAT THE BRIDE IS LIKE.
LISTEN TO THIS! THEY WENT TO SCHOOL TOGETHER! AND SHE'S A QUIN-
PARDON THIS INTER-RUP-TION.
BUT IT IS TIME. ALLOW ME TO INTRO-DUCE THE FAMILY.
I KNOW YOU'LL BE SURPRISED, GRANDMA.
RATTLE
RATTLE

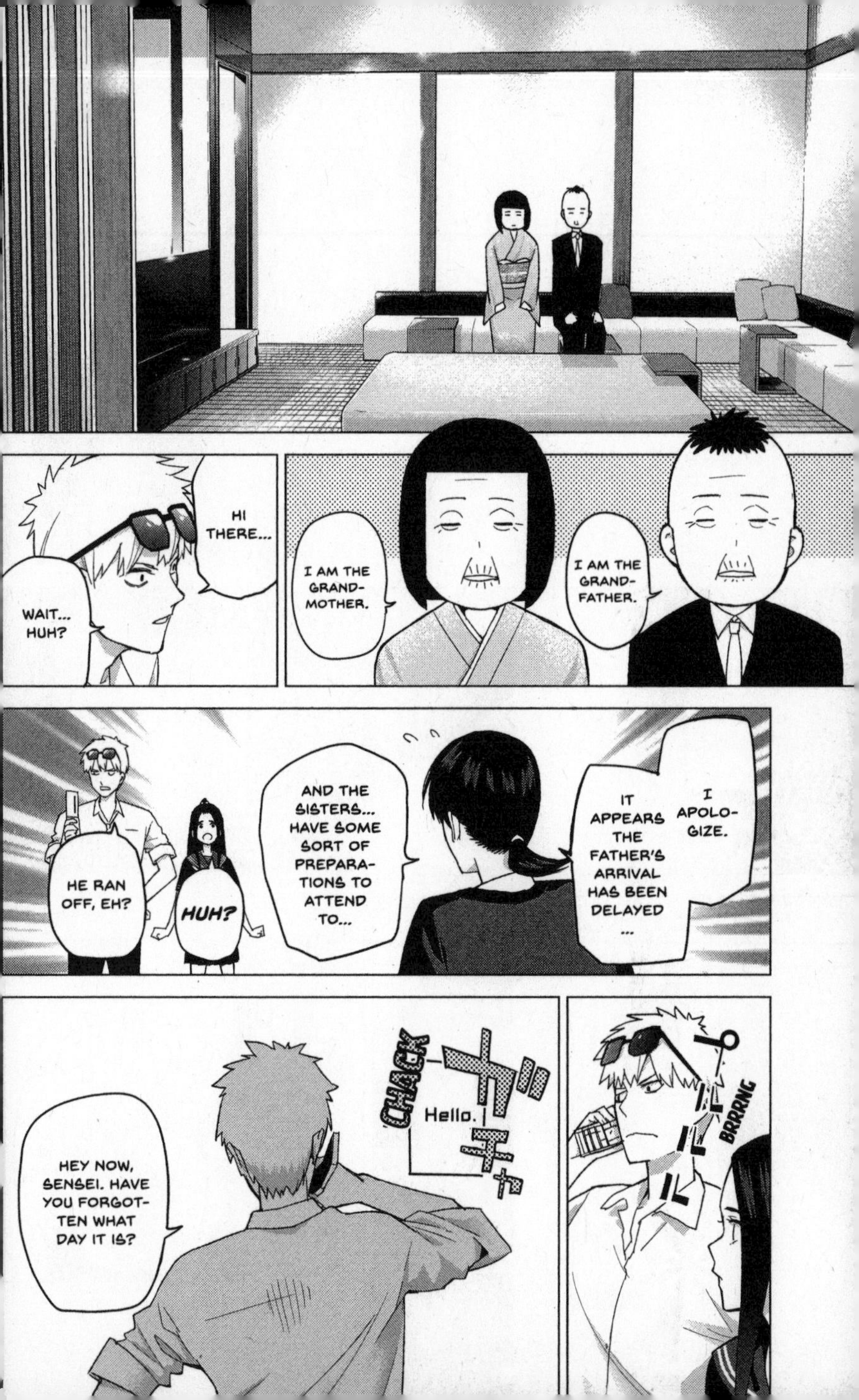
I AM THE GRAND-FATHER.
I AM THE GRAND-MOTHER.
HI THERE...
WAIT... HUH?
I APOLOGIZE.
IT APPEARS THE FATHER'S ARRIVAL HAS BEEN DELAYED...
AND THE SISTERS... HAVE SOME SORT OF PREPARATIONS TO ATTEND TO...
HUH?
HE RAN OFF, EH?
BRRRING
ガチャ
CHACK
Hello.
HEY NOW, SENSEI. HAVE YOU FORGOTTEN WHAT DAY IT IS?

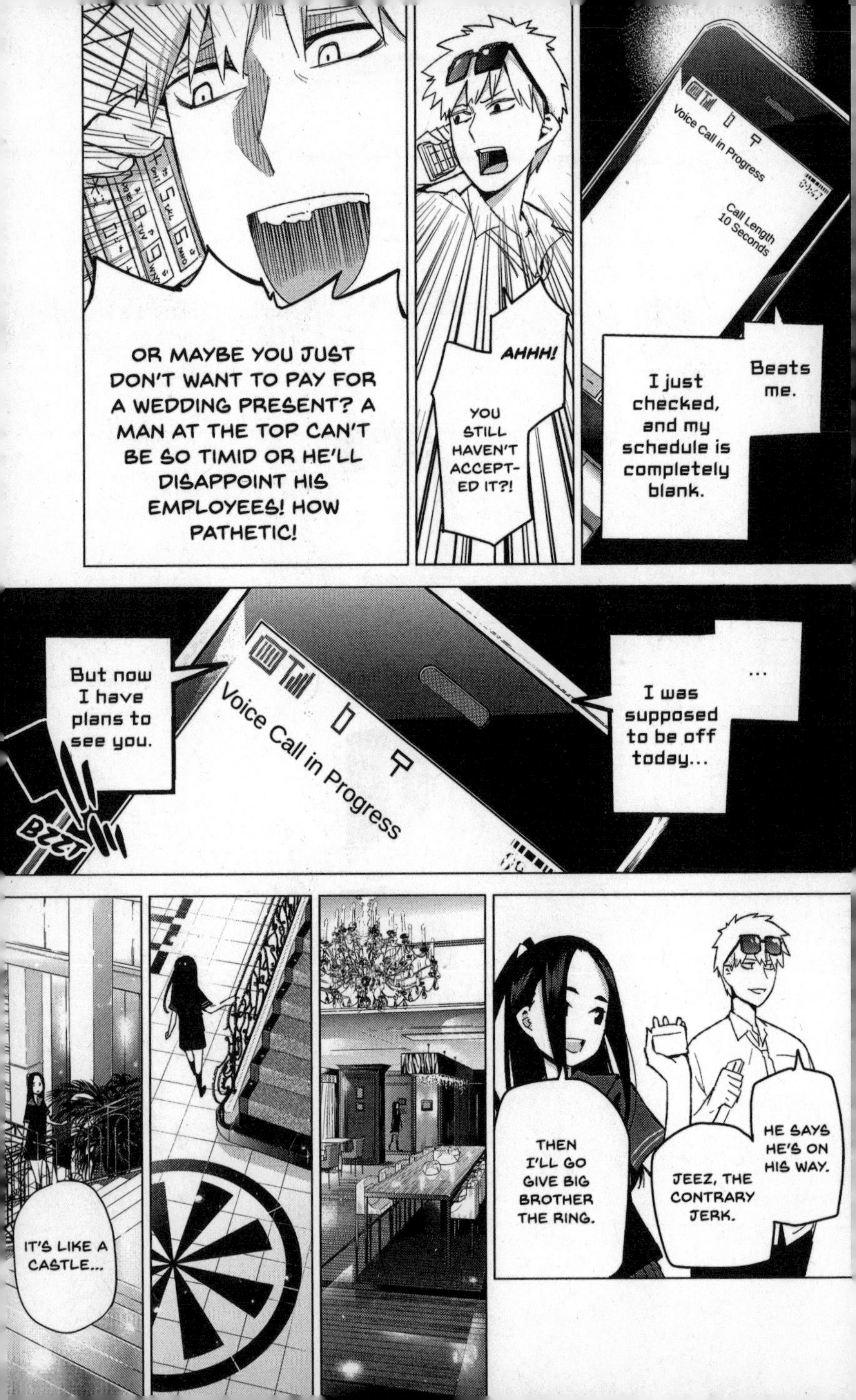
Voice Call in Progress
Call Length 10 Seconds
Beats me.
I just checked, and my schedule is completely blank.
AHHH!
YOU STILL HAVEN'T ACCEPT-ED IT?!
OR MAYBE YOU JUST DON'T WANT TO PAY FOR A WEDDING PRESENT? A MAN AT THE TOP CAN'T BE SO TIMID OR HE'LL DISAPPOINT HIS EMPLOYEES! HOW PATHETIC!
...
I was supposed to be off today...
Voice Call in Progress
But now I have plans to see you.
BZZZT
HE SAYS HE'S ON HIS WAY.
JEEZ, THE CONTRARY JERK.
THEN I'LL GO GIVE BIG BROTHER THE RING.
IT'S LIKE A CASTLE...

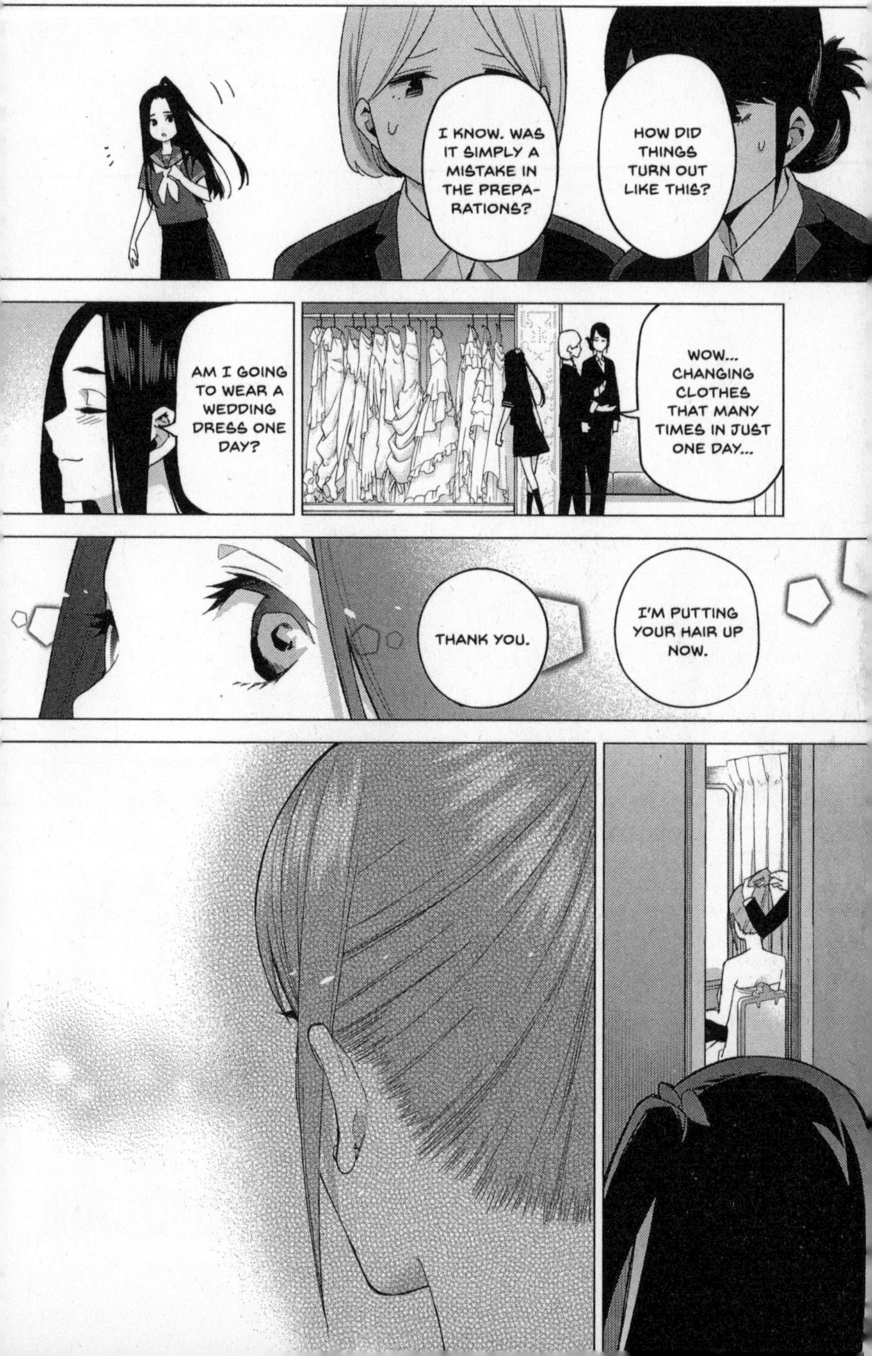
HOW DID THINGS TURN OUT LIKE THIS?
I KNOW. WAS IT SIMPLY A MISTAKE IN THE PREPARATIONS?
WOW... CHANGING CLOTHES THAT MANY TIMES IN JUST ONE DAY...
AM I GOING TO WEAR A WEDDING DRESS ONE DAY?
I'M PUTTING YOUR HAIR UP NOW.
THANK YOU.

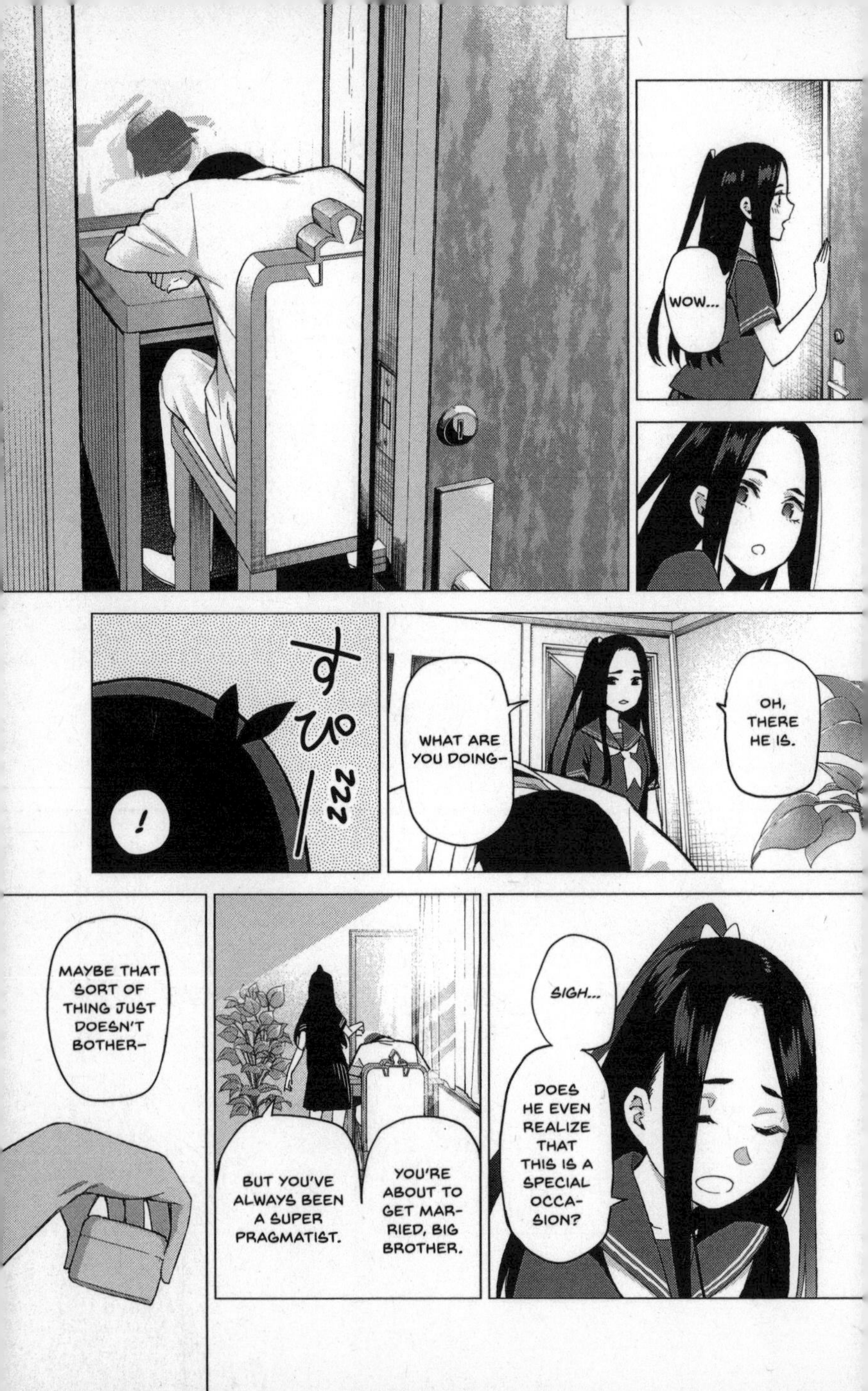
WOW...
OH, THERE HE IS.
WHAT ARE YOU DOING—
すぴー
zzz
!
SIGH...
DOES HE EVEN REALIZE THAT THIS IS A SPECIAL OCCA-SION?
YOU'RE ABOUT TO GET MAR-RIED, BIG BROTHER.
BUT YOU'VE ALWAYS BEEN A SUPER PRAGMATIST.
MAYBE THAT SORT OF THING JUST DOESN'T BOTHER—

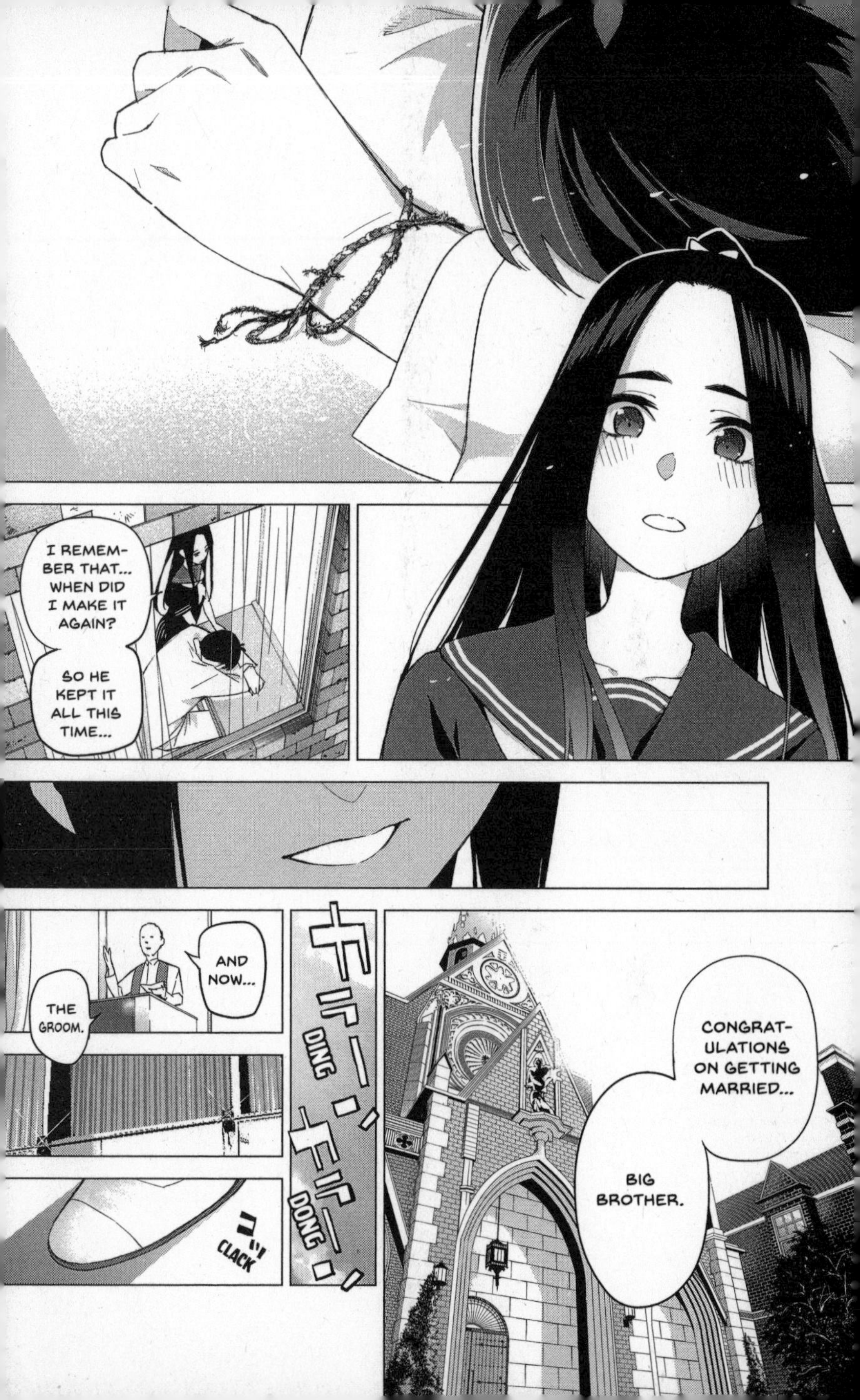
I REMEMBER THAT... WHEN DID I MAKE IT AGAIN?
SO HE KEPT IT ALL THIS TIME...
CONGRATULATIONS ON GETTING MARRIED...
BIG BROTHER.
DING
DONG
AND NOW...
THE GROOM.
CLACK

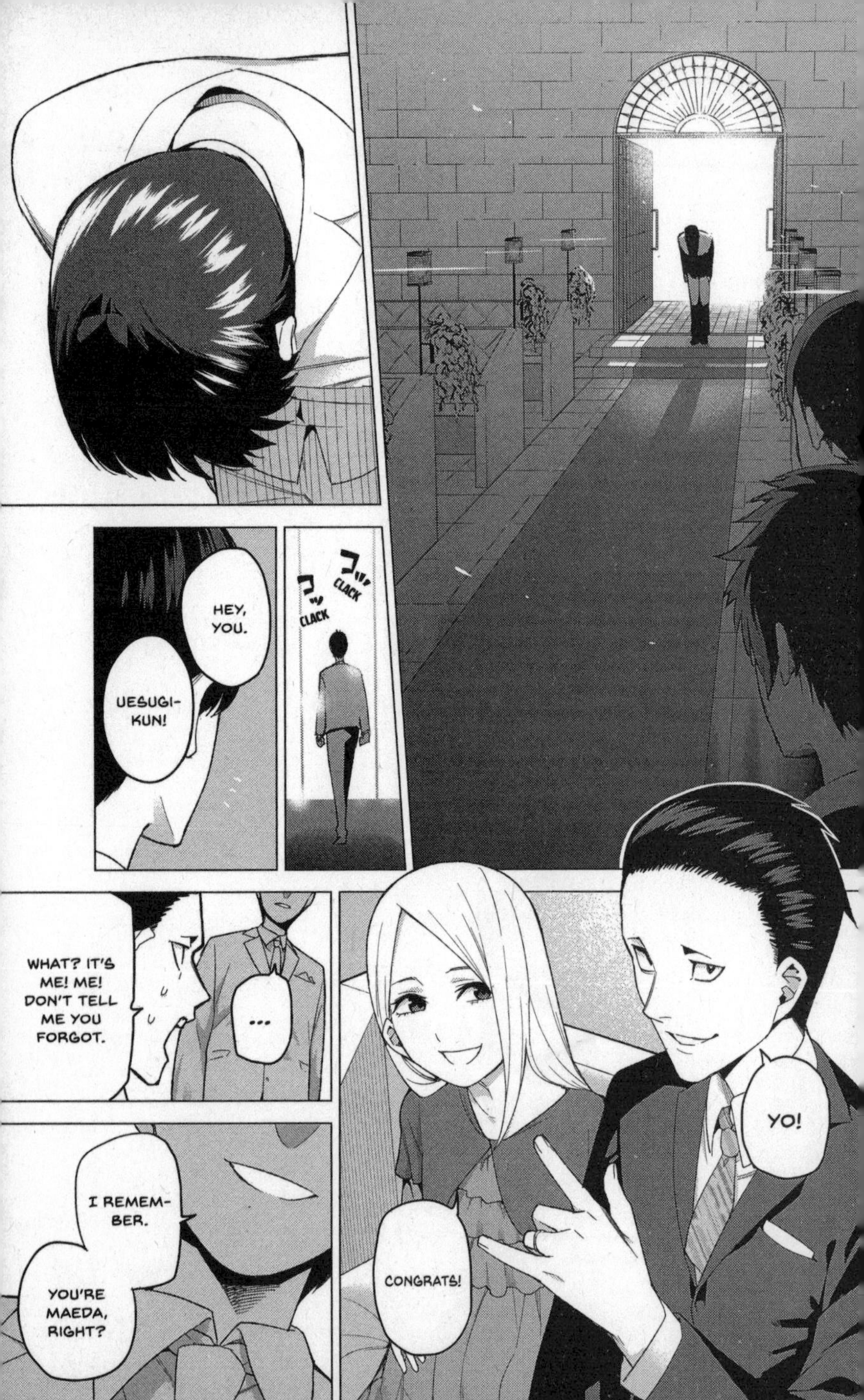

コッ
CLACK
コッ
CLACK
HEY, YOU.
UESUGI-KUN!
YO!
CONGRATS!
WHAT? IT'S ME! ME! DON'T TELL ME YOU FORGOT.
...
I REMEMBER.
YOU'RE MAEDA, RIGHT?

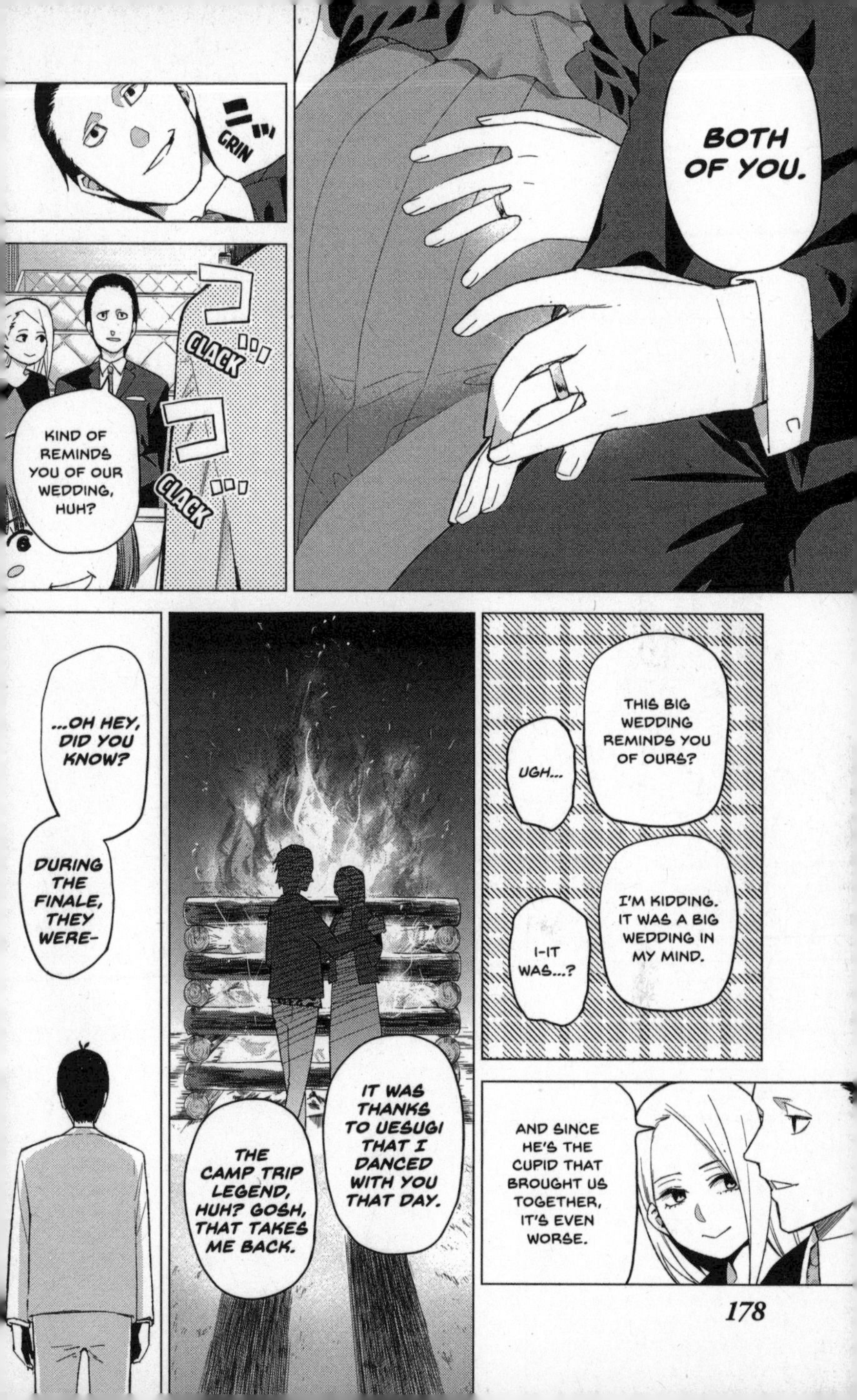
BOTH OF YOU.
GRIN
KIND OF REMINDS YOU OF OUR WEDDING, HUH?
CLACK
CLACK
THIS BIG WEDDING REMINDS YOU OF OURS?
UGH...
I'M KIDDING. IT WAS A BIG WEDDING IN MY MIND.
I-IT WAS...?
AND SINCE HE'S THE CUPID THAT BROUGHT US TOGETHER, IT'S EVEN WORSE.
IT WAS THANKS TO UESUGI THAT I DANCED WITH YOU THAT DAY.
THE CAMP TRIP LEGEND, HUH? GOSH, THAT TAKES ME BACK.
...OH HEY, DID YOU KNOW?
DURING THE FINALE, THEY WERE-

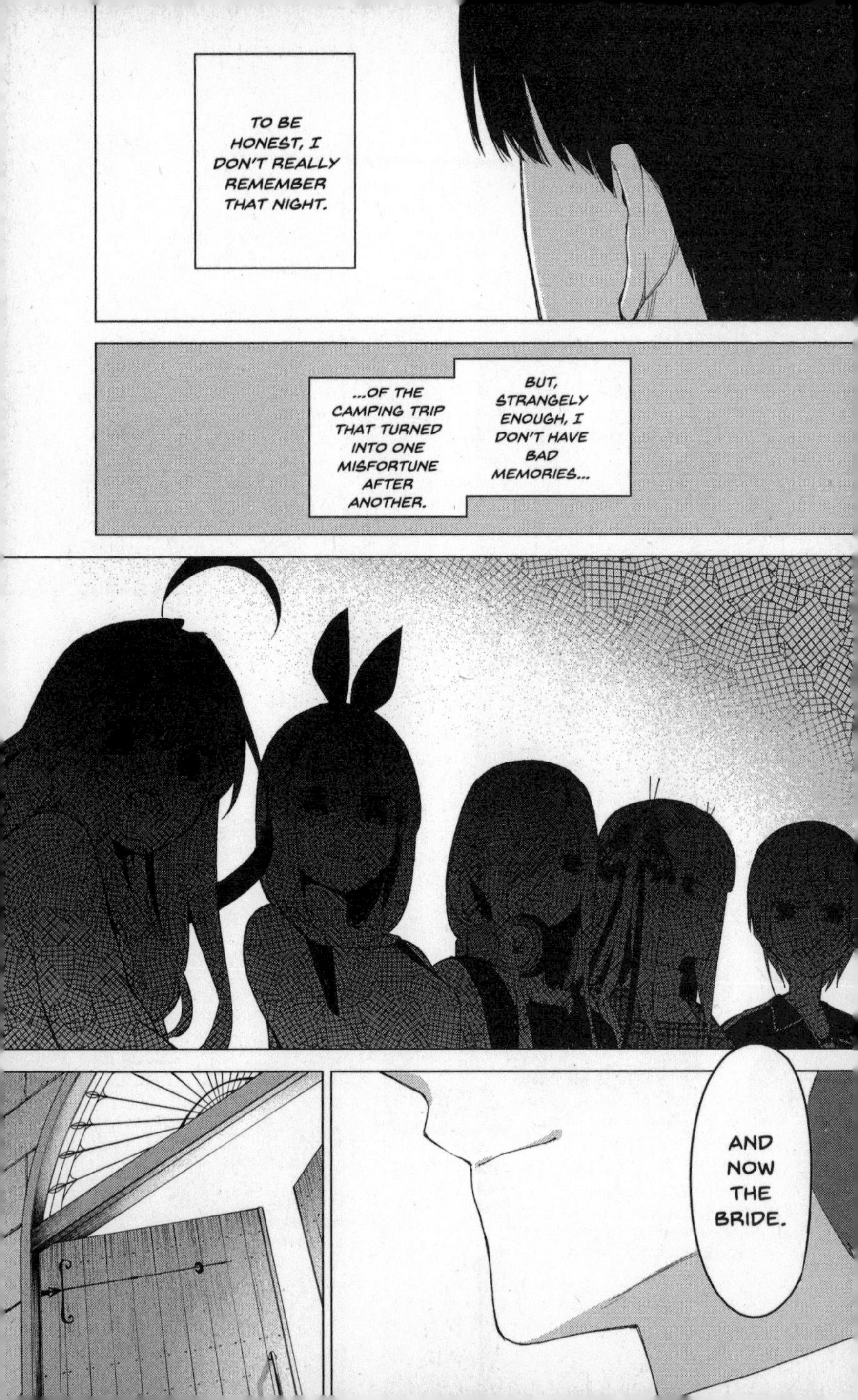
TO BE HONEST, I DON'T REALLY REMEMBER THAT NIGHT.
BUT, STRANGELY ENOUGH, I DON'T HAVE BAD MEMORIES...
...OF THE CAMPING TRIP THAT TURNED INTO ONE MISFORTUNE AFTER ANOTHER.
AND NOW THE BRIDE.

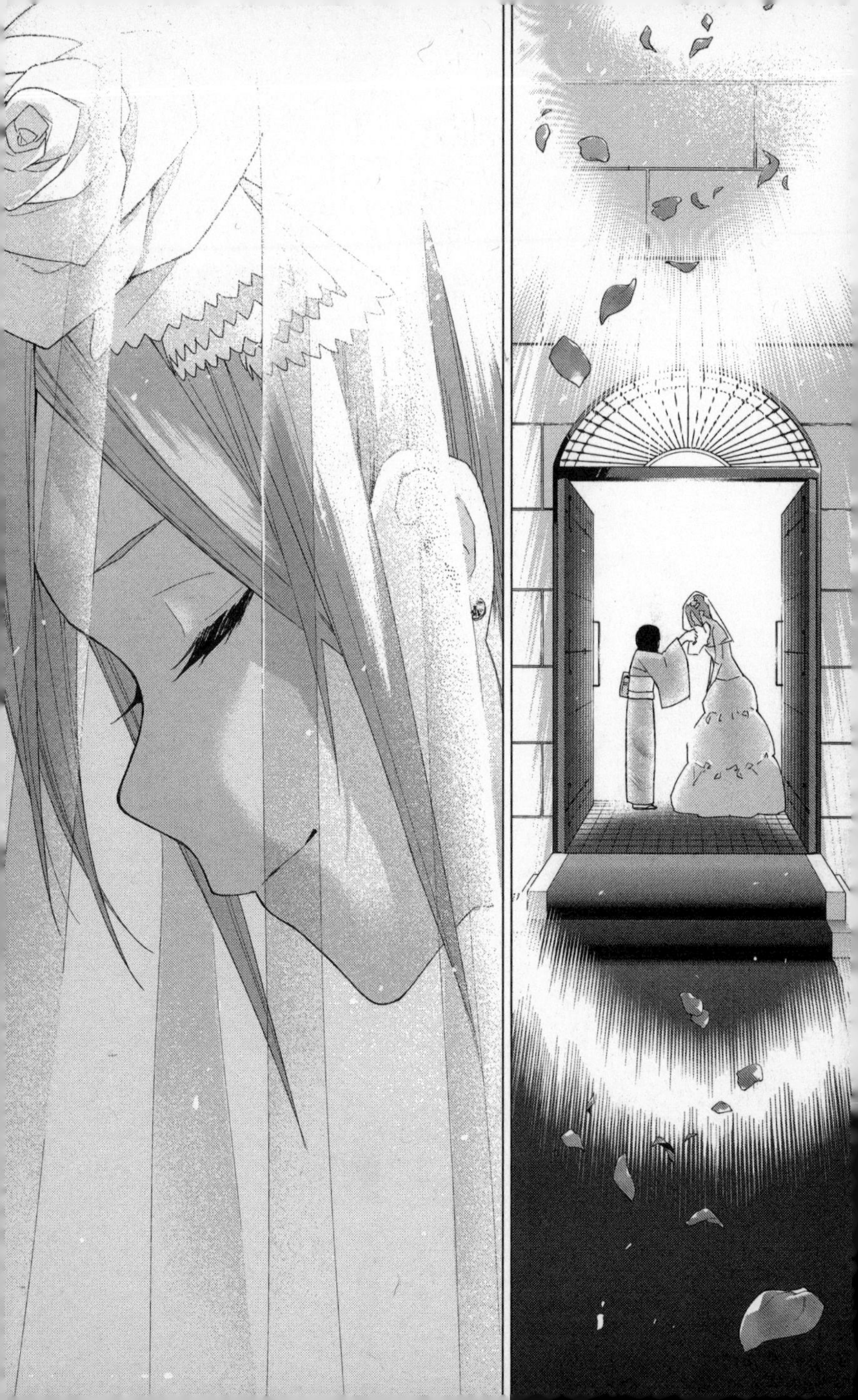

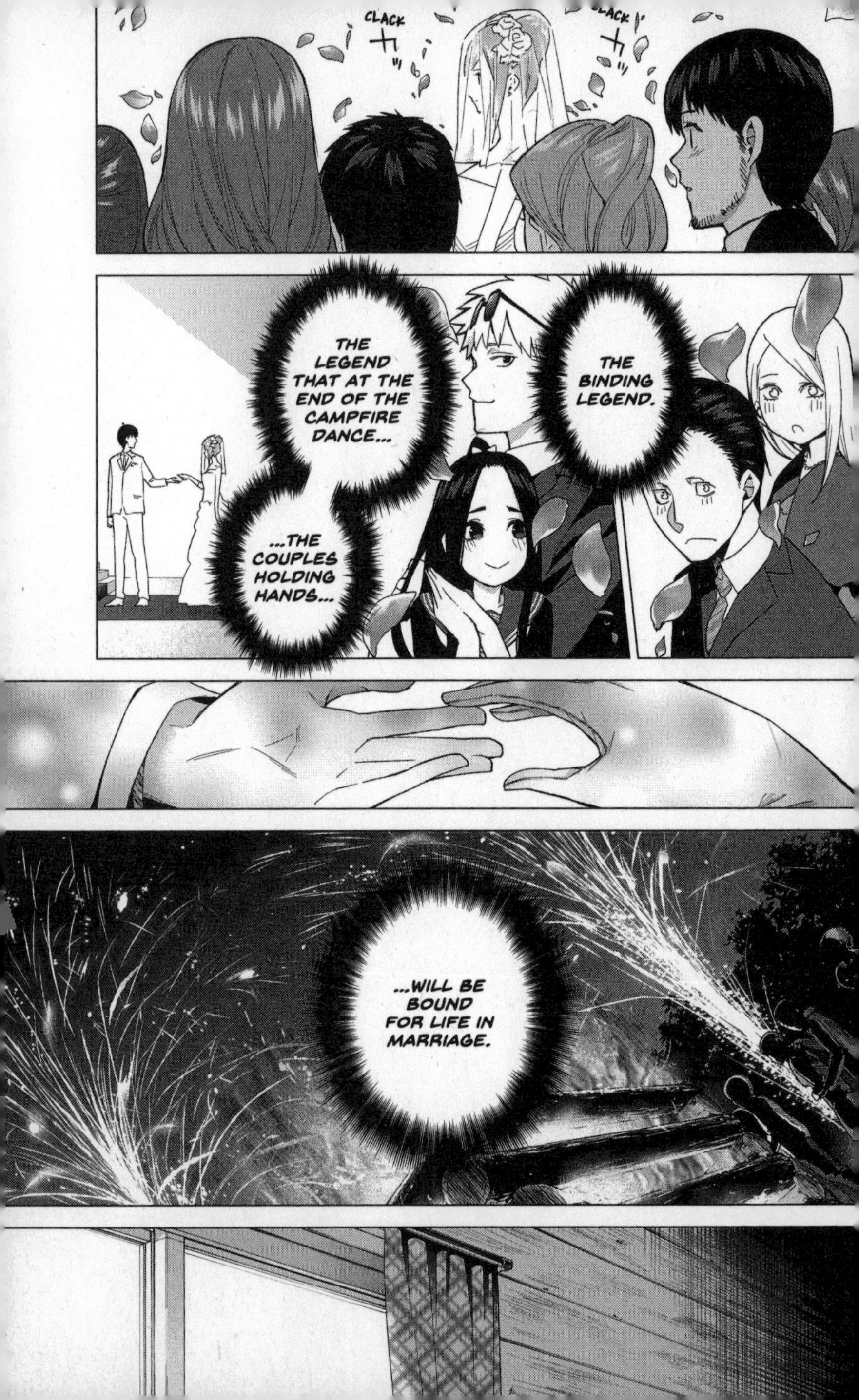
LACK
CLACK
THE BINDING LEGEND.
THE LEGEND THAT AT THE END OF THE CAMPFIRE DANCE...
...THE COUPLES HOLDING HANDS...
...WILL BE BOUND FOR LIFE IN MARRIAGE.

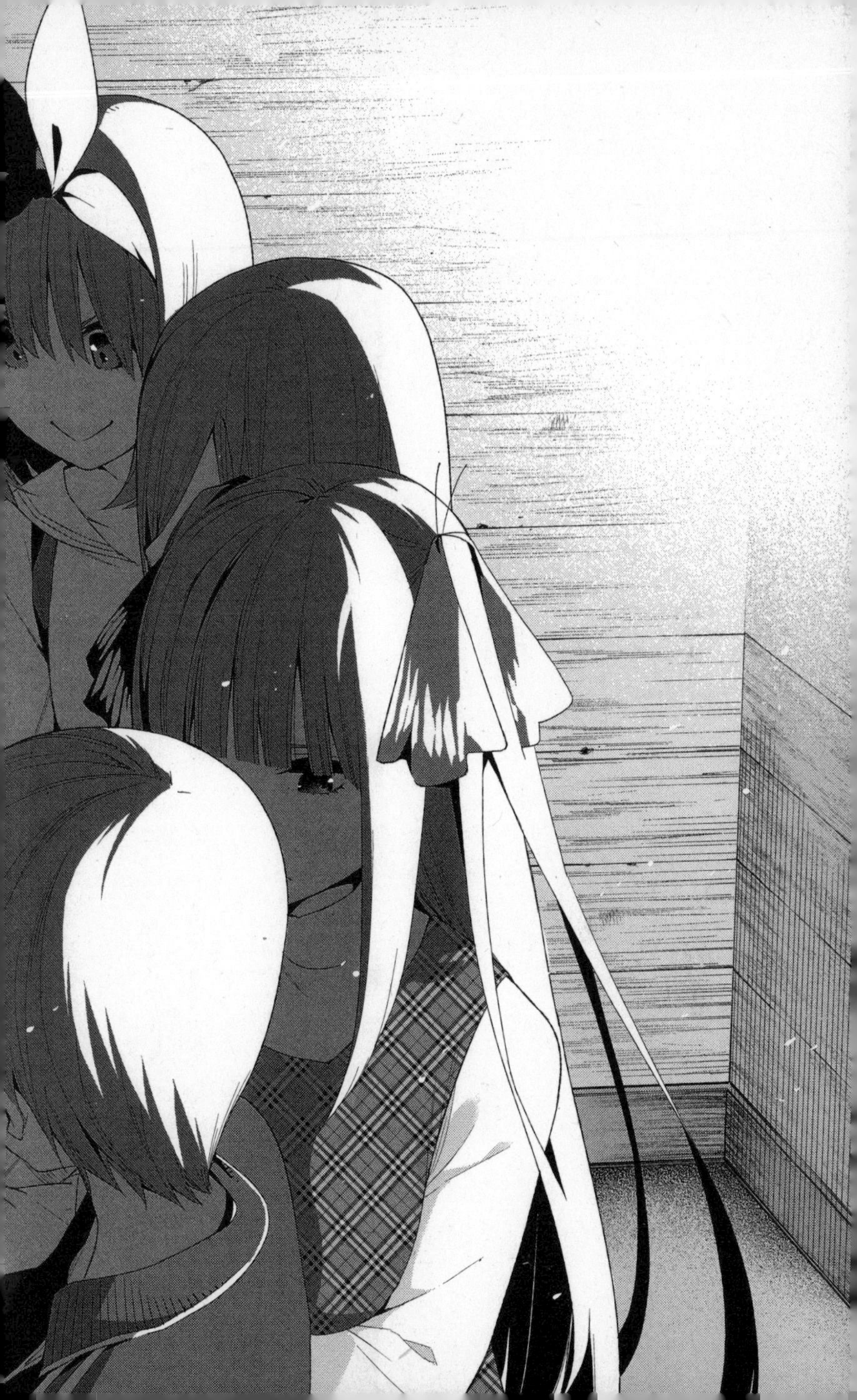

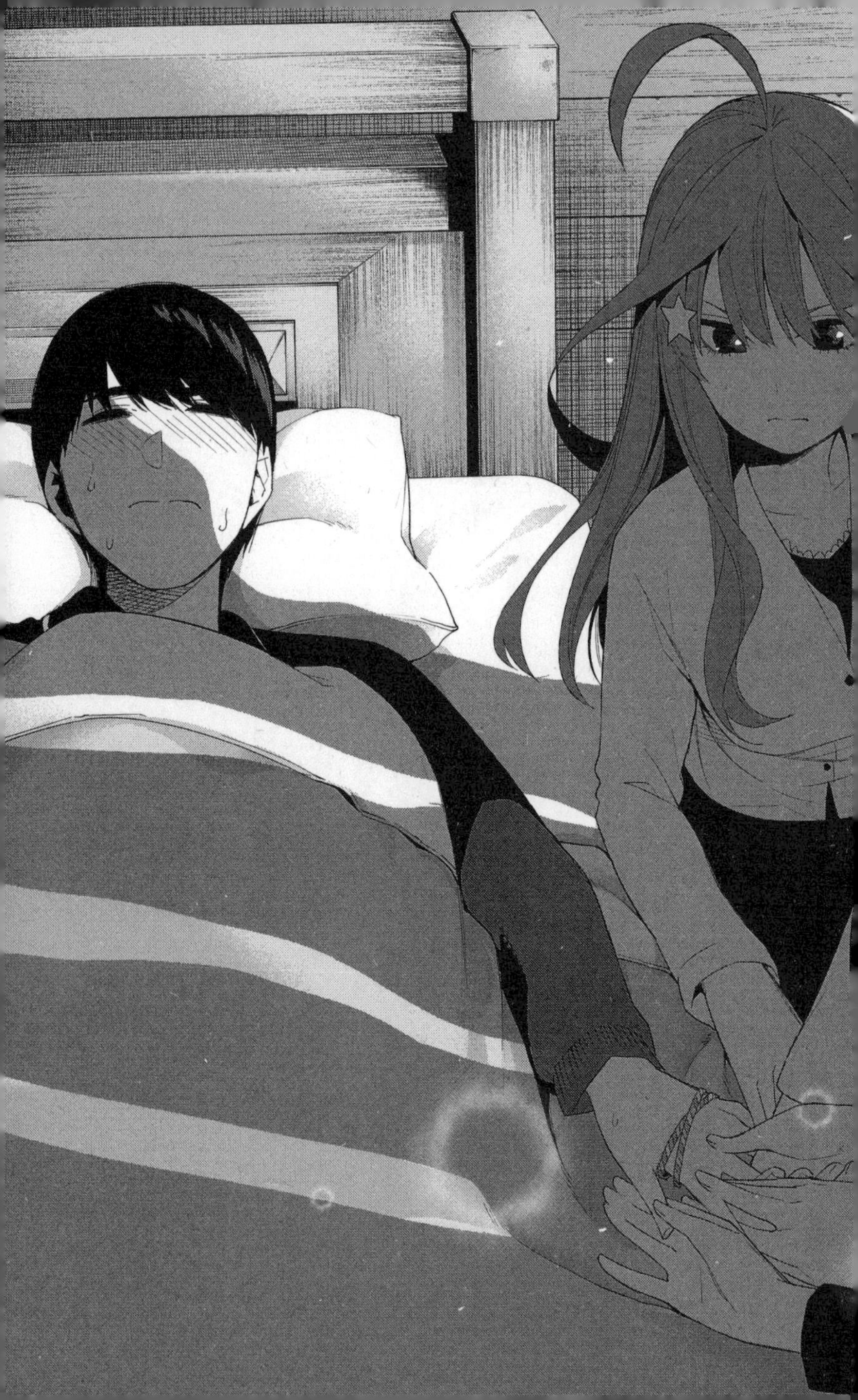

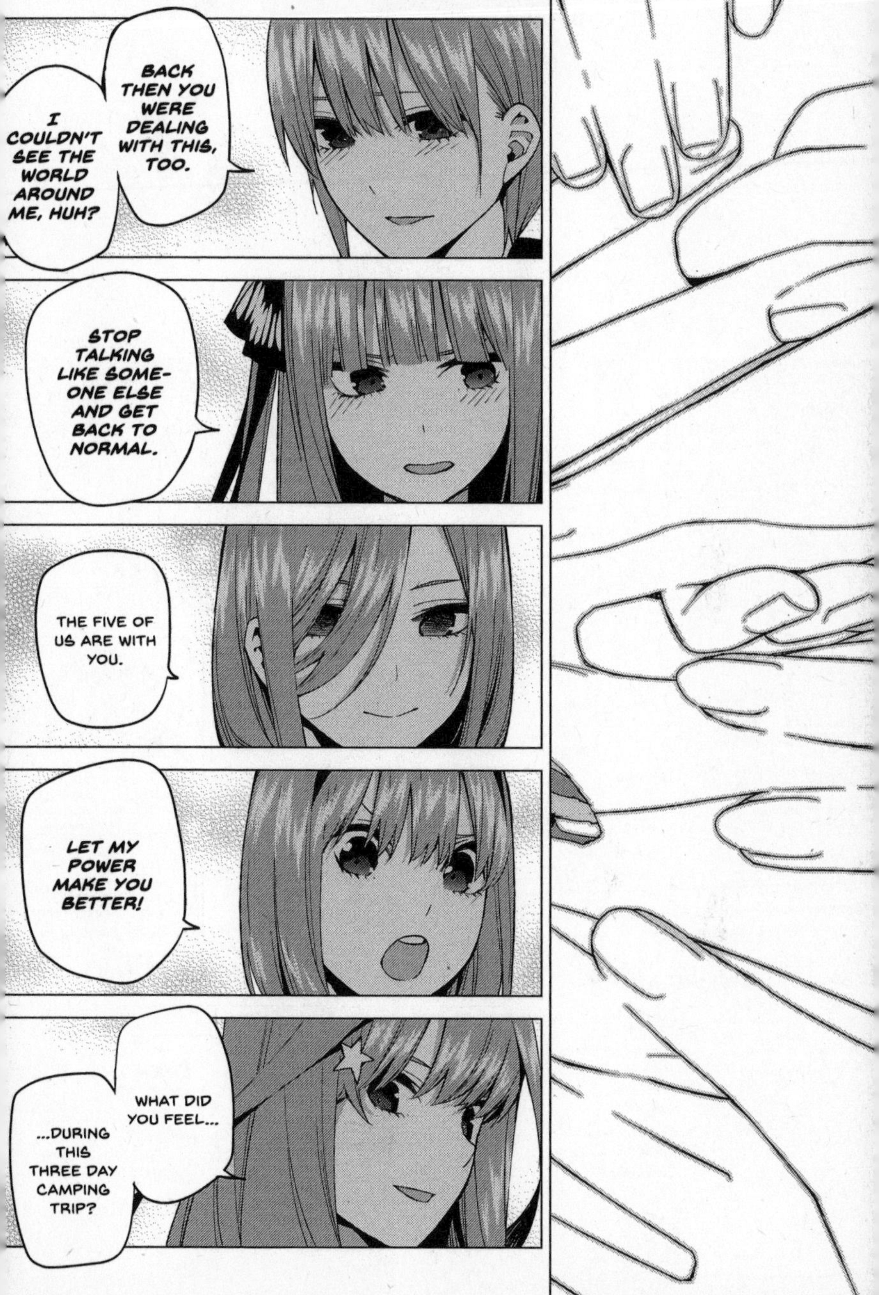
BACK THEN YOU WERE DEALING WITH THIS, TOO.
I COULDN'T SEE THE WORLD AROUND ME, HUH?
STOP TALKING LIKE SOME-ONE ELSE AND GET BACK TO NORMAL.
THE FIVE OF US ARE WITH YOU.
LET MY POWER MAKE YOU BETTER!
WHAT DID YOU FEEL...
...DURING THIS THREE DAY CAMPING TRIP?

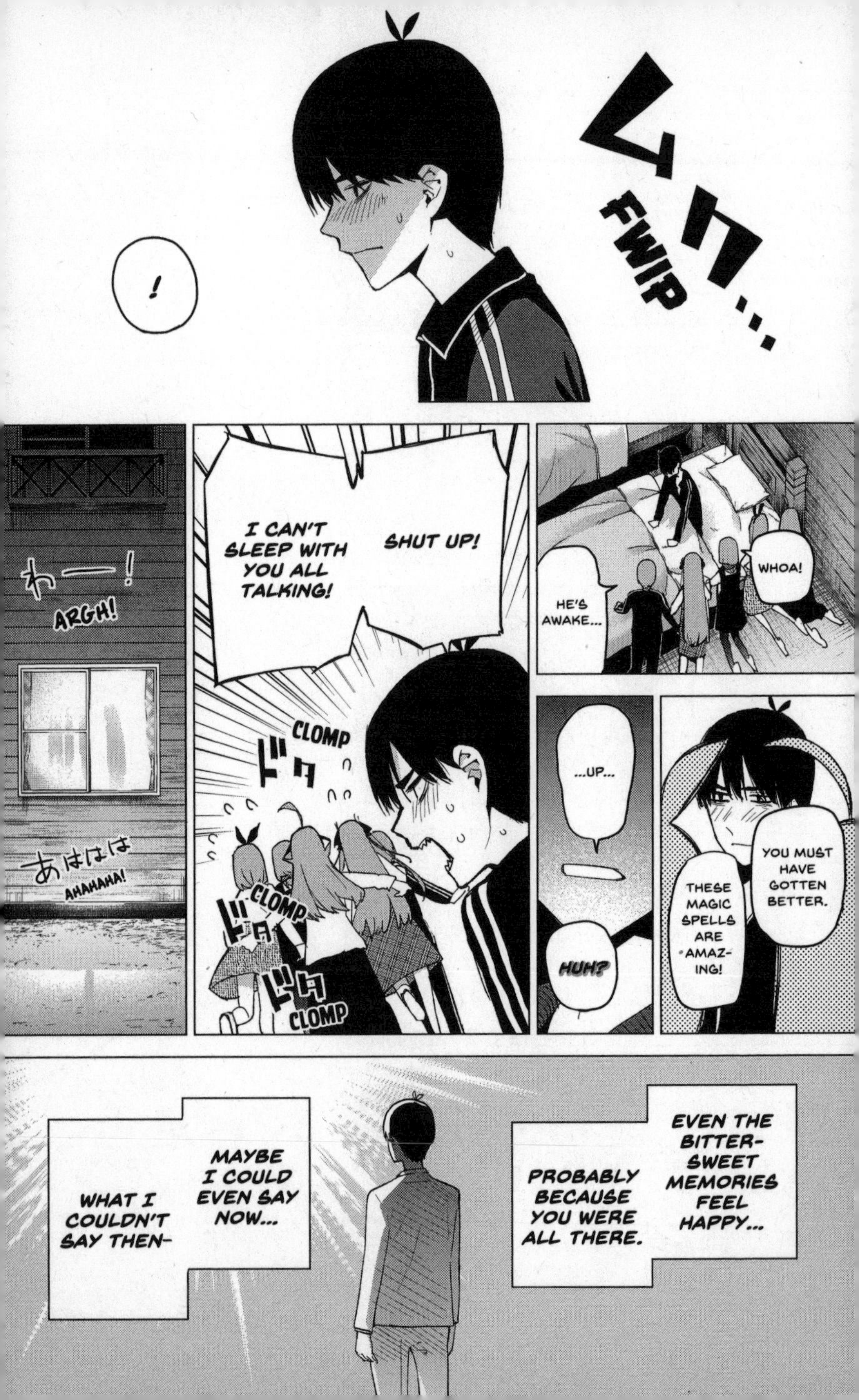
ムク…
FWIP
!
WHOA!
HE'S AWAKE...
YOU MUST HAVE GOTTEN BETTER.
THESE MAGIC SPELLS ARE AMAZ-ING!
...UP...
HUH?
SHUT UP!
I CAN'T SLEEP WITH YOU ALL TALKING!
ドッ
CLOMP
ドッ
CLOMP
ドッ
CLOMP
わー！
ARGH!
あははは
AHAHAHA!
EVEN THE BITTER-SWEET MEMORIES FEEL HAPPY...
PROBABLY BECAUSE YOU WERE ALL THERE.
MAYBE I COULD EVEN SAY NOW...
WHAT I COULDN'T SAY THEN-

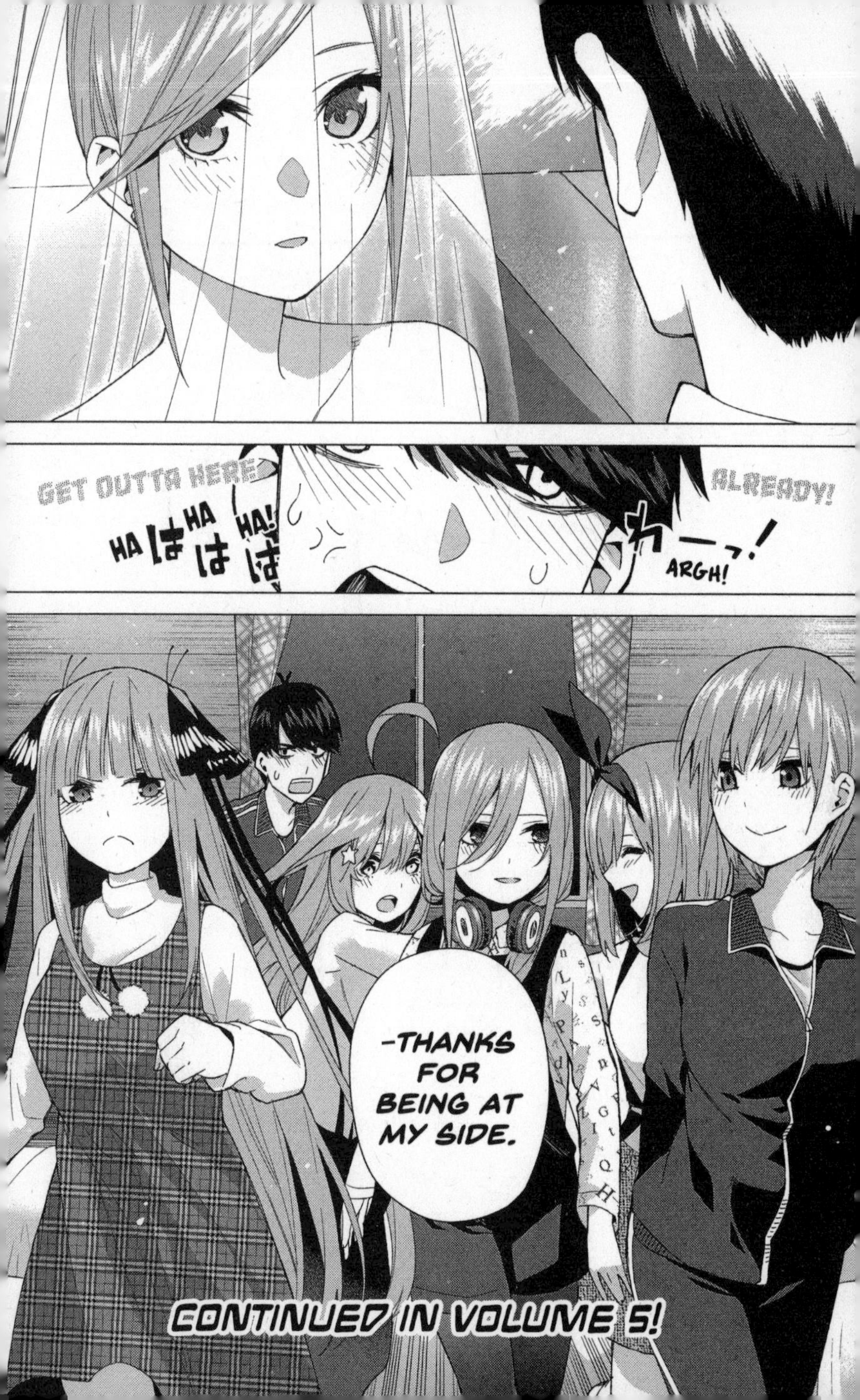
GET OUTTA HERE ALREADY!
わーっ!
ARGH!
HA は HA は HA! ば
-THANKS FOR BEING AT MY SIDE.
CONTINUED IN VOLUME 5!

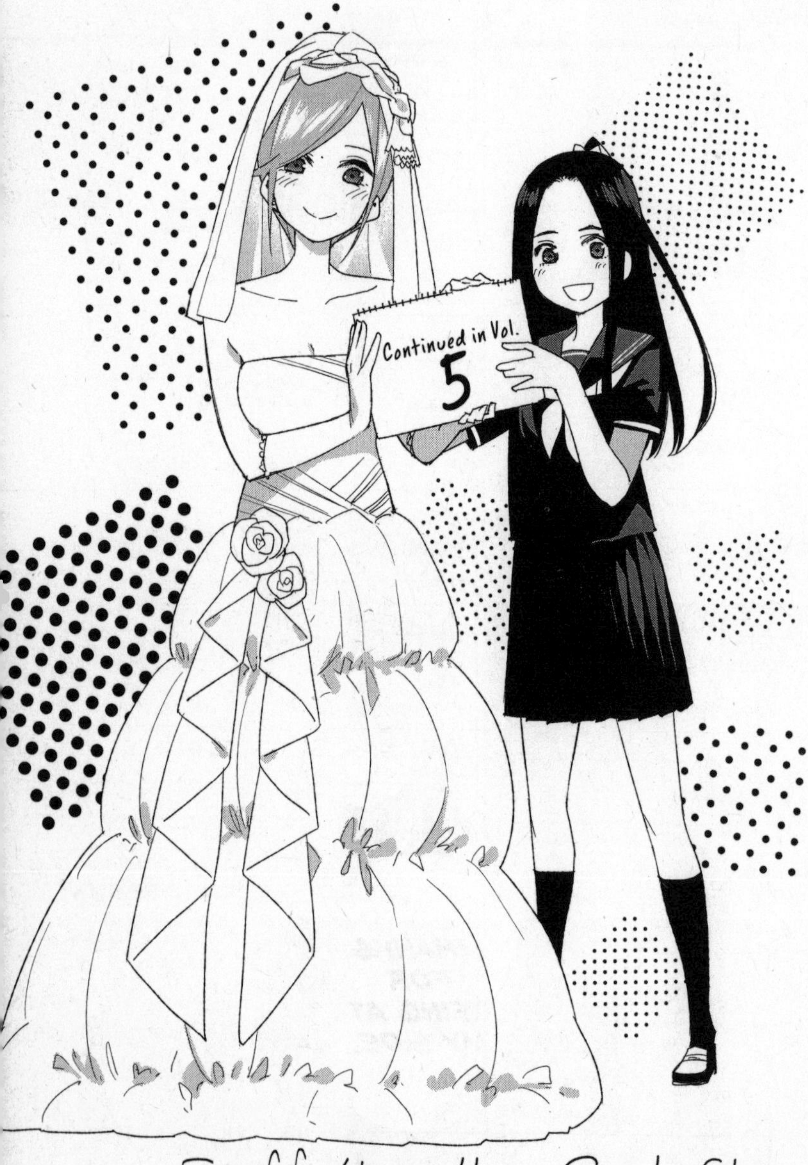
Continued in Vol.
5
Staff Ueno Hino Ogata Cho

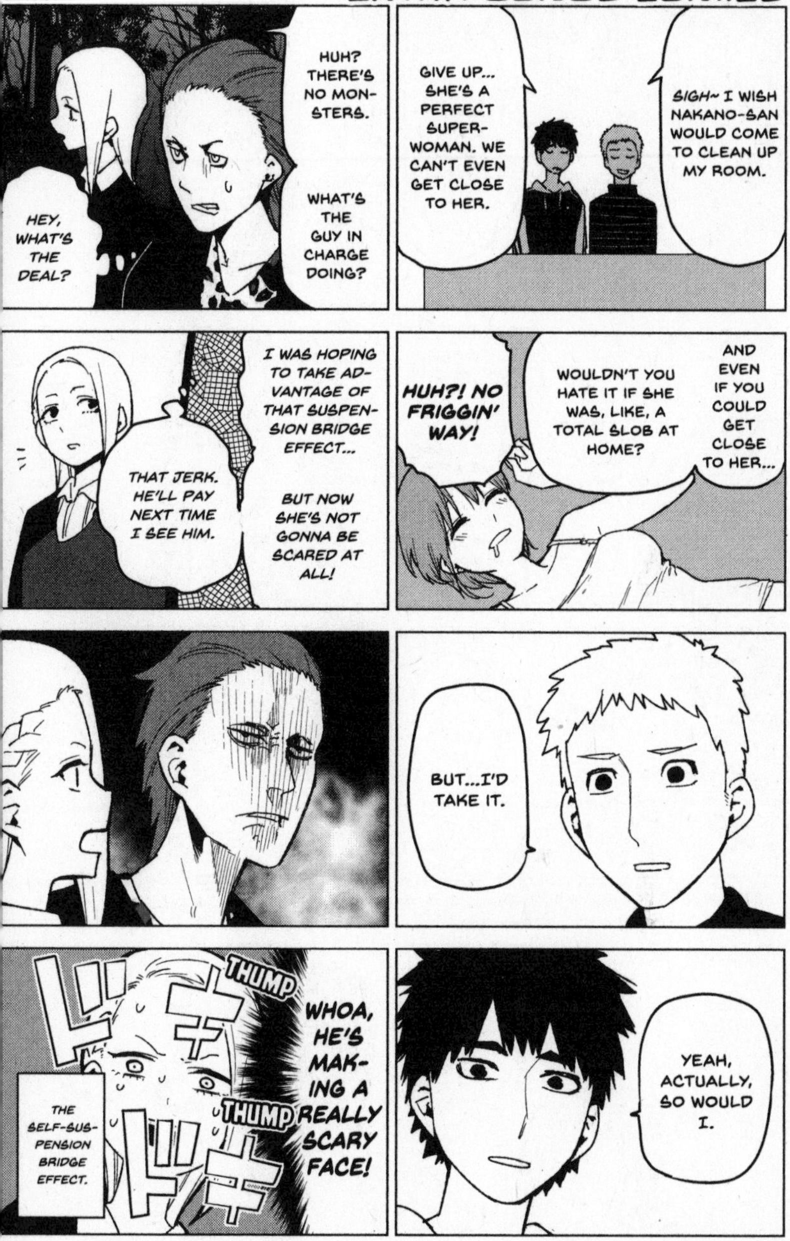
SIGH~ I WISH NAKANO-SAN WOULD COME TO CLEAN UP MY ROOM.
GIVE UP... SHE'S A PERFECT SUPER-WOMAN. WE CAN'T EVEN GET CLOSE TO HER.
AND EVEN IF YOU COULD GET CLOSE TO HER...
WOULDN'T YOU HATE IT IF SHE WAS, LIKE, A TOTAL SLOB AT HOME?
HUH?! NO FRIGGIN' WAY!
BUT...I'D TAKE IT.
YEAH, ACTUALLY, SO WOULD I.
HUH? THERE'S NO MON-STERS.
WHAT'S THE GUY IN CHARGE DOING?
HEY, WHAT'S THE DEAL?
I WAS HOPING TO TAKE AD-VANTAGE OF THAT SUSPEN-SION BRIDGE EFFECT...
BUT NOW SHE'S NOT GONNA BE SCARED AT ALL!
THAT JERK. HE'LL PAY NEXT TIME I SEE HIM.
THUMP
THUMP
WHOA, HE'S MAK-ING A REALLY SCARY FACE!
THE SELF-SUS-PENSION BRIDGE EFFECT.

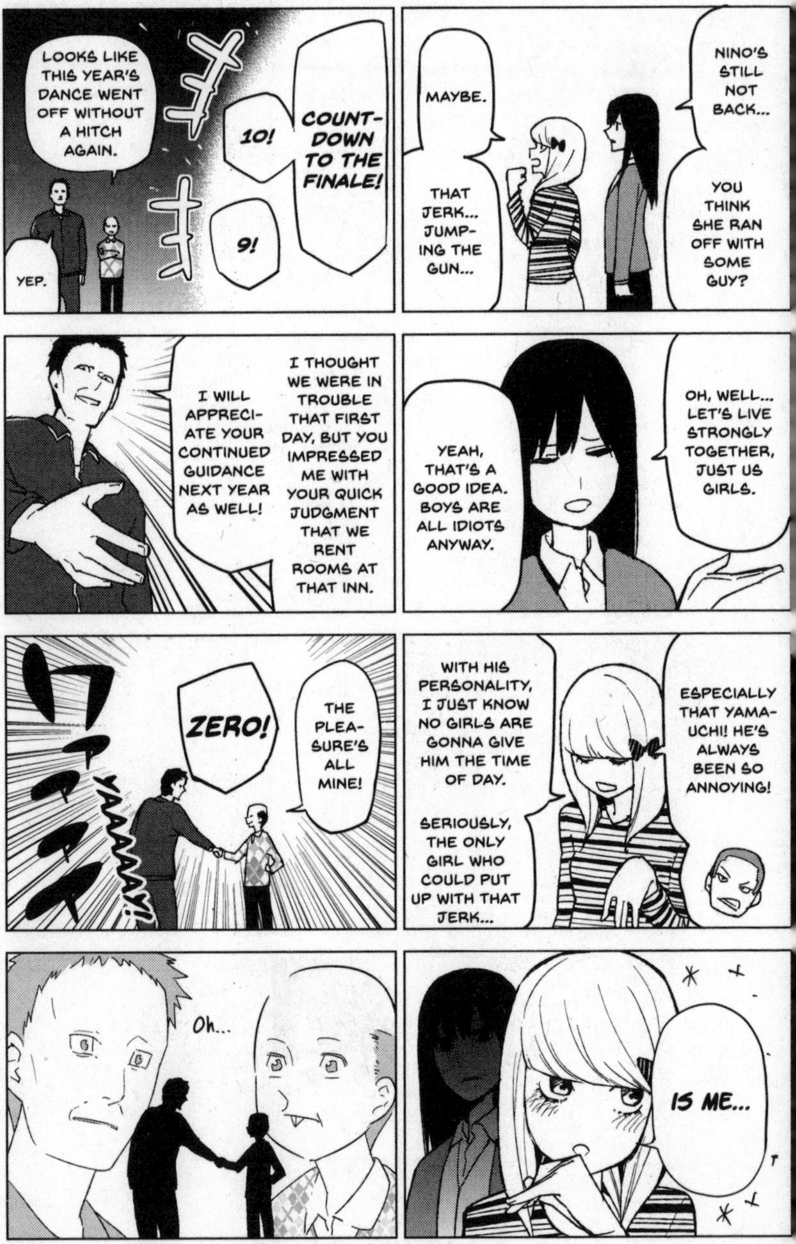
NINO'S STILL NOT BACK...
YOU THINK SHE RAN OFF WITH SOME GUY?
MAYBE.
THAT JERK... JUMPING THE GUN...
COUNT-DOWN TO THE FINALE!
10!
9!
LOOKS LIKE THIS YEAR'S DANCE WENT OFF WITHOUT A HITCH AGAIN.
YEP.
OH, WELL... LET'S LIVE STRONGLY TOGETHER, JUST US GIRLS.
YEAH, THAT'S A GOOD IDEA. BOYS ARE ALL IDIOTS ANYWAY.
I THOUGHT WE WERE IN TROUBLE THAT FIRST DAY, BUT YOU IMPRESSED ME WITH YOUR QUICK JUDGMENT THAT WE RENT ROOMS AT THAT INN.
I WILL APPRECIATE YOUR CONTINUED GUIDANCE NEXT YEAR AS WELL!
ESPECIALLY THAT YAMAUCHI! HE'S ALWAYS BEEN SO ANNOYING!
WITH HIS PERSONALITY, I JUST KNOW NO GIRLS ARE GONNA GIVE HIM THE TIME OF DAY.
SERIOUSLY, THE ONLY GIRL WHO COULD PUT UP WITH THAT JERK...
THE PLEASURE'S ALL MINE!
ZERO!
YAAAAAY!
IS ME...
Oh...

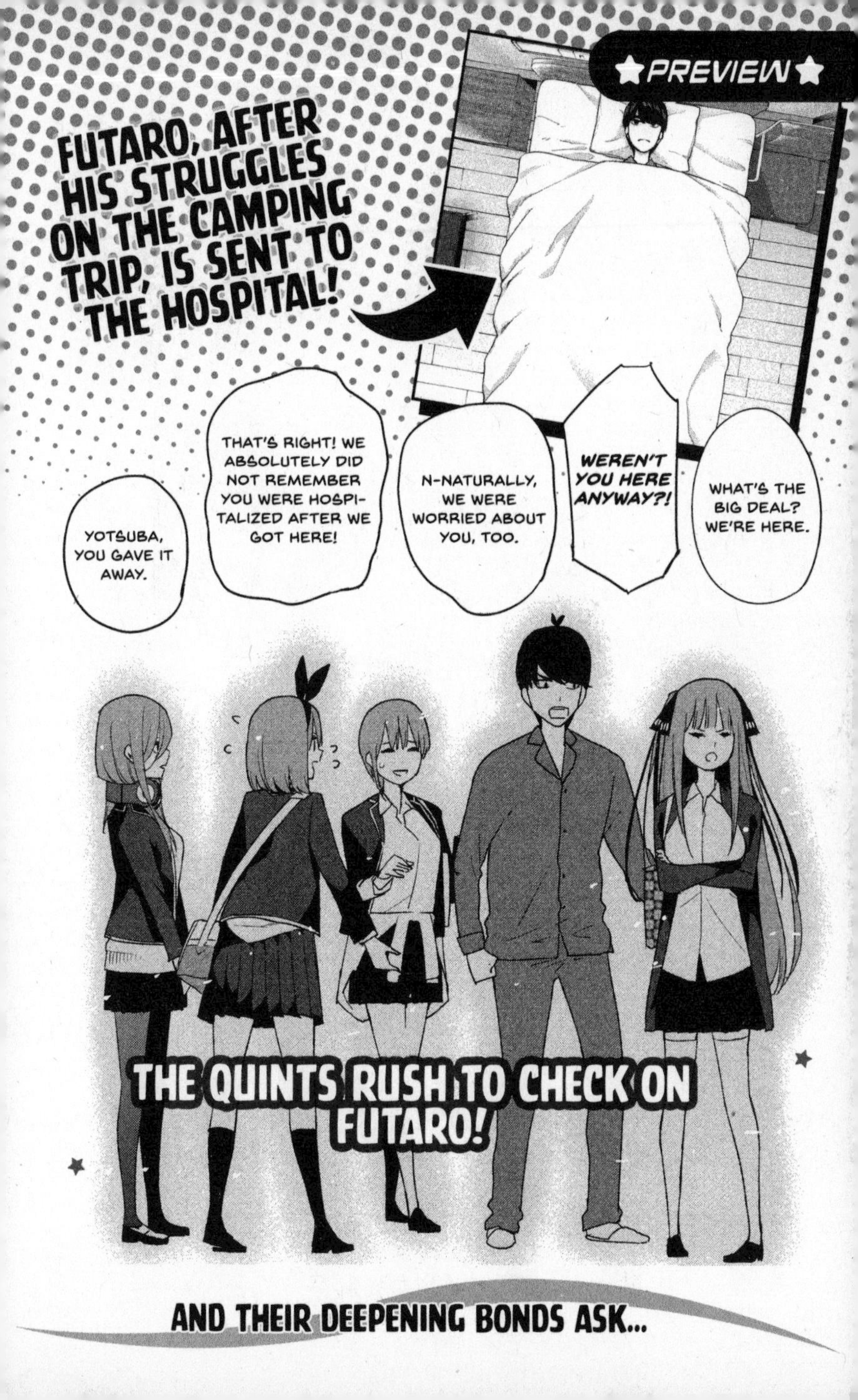
★PREVIEW★
FUTARO, AFTER HIS STRUGGLES ON THE CAMPING TRIP, IS SENT TO THE HOSPITAL!
WHAT'S THE BIG DEAL? WE'RE HERE.
WEREN'T YOU HERE ANYWAY?!
N-NATURALLY, WE WERE WORRIED ABOUT YOU, TOO.
THAT'S RIGHT! WE ABSOLUTELY DID NOT REMEMBER YOU WERE HOSPI-TALIZED AFTER WE GOT HERE!
YOTSUBA, YOU GAVE IT AWAY.
THE QUINTS RUSH TO CHECK ON FUTARO!
AND THEIR DEEPENING BONDS ASK...

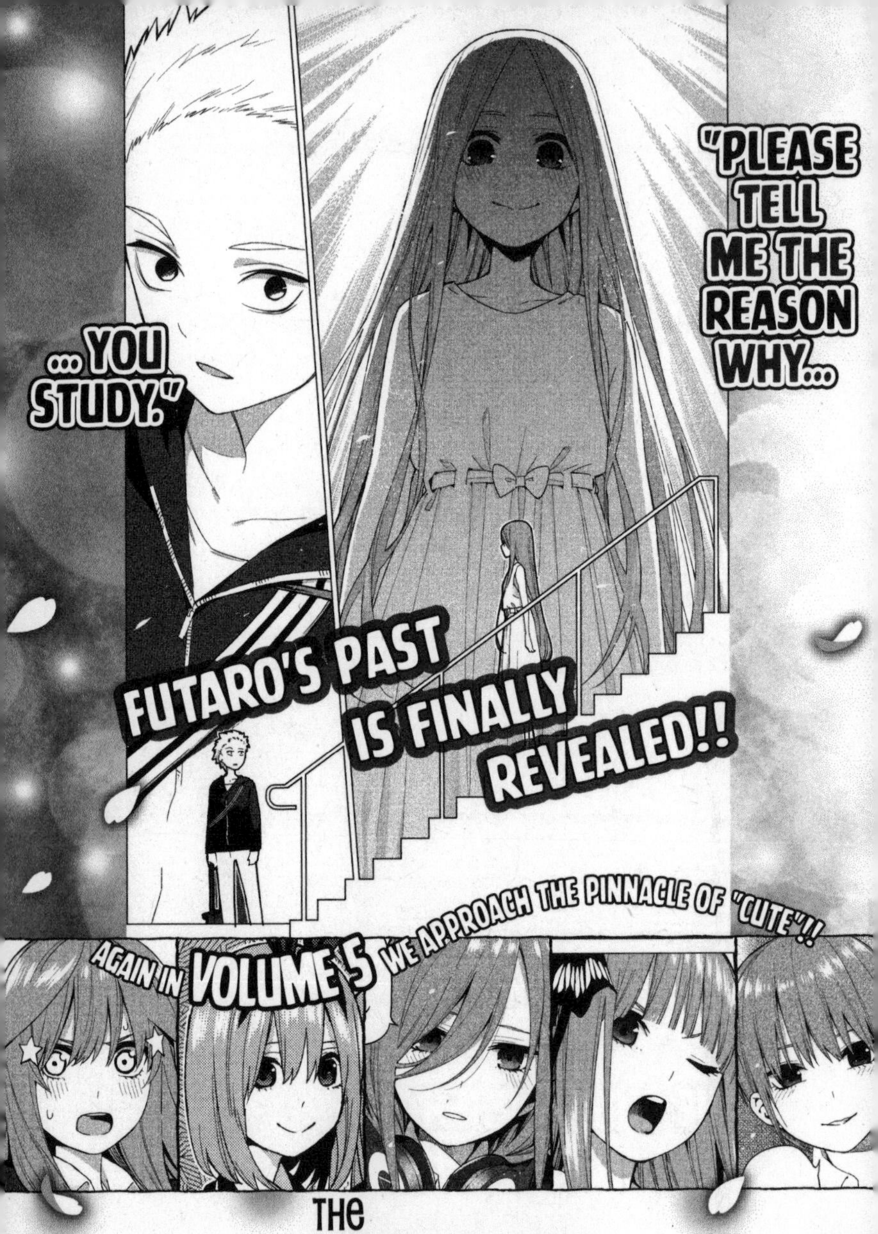
"PLEASE TELL ME THE REASON WHY...
...YOU STUDY."
FUTARO'S PAST IS FINALLY REVEALED!!
AGAIN IN VOLUME 5 WE APPROACH THE PINNACLE OF "CUTE"!!

THE QUINTESSENTIAL QUINTUPLETS 5

The Quintessential Quintuplets volume 4 is a work of fiction. Names, characters, places, and incidents are the products of the author's imagination or are used fictitiously. Any resemblance to actual events, locales, or persons, living or dead, is entirely coincidental.

A Kodansha Comics Trade Paperback Original.

Published in the United States by Kodansha Comics, an imprint of Kodansha USA Publishing, LLC, New York.

Publication rights for this English edition arranged through Kodansha Ltd., Tokyo.

First published in Japan in 2018 by Kodansha Ltd., Tokyo, as *Gotoubun no Hanayome* volume 4.

Cover Design: Saya Takai (RedRooster)

ISBN 978-1-63236-853-9

Printed in the United States of America.

www.kodanshacomics.com

9 8 7 6 5 4 3 2 1

Translation: Steven LeCroy
Lettering: Jan Lan Ivan Concepcion
Additional Layout: Belynda Ungurath
Editing: David Yoo, Thalia Sutton
Editorial Assistance: YKS Services LLC/SKY Japan, INC.
Kodansha Comics Edition Cover Design: Phil Balsman